POLICING NOT PROT

MW01258511

CRITICAL PERSPECTIVES ON YOUTH SERIES

General Editors: Amy L. Best, Lorena Garcia, and Jessica K. Taft

Policing Not Protecting Families

The Child Welfare System as Poverty Governance

Edited by
Jennifer Randles *and* Kerry Woodward

NEW YORK UNIVERSITY PRESS
New York

NEW YORK UNIVERSITY PRESS
New York
www.nyupress.org

© 2025 by New York University

Please contact the Library of Congress for Cataloging-in-Publication data.

ISBN: 9781479820603 (hardback)
ISBN: 9781479820610 (paperback)
ISBN: 9781479820634 (library ebook)
ISBN: 9781479820627 (consumer ebook)

This book is printed on acid-free paper, and its binding materials are chosen for strength and durability. We strive to use environmentally responsible suppliers and materials to the greatest extent possible in publishing our books.

Manufactured in the United States of America

10 9 8 7 6 5 4 3 2 1

Also available as an ebook

CONTENTS

Introduction

Policing Parents Not Providing for Children

KERRY WOODWARD AND JENNIFER RANDLES

During a 2020 presidential candidate debate between incumbent Donald Trump and Democratic nominee Joseph Biden, the moderator turned to the topic of immigration and family separation. The question referred to the Trump administration's "Zero Tolerance" policy implemented in 2017, which involved the forcible separation of around four thousand children from their parents at the US-Mexico border (USDHS 2023b), a practice ostensibly put in place to discourage adults from crossing the border without authorization. Many of these migrant adults were seeking asylum and had immigrated to escape violence and poverty in their home countries.

Nevertheless, undocumented adult asylum seekers were detained, and their accompanying minor children were handed over to the US Department of Health and Human Services (DHHS). DHHS then sent them to more than one hundred Office of Refugee Resettlement shelters and other care facilities—including group and family foster care— scattered across the country, often hundreds of miles away from their parents (Kandel 2021). Many of these children were infants and toddlers younger than five.

Using family separation as a deterrent to migration prioritized racialized immigration objectives over children's best interests and egregiously violated children's rights specified in Article 9 of the United Nations Convention on the Rights of the Child (1989): "a child shall not be separated from his or her parent against their will, except when . . . separation is necessary for the best interest of the child." Children's rights to family preservation are core to the Convention, the preamble of which states, "the family, as the fundamental group of society . . . ,

1

should be afforded the necessary protection and assistance so that it can fully assume its responsibilities within the community. . . . The child, for the full and harmonious development of his or her personality, should grow up in a family environment, in an atmosphere of happiness, love and understanding." The United States remains the sole country yet to ratify the Convention on the Rights of the Child.

Family separation at the border was thus widely condemned by human rights experts, who described the practice as "punitive" and one that "severely hampers [children's] development, and in some cases may amount to torture" (UN OHCHR 2018). Other organizations such as the American Academy of Pediatrics described the practice as inhumane and likely to cause toxic childhood stress—severe, prolonged stress that can disrupt children's cognitive, emotional, social, and physical development, with potentially lifelong negative consequences (Kraft 2018). Others denounced the policy as a form of punishment for families who fled their homes, and often extreme violence and poverty, in search of safer conditions for their children. In that now-infamous presidential candidate debate, Biden concluded that the family separation policy "violates every notion of who we are as a nation."

But in fact, the state-sanctioned child taking that resulted from this particular immigration policy falls in line with the long history of family separation in the United States, especially among poor children of color. African Americans, enslaved in this country for hundreds of years, were routinely sold off from their families and further controlled by the threat of family separation. American Indians, their populations decimated after the disease and war brought by colonization, were confined on reservations, only to have their children taken by the federal government and other entities and placed in boarding schools—often too far away to visit—where they were methodically stripped of their cultural heritage and at times exposed to physical and sexual violence and even death. Migrant family separation at the border—which has not been confined only to Trump's Zero Tolerance policy—is just the latest example of large-scale, racialized, forced family separations in the United States. Rooted in white supremacy, forced family separations are built into the fabric of the United States; they continue today, largely through the separation of marginalized families "in the best interest of the children" by the child welfare system.

Thus, how we purport to protect children from abuse and neglect in the United States is based on a strikingly similar logic as that underlying the forced separation of poor migrant parents from their children. Rather than protecting and providing support for immigrant families legally seeking asylum and refuge, the policy effectively policed and punished families for their home countries' economic and social circumstances, over which they had no control. Similarly, rather than providing poor, struggling families with the economic and other assistance they need to keep their kids safe and healthy, we routinely remove children and place them in out-of-home care away from their families. But as the United Nations Convention codified, children have the right to grow up with their parents, even if their families need protection and assistance in order to provide nurturing environments where children's rights can be fully realized.

Sadly, Biden was wrong. Family separation at the border did not "violate every notion of who we are as a nation." Rather, it was a continuation of our nation's long history of separating families whose sanctity is not valued and denying children their fundamental rights to safety and security. As the chapters in this volume reveal, this history is reflected not only in our recent policy and practices at the border but also in how we treat the many children and youth who find themselves involved in a child welfare system that more often polices poor families, especially poor families of color, instead of providing for and protecting them.

* * *

In a typical year in the United States, one in twenty-five US children has some interaction with the child welfare system. Over one-third of US children experience a child maltreatment investigation at some point during their youth (Kim et al. 2017). For poor children and Black children, the rates of investigations are significantly higher. The evidence on investigation disparities among American Indian families is mixed; however, a California study (Putnam-Hornstein et al. 2021) showed that Native children were disproportionately investigated at a rate similar to Black children. While only about one-third to one-half of investigated cases are substantiated as cases of child maltreatment (Kim et al. 2017; Putnam-Hornstein et al. 2021), and not all of those result in placement in foster care, more than one in ten Native American children and nearly one in ten Black children in the United States will spend time in foster care during their childhoods. Although nationally Latine children are not disproportionately represented in the child welfare system, they are overrepresented in some state systems, and immigrant families are particularly vulnerable (Davidson, Morrissey, and Beck 2019).

The 2010 reauthorization of the Child Abuse Prevention and Treatment Act (CAPTA)—originally enacted in 1974—defines child abuse and neglect as "any recent act or failure to act on the part of a parent or caregiver that results in death, serious physical or emotional harm, sexual abuse, or exploitation, or an act or failure to act that presents an imminent risk of serious harm" (42 U.S.C. § 5106g [2010]). States may expand on these definitions to specify the situations that mandated reporters must report to child protective services. In 2021, almost two-thirds (64 percent) of family separations leading to children's placement in foster care were due to substantiated cases of neglect (USDHHS 2023); this is true across racial groups (USDHHS 2022a, 2022b). Neglect, even more than other forms of maltreatment, is closely linked to poverty (Sedlak et al. 2010). One key reason for this linkage is that explicitly poverty-related problems—such as a lack of adequate housing—can be considered neglect in many states. Only twenty-seven states and the District of Columbia specifically exempt an inability to provide for a child financially from the definition of neglect (CWIG 2022a). In other states—including California, the state with the greatest number of children—a failure to provide adequate housing, food, or other basic needs, even when parents are making every effort to do so, could cause them to lose custody of their children. Parental drug and alcohol use, which usually falls under the category of "neglect," is another common cause of child removal (USDHHS 2022a). The murkiness of individual states' laws (CWIG 2022a) regarding substance use and child maltreatment, and the endless unique situations they aim to cover, mean that individual caseworkers' interpretations and discretion play a major role in life-altering decisions about which children stay with, and which are taken away from, their parents.

In 2019, 14.4 percent of children in the United States lived in poverty, with 6.2 percent in deep poverty, or below half the poverty threshold (less than about $10,300 a year for a family of three with two children) (US Census Bureau 2020). Children of color are significantly more likely than white children to experience poverty; 26.4 percent of Black children, 21.5 percent of American Indian and Alaska Native children, and 20.9 percent of Latine children were living in poverty before the COVID-19 pandemic hit, compared with only 12.3 percent of white children (US Census Bureau 2022a). Although temporary stimulus payments and child tax credits during 2021 plunged child poverty rates to historic lows (Cox, Jacoby, and Marr 2022), the government's failure to pass permanent antipoverty policies was quickly met with dramatic increases in child poverty rates—from 5.2 percent (3.8 million) of children living in poverty in 2021 to 12.4 percent (9 million) a year later (Shrider and Creamer 2023). The United States is unusual among wealthier nations in that it does not provide either universal or income-based cash allowances for families with children (ODI and UNICEF 2020). Hence, it is ironic that when children are removed from their family of origin due to child maltreatment, usually "neglect," their foster parents receive funding from the state to support the children's care—yet children's own parents were not eligible for this assistance to help them care for those children at home.

In addition to the millions of families who encounter the child welfare system directly, countless other families—those who struggle to feed, house, and supervise their children due to poverty—live in fear of the child welfare system knocking on their doors (Fong 2023). While the "sanctity of the family" is touted as an American value—a central and lauded freedom from government intervention—in fact, only some families' autonomy has ever been respected (Vasquez-Tokos and Yamin 2021). Imagined by many people as a system that ensures the care and safety of children, which is sometimes accurate, the child welfare system also separates families and punishes parents who are unable to meet parenting standards due to structural inequalities of race, gender, class, and other axes of inequity. Yet despite the wide reach of the child welfare system, critical scholarship on this system, its interactions with other state systems, and its broad social implications has been rare until recently, with Dorothy Roberts's (2002) early work in this area a notable exception.

As Roberts (2022) has more recently argued, how we refer to the system reflects distinct understandings of the system's intent and impacts. "Child welfare system" and "child protective services" imply that the system's purpose is to improve, protect, and promote the welfare of children via services designed to address their physical, emotional, cognitive, and social needs. Yet critics of the system, including many of the authors in this volume, prefer "family regulation" or "family policing" system to underscore its coercive and harmful impacts on families. "Family policing system" specifically highlights the links and parallels between the criminal legal system and the "child welfare system," which polices, punishes, and separates families. As such, we use both "child welfare system" and "family policing system" to signal its contested aims and effects.

Since the 1970s, scholars have explored how state programs that provide aid and services to poor people also exert social control over recipients. More recently, scholarship on poverty governance, or the ways the state and its programs and institutions manage and discipline poor populations, has grown. The US criminal justice system and welfare programs have been examined through the framework of poverty governance, with particular attention to the unique histories of colonialism, slavery, and immigration that have shaped the United States and its institutions. Yet only recently has the child welfare system been analyzed through this lens (Fong 2020, 2023; Woodward 2021). This book aims to bring together many of the scholars across numerous disciplines who are working to investigate the US family policing system and how it governs the mostly low-income families it entraps. We bring into conversation emerging and established scholars, practitioners, and legal experts who are uniquely positioned to offer both macro-policy analyses and micro-level insight into the lived experiences of the children and families the system is supposed to provide for and protect but all too often polices and punishes instead. While no volume could possibly provide a comprehensive look at the US child welfare system, which varies by state and encompasses thousands of private organizations in addition to public agencies, we believe that an interdisciplinary volume can best illustrate the current scope of the literature on the family policing system. We hope this book contributes to this emerging critical scholarship and encourages a full-scale reassessment of how we think about child welfare and the system that surveils and polices poor families.

This reassessment must entail a holistic consideration of children's rights. As family separation at the US-Mexico border during the Trump administration reminded us, we have an ethical obligation to protect children's rights to family preservation. However, as the Convention also codified, children also have rights to protection from injury, abuse, violence, neglect, and exploitation while in their parents' care. Families are not always cohesive units that protect and support children. There are some extreme cases of harm and violence inflicted on children— even when their parents and families have adequate resources and support—that necessitate finding alternative homes for them. Children's rights are not solely rooted in their roles as members of families; children are individuals who deserve a safe and caring environment that meets their physical, social, and emotional needs, and we have a collective responsibility to protect children's well-being by ensuring that these needs are met. Truly promoting child welfare would entail creating a society in which child maltreatment does not stem from a family's lack of economic and social resources. Yet the child welfare system has never focused on providing economic and other support to struggling families; instead, it relies heavily on family separation—or the threat of separation—which it wields as a widespread strategy for governing people living in poverty.

Poverty Governance and the Child Welfare System

Contemporary theorizing about poverty governance can be traced to Frances Fox Piven and Richard Cloward's 1971 book *Regulating the Poor* and Michel Foucault's late 1970s lectures at the College of France. First, Piven and Cloward showed that welfare programs serve political and economic purposes beyond simply aiding the poor. Specifically, programs that provide resources to poor populations also mitigate social unrest by easing hardship and enforce work by providing limited assistance, much of which is dependent on or otherwise promotes employment. Today, scholars regularly grapple with and explore the ways that supposedly assistive social programs exert social control over recipients of aid.

A second influence on many scholars' understandings of state poverty governance today stems from Foucault's (1982, 2008) theorizing on governmentality, or how the state and other sources of power shape people's behavior. Foucault (2008) identified three key elements of neoliberal governance, which arose in the 1970s and 1980s: (1) the dominance of the market and centrality of market logic; (2) the rise of punitive approaches and focus on "crime"; and (3) the growing belief that people are rational actors who are free and motivated to make rational decisions with few, if any, constraints. Foucault explored how these neoliberal tenets were becoming embedded in state institutions, which then sought to shape the subjectivities of poor, marginalized populations who rely on—or become entangled within—these institutions.

About a decade after Foucault, Pierre Bourdieu explored the emergence of the state and its transformation over time. Bourdieu (1999; Wacquant 2009) theorized that there are two hands of the contemporary state that are in constant tension: a masculine right hand focused on economic deregulation and what could be called market fundamentalism, and a feminine left hand focused on social functions, such as education and health. To Bourdieu's conceptualization of the right hand of the state, Loïc Wacquant (2009, 289) added the punitive role of the penal system, arguing that "we need to bring penal policies from the periphery to the center of our analysis of the redesign and deployment of government programs aimed at coping with the entrenched poverty and deepening disparities" of the contemporary era.

In the past decade and a half, scholars have done just that by centering not only the US criminal justice system but also the punitive policies and practices that have spread throughout many public institutions. Wacquant (2009, 79) described the punitive turn of assistive programs—most notably the enactment of the Personal Responsibility and Work Opportunity Reconciliation Act (PRWORA) of 1996, or "welfare reform"—as "fostering a programmatic convergence with penal policy." Focusing on welfare reform implementation, Joe Soss, Richard Fording, and Sanford Schram (2011, 6) similarly argued that the two hands of the state "now work together as integrated elements of a single system." They view this contemporary approach to poverty governance—neoliberal paternalism—as unique in its expansion of state programs aimed at poor populations and its extension of state efforts to bolster markets and organize policies around market principles.

Drawing heavily on this line of scholarship, we understand "neoliberalism" to mean processes through which the state actively promotes market logic. Key tenets of neoliberalism include privatization (promoting private enterprise in traditionally state-run functions, e.g., private foster care agencies); decentralization, devolution, and deregulation (advocating for local over central decision-making and loosening regulations to allow for unhindered market forces); and personal responsibility (promoting—or coercing—economic self-sufficiency among low-income populations and requiring work in exchange for aid). Combined with "paternalism," or efforts to manage and discipline poor populations who are presumably unable to manage themselves, neoliberalism not only shapes how state institutions and markets interact but also seeks to "teach" poor, racialized populations how to transform themselves by embracing market rationality (Soss, Fording, and Schram 2011). This disciplinary strategy is aimed at creating "good neoliberal citizens" (Randles and Woodward 2018) or, in relation to the child welfare system, "good neoliberal citizen-parents" (Woodward 2021).

Today, the public assistance, criminal justice, and child welfare systems, along with corporate entities, expect poor people—especially poor people of color—to achieve and maintain economic self-sufficiency. Simultaneously, the state and corporations profit from poor people's attempts to survive in the marketplace, raking in profits and tax dollars while keeping wages low. They then profit off poor people's misfortunes by collecting legal fees and interest payments to fund local governments and bankroll private collection agencies. Governments also benefit from financial incentives given to states for placing poor children in foster and adoptive families and from child support payments required of poor parents whose children have been taken. These neoliberal paternalistic practices exemplify how the contemporary state manages poor people today, but their roots trace back to the capitalist accumulation by means of racial violence—including family separation—on which the United States was founded (Dettlaff 2023).

Despite the broad reach of the child welfare system in the same communities of color in which welfare and penal system involvement is common, most scholarship on neoliberal poverty governance has not considered it. Developing as a federal system just as neoliberalism was arising, the contemporary child welfare system emerged from local agencies and state efforts and has retained a decentralized and privatized structure. Nearly always omitted from discussions about the state and its central institutions, the family policing system has long operated at the nexus of its right and left hands. Claiming to protect children and assist struggling families, the system operates largely through a combination of the punitive power to separate children from parents and the paternalistic power to require an array of "services" and conformity to parenting norms under the guise of "children's best interests."

While a few scholars have begun in recent years to look at the child welfare system through the lens of poverty governance, this line of scholarship remains underdeveloped. Understanding the child welfare system as one state system in a web of systems that primarily manage and control poor, disproportionately Black and brown populations allows for a deeper analysis of how laws and practices regulate poor families. This approach reveals the need for empirical research on the relationships between state systems that govern poor populations and calls for an analysis that attends to race, class, *and* gender.

Turning our attention to the child welfare system—a system that by its very design has never fit neatly into either the right or left hand of the metaphor—we have an opportunity to explore the unique ways that mothers, especially, are forced to engage with what is widely conceived as an assistive system. Intended to protect children, the child welfare system is more often experienced by low-income mothers as punitive— policing and punishing poor parents and leaving poor children as collateral damage. While official data on the gender of caregivers involved in the family policing system and the proportion who are female heads of households are lacking, we know that it is mostly mothers, and disproportionately single mothers, who are impacted by the system (see, for example, Dolan 2011). This impact includes the surveillance and fear experienced by many poor mothers, including many who are not officially involved with the child welfare system (Fong 2023). This book, therefore, seeks to bring the child welfare system—recently called the "New Jane Crow" (Clifford and Silver-Greenberg 2017) because of its gendered, racialized, and pervasive power and its parallels with the criminal justice system—to the fore of academic and political debates as a system that shapes the lives of poor families, especially those of poor Black and American Indian women and children.

Two Interlocking Histories: State-Sanctioned Child Separation and State Efforts to Regulate Child Welfare

In 1662, the colony of Virginia passed a law ensuring that the free or enslaved status of children would stem from their mother's status, unlike in British law, in which the father's status determined his children's. This law ensured the power of white enslavers to rape enslaved women and own the resulting children, thereby increasing their wealth (Briggs 2020). For two centuries, children, mothers, and fathers were sold, often far away from the rest of their families, at the will of enslavers who separated families for profit and control. Laura Briggs (2020) argues that while family separation was often justified by the racist belief that Black mothers did not grieve as white mothers did, enslavers were also likely to downplay the frequency with which family separation occurred, instead painting slavery as a benign, mutually beneficial "arrangement." Meanwhile, family separation, especially the threat of being sold away from one's children, became a primary tool for controlling the enslaved population.

While the slaughter and displacement of American Indians began with the arrival of Europeans in what became the United States, the codification of family separation began in 1870 with the advent of Indian boarding schools and the forced separation of American Indian children from their families. Stripped of their languages, traditional clothes, cultural and religious practices, and families, children were removed and trained for menial jobs and in "American" (white, middle-class) cultural norms in order to coerce the acquiescence of tribes that were revolting over broken treaties (Briggs 2020). Family separation was again a key way that people in power compelled compliance. While neither enslaved people nor American Indians ever stopped resisting, threats of family separation and harm to those who sought to reunite quelled revolts.

The dehumanization involved in these family separation tactics also served another purpose: the creation and entrenchment of modern racial categories developed with colonization and slavery. Both the ability and willingness to forcibly separate enslaved Black families reinforced their legal status as property rather than people and further differentiated the status of those who were enslaved from poor, but free, whites. This distinction was essential for establishing the collusion of poor whites, whose economic interests positioned them closer to those who were enslaved than to white, wealthy enslavers. However, once the racial caste system was codified and the status of Black enslaved people as less than human was established, poor whites were more likely to identify with the powerful people who owned property than with those who were considered chattel. While the color line did not bend for Black people even after slavery ended, post–Civil War state-level efforts to manage American Indians were aimed at long-term assimilation (i.e., cultural genocide) (Briggs 2020). Native Americans were deemed a unique race, but unlike Blacks, they were seen as potentially "assimilable." In addition to a racial category, "Native American" became a political category, with individual tribes determining membership (i.e., citizenship) and making claims for land and rights. The threat of family separation— and separation itself—aimed both to assimilate Indian youth into white "American" culture and to undermine the political power of American Indian nations.

Although state-sanctioned family separation of poor "white" families has been far less systematic than that experienced by enslaved Black families and American Indian families, it has occurred. By 1850, with the number of abandoned and orphaned children reaching as high as forty thousand in New York City alone (Rymph 2017), local wealthy, white organizations sought a solution to this "unruly" population: Orphan Trains. The Orphan Trains, which continued operating through the 1920s, brought poor, abandoned, or orphaned children from East Coast cities west to families seeking to adopt or care for children, often because they sought the unpaid labor of youth to help on family farms. Most of these children came from European immigrant parents who were racialized as nonwhite at the time, underscoring the consistent role of white supremacy in both family separation and coercive efforts to "protect" children. It is estimated that the majority of urban, East Coast "orphans" from this time were not, in fact, orphans but had been left at orphanages by family members who were unable to provide for them due to poverty (Gordon 1999). Even though this precursor to today's foster care system was not a systematic attempt at separating families, it was a class- and race-based poverty management system that disregarded the humanity and family bonds of poor, white immigrants. As the historian Linda Gordon (1999, 10–11) has claimed, to poor parents pressured to surrender children to orphanages due to economic constraints or those who feared that their children would be "snatched" off the streets because of their poverty, "the child savers were actually child stealers."

Over the next several decades, reformers' efforts to "save" children from poverty and urban streets grew into a concern about cruelty against children. Though not a new problem, cruelty toward children perpetrated by their own families arose as a new concern amid anxiety-producing structural changes of rising urbanization, industrialization, and immigration. Gordon (1988, 28) described nineteenth-century child-protection reformers as turning their "class, ethnic, and cultural anxieties" into alarms about the morality and lack of self-control practiced by "inferior classes and cultures." By 1880, thirty-four Societies for the Prevention of Cruelty to Children (SPCCs) had arisen throughout the United States. While SPCCs were led by upper-class, Protestant men, many of the reformers and volunteers were religious, upper-class women engaging in seemingly charitable efforts to improve the lives of needy children and their presumptively drunken, cruel immigrant fathers. SPCCs also aided abandoned children and took on the issue of "baby farmers"—those who were paid to take care of young children when poor families could not—among whom child death rates were high. Yet as Gordon (1988) has written, poor immigrant residents often feared the punitive approach of SPCCs and their close relationship with local police (much like today; Fong 2023), sometimes referring to them as "The Cruelty."

During the Progressive Era, women social reformers shifted their attention away from the assumed cruelty of drunken fathers and toward poor immigrant mothers and their supposed role in child neglect. The Progressive Era led to the professionalization, secularization, and feminization of social work. Solutions became less punitive and more preventative, albeit still largely excluding Black families and others positioned as undeserving, such as unmarried women, from receiving government aid to help support their children (Gordon 1994). A 1909 White House conference sought to increase state support to poor families specifically to limit out-of-home care for children, yet it failed to address the specific needs of communities and families of color (Rymph 2017).

Three years later, the Children's Bureau, first imagined by Lillian Wald and Florence Kelley, was established. While supportive of providing services to women of color, the Children's Bureau also promoted state-level autonomy, which allowed for significant discrimination against Black and Latina women, especially in southern states (Gordon 1994). Through the Children's Bureau and the subsequent Women's Bureau, mostly white women reformers pushed for state mothers' aid laws for "deserving" single mothers, generally widows, and later "deserted" women with children.

Women reformers also played vital roles in establishing the first federal welfare program, the Sheppard-Towner Maternity and Infant Protection Act of 1921, which offered health care and educational services to mothers and infants, seeking to assimilate poor, often immigrant women into Anglo, middle-class norms of child rearing. Though racist and ethnocentric, the program was less punitive than family separation initiatives and helped decrease maternal and infant mortality rates before it was repealed in 1929 (Gordon 1994; Mink 1990).

Gordon's (1988) study of Boston-area child welfare and family violence agencies showed that, like today, between 1880 and 1960, neglect was the most commonly identified form of child maltreatment. Single-mother-headed families made up about a fourth of families known to agencies in the study, with over 80 percent of those mothers accused of child neglect, often meaning inadequate supervision. Finding work at all as a single mother in the early 1900s was difficult, but finding child care was even harder. Some mothers left their children home alone, risking agency involvement, while others voluntarily placed their children in informal boarding arrangements to be looked after by other poor mothers. Other survival tactics included taking in boarders (usually men), establishing new romantic relationships with men, and engaging in explicitly illegal (yet common) prostitution or bootlegging. All these strategies conflicted with accepted standards of women's behavior and risked accusations of child neglect due to immorality and ineligibility for means-tested government assistance, which was tied to morality tests at the time. In Gordon's study, three-quarters of cases of child neglect based on accusations of an "immoral" home involved single mothers accused of drinking, smoking, having sex outside marriage, or other similar behaviors deemed unacceptable for women.

According to the historical records that formed the basis of Gordon's study, although single mothers were less likely than two-parent families to voluntarily place their children in agencies' care, single mothers were far more likely to have their children removed—and disproportionately without due process. Thus, the "solution" of child taking rather than providing families necessary aid was already becoming entrenched. Meanwhile, by the late 1800s, states began to subsidize both orphanages and care provided by individual "substitute mothers," a precursor to modern foster care (Rymph 2017). For poor women today, especially poor women of color, socially condemned sexual behavior and especially substance use continue to be key causes of state-sanctioned child taking.

The connection between poverty and child welfare did not go unnoticed by reformers, many of whom worked to bring government aid to poor families. Following the Progressive Era's state-administered Mothers' Aid Laws, the New Deal instituted Aid to Dependent Children (later Aid to Families with Dependent Children, or AFDC) in 1935. Yet this means-tested cash aid program was available only to the most "deserving" mothers and children, further embedding racism and religious moralism into the emerging left hand of the state. Those who were deemed deserving were disproportionately white widows and occasionally "deserted" mothers, that is, those who could pass the strict morality tests enacted by states and administrators and implemented by local caseworkers (Gordon 1994).

While the first half of the twentieth century was marked more by highly gendered and racialized provision of services to women and children than by state-sanctioned family separation, the moralistic and deeply gendered structure of the welfare system has had long-term consequences for children and family well-being. White women reformers who largely shaped social welfare policies of the early 1900s codified both women's responsibility as primary parents and a patronizing approach to assisting low-income, often racialized families that conditioned aid on tests of mothers' moral fitness (Gordon 1994; Mink 1990).

Not until the 1960s and 1970s did a combination of the Civil Rights, Welfare Rights, and Women's Liberation Movements and the court cases they instigated significantly lessen the racialized discretion that defined the welfare system. The result was greater racial equity in accessing welfare assistance and, given the disproportionate poverty among Black families, a rise in the number of Black welfare recipients. Once largely reserved for white, previously married mothers and their children, AFDC became associated with "unwed" Black mothers and children as more Black mothers were able to access cash aid. The result was a decrease in public support for welfare (Abramovitz 1996; Quadagno 1994), putting more children at risk of family separation.

The Child Welfare System in an Era of Academic Scholarship

While the World War II era and the 1950s saw little interest in the topic of child maltreatment, the issue reentered public discourse and made its way into federal legislation in the early 1960s (Raz 2020). The pediatrician C. Henry Kempe and colleagues published an influential article in 1962 that made the case that children enduring persistent abuse may experience "battered-child syndrome"; however, it also framed the problem as one of individual families. Abusing parents were framed as "mentally ill" and in need of psychological help (Raz 2020). Medical literature on child abuse flourished in the aftermath of this article, again with a focus on the medical and psychological causes and solutions to deliberate violence against children. Instead of paying attention to structural inequalities—such as poverty and racism—the literature focused on the individual flaws of parents accused of child abuse and advocated for their "treatment" rather than financial support and social services. Stemming from this medicalization of child maltreatment, the Children's Bureau published model legislation in 1963 to require mandatory reporting to law enforcement by physicians in cases of suspected child abuse. Other organizations, including the American Medical Association, followed suit, and by the late 1960s, states began enacting mandatory reporting legislation (Raz 2020).

This era also saw the passage of the Public Welfare Amendments of 1962, which created the AFDC–Foster Care program, marking the first time that foster care was publicly funded or run by government agencies. This law codified the connection between poor families and child welfare services by enabling Title IV AFDC funds to be used to provide financial support for children in foster care. Mical Raz (2020, 74) explains, "The stated goal of this program was that children in poor families could be temporarily placed in foster homes while their parents worked toward rehabilitation." But while foster care had until then been a mostly voluntary, albeit coercive, system to aid poor, white parents who needed help caring for their children, this soon changed. AFDC–Foster Care created a "disturbing incentive" to shift away from "voluntary place-ments" and instead force placements of AFDC-eligible children, mean-ing poor children with single mothers (Rymph 2017, 170). This shift and reports of punitive implementation of AFDC–Foster Care, particularly for mothers newly applying for AFDC, occurred while welfare rolls were rapidly expanding, particularly among Black mothers, due to the over-turning of racist policies and practices that had prevented them from receiving aid in the past. As efforts to extend the left hand of the state to people of color gained ground, simultaneous efforts to merge assistance with disciplinary elements of the state's right hand unfolded, marking a key feature of the contemporary era of punitive poverty governance.

While media and public policy debates continued to frame child mal-treatment as an individual pathology of disturbed parents (Raz 2020), scholarship and efforts by social workers to call attention to the systemic connections between poverty, racism, and child welfare system involve-ment were growing. A 1970 sociological study of child abuse conducted by David Gil and funded by the Children's Bureau identified a higher prevalence of child abuse among poor families and families of color. Gil (1971, 647) argued that "multiple links between poverty and racial discrimination and physical abuse of children suggest that one essential route toward reducing the incidence and prevalence of child abuse is the elimination of poverty and structural social inequalities." During the 1970s, academics called for the problems of child abuse and neglect to be alleviated through antipoverty measures and increased social services for poor communities of color, while Black and Indigenous social work-ers called attention to the racism embedded in the system. However, the notion of protecting children from pathological parents continued to guide policy and practice (Raz 2020), and the child welfare system's focus on disciplining and controlling poor populations—rather than al-leviating poverty—became more entrenched.

Meanwhile, burgeoning research into child maltreatment and the surrounding media attention led to the passage of the Child Abuse Prevention and Treatment Act (CAPTA) in 1974. Sponsored by Demo-cratic Senator Walter Mondale, the Act provided funds for child abuse prevention and services and made mandatory reporting requirements a condition of states' eligibility for federal funding. Rather than draw-ing on David Gil's structural analysis, the bill stayed tightly wedded to psychological and medical theories of child abuse (Raz 2020), reflecting the influential congressional testimonies of members of Parents Anonymous, a mostly white, middle-class self-help group for parents who had abused or feared that they would abuse their children. By broadening definitions of child abuse to include emotional abuse and neglect and promoting the view that child abuse was a problem that crossed socioeconomic lines, congressional hearings leading to CAPTA's passage focused on individual reasons for parents' abusive and neglectful behavior, rather than structural and systemic problems (Raz 2020).

Consistent with the era's emphasis on "personal responsibility" and market logic as part of a broader neoliberal shift, CAPTA provided funds to local, often private organizations focused on child abuse prevention and related services. While perhaps useful in understanding childhood trauma and psychology, broadening definitions of child abuse to include emotional abuse and neglect opened the doorway to more state intervention into families, particularly families unable to meet the emerging white, middle-class expectation of emotionally intensive parenting (Hays 1996). With the structural barriers that many families faced in meeting these new standards of care ignored, the result was a rise in the number of children—most of them low income—separated from their families by the state (Lee 2016; Raz 2020).

While unmoved by research indicating the need to address the structural factors behind child abuse and neglect, policy makers were more interested in new scholarship about children's psychological well-being. The 1973 book *Beyond the Best Interests of the Child*, by Joseph Goldstein, Anna Freud, and Albert Solnit, a legal scholar, child psychoanalyst, and child psychiatrist, respectively, argued that children need a primary "psychological parent"—often but not necessarily a biological parent— and that separation from that person can cause harm.

Ironically, this attachment-based theory shifted the way courts and child welfare professionals thought about child placement and permanency and was used to justify adoption by foster parents, based on the logic that separating children from foster caregivers with whom they had formed deep attachments would be harmful (Lee 2016; Raz 2020; Reich 2005). Although the authors' subsequent book *Before the Best Interests of the Child* (Goldstein, Freud, and Solnit 1979) made clear that children should *only* be removed from their biological families in severe cases of maltreatment, their initial focus on continuity of care for children placed outside of their homes was often used in court cases to support termination of parental rights when a child had grown "attached" to their foster parents who were hoping to adopt them (Raz 2020). In other words, instead of preventing forced separation of biological parents and children or ensuring that children were placed with relatives and/or in stable foster homes, this research was largely used to justify adoption by (often white, middle-class) foster parents.

The Rise of Neoliberal Poverty Governance and Racial Disparities in the Child Welfare System

In response to progressive social movements and rising economic insecurity, a coalition of fiscal and social conservatives promoted market-based strategies for addressing nearly all social problems, ushering in a new era of neoliberal poverty governance. The focus of state systems shifted from providing government aid to people in need—particularly during times of economic crisis to stimulate the economy—to promoting "personal responsibility," adopting punitive approaches, and instilling market logic into all areas of life (Soss, Fording, and Schram 2011). Over the next several decades, this shift resulted in a dramatic increase in the incarceration of poor—and especially poor, Black—men; a punitive and stingy approach to welfare provision codified in PRWORA; and the growth of the child welfare system, including a rise in the number of children in foster care, due in part to a shrinking social safety net (Ginther and Johnson-Motoyama 2022). The assistive left hand of the state became weaker as it was overtaken by an increasingly stronger right hand and its punitive and conditional approach to social provision.

Vast racial disparities in the number of children forcibly placed in out-of-home care were already apparent by the early 1970s, as Black and American Indian children were disproportionately removed from their families. North Dakota, a state with a large Native population, had gone so far as to pass a law declaring that "chronic dependency"—or long-term welfare use—was evidence of an "unsuitable home" and thus cause for child removal. By the mid-1970s, an astounding 25 to 35 percent of American Indian children were in out-of-home care (Briggs

2020). Native resistance—especially Native women's resistance—to this new form of state-sanctioned child taking resulted in the 1978 passage of the Indian Child Welfare Act (ICWA). Still in effect, though the focus of many legal challenges, including the 2023 Supreme Court case *Haaland v. Brackeen*, the ICWA affirms the authority of Indian tribes in child welfare decisions for Indian children—children who are members of, or eligible for membership in, a federally recognized tribe. In addition, crisis intervention services must be offered to a family before a child is removed. The Act also requires a multitiered preference system for out-of-home care: family members, then tribal members, then Native members of another tribe, and only then placement with non-Native families. While the Act itself is considered a success, its implementation by child welfare agencies and family courts has been inconsistent, partly due to the lack of federal funding for oversight, and compliance remains a significant problem more than four decades later (Linjean and Weaver 2022).

Like American Indian children, African American children became vastly overrepresented in foster care. Severe poverty in the Black community was exacerbated by discriminatory welfare policies, particularly "suitable home" rules that required welfare recipients to comply with whatever white, middle-class norm the local welfare workers thought appropriate. "Good housekeeping" rules, for example, could be used to deny support if a "white glove test" deemed a home to be poorly maintained. In 1961, the head of the Department of Health, Education, and Welfare, Arthur Fleming, directed states not to deny families Aid to Dependent Children (ADC) payments based on "suitable home" rules unless they had attempted to "rehabilitate the family," which would presumably coerce compliance with housekeeping and morality expectations. Then he allocated federal money for foster care for those children whose families could not be rehabilitated. As federal dollars flowed to foster care, the number of children taken from their families increased, and foster care rolls grew, disproportionately among Black children (Roberts 2022).

More children in foster care led to more children whose parents had their parental rights terminated and thus more children available for adoption. With too few Black families approved as foster or adoptive parents, liberalizing views of race in the United States, and fewer single, white mothers placing (or coerced into placing) their babies for adoption, transracial placements increased. Transracial adoptions, however, were still relatively rare in the 1970s; thus, many Black children were separated from their families—often via placement in white foster homes—with little hope of permanence. The National Association of Black Social Workers (NABSW) famously responded in 1972 with a scathing statement that called transracial adoption and foster care placements a form of genocide (Roberts 2002). In addition to their claims that transracial placements were psychologically detrimental to Black children, the NABSW argued in favor of kinship care and pointed to the structural barriers Black families faced in pursuing adoption (NABSW 1972; Raz 2020).

Transracial placements declined in the years that followed, but child removal did not. In 1977, approximately 25 percent of out-of-home placements were of Black children, who made up just under 11 percent of American children at the time. Once placed, Black children also spent twice as long as white and Latine children in foster care (Raz 2020). While one might be inclined to blame the NABSW's position on transracial placements for large numbers of Black children remaining in foster care, including many who age out before being adopted, this would obscure how most white families preferred and continue to prefer to adopt children who match them racially or who are seen as "closer to white" (i.e., Asian, Latine, and American Indian) (Woodward 2016).

Despite concern in the 1970s around large numbers of Black children in out-of-home care, little was done to curtail the numbers of Black children in the system or to alleviate the poverty caused by centuries of structural racism in Black communities (Raz 2020; Roberts 2022). A few organizations, including the Black Administrators in Child Welfare Action Group, were alarmed by the racial disparities in every aspect of the child welfare system. However, they were mostly unsuccessful at shifting the national conversation away from how to deal with so many Black children in foster care and toward addressing the causes of this disparity and ensuring that Black (and all) families have the necessary support to stay together safely (Raz 2020).

Alarm over the number of children in foster care—especially Black children—and the time they spent there did, however, lead to the passage of the Adoption Assistance and Child Welfare Act (AACWA) in 1980. Promisingly, the bill provided funding for services to keep children in their homes and to promote both reunification and adoption by making "reunification or permanent adoption as financially attractive [to states] as foster care" (Reich 2005, 42–43).

The AACWA also enacted the federal Adoption Assistance Program to financially support families who adopt through the foster care system, thereby increasing opportunities for lower-income families—and thus many families of color—to adopt children. Yet funding intended for family preservation services was quickly limited by the Reagan administration, while funding for foster care placement grew. In the years leading up to and immediately following the AACWA, rates of children in foster care decreased, primarily due to fewer white children in out-of-home care; but by 1983, foster care rates were rising again, and racial disparities were growing (Raz 2020).

The next significant policy change came in 1993, when President Clinton signed into law the Family Preservation and Family Support Services Program, which was expanded and renamed the Promoting Safe and Stable Families Program (PSSF) in 1997. The PSSF increased funds for family support, provided services to prevent unnecessary separations, and promoted reunification and permanency for children (Capacity Building Center for States 2023; Casey Family Programs 2011). Also in 1997, in response to the growing number of children in foster care nationally, which increased from about 280,000 to almost 500,000 between 1985 and 1995, Clinton signed the Adoption and Safe Families Act (ASFA). ASFA did nothing to alleviate the underlying poverty and related hardships that undergirded most families' involvement with the child welfare system. Instead, it created strict time limits for out-of-home care, which are still in effect today. States must move to terminate parental rights for children who have been in out-of-home care for fifteen out of the past twenty-two months, with limited exceptions. Thus, parents who are incarcerated or otherwise unable to meet the stringent requirements to regain custody in this arbitrary time frame are at risk of having their parental rights permanently terminated, with the expectation that the children will be adopted into "permanent" families.

Policies like ASFA aimed at speeding up or promoting the severance of ties between biological parents and their children—with little recourse and no right to any further contact—can only be understood as disregarding poor families, particularly Black and American

Indian families, and violating children's rights to protection from injury and care in stable environments that meet their physical, social, and emotional needs. A permanent, state-sanctioned severing of ties between parents and their children is unthinkable in all but the most heinous cases of child abuse—and yet the vast majority of child removals are in cases of poverty-related neglect (Human Rights Watch 2022; Roberts 2002; see also Sedlak et al. 2010; USDHHS 2022a).

Not coincidentally, the implementation of the quintessentially neoliberal PRWORA "welfare reform" in the mid-1990s coincided with Clinton's signing of ASFA. PRWORA replaced AFDC with the Temporary Assistance for Needy Families (TANF) program, ending poor families' entitlement to at least some monthly income. Based on block grants to the states, TANF devolved power over welfare policy design and implementation to states and counties, marking a return to when local laws and caseworker discretion determined the availability of aid. However, PRWORA also ensured nationwide work requirements to receive aid and time limits on the receipt of aid. As a result, welfare rolls that had grown during the 1970s as more families of color were finally able to access aid dropped dramatically, leading to a rise in deep poverty and putting more children at risk of "neglect" as defined by the child welfare system (Trisi and Saenz 2020). PRWORA gutted public aid across the country, and states with the greatest declines in their welfare caseloads also saw significant increases in the number of children in foster care (Ginther and Johnson-Motoyama 2022), children who now had little more than a year before they could be physically and legally severed from their biological parents. Meanwhile, the neoliberal logic of "personal responsibility" justified these family separations as the result of "choices" made by failed parents.

ASFA and welfare reform had particularly harsh consequences for those youth—disproportionately Black (Cho et al. 2023) and/or queer (Fish et al. 2019)—who did not get adopted after their parents' parental rights were terminated. Research suggests that children who encounter child welfare services (Evangelist, Thomas, and Waldfogel 2023) and those who spend time in foster care (Doyle 2007) have worse outcomes than otherwise-similar youth without child welfare system involvement. Youths who age out of foster care without a permanent family are disproportionately youths of color and fare particularly poorly, with high rates of homelessness, teen parenthood, incarceration, joblessness, substance abuse, and mental health challenges (Annie E. Casey Foundation 2023d), among other struggles. In 2021, more than nineteen thousand youths aged out of foster care and transitioned to adulthood without either the support of a stable family or access to the services they previously received through the foster care system (Annie E. Casey Foundation 2023d). This is a particularly dire outcome of child welfare system involvement that accords with neoliberal welfare reform's emphasis on "personal responsibility" and "self-sufficiency."

Growing awareness of the racial disparities in the child welfare system has led to attempts at policy reforms, most significantly the Family First Prevention Services Act of 2017 (FFPSA, P.L. 115-123 [2018]). This historic law provides federal funding for state programs aimed at keeping children safely in their families and restricts federal funding for congregate care—highly supervised residential group homes for children—to keep more youth in family settings. While intended to limit family separation while providing needed services, recent assessments of FFPSA suggest that administrative barriers to access funding, insufficient services for families, and workforce gaps among specialists have all prevented a full embrace and implementation of the act (Vivrette et al. 2023). Yet many stakeholders remain hopeful as child welfare professionals work to expand constructive partnerships between child- and family-focused agencies using funding provided through the FFPSA. Even more recently, the Administration for Children and Families issued a final rule allowing separate approval standards for kinship foster care arrangements, which should increase the number of children able to remain with their extended families while also receiving financial assistance (ACF 2023).

* * *

State-sanctioned child taking did not end with the abolition of slavery, the closure of American Indian boarding schools, the conclusion of the Orphan Trains, or the development of social welfare programs and a formal child welfare system. Although lower than in the previous decade (Wildeman and Emanuel 2014), recent estimates suggest that more than 5 percent of all children in the United States will spend time in foster care; the rates for American Indian (11.2 percent) and

Black children (9.2 percent) are substantially higher (Yi, Edwards, and Wildeman 2020). The vast majority of these children come from poor or low-income families.

Disproportionate rates of maltreatment—and child welfare system involvement—among poor families are considered normal and expected, so much so that the higher poverty rates of Black people and American Indians are often the primary explanation and justification for their greater involvement in the child welfare system (Bartholet 2009; Kim and Drake 2018; for a critical assessment of the poverty versus racial bias debate, see Dettlaff et al. 2021). Chapters throughout this book collectively point to a fundamental truth about this disproportionality: families in poverty are policed, but neither the parents nor children are protected or provided for.

In addition to long histories of structural racism that increase the likelihood of Black, American Indian, and Latine families living in poverty and in poor neighborhoods, these families live at the intersection of race and class oppression in two other ways. First, they face greater structural barriers to escaping poverty, poor neighborhoods, substandard housing, and systems of surveillance. Second, they face biased state systems—including the child welfare system—that are more likely to criminalize, penalize, and dehumanize the experiences of poor people of color and the families in which they live. The chapters in this volume explore myriad ways the family policing system governs poor families, frequently at the expense of aiding the children it claims to protect. With attention to the racialized and gendered underpinnings and ongoing practices of the child welfare system, chapters highlight the family policing system's significant influence in the lives of low-income families, especially those facing other challenges, such as drug addiction and intimate partner violence.

Book Organization

Organized in five parts, this book demonstrates that the child welfare system is an important, yet often neglected, institution of racialized and gendered poverty governance, with often harmful consequences for families and especially children and youth. Chapters illustrate how the system privileges market logic and seeks to control the behavior and subjecthood of poor people through racialized, gendered, and increasingly punitive strategies. Together, these chapters show how the child welfare system, working in tandem with other state systems, governs poor and other marginalized families through its power to determine who is a "good enough" parent.

Chapter 1, by Matty Lichtenstein, provides a historical look at how the professionalization of the child welfare field led workers and then policy makers away from the structural issue of poverty and instead toward an individualized, rehabilitative approach to child welfare. By "unseeing" poverty and pathologizing poor families and other marginalized families, racial disparities in child welfare involvement grew.

The volume's second part bridges the gap between the history of the child welfare system and how it systematically governs poverty in racialized and gendered ways. The three chapters in this part address key child welfare policies and illustrate how they have been implemented—or not. The authors show the child welfare system's embrace of neoliberal paternalism; rather than providing much-needed services and support, the family policing system expects families to meet white, middle-class parenting standards with little government support. Failure to do so is met with punitive measures, including removing children from their parents' care.

Chapter 2, by Amy Casselman-Hontalas, examines the contemporary child welfare system and its pervasive involvement in American Indian families and communities to show the historical continuity of family separation as a tactic to control American Indians. Looking specifically at the Indian Child Welfare Act and the *Haaland v. Brackeen* case's challenge to it, she explores the future of Indian child welfare and tribal sovereignty. In chapter 3, Stephanie A. Bryson explores the impact of the Adoption and Safe Families Act of 1997, revealing the impact of class, gender, and caseworker discretion in the implementation of this tool of poverty governance, which is responsible for the dissolution of millions of families. Next, in chapter 4, Tina Lee shows how race and local context shape the state's response to poor families with drug-using mothers, leading to varying degrees of policing, punitive legal actions, and surveillance.

The volume's third part explores the relationship between systems that are seemingly focused on social provision—the assistive "left hand" of the state—and the child welfare system. These chapters address how government and private organizations have attempted to help struggling families, but in ways that are often insufficient given the punitive structure of the family policing system and the entrenched disadvantages that many families who are mired in it face.

Chapter 5, by Shanta Trivedi and Erin Carrington Smith, examines how the state fails poor mothers who have experienced intimate partner violence, frequently causing more harm by accusing mothers of "failing to protect" their children from violence inflicted by someone else, often the child's father or father figure. Focusing specifically on the experiences of mothers who use opioids and their interactions with child welfare workers and mandated reporters, in chapter 6, Kristina P. Brant shows how the threat of child removal deters mothers living in poverty from voluntarily interacting with social services and public health institutions. Next, chapter 7, by Cyleste C. Collins and Rong Bai, examines the role of housing insecurity in child welfare system involvement and how housing assistance programs provide necessary but insufficient support for families experiencing deep poverty and related adversities.

The fourth part examines the punitive "right hand" of the state and its relationship with the child welfare system. Its four chapters delve into connections between the family policing system and family drug treatment courts, the police, carceral institutions, and immigration enforcement. Entanglements among these supervisory and disciplinary practices and institutions reveal how surveillance of poor families, especially families of color, perpetuates patterns of family separation as a punitive control tactic to police the boundaries of acceptable parenting.

In chapter 8, Laura Tach, Elizabeth Day, and Brittany Mihalec-Adkins show how family drug treatment courts, while providing a range of supports and services as alternatives to incarceration and termination of parental rights, fail to center children's needs and may therefore further children's trauma. In the following chapter, Kelley Fong and AshLee Smith examine the overlaps between two distinct systems of poverty governance—child protective services and police—to reveal how they systematically collaborate through routine patterns of activity, including sharing information about families and accompanying each other during investigations. Next, Kristina K. Lovato looks at how the US child welfare system impacts Latine immigrant families and children—many of whom have undocumented parents, putting them at greater risk of child welfare system involvement. The final chapter in part 4, chapter 11, by Frank Edwards, reveals the existence of racialized state policy regimes, as he demonstrates that states with disparate rates of African American and Native American incarceration also have large racial disparities in child protection interventions and outcomes.

The collection concludes with a discussion of whether the US child welfare system is so flawed and oppressive for families that it must be abolished entirely or whether it should be restructured to amplify supportive functions for marginalized families. Chapter 12, by Alan J. Dettlaff and Maya Pendleton, presents a vision for abolition of the current system. They argue that ending the oppression of Black families, in particular, requires envisioning and then implementing responses to children and families in need that do not rely on forcible family separation or coercive control. Conversely, in chapter 13, Dee Wilson and Erin J. Maher propose a framework to guide child welfare system reforms. They advocate for poverty reduction strategies and comprehensive services, as well as revisions to states' neglect statutes, to require public child welfare agencies to provide assistance so that families can safely stay together or reunify. Our concluding chapter highlights key takeaways from the preceding thirteen chapters and discusses several issues that are largely absent from the book but that require more research and critical discussion. We conclude with concrete recommendations that focus on ending poverty and increasing support for marginalized children and families.

By bringing together historical, quantitative, and qualitative analyses, each addressing a different aspect of the system, this book collectively catalogs how the family policing system surveils and disciplines poor families, especially Black and Native families, more than it provides concrete assistance. The chapters also show how the child welfare system interacts with other state systems and how these collaborations, intended to protect children, can actually harm children and families. Collectively, the volume fills crucial gaps in our knowledge about racialized poverty governance, the inner workings of the child welfare system, and child and family well-being among the most vulnerable families.

PART I

Theoretical Approach and Historical Context

1

Unseeing Poverty

The Origins of Inequality in US Child Welfare

MATTY LICHTENSTEIN

In 1974, the United States Congress passed the Child Abuse Prevention and Treatment Act (CAPTA). Several years in the making, this legislation was the first in which the federal government allocated funding for research and resources to promote child abuse prevention. To pass this unprecedented law, advocates presented child abuse as a classless, deracialized issue in legislative debates and hearings, linking it instead to parental pathology (Nelson 1984; Raz 2020). In this framing, parents who abused their children were damaged individuals, and they required a psychological diagnosis and personalized treatment. Little mention was made of the facts that many child welfare workers knew: most child maltreatment investigations involved families in poverty, and families of color faced disproportionate surveillance and child removal.[1]

The racial and class inequalities in child welfare services and surveillance are well documented in both historical and contemporary scholarship (Fong 2017; Gil 1970; Kim et al. 2017). This chapter aims to explain how these inequalities are rooted in the development of child welfare practices and norms, an analysis that helps answer the following question: Why did policy advocates delink child maltreatment and poverty interventions in the 1970s, during a crucial period of child welfare advocacy? The current literature argues that advocates for child abuse prevention laws were facing the powerful conservative and antiwelfare attitudes of the Nixon administration, as well as a broader public backlash to poverty aid in the early 1970s. In the face of these challenges, these advocates believed that CAPTA could only pass if child abuse was framed as an individualized family problem, not a broader race and class issue that would require systemic policy solutions (Nelson 1984; Raz

2020). Yet I show that the political separation of two deeply overlapping social issues, poverty and child maltreatment interventions, had deep roots in child welfare's professional development.

This chapter tells the story of how, influenced by administrative and policy shifts in the 1940s that emphasized a rehabilitative approach to poverty, leading child welfare advocates promoted specialized child welfare worker training that focused on psychotherapeutic interventions for struggling children and their families, not poverty mitigation measures. A rehabilitative approach shaped the child welfare profession into a tool of poverty governance, through which a national network of agencies regulated disproportionately poor families and families of color, while largely overlooking the intertwined effects of racial discrimination and financial hardship on the challenges these families faced. The story of the professionalization of child welfare workers in the US child welfare system demonstrates the early and persistent roots of the US neoliberal approach to family poverty governance, in which structural inequalities are framed as individual problems, thereby justifying policing and punishing families for suffering from the impact of policy failures.

Analyzing Child Welfare

To explain how child welfare's professionalization process unfolded, this chapter offers an analysis of texts produced by some of the influential organizations and street-level practitioners that shaped child welfare into the system we know today. These historical texts include archival data; publications and statistical reports from the Children's Bureau, a federal agency representing children's interests; and articles in *Child Welfare*, a landmark journal published by the Child Welfare League of America (CWLA), a nonprofit association representing both state and private agencies. In addition to systematically collecting and triangulating data on historical trends in child welfare policy and professional norms, I analyzed *Child Welfare* articles published from 1950 to 1974 using a large-scale qualitative coding method that accounts for trends over time (Lichtenstein and Rucks-Ahidiana 2020).

These administrative and professional publications were distributed widely to child welfare professionals and organizations during the crucial era of 1935–70, as the US welfare state and the child welfare profession evolved in response to new demands for social equality. The authors of these texts included child welfare advocates, agency leaders, researchers, and practitioners. In exploring the formational ideologies of child welfare institutions and the individuals who inhabited them, we gain a deeper understanding of how the child welfare professionalization process tethered it to an individualized approach that reinforced class and racial inequalities.

Drawing on these data and existing scholarship, I begin this chapter with a brief historical background to situate the roots of the US child welfare profession in the early twentieth century. I then use my analysis of *Child Welfare* journal articles, supplemented by historical reports and data, to explain how child welfare practitioners, leaders, and advocates professionalized the field by advocating for widespread practitioner training in specialized psychotherapeutic skills focused on child and family rehabilitation. This professionalization process reinforced and institutionalized broader US welfare state policies that avoided directly addressing poverty issues in favor of a psychologically based and individually oriented "rehabilitative" approach to marginalized families. Finally, I use my analysis of historical reports and *Child Welfare* articles to show how this professionalization process shaped how child welfare workers engaged with poor families and families of color, both in their knowledge production processes and in their practices.

From Patchwork to Profession

Until the 1930s, a far-flung set of mostly private local organizations, occasionally propped up by some state funding, constituted most US organizational efforts to protect children's welfare. Family and child welfare agencies provided foster care, adoption, and financial assistance services to predominantly poor and white families, often engaging in significant and invasive surveillance of these families in the process, while frequently ignoring the needs of families of color altogether (Abramovitz 1996; Katz 2013; Rymph 2012). Despite the fragmented nature of child welfare services in the early twentieth century, a few national organizations helped provide a unifying voice in the emerging field, chiefly the Child Welfare League of America (CWLA; est. 1921), the Children's Bureau (est. 1912), and the Children's Division of the American Humane Association (AHA; est. 1877).

The Great Depression catalyzed a significant shift in the US child welfare field and in turn the profession. In response to overwhelming financial need, the federal government funneled unprecedented sums of money into a massively expanded welfare state, culminating in the passage of the Social Security Act in 1935 and the establishment of financial relief programs like Aid to Dependent Children (ADC), which provided financial assistance to poor, unmarried mothers and their children. In contrast to such financial assistance programs, public child welfare services focused mostly on "social services," broadly defined as psychological counseling and referrals to a variety of medical and other services, which were framed as distinct from financial need.

Resources for public social services grew steadily during the late 1930s and the 1940s, stimulated by Social Security Act funding. In the context of these increasing resources, child welfare professionals sought to clarify the purpose of the child welfare field: What did this field actually do, and how did it differ from public financial assistance services? In response to these questions, multiple Children's Bureau reports presented child welfare services as providing for—at least in theory—a comprehensive array of children's needs. Services included foster care and adoption placement, counseling services in the home, homemaker services, referrals and counseling for medical needs, counseling for "crippled" children both at home and in clinics or institutions, and prenatal services.[2]

While presented as universally available to all children, in practice, the provision of child welfare services was inconsistent, insufficient, and deeply racialized, evolving in the context of a historically racist welfare state. Unlike the contemporary child welfare system, in which families of color are disproportionately targeted for interventions, the early twentieth century was marked by a severe underprovision of services to Black, Latine, and Indigenous families (Bernstein 2002; Billingsley and Giovannoni 1972; Rymph 2017; Simmons 2020). It was in this context of class and racial inequalities that child welfare agencies and leaders sought to define their function and purpose in the US social welfare state.

Rehabilitation and Unseeing Poverty: From Policy to Specialized Practice

Child welfare agencies' focus on a wide range of social and psychological services did not directly address one of the most urgent challenges that many US children faced: poverty. Indeed, the National Commission on Children and Youth in 1947–48 noted that expanding economic aid to needy families was its first priority.[3] Similarly, in a 1950 article published in *Child Welfare*, Neota Larson, the assistant chief of the Children's Bureau, noted that economic need is a leading problem for children. Yet, as she explained, "Some countries, like Great Britain, Canada, Australia and Sweden, have set up programs to augment family income through a system of family allowances. This is one way to approach the problem. Another is to supplement family income with community services, public and private. This has been our way" (Larson 1950, 6).

Larson contrasted socioeconomically similar countries' approach of providing money to needy families with the US system of providing rehabilitative services. The reason a focus on "services" had become "our way," or the American way, becomes clearer when understood against the backdrop of the deeply entrenched race and class biases of US welfare politics (Quadagno 1994). Child and family welfare advocates fought fiercely for expanded funding for cash assistance programs in the 1940s, but conservative US legislators were simply unwilling to provide it. In response to intensified political opposition to improving poverty relief, welfare administrators and advocates increasingly turned toward social services as a way to "rehabilitate" the needy by focusing on their presumed social and psychological shortcomings.

This individualized casework-based approach was promoted as a means to enable poor people to find their own way out of poverty and its related social ills, efforts that both echoed a long history of emphasizing personal responsibility in US poor relief organizations and foreshadowed later neoliberal efforts to "discipline the poor" (Katz 2013; Soss, Fording, and Schram 2011). This framing resonated with US lawmakers. Rehabilitative services, framed as distinct from direct economic aid because of their focus on the psychological roots of the individual aid recipient's poverty, were more likely than direct aid to receive government funding (Mittelstadt 2005).

This broader trend toward rehabilitative services in the US welfare state had a profound influence on child welfare professional discourses and practice. As early as 1947, a Children's Bureau researcher argued that assistance for children should go "beyond economic security" and should include guidance on how to manage a household and services for neglect and abuse, family relations, mental and physical disabilities, juvenile delinquency, and a long list of other issues that were framed as noneconomic in nature (Arnold 1947). In Children's Bureau reports on child welfare services, financial assistance—or "direct service" (US Children's Bureau 1949, 15)—was noted in the 1940s, but by the 1950s and 1960s, reports rarely mentioned financial assistance as a service that child welfare agencies provided to families.

Yet a turn away from poverty relief to rehabilitative services was not simply a pragmatic response to a lack of funding—or to improved economic prospects for white Americans in the 1950s. Instead, this change was rooted in factors unique to the professionalization of child welfare work that began decades earlier. By the 1920s, social work, the parent profession of the child welfare field, had shifted away from advocating for broader structural policy reform aimed at poverty relief and toward a casework method that focused on the individual psychological needs of clients (Popple 2018; Trattner 1999). Trained in the social work tradition, child welfare administrators and advocates writing in the 1930s and 1940s sought to show that they were uniquely qualified to provide rehabilitative services to children and their families using specialized casework skills. This focus on casework skills tailored for children's issues merged child welfare workers' professionalization agenda with a rehabilitative logic of resolving problems through an individualized psychological focus, a logic that was increasingly driving US welfare policy by the 1950s.

As Charles Schottland, the United States Social Security Commissioner, wrote in 1955, private social service agencies had moved away from financial relief as a primary focus because federal programming now provided economic relief to millions of poor Americans.[4] Instead, these agencies now provided services focused on "social rehabilitation," which Schottland defined quite vaguely as restoring "a person to maximum happiness and maximum usefulness" (1955, 6). This framing recast the issue as less a matter of insufficient funds and more a matter of professional function.

Child welfare organizational leaders, from the Children's Bureau to the Child Welfare League to social work educators, integrated this rehabilitative framing into their efforts to professionalize the still struggling and understaffed field of child welfare. Publications described concerted efforts to develop "specialized" child-welfare-specific professional training focused on psychotherapeutic approaches to families' and children's problems (CWLA 1951; Mayo et al. 1950; see also US Children's Bureau 1957). The goal was to develop a consistent set of standards for child welfare practices across the many private and public agencies that were scattered across the nation, and indeed, discussions of child welfare practices featured prominently in the *Child Welfare* journal in the 1950s.

In a 1958 statement, CWLA leaders also promoted a focus on rehabilitative services, arguing that now that federal public assistance programs like ADC allowed poor families to keep their children at home—instead of, as in the past, giving them up to child welfare organizations due to an inability to support them—child welfare agencies could focus on in-home services, through which agencies "strive[ed] to maintain the family through emphasis on prevention" (CWLA 1958, 3). This aspirational perspective was reinforced in the influential statement by the 1959 Advisory Council on Child Welfare Services, whose writers constituted a "who's who" of child welfare leaders. Despite administrative restrictions that blocked many struggling families from accessing government aid, the council members claimed that ADC was the primary resource for impoverished families, leaving child welfare professionals to focus on services aimed at "behavior and social adjustment"; to support this claim, the report trumpeted that only 9 percent of children receiving child welfare services were poor.[5] Yet this claim was factually problematic because it defined poor children as those in families receiving ADC. However, ADC recipients were, in fact, only a small portion of poor families at the time, and most "working poor" two-parent families were ineligible for the program, as were those deemed by ADC administrators to be "undeserving" of aid, which included a disproportionate number of African American families (Abramovitz 1996; Frame 1999). Indeed, there were approximately 16.6 million children living below the poverty line in the United States in 1959, and only a small portion (less than a million) received federal cash assistance (US Census Bureau 1968).[6] Yet it is likely that many families receiving child welfare services—whether voluntarily, coercively, or forcibly—were among those poor families who were not receiving ADC, a fact ignored by the Child Welfare Advisory Council.

Despite the council's problematic assumptions, its statement was read and reprinted in full in the 1962 Public Welfare Amendments (PWA) hearings, which strongly reinforced the idea that rehabilitative services were central to the child welfare profession. The PWA increased funding for child welfare services and required that every family receiving Aid to Families with Dependent Children (AFDC), the newly named ADC, receive social services (Cohen and Ball 1962). A 1962 editorial celebrated this shift, noting, "In these decisions government has at last recognized that the unmarried parent on ADC, the family with the deserted father, the parents who abuse and neglect their children, must receive social work service and not just a check if children are to be protected. The [Department of Health, Education, and Welfare] Secretary's statement acknowledges that many of the parents receiving assistance are persons with problems who may be assisted with social work help to become more responsible mothers and fathers to their children" (E.E.G. 1962, 50).[7]

This shift from poor families to "problem" families is also documented in recent scholarship on how US foster care norms evolved in the mid-twentieth century. In the decades after the Social Security Act passed, child welfare agencies providing foster care to mostly poor families began labeling the families they worked with as pathologically damaged due to issues like divorce, mental illness, or children born to unmarried parents. Little attention was paid to economic need as a contributing factor to family challenges (Rymph 2012, 2017). This chapter argues that this shift in how both poor families and the purpose of foster care were understood was part of a broader evolution of professional child welfare practices that emphasized "specialized" social services—such as referral and psychological services—but deprioritized addressing poverty.

(Un)seeing Poverty: Knowledge Production and Professional Practice

Avoiding substantive engagement with the issue of poverty was baked into the processes of knowledge production in midcentury US child

welfare. From the 1940s through the 1960s, the Children's Bureau produced a wide array of reports, including an annual series of statistical
reports on children served by child welfare agencies, which provided
a rich source of knowledge about American children in need. Yet the
reports' detailed descriptions of children served by child welfare agencies across the nation did not include data on family income level,
which meant that national child welfare data gave policy makers and
practitioners little insight into how many children receiving services
were poor, a problem that persists to this day.[8] By overlooking the
prevalence of poverty among families who received child welfare interventions, the knowledge producers at the Children's Bureau and other
child welfare advocacy organizations rendered these families' poverty
essentially invisible.

These efforts to "unsee" poverty at the administrative and policy levels, however, were often in active conflict with the poverty that many
child welfare workers engaged with on the ground, as documented in
publications by practitioners and administrators. Child welfare leaders
and professionals gilded over this conflict by simultaneously advocating
for policies that improved funding for poor families while also insist-
ing that they did not see child welfare work as the professional space in
which to actually implement such policies (Eliot 1954; Reid 1956a, 1962;
Winston 1960, 1966). Child welfare leaders seemed to recognize the intertwined nature of child welfare services and poverty relief yet generally
advocated for a clear demarcation of child welfare as a field focused on
social services (Gaughan 1954), such as psychological services, medical
or financial aid referrals, homemaker services, or child placement.

A systematic review of *Child Welfare* articles during this period reveals that for street-level practitioners, poverty was a frequent concern,
though it was often reframed in psychological or rehabilitative terms. In
a striking example, a 1966 article discussed "community group therapy,"
an effort to provide activities in a group setting for "emotionally and
socially deprived girls." Described entirely in psychological terms, the
girls' issues were viewed as the outcome of having "depressed, impulsive,
nonprotecting [sic] parents." In turn, they were seen as requiring a
series of psychological interventions. Yet, buried in the description of
the group participants were statements that make clear that they and
their families were indeed severely deprived—of financial security. These

were very poor families, described as on public assistance or otherwise financially struggling. At least some of them were African American, and all of them were so poor that the girls' primary interest was in the food provided at the program.[9] Yet the authors did not link this poverty and material deprivation to their primary diagnosis of sociopsychological deprivation (King 1966).

This sort of "unseeing" of poverty—to the point that even when explicitly dealing with poor children, child welfare practitioners reframed poverty as a matter of psychological deprivation—pervaded a profession insistent on a rehabilitative focus. Even if child welfare administrators and organizations recognized that poverty was a paramount issue, the profession's practical response to poverty was usually what they considered to be "social services."

Articles in the early 1970s linked poverty with pathology, specifically describing children in foster care from poor, inner-city families of color (usually Black) as having experienced "psychological deprivation" and linking race, poverty, and maltreatment (Kappelman et al. 1970; Kavaler and Swire 1972, 575). One article (Littner 1972, 217) categorized some poor families as "emotionally disorganized and disintegrating" and noted that poor children from the "ghetto" (code for Black) who have been exposed to violence and then face "even more severe external pressures" may resort to their own violent behavior as adults (Littner 1972, 212). Such interpretations, particularly common in *Child Welfare* articles in the 1960s and 1970s, echoed broader scholarly claims at that time about a "culture of poverty" in which poor communities developed values and behaviors that kept them in poverty (Lewis 1968). This framing characterized financial hardship as the result of parental shortcomings, suggesting that rehabilitative psychological interventions, instead of financial assistance and systemic policy changes, were the solution to both poverty and child maltreatment.

Pushback and Ambivalence: Poverty Governance in Practice

The intertwining of sociopsychological needs and poverty—and the active effort to reframe the latter as the former—received some pushback. In a study of child neglect published in 1964, the author noted that families referred to agencies for neglect issues were generally poor, unemployed, on financial assistance, and supporting many children. Specific behaviors described as "frequently cited in neglect complaints in order of frequency" included "excessive drinking, inadequate control or discipline, inadequate housekeeping, illicit sex relations of parents, and leaving children untended." The author argued that the predominance of poor families—with families of color also overrepresented—in neglect reports undermined the assumptions of the "psychodynamic orientation" of social work that dominated child welfare practice and that disassociated family problems from financial issues: "Because of the strong psychodynamic orientation of social work, attention has been focused largely upon the personality disturbance of parents as a major causal factor in neglect. Thus, this focus would make it logical to assume that such disturbances would occur among families regardless of social class or other demographic characteristics" (Boehm 1964, 459). In fact, the author argued, her analysis of families reported to child welfare indicated that this assumption was wrong and that child welfare engaged with families that were not pathological but often simply poor or socially disadvantaged: "For the most part, [families reported as neglectful in the study] represent the most socially and economically disadvantaged sectors of the population and differ from the general population of the community in the significantly higher proportion of broken homes, minority group membership, and lower socioeconomic status" (Boehm 1964, 459).

Another critique of the psychotherapeutic approach came from a nonprofit worker who argued that "casework simply has not been very successful with lower-class families." This critique was part of the author's larger argument that social work's hyperemphasis on "intrapersonal and intrafamilial conditions as sources of difficulty," instead of "lower class culture," impeded effective casework (Hunter 1962, 391). The author, however, retained the assumptions of the broader discipline and did not suggest that social workers should actively work on poverty reduction. Instead, he advocated for more sensitivity to class differences between social workers and clients and to broader cultural issues tied to class.

That even a critique of social work's framing of poverty culminated in a recommendation for a psychological reorientation, not a shift to structural issues, indicates the deep roots of the rehabilitative framing in the fields of social work broadly and child welfare specifically. These roots were linked to child welfare's professional emphasis on "specialization," which sought to frame the profession as focused on psychotherapeutic issues, distinct from structural and economic ones. While generally accepted as vital to the professionalization of the field, specialization was singled out for strong critique in 1962 by Jerome Sampson, a California welfare administrator. Sampson argued that the specialized training of child welfare workers in social casework and psychotherapeutic interventions led to "separation and isolation of services within agencies, . . . unhealthy competition for trained caseworkers, a struggle for tax dollars, . . . and retardation of the development of urgently needed services" (1962, 395). Specifically, Sampson claimed that while specialization improved child welfare professional practices, it also meant that child welfare interventions were too disconnected from public aid and poverty issues—that is, "public child welfare services have been too fat and too enriched as compared with public assistance" (1962, 396)—and that social services should be provided together with financial assistance. The article, however, was paired with a response by a different author, who wholly rejected this argument, claiming that all of Sampson's critiques would be resolved by simply increasing funding and by staffing child welfare agencies with properly trained employees (Turitz 1962). This response reflected broader child welfare discourse and practices that tended to overlook the intersecting problems of poverty and racial discrimination in shaping who needed services and who received them.

Yet even as child welfare's professional framing remained rehabilitative, the facts on the ground began to change. The 1960s saw a rise in the proportion of poor children involved in the child welfare system (Jeter 1960, 50; 1963, 131). This was due both to the PWA's new requirement that states provide child welfare services to families receiving AFDC and to the dramatic increase in eligibility for AFDC in the aftermath of court rulings pushing back on racially discriminatory practices at the state and local levels, specifically state agencies withholding aid to eligible families of color (Abramovitz 1996; see also Cohen and Ball 1962). Child welfare agents had to contend with a growing number of poor children—increasingly children of color—to "rehabilitate."

This paradox was recognized by child welfare leaders, who continued to push for policies that increased poverty relief funding, even as they promoted a rehabilitative framework for child welfare practice (Eliot 1954; Reid 1956a, 1962; Winston 1960, 1966). In 1962, Joseph Reid, a CWLA director, noted that rehabilitation would be most effective when conjoined with adequate poverty relief: "In order for a public assistance recipient or a child in a foster home to receive casework help [and] rehabilitation service . . . he first has to eat. . . . Neither rehabilitation programs nor reorganization of public welfare agency structure will solve the problem of inadequate public financing" (1962, 483).

In practice, however, child welfare's professional focus remained firmly rehabilitative, in keeping with decades of social work training and child welfare professionalization. A 1968 article by Rebecca Smith, a CWLA director, noted critiques by "some leaders in the child welfare field" that child welfare was too focused on placing children in foster care, rather than on the causes of placement: "Has the field forgotten the abject misery caused by unspeakably wretched housing, hunger, illness, illiteracy, lack of job opportunities, and racial bigotry? Has it overlooked the fact that skilled counseling and treatment of psychological conflicts alone cannot erase such misery?" (1968, 130).

Yet despite Smith's concerns with these issues, her recommendations were still deeply rooted in the dominant views of the social work field of the time, avoiding direct responses to poverty in favor of a psycho-therapeutic approach. Specifically, Smith suggested that child welfare agencies should seek to address such issues through an array of social services, from tutoring to homemaker guidance and therapeutic programs. The only hint at economic relief was job training for unmarried mothers—probably as part of increasing requirements for AFDC eligibility (R. Smith 1968). Smith's response thus encapsulated the complexities of professionally intervening in issues linked to poverty, even while hamstrung by the political and social constrictions of the US welfare state.

Race and Child Welfare Interventions

The growth of public child welfare services in the aftermath of the Social Security Act of 1935 was linked to a deepening racialization of the child welfare field's target population. While private agencies had long avoided working with children of color, primarily Black children, these same Black children were increasingly overrepresented in public child welfare interventions in the 1940s and later, as these agencies' resources grew due to increased federal and state funding. By 1959, "nonwhite" children constituted 25 percent of child welfare cases (up from 14 percent in 1945) and 30 percent of foster care placements, although they only made up about 13 percent of the child population during this entire period (US Census Bureau 2021). This overrepresentation only intensified in later decades, as public child welfare agencies shifted their focus to child maltreatment and increasingly targeted poor families and parents of color (Freundlich and Barbell 2001).

As public child welfare leaders made clear in multiple documents, they believed their duty was to serve every child, regardless of "race, color, or creed" (CWLA 1958; Mayo et al. 1950). Yet this was a quixotic challenge in a welfare state built on a long history of racially discriminatory policy development, which was further exacerbated by fragmented state- and local-level implementation of welfare programs in the US federalist polity. African American, Latine, and Indigenous families were historically excluded from state assistance programs and then were increasingly targeted for oversurveillance and punitive interventions beginning in the 1960s. When services were provided, the quality was often abysmal, with Black children frequently placed in harsh institutional settings due to agencies' refusal to provide foster care services for them and with American Indian children forced to attend often-abusive boarding schools (Bernstein 2002; Billingsley and Giovannoni 1972; Rymph 2017; Simmons 2020).

Yet child welfare leaders rarely wrote about the clear racial double standards in services. Instead, in ways that both paralleled and diverged from their response to poverty, child welfare practitioners tended to avoid active engagement in the broader issues of race and racial discrimination, which their casework-focused training and available child welfare funding and resources generally did not equip them to address. This systemic disengagement is reflected in *Child Welfare*. Unlike the repeated discussions of poverty in *Child Welfare* during the 1950s, I found almost no substantive discussions of race or racism in the articles examined from this decade (397 articles from all even-numbered years were coded). However, the number of articles focused on race jumped in the 1960s—of the 936 articles coded for 1950–68, only two articles discussed race as the main article topic in the 1950s, while twelve articles did so in the 1960s. At least one hundred articles mentioned race as part of broader discussions in the 1960s, but often as a brief aside, with little substantive discussion of racial discrimination.

During the 1950s, and far more frequently in the 1960s, discussions of race in *Child Welfare* focused primarily on the challenges of finding adoptive and foster care homes for children of color, in particular African American children. As public agencies with newly expanded resources took more interest in adoption and foster care—issues that had previously been dominated by private agencies that largely ignored Black children—social workers repeatedly noted the difficulty of finding families willing to take Black children due to their race (Hawkins 1960; Reid 1956b). But these statements rarely acknowledged what recent scholarship has shown: deeply discriminatory child placement practices placed Black children in particularly abysmal institutional and foster care conditions (Bernstein 2002; Simmons 2020). During the 1960s, *Child Welfare* published at least seven articles focused entirely on the issue of placing Black children in foster and adoptive homes, and authors also paid increasing attention to the racial dynamics of the rise in "illegitimate" children born to unmarried parents (Garland 1966; Wrieden 1960). Articles in that decade discussed concerns that ADC would increase the likelihood of poor women, especially African American women, bearing children without marrying the fathers, while echoing a growing public sentiment: the resentment of many white Americans at the rising numbers of Black children receiving ADC (Hollander 1960; Wrieden 1960).

To some degree, in the 1950s and 1960s, child welfare professionals' attitudes toward race and poverty were both intertwined and the inverse of each other. Advocates and child welfare administrators pushed for broader structural changes to reduce poverty, including legislative action to increase ADC/AFDC funding, in the face of legislative and public resistance to increasing direct support for poor families (Winston 1966). Still, they did not see direct professional engagement in poverty relief as their responsibility, seeking instead a rehabilitative approach that shaped the professional roots of contemporary US child welfare practices. In contrast, the challenges of finding adoption and foster care placements for children of color was a practical problem that fell directly under child welfare agencies' purview. Yet, even as public child welfare advocates declared that they would serve all children regardless of demographics, there was little discussion or advocacy regarding the structural problems of racism during this period, specifically the discrimination that mothers and families of color faced, the poverty they suffered as a result of that discrimination, and the deeply rooted alienation of these families from the agencies that had long underserved them. By abdicating professional responsibility for directly and practically addressing poverty, child welfare's rehabilitative approach deeply and negatively affected families of color in particular, who were disproportionately represented among the US poor.

Child Maltreatment in a Rehabilitative Framing

During the 1960s, all fifty states passed laws mandating that professionals report suspicions of child abuse and neglect to social service or law enforcement authorities. The shift to a focus on child maltreatment unfolded during a period of increasing backlash to poverty support in the late 1960s and the 1970s, as epitomized by the Nixon administration's open contempt for social welfare programs. Current scholarship points to this backlash as an explanation for why the 1974 enactment of CAPTA, the Child Abuse Prevention and Treatment Act, hinged on the white, middle-class child as the paradigmatic case of abuse and the victim of psychologically damaged parents. Scholars argue that this was the only way such a bill could pass during the Nixon administration (Nelson 1984; Raz 2020).

While correct about the legislative moment, this reading misses an important point: child welfare workers were not trained or equipped to deal with child abuse as a structural issue intimately linked to poverty and race. Their lack of preparedness was the product of both broader policy trends and factors internal to the profession. From a policy perspective, state and federal legislators did not provide child welfare agencies with the resources to alleviate financial need, and the existing financial relief resources that parents could access through public aid offices were woefully insufficient and deeply stigmatized (Abramovitz 1996; Katz 2013). A concurrent push in the broader US welfare administration for a focus on "rehabilitative" social services, as distinct from financial aid (Mittelstadt 2005), heavily influenced child welfare leaders of institutions like the Children's Bureau, who worked to shape the child welfare field into a profession of trained practitioners focused on social rehabilitation using individualized psychotherapeutic tools. "Unseeing poverty"—or delinking family challenges from broader issues of racial discrimination and poverty and instead focusing on surveilling individual parental inadequacies—thus became "our way," the American way, of governing poor families in the United States (Larson 1950).

This chapter reveals how the delinking of structural disadvantage and child maltreatment was rooted in child welfare's decades-long professionalization process, which primed child welfare actors to treat child maltreatment as a psychological problem of individual parents, not as a problem linked to broader social conditions or policies. Although some social workers certainly advocated for a greater focus on poverty and race issues (Raz 2020), institutionalized professional norms reinforced a political strategy of pathologizing marginalized families. In the aftermath of CAPTA's passage, an increased focus on child abuse and neglect, delinked from issues of poverty, further entrenched child welfare as a system of poverty governance that reinforced socioeconomic inequalities. Research has consistently indicated that poor children are overrepresented in child welfare interventions (Dolan et al. 2011; Sedlak et al. 2010; USDHHS 1988). For decades, Black and Indigenous families have been disproportionately affected by child welfare investigations and child removals due to the child welfare system's oversurveillance and separation of families facing intersecting racial and economic discrimination.

By the mid-1970s, American Indian children suffered from such egregiously high levels of family separation that advocates convinced Congress to pass the Indian Child Welfare Act (1978), although Indigenous children continue to be overrepresented in child welfare cases (Kim et al. 2017; see also USDHHS 2022a). These numbers have been particularly glaring in foster care. In 1980, children of color made up 47 percent of foster care placements, but by 1990, they made up 60 percent, a vast overrepresentation of their proportions in the population and a powerful indicator of the racialization of the child welfare system (Freundlich and Barbell 2001).

The class and racial inequalities that are so deeply embedded in child welfare practices are linked both to child welfare's professionalization process and to the political and administrative context in which it evolved. In fact, it is possible that an approach based on psychological rehabilitation might have been helpful—or, at minimum, not harmful—to marginalized families if it functioned in concert with adequate and nondiscriminatory financial assistance programming. But the US child welfare profession has always been embedded in a broader welfare state that has never substantively addressed socioeconomic inequalities (Abramovitz 1996; Hutchinson 2002). In this context, a rehabilitative approach translated problems linked to systemic poverty and racial discrimination into individualized issues of child-specific parental or family dynamics, obscuring, to workers and policy makers alike, the challenges these families faced.

The legacy of a proto-neoliberal professionalization process has lingered in the US child welfare system to this day. With an outsized focus on poor and marginalized families, the child welfare system functions as a form of racialized poverty governance, despite persistent calls for reform (Pelton 1978, 2015) or outright abolition (Roberts 2022). As the United States faces concerning levels of socioeconomic inequality and high numbers of child welfare investigations (Kim et al. 2017), the "unseeing" of poverty in family governance persists, and we still remain far from a society in which all families have the support they need to truly protect their children.

NOTES

1 This was in part because child welfare practices often treated—and still do—conditions of poverty as evidence of bad parenting. Challenges that poor parents were more likely to face, like fewer childcare and educational resources, were often framed as parental neglect and as indications that the parents might cause the child harm (Fong 2020; Pelton 2015).

2 See the US Children's Bureau's *Children's Bureau Statistical Series* (CBSS), published 1949–69.

3 "National Commission on Children and Youth. Action Program 1947–1948," FS 1131-3.202, Box 571, RG 287, National Archives and Record Administration, College Park, MD.

4 For more on how family agencies ceased to focus on financial assistance by the early 1950s as a result of federal poverty relief funding, see Shyne 1951, 1953.

5 "Report of Advisory Council on Child Welfare Services, 1959," Box 572, RG 287, National Archives and Record Administration, College Park, MD.

6 Data on the number of children receiving cash assistance from 1959 to 2011 is available in the US House of Representatives, Committee on Ways and Means,

Greenbook (2012). Figure 7-2 shows the number of families receiving cash assistance in 1959.

7 This editorial was written in response to administrative regulations that preceded the passage of the PWA by several months, but the regulations and PWA overlapped; Abraham Ribicoff, the secretary of the US Health, Education, and Welfare Department (the predecessor to today's Department of Health and Human Services) required welfare departments to provide social work services to ADC families, among other requirements for aid disbursement. The PWA made these regulations federal law.

8 See US Children's Bureau (1949–69). Note that in the early 1960s, the Children's Bureau did publish three reports on child welfare services that addressed family income level data (see Jeter 1960, 1962, 1963). However, the National Child Abuse and Neglect Data System, the basis for the "Child Maltreatment" reports issued annually by the Children's Bureau (1995–present), does not collect data on income level.

9 The article noted that the group "consisted of seven Negro and white girls" but does not specify how many of each (King 1966, 527).

PART II

The Child Welfare System as Poverty Governance

Taking the Children to Take the Land

Indian Child Welfare and the Enduring Epidemic of Family Separation

AMY CASSELMAN-HONTALAS

At the height of public outrage over the Trump administration's forced separation of children from their parents at the US-Mexico border, the rallying cry of "This is not who we are!" was echoed by television pundits, plastered on social media, and paraded through streets in protest. As a caseworker for a federally recognized tribe and an adjunct professor of American Indian history and law, I was baffled by such a statement.

The United States was founded on American Indian genocide and the enslavement of Africans, both of which were structured by the logic of family annihilation. In the case of Indigenous people, the survival of Native families was problematic for a country that, by definition, can only exist through the consumption of Native resources. Due to Native people's preexisting right to land, they were viewed by the United States as a "problem" to be "solved." And, because resources are passed down generationally, "solving" the "problem" that is a People resulted in centuries of physical and cultural genocide that targeted Native families. Policies designed to destroy Native communities in service of appropriating their land focused on children, under the logic that disappearing the youngest generation was the most direct route to disappearing all future generations. Historically, this included state-sponsored infanticide, the incarceration of Native children in government-run boarding schools, and the transfer of Native children to white foster and adoptive families. Placing children in non-Native settings was designed to sever the bonds between children, their parents, and their communities in order to disrupt intergenerational transfers of resources and reduce the number of people who could assert claims over the lands and resources that the United States desired.

Further, maintaining physical custody of Native children gave the United States leverage to coerce Native parents into behavior that benefited the settler state, including relocating Native people to smaller parcels of land. Thus, the welfare of Indian children has always been enmeshed with the welfare of Indian nations, including the wealth associated with their land. From contact to present, government-sponsored family separation has contributed to the cumulative loss of approximately 98.9 percent of Native land in the United States, leaving approximately 42.1 percent of Native nations without any land base at all (Farrell et al. 2021). Because Indigenous economies were rooted in their land, catastrophic land loss meant an unfathomable loss of wealth. All Native communities were profoundly affected, and many were driven into severe poverty.

As has always been the case, Native people continue to resist and rebuild in the face of centuries of genocide. Native communities are incredibly diverse, and many individuals and nations are economically thriving. That said, when taken as a whole, Native people are the most impoverished demographic in the United States vis-à-vis their non-Native peers. While this is the case in both rural and urban settings, many reservation communities are especially impoverished, some with poverty and unemployment rates that exceed 50 percent (Bear Runner 2019; Shrider and Creamer 2023).

When we consider that poverty and unemployment did not exist before the arrival of Europeans, it is impossible to ignore the causal relationship between colonization and Indigenous poverty. Because mainstream child welfare literature does not typically focus on the state's role in creating poverty, it often overlooks the complex historical relationships between the government and the governed. Scholarly literature (see, for example, Soss, Fording, and Schram 2011) frequently uses the 1996 Personal Responsibility and Work Opportunity Reconciliation Act, often referred to as "welfare reform," as a temporal marker to discuss the neoliberalization of welfare, which—among other things—increased state surveillance of recipients, heightened punitive measures for noncompliance, and implemented policies designed to shape the behavior of poor parents. While the 1996 reforms certainly impacted poor

Native families, a more comprehensive examination reveals that the most relevant temporal marker in Indian child welfare is the formation of the United States itself. In other words, Native children and families have endured state surveillance, punitive measures for noncompliance, and the use of Native children to shape the behavior of their parents for as long as the United States has existed as a country.

Pushing the boundaries of traditional scholarship on child welfare by placing it in a historical context is essential if we are to create a more comprehensive body of research on US poverty governance, or ways the state manages and disciplines poor populations (Soss, Fording, and Schram 2011), particularly as it relates to historically marginalized groups. For example, (re)considering the state's role in creating Native poverty can shed light on similar but distinct cases of racialized poverty governance, such as the enslavement and exploitation of Black Americans and their descendants. Viewing contemporary state exploitation of Black and Native children as logical manifestations of an uninterrupted history reveals that public programs merely recirculate wealth by returning an infinitesimal sum to the very communities whose exploitation made funding these programs possible (see Roberts 2022). This is especially true for the large number of Black Americans in the United States who also have Native ancestry and thus experience the legacy of both enslavement and colonization. Viewing poverty governance as an ongoing, historical process better equips us to develop strategies to address family poverty. Contemporary literature frequently suggests the augmentation or implementation of social programs to assist the economically marginalized. While such programs would probably benefit many families of color on a surface level, failing to address the root cause severely limits their efficacy. This is particularly true for Native people who, prior to European contact, had cared for their families on the land that would become the United States. Thus, any initiative that does not consider colonization and tribal sovereignty is incomplete. Assistive programs implemented by colonial structures that are designed to "help" Native people overlook the fact that Native communities are perfectly capable of taking care of themselves. Instead, what is needed is the reclamation of the tools necessary for self-sufficiency. While I discuss this issue at length in the conclusion, a crucial first step would be for the United States to simply fulfill its constitutional obligations to Native people.

This chapter theorizes US poverty governance as a tool of settler co-lonialism by illustrating how historical constructions of Native people translate into contemporary child welfare policies. First, I offer context by discussing the unique space that Native children, families, and communities occupy in the contemporary welfare state. Second, I submit a historical analysis, detailing how child separation has been used to control Native people and, by extension, their land. In doing so, I illustrate the unique ways that colonial exploitation and punitive poverty governance have been woven throughout the fabric of American Indian history by way of Indian child welfare. As my historical analysis transitions into the present day, I demonstrate how the modern Indian child welfare system parallels the function, form, and outcome of policies established in previous centuries. Using South Dakota as a case study, I show how the contemporary child welfare industrial complex is designed to profit from the bodies of Native children in ways that are remarkably similar to previous eras. As in the past, this case study demonstrates that child removal is characterized by an aversion to Native culture, a lack of cultural competency, the failure to fulfill legal obligations to Indian nations, the erroneous conflation between poverty and abuse, and the false assumption that placing Indian children in white settings is in their best interest. While these justifications are part of a remarkably consistent state attitude toward Native people, the case study indicates that the removal of Native children by the state is exacerbated by the contemporary neoliberalization of child welfare in an increasingly privatized environment. Next, I examine the landmark 2023 US Supreme Court decision in *Haaland v. Brackeen*. My analysis exposes how a civil suit ostensibly about Indian child welfare was ultimately about the appropriation of Native land. In doing so, I illustrate how controlling Native children perpetuates the colonization of Native people, forcing us to confront the ways in which neoliberalism intersects with neocolonialism. Finally, I comment on the future of Indian child welfare by discussing Native-led strategies to end genocide-by-separation.

Indian Children in the Child Welfare Landscape

While it is vital for scholarly research to study how child welfare is structured by race, gender, and class, the integration of Native children into existing frameworks is often problematic because it generally fails to consider settler colonialism. Like all people of color, phenotypically Native people experience racism under white supremacy. However, as the only (legally recognized) Indigenous group in the United States, Native people have a unique relationship to the land and, consequently, a radically different relationship to the federal government. As a result, there is an entire body of law that governs Native people, which includes policies that apply to Indian children only, thus differentiating them from all non-Native children (Pevar 2012).[1] Despite these differences and distinctions, child welfare literature tends to collapse Native children into analyses that theorize children of color broadly.

The unique body of law that governs Native people primarily flows from the hundreds of treaties signed between the United States and Native nations. Federal Indian policy generally only applies to "federally recognized tribes," of which there are currently 574 (US Department of the Interior, Bureau of Indian Affairs, n.d.).[2] Under current law, federally recognized tribes are semiautonomous nations that may exercise all rights of self-governance other than those that have been specifically extinguished by Congress. Like all sovereign nations, one of the most important rights that all federally recognized tribes exercise is the ability to self-determine criteria for citizenship. While citizenship requirements are different for each tribe, each has some sort of descendant criteria. This typically means that a prospective tribal citizen must prove that they are a descendant of someone listed on a tribal census. Congress and the US Supreme Court have consistently held that tribal citizenship is a political designation, not a racial one (Pevar 2012).

The primacy of race as a definitional category in the United States, coupled with an inadequate understanding of American Indian history, makes the race/citizenship distinction exceedingly difficult for many Americans to grasp. Like all racial categories, "Indian" is socially constructed and reductive, homogenizing a diverse group of people on the basis of meanings assigned to phenotype and perceived group identity. Yet "Indian" is also a legal term used by the federal government whose definition is based on political membership (i.e., tribal citizenship) independent of race. Thus, any discussion of Indian child welfare is complex because it requires us to consider both children who are phenotypically Native and children who appear racially non-Native but are nevertheless

"Indian" under the law. This speaks to the racialization of child welfare, as state actors frequently operate on essentialized notions of race, making it difficult for many to understand that a child who is phenotypically white or Black can also be American Indian (Brown 2020). Understanding this distinction is crucial for state social workers because federal law significantly limits state jurisdiction over Indian child welfare cases. This has been the case since the passage of the Indian Child Welfare Act (ICWA) in 1978, a law designed to reduce the staggering number of Native children who were being taken from their parents and placed in white settings. While congressional support for the Act relied heavily on child welfare statistics from the 1960s and 1970s, the Native architects of ICWA designed the law to account for a larger colonial history (Echo-Hawk 2010). The following section offers a brief description of this history, illustrating how the US settler state has created and governed poverty among Native families since its inception.

Taking the Children to Take the Land: A Brief History of Indian Child Welfare

In May 2021, ground-penetrating radar revealed the mass grave of 215 Native children who perished in one of Canada's 139 residential schools (BBC News 2021). For those who followed the story, it was a point of entry for many Americans who were previously unaware that beginning in 1819, the United States developed a vast network of more than four hundred boarding schools, which, at times, imprisoned nearly 83 percent of all school-age Native children. Predating the Canadian system and exceeding it in scope, American Indian boarding schools were designed with the express purpose to "kill the Indian, save the man" (Adams 1995; Echo-Hawk 2010; Newland 2022).

Symbolic murder in the form of using schools to kill the Indian (child) to "save the man" came on the heels of decades of warfare that used the logic of infanticide to acquire Native resources. For example, during the 1813–14 Creek War, which led to the loss of twenty-three million acres of Native land, the future US president Andrew Jackson instructed his troops to kill Native children to "complete the extermination" (Toensing 2018). Similarly, in an 1864 effort to protect white settlers invading

Cheyenne and Arapaho land, Colonel John Chivington instructed his troops to target Native children because "nits make lice" (Casselman 2016). By the 1870s, physical genocide against Native people became a financial burden to the United States. As the government looked for a cheaper alternative, it contracted Brigadier General Richard Henry Pratt to create a system of off-reservation boarding schools for American Indian children.

Starting with the Carlisle Indian Industrial School in 1879, these boarding schools were designed to strip Native children of their identities and assimilate them into white culture. When children arrived at boarding school, their hair was cut, their clothes were replaced with uniforms, and their possessions were confiscated and destroyed. Children were forced to take new Anglo-American names, speak English, and practice Christianity. In addition to the trauma of being separated from their parents and stripped of their identities, boarding schools were sites of rampant physical and sexual abuse, leading to intergenerational trauma that is still felt today (A. Smith 2005).

Boarding schools were also money-making institutions for a variety of actors. In addition to providing jobs and stimulating local economies, boarding schools were lucrative for unscrupulous administrators, who pocketed budget surpluses by purchasing inadequate supplies of food and medicine. As a result, children were often malnourished and went without medical care, leading to the death of untold thousands. Further, under the guise of "work experience," children were contracted out to farms and factories to learn the so-called industrial arts of domestic and manual labor. Here, federal dollars flowed to school administrators while local economies benefited from child labor (Hilleary 2021; A. Smith 2005).

Compulsory boarding-school attendance led to the surveillance of Native parents, along with heightened punitive measures exacted against entire communities. Parents who refused to surrender their children were imprisoned, and communities found to be withholding children faced cuts to the rations and monies that constituted the majority of their economy (Echo-Hawk 2010; A. Smith 2005). Once children were acquired by the state, they could then be used as leverage to control their parents. As Native people continued to resist encroachment onto their land, Commissioner of Indian Affairs Ezra Hayt noted that the state could use Native children at boarding schools to quell their parents' "hostile attitude toward the government" (Brown and Estes 2018). The best example of this is the 1887 General Allotment Act (also known as the Dawes Act), which privatized communally held tribal land. According to the superintendent of schools, if Native people were to resist privatization, "the children would be hostages for the good behavior of their people" (Brown and Estes 2018). With their children used as leverage by the state, Native communities were forced to accept the division of their land into privately owned parcels. In the process, the United States seized about two-thirds of all remaining Native land. This is the single greatest transfer of wealth from Indigenous communities to the settler state and is frequently cited as a turning point during which reservation communities were driven into profound poverty (Ahlstedt 2016; Echo-Hawk 2010).

Despite the devastation wrought upon Native children and communities, both boarding schools and land privatization were framed as in the "best interest" of Indian children and their parents. In the case of boarding schools, state actors—frequently white women reformers who styled themselves as "friends of the Indian"—viewed their work as "rescuing" Native children from what they perceived as economic and cultural poverty. Reformers failed to acknowledge their role in creating Indigenous poverty—such as supporting the withholding of rations in order to discipline Native communities—and insisted that departures from an idealized norm of a white, middle-class nuclear family rendered Native homes unfit. Such assessments were highly gendered, as Native women whose homes lacked "furniture, decorations, curtains, tablecloths, and other accoutrements" were deemed to be "utterly inadequate" mothers whose parenting was "virtually pathological" (Jacobs 2009, 127–31).

In addition to boarding schools, land privatization—designed primarily to appropriate Native land—was also favored by cultural reformers because the land distribution process favored male heads of nuclear families. Thus, privatization worked as a corollary to boarding schools in which Native children would be raised in a "superior" culture, while their parents would be "civilized" by learning the value of patriarchy, the nuclear family structure, and private land ownership (Ahlstedt 2016). Here, both boarding schools and land privatization created spaces in which Indigenous people could be "simultaneously nurtured and disciplined, gently guided and closely monitored" (Jacobs 2009, 112).

The 1950s ushered in what was dubbed the "Termination Era," in which lawmakers stated that they wanted to "get out of the Indian business" once and for all. This involved abrogating treaties, seizing reservation land, and continuing to target Native children for removal. Boarding schools continued to operate, reaching their peak enrollment in the 1960s. At the same time, it is estimated that up to seventy thousand Native women were sterilized in government hospitals in order to prevent Native children from being born (Johansen 1998). For those children who were born, the federal government instituted the Indian Adoption Project with the explicit goal of placing Native children in non-Native homes (Ono 2016b).

While Native children were being adopted en masse by non-Native families, they were also being placed in foster care at epidemic levels. Even though decades had passed since nineteenth-century reformers advocated for American Indian boarding schools, by the 1960s and 1970s, state actors continued to believe that Indian families and reservation communities were inherently unfit for children. Cultural bias and racial animus fueled an industrial complex with far-reaching economic outcomes. Not only did residential facilities for Native children inject federal dollars into state economies, but non-Native foster families benefited from monthly stipends and the use of Native children as a source of unpaid labor. As one report revealed, non-Native communities eager to foster Native children for the economic benefits would frequently petition their local governments to make more Native children available for fostering. This created what were known as "baby farms" in cities across the United States, where local governments systematically removed Native children to satisfy the demands of their white constituents (Byler 1977, 6).

The Indian Child Welfare Act and a New Era of Indian Child Welfare

By the mid-1970s, up to one-third of all Indian children were in either foster care or adoptive homes. Between 85 and 95 percent of these children were in non-Native settings. And, depending on the state, Native children were between five and twenty-five times more likely to be in foster care or an adoptive home compared to their non-Native peers, even when "fit and willing relatives were available to care for them" (Echo-Hawk 2010; Hopkins 2018). A 1977 investigation by the American Association of Indian Affairs concluded that these removals were due not to abuse but rather to "the widely shared ideology that appreciated middle-class nuclear family orientation over the extended family orientation of Indian families" (Ono 2016a, 112).

To halt the abduction of Native children, Native activists, attorneys, and organizations worked with allies in Congress to pass the Indian Child Welfare Act of 1978. ICWA is not only regarded as one of the most important victories for tribal sovereignty in recent history, but it has also been hailed as "the gold standard" for *all* child welfare policy because of its focus on preserving a child's ties to their family and community of origin.[3] ICWA includes several components that are critical to protecting Native children and nations. Perhaps most importantly, ICWA institutes a priority placement schedule in which an Indian child may not be placed in a non-Indian setting until the following sequential placement options have been exhausted: (1) the child's extended family; (2) other members of the child's tribe; (3) any other Native family.[4] Importantly, ICWA applies to all Indian children no matter where they live. Thus, US states have a due diligence requirement to determine if any child that enters their welfare system is eligible for ICWA. Under ICWA, an "Indian child" is "any unmarried person who is under age eighteen and is either (a) a member of an Indian tribe or (b) is eligible for membership in an Indian tribe and is the biological child of a member of an Indian tribe" (25 U.S.C. 1903 [1978]). Crucially, the definition of an "Indian child" is based on tribal citizenship, which empowers tribes to protect their children from colonial racial classifications.

Since the passage of ICWA, it has prevented unnecessary removals, facilitated family reunification, and significantly increased the likelihood that Native adoptees and foster children are placed in Indian homes. In areas where compliance is high, data show that Native children thrive, exceeding the outcomes of their peers placed in non-Native settings (Akee 2018; Austin 2009). Despite this progress, ICWA is flagrantly violated in many areas of the country. The following are two high-profile case studies that expose the colonial motives behind such violations.

Twenty-First-Century Kidnapping: Foster Care and the Commodification of Native Children

They make a living off our children.
—Juanita Sherick, tribal social worker, Pine Ridge Indian
Reservation (Sullivan and Walters 2011)

In *The Poverty Industry: The Exploitation of America's Most Vulnerable Citizens*, author David Hatcher (2016) analyzes state and federal data to argue that foster care in the United States has become a for-profit industrial complex. Because states receive more federal dollars for children in foster care than they spend on related services, placing children in foster care is a boon to state economies. This is exacerbated by neoliberal shifts in state programs as child welfare services are outsourced to private industries. Such a system works to the detriment of poor children as it disincentivizes providing support services directly to poor families.

Hatcher's analysis is especially relevant in states with large Native populations. Because Native children are more likely to be classified as "special needs"—a designation that signals additional federal funding—they generally bring more federal dollars to the state than do non-Native children. Such is the case in South Dakota, where *all* Native children are classified as special needs (Sullivan and Walters 2011). In 2011, National Public Radio's investigative series "Native Foster Care: Lost Children, Shattered Families" exposed the perverse financial incentives that states like South Dakota have to violate the Indian Child Welfare Act.[5] In the course of their reporting, the investigative journalists Laura Sullivan and Amy Walters found that while Native children were 13.5 percent of the state's child population, they constituted 54 percent of children in foster care. And, despite ICWA's priority placement schedule, a staggering 90 percent of Native children removed by the state were placed in non-Native settings.[6]

While it is unlikely that state social workers see dollar signs when they make home visits, the role that child welfare plays in the South Dakota economy is undeniable. For example, when former South Dakota governor Bill Janklow was asked how important federal social service funds were to the state economy, he replied, "Incredibly important. Look, we're a poor state. We're not a high-income state. . . . We don't have factories opening here, hiring people in high wage jobs." Further, former South Dakota state senator Bill Napoli described the link between federal funding and child removal: "When [federal dollars] came down the pike, it was huge. That's when we saw a real influx of kids being taken out of families. Families were being disrupted because the money was there."

South Dakota is among the states that are the most dependent on federal support to drive their economies and, thus, one of many incentivized to expand the foster care industrial complex. While Janklow and Napoli are referring to South Dakota state child welfare in general, Sullivan and Walters's reporting shows that South Dakota's state budget was disproportionately rooted in federal funds apportioned for Native children.

Of course, state welfare agencies provide vital services to children in need, and there are times when it is unsafe for a child to remain in their home. Individual social workers are usually caring people who work hard for little pay in an effort to protect a vulnerable population. Unfortunately, as the history of American Indian boarding schools demonstrates, even well-meaning people have done great harm. Just as it was in the nineteenth century, today many child welfare workers' decision-making remains rooted in cultural biases that view the homes of white, middle-class nuclear families as ideal. When such ideals are the norms against which all other homes are compared, it is often deviance rather than abuse that forms the basis for removal (Roberts 2002). This is evidenced by the fact that the vast majority of Native children are taken from their parents due to "neglect" rather than physical abuse. Abuse in the form of physical violence is generally objective and accounts for a very small fraction of Indian child welfare cases. In contrast, neglect is subjective in nature, which allows cultural bias to impact on-the-ground decisions (Lakota People's Law Project 2013).

Bias against traditional kinship systems is one of the most common reasons that children are deemed "neglected." For example, kinship structures frequently dictate that every adult is responsible for the welfare of every child. This creates a large, loving family with many caregivers. Thus, leaving a child in the care of a relative or community member is a common practice. However, non-Native social workers may label this "child abandonment," which is grounds for removal (Byler 1977;

Jacobs 2009). Further, Native family units frequently consist of multiple generations, extended family members, and people who are not biologically related but are nevertheless considered family. In many Native communities, large family units traditionally cohabitated and coslept in a large room together. Such traditions are frequently misunderstood by state actors who are concerned about overcrowding. Further, cohabitation and cosleeping may also be a necessity for communities with limited economic resources. Thus, what is incorrectly observed as abuse exists at the intersection of culture and poverty.

Bias against Native cultures intersects with poverty in many ways. Due to centuries of colonization, many Native communities are, indeed, poor. However, poverty does not equal neglect (Nagle 2021). Further, cultural biases lead to incorrect assessments of the economic well-being of families. Based on traditions that reach back centuries, Native communities provide social safety nets through kinship care, resource sharing, and in-kind services. This type of economy, however, is often invisible to outsiders (Akee 2019). For example, a social worker might observe an empty refrigerator and conclude that children in the home were not being fed. Such a conclusion discounts the practice of sharing meals at a community center or taking regular meals at the home of a relative.

While cultural bias may lead to unnecessary removals, once Native children are taken by the state, reunification is often difficult due to state bureaucracy, which itself is frequently structured by non-Native worldviews. Reunification commonly requires participating in numerous mandated "services," continually passing drug tests, demonstrating adequate and clean housing, and removing any people who are deemed "risky" from one's home (see, for example, in this volume, Bryson's chapter 3; Lee's chapter 4; Trivedi and Smith's chapter 5; Collins and Bai's chapter 7; and Tach, Day, and Mihalec-Adkins's chapter 8). For Native families, poverty, location, access to services—such as drug treatment programs and parenting classes—and different cultural norms (e.g., what is considered suitable housing) can make reunification especially difficult. Barriers to reunification help explain why Native children spend more time in foster care than do their non-Native peers (Edwards, Beardall, and Curtis 2023). This is especially troubling because extended time in foster care can be grounds to terminate parental rights under the logic that it is in the "best interest" of an Indian child to remain with the family with whom they have bonded, even when that family is non-Native. The next section concerns one such family and highlights how the welfare of any single Indian child is enmeshed with the welfare of all Indian children and tribes.

Still Taking the Children to Take the Land: *Haaland v. Brackeen* and the Future of Indian Child Welfare

To the spirit eater, nothing is sacred and everything has a price tag. But our children are not for sale. They are our future.
—Ruth Hopkins (Dakota/Lakota) (Hopkins 2018)

Chad and Jennifer Brackeen are a white evangelical Christian couple with a substantial income.[7] They live in a four-bedroom, three-bathroom home in Texas with a swimming pool and a zipline. Despite the Indian Child Welfare Act's priority placement schedule, they were allowed to foster a boy who is an Indian child under the Act. He is referred to in court documents as "ALM." After ALM was born, the rights of his biological parents were terminated for reasons not included in the public record. The state temporarily placed ALM with the Brackeens while the Navajo Nation pursued a permanent placement for him. Days before his placement with a Navajo family, the Brackeens obtained an emergency stay to stop the custody transfer. Due to what became a prolonged legal process, ALM's original Navajo placement fell through, and the Brackeens were able to legally adopt him in 2018.

Alvetta James is ALM's biological great-aunt. She is a traditional Navajo homemaker who lives in a two-bedroom home in the Navajo Nation. Raised speaking Navajo, she lives with her extended family, who support themselves through tending livestock, weaving traditional textiles, and performing Navajo ceremonies. When ALM's sister "YJ" was born, the Brackeens wanted to adopt her too. However, the Navajo Nation had already made the necessary arrangements for Ms. James to adopt YJ. As a biological relative, Ms. James was first on ICWA's priority placement schedule. Thus, when Ms. James arrived at family court in the state of Texas, where YJ was born, she expected to return home with her grandniece.

At the hearing, both Ms. James and Mr. Brackeen had the opportunity to speak. Ms. James, wearing moccasins, a traditional Navajo skirt, and turquoise jewelry, stressed her love for YJ and her desire to raise her. Mr. Brackeen, dressed in a Western business suit, expressed his concerns about the fitness of Ms. James as a parent as well as the environment in which YJ would be raised. For example, Mr. Brackeen noted that with Ms. James, YJ might find herself "in a smaller, confined home." He also stated that he was "concerned with the limited financial resources [that Ms. James and her family have] to care for [YJ]." In a ruling that shocked both sides, family court judge Alex Kim awarded the Brackeens primary custody of YJ, with the stipulation that she visit her Navajo family over the summer.

The placement of ALM and YJ with the Brackeens illustrates how race and class intersect in Indian child welfare cases. The Brackeens are the embodiment of the white, middle-class nuclear family that has always been viewed as ideal for Native children. In contrast, Ms. James represents the archetypal extended Native American family living in a traditional Indigenous community, whose economic status—while self-sustaining—is foreign and viewed with concern. Yet beyond the case's significance as an individual case study, the Brackeens set in motion what became one of the most important legal battles in contemporary American Indian history. Despite winning custody of both ALM and YJ, the Brackeens filed a lawsuit now known as *Haaland v. Brackeen*, alleging that the Indian Child Welfare Act is unconstitutional because it discriminates based on race.

On October 4, 2018, US District Court Judge Reed O'Connor ruled that ICWA's provisions were "equivalent to racial discrimination." The decision was appealed, and on November 9, 2022, the US Supreme Court heard oral arguments on the case. In *Haaland*, the justices were asked to consider a question whose answer could radically redefine tribal sovereignty in the United States: Is Indian identity a matter of race or a matter of citizenship? The ability of tribes to exist as distinct political entities is based on the bedrock principle that tribal citizenship is a political classification, not a racial one. Thus, if the US Supreme Court agreed that ICWA is "equivalent to racial discrimination," it would undermine tribal sovereignty as we know it.

On June 15, 2023, in a major victory for Native nations, the US Supreme Court ruled against the Brackeens in a seven-to-two decision.

After the decision was handed down, the joy and excitement across Indian country was palpable. While the ruling is worthy of celebration, the outcome is more a relief than a vindication. In a somewhat technical ruling, the Court found that the Brackeens lacked standing (i.e., were ineligible) to bring their argument before the Court. As a result, the justices could not consider the central issue that motivated the case. Thus, the question "Is the Indian Child Welfare Act unconstitutionally race-based?" went unanswered.

Therefore, even though the Brackeens lost, proponents of ICWA did not win. Indeed, Justice Brett Kavanaugh emphasized that he ruled against the Brackeens because they lacked standing, not because their argument lacked validity. In his concurring opinion, Justice Kavanaugh described ICWA as a law that could undermine a "child's best interests" simply because of their race. He concluded by noting that the constitutionality of the law should be reexamined by the Court if and when it has the opportunity.

Justice Kavanaugh's remarks seem to invite future cases that could accomplish what the Brackeens could not. If history has taught us anything, there is every reason to believe that as long as there are Native children, there will be non-Native people who want to adopt them, a foster care industry that wants to profit from their bodies, and non-Native entities that will lobby to overturn the laws that protect them. For example, the Goldwater Institute, a conservative think tank, has filed thirteen separate lawsuits alleging that ICWA is unconstitutionally race based. As the Goldwater Institute is just one of many entities pursuing similar cases, it is likely that the US Supreme Court will face the question of ICWA's constitutionality again. Should the Court rule that ICWA is unconstitutionally race based, it could effectively deem *all* federal Indian law unconstitutional, abrogating all rights that tribes exercise as sovereign entities. This outcome could eliminate funding for housing, education, and medical care; prohibit economic development activities including hunting, fishing, and tribal gaming; and abrogate tribal rights to water, natural resources, and land. Thus, it is unsurprising that financial supporters of anti-ICWA advocacy groups have ties to extractive energy corporations. For example, The Goldwater Institute is funded in part by entities associated with Koch Industries, an energy-production company that has already started the process of extracting oil from Indian land (Associated Press 1989; Chen 2021; Clarren 2017; Nagle 2021; Pember 2019). The fact that a law about Indian children could be used to dismantle tribal sovereignty in service of the colonization of Native resources illustrates the enduring relationship between Native children and the survival of their nations. In that way, *Haaland v. Brackeen* forces us to consider how neoliberalism works hand in hand with neocolonialism, as the dismantling of ICWA would serve the dual purpose of taking a nation's two most precious resources: its children and its land.

Conclusion: Activism, Sovereignty, and the Future of Indian Child Welfare

There is no resource that is more vital to the continued existence and integrity of Indian tribes than their children.
—Indian Child Welfare Act (25 U.S.C. 1901 [1978])

This chapter argues that centering colonization in our analysis allows us to better understand how the welfare of Indian children is enmeshed with the welfare of Native communities, particularly as it relates to state acquisition of wealth via settler colonialism. When we consider that prior to European contact, Native poverty did not exist and Native children were cared for by large, loving communities, it becomes abundantly clear that Native people are perfectly capable of managing their economies and caring for their children. Therefore, policy recommendations to improve the welfare of Indian children must transcend traditional models, focus on Native-centered solutions, consider the impact of colonization, and acknowledge that the best place for Native children is with their families in a setting that is safe and conducive to their well-being. Further, no matter where they live or what they look like, all Native children should have the opportunity to develop a sense of identity as members of distinct Indigenous communities. The Indian Child Welfare Act was designed to accomplish all of these goals and therefore must be protected, expanded, and enforced.

As is often the case, contemporary issues in Native communities would be improved if the United States simply enforced its own laws. Many of the problems I have identified in this chapter would not exist if

ICWA was correctly implemented and enforced. For example, ICWA requires that "active efforts" be made to alleviate any condition that might be grounds for removal, including implementing family-focused anti-poverty measures. "Active effort" requirements are unevenly enforced by states and can be difficult to implement at the tribal level due to chronic underfunding (Pevar 2012). Fully funding ICWA would help tribes develop court infrastructure, hire tribal lawyers, train tribal social workers and caretakers, and fund "active effort" plans, all of which would prevent Indian children from being appropriated in violation of the law. Further, the Indian Child Welfare Act is most effective in states that have expanded ICWA protections via state law, implemented robust ICWA training programs for state employees, and promoted positive working relationships with local tribal nations. Encouraging other states to adopt similar models could expand ICWA's efficacy across the country (Tidwell 2023).

Contemporary research indicates that tribal sovereignty is the most important factor in the economic welfare of Native nations and the well-being of Native children.[8] The best way to strengthen tribal sovereignty is to support Native-led efforts to ensure that the United States fulfills its constitutional obligations to Native nations. Despite common misconceptions, treaties signed between Native nations and the United States are still legally binding. By the United States honoring its promises, Native nations stand to regain land, resources, and political power, which, in turn, will allow them to improve their economies and better protect their children. Unlike policies designed by outsiders to "help" Native people, honoring treaties and other legal commitments promotes prosperity by facilitating self-determination.

The history of Indian child welfare is one of an enduring battle between a settler state whose existence depends on the disappearance of Native people and the millions of Native people who have refused to disappear. Central to Indigenous survival is protecting the integrity of Native families, preserving tribal sovereignty, and maintaining intergenerational transfers of cultural traditions (Echo-Hawk 2010). The Native leaders who negotiated treaties with the United States and the architects of the Indian Child Welfare Act recognized this. It is now up to the United States to uphold its end of the bargain by fulfilling its promises and enforcing its laws.

I opened this chapter by expressing my shock when Americans insisted that separating children from their parents is "not who we are!" As this chapter has shown, this is exactly who we are and who we have always been. But it is not who we have to be. Exploring poverty governance in the context of settler colonialism helps us understand the important role that Indian child welfare has always played in the United States' history. It is my hope that by confronting this history, one day we will instead see a sign that reads, "This is who we were but who we ceased to be. It is now what we endeavor to repair."

Positionality Statement

This chapter is based on my experience as a caseworker for the Washoe Tribe of Nevada and California, as well as my experience teaching American Indian history and federal Indian policy. I have received an overwhelming amount of support from Native colleagues and community members as I endeavor to leverage my privilege to provide a platform for voices and experiences that are often marginalized. Yet, as a non-Native scholar, I recognize my positionality as someone who has benefited from the historical and continued colonization of Native people. As part of my commitment to serving the community, I am pleased to donate my time to Native organizations that believe they can benefit from my background and experience. All personal proceeds from this chapter will be donated to the Native American Rights Fund and the National Indian Child Welfare Association.

NOTES

1 Indian children, their biological parents and extended family, and their tribes are entitled to special protections under federal law.

2 I focus on federally recognized tribes because, in most cases, they are the only entities subject to federal Indian law. These laws make distinctions between Alaska Natives and Native Hawaiians vis-à-vis people Indigenous to the continental United States. Generally, Alaska Natives are members of federally recognized tribes; thus, federal Indian law usually applies to them. However, unless otherwise specified, Native Hawaiians are not considered Indigenous people under the law, primarily because Hawaii was annexed by the United States without a treaty. The process of becoming federally recognized is complex and warrants its own discussion, including how it impacts Indigenous children; however, such an analysis is beyond the scope of this chapter.

3 See, for example, Brief of Casey Family Programs et al. as Amici Curiae in Support of Respondent Birth Father, *Adoptive Couple v. Baby Girl*, 570 U.S. 637 (2013) (no. 12-399).

4 This description best captures ICWA's priority placement schedule as a whole; however, regulations for adoption versus foster care placements differ slightly. There is also a "good cause" exemption that allows courts to circumvent the schedule in some cases.

5 Unless otherwise noted, data from this case study are derived from this series, including quotations by politicians. Despite being published more than ten years ago, this investigation is still an important source. Subsequent research shows that the problems that Sullivan and Walters document persist and, in some cases, have worsened (Pevar 2017; Puzzanchera et al. 2023).

6 The data in Walter and Sullivan's reporting were further confirmed by a congressional report published by the Lakota People's Law Project (2013).

7 This section draws on *Haaland, et al. v. Brackeen, et al.*, 599 U.S. 255 (2023), including the lower court rulings *Brackeen, et al. v. Haaland, et al.*, No. 18-11479 (F.3d. 5th Cir. Apr. 6, 2021), and *Brackeen, et al. v. Zinke, et al.*, No. 4:17-cv00868-O (N.D. Tex. Oct. 4, 2018). For family court testimony and descriptions of litigants, see Nagle 2021; and Hoffman 2019.

8 See broadly the work of Randall Akee, including his articles for Brookings (2018, 2019).

3

"'Oh, This One Has Money.' I Mean, of Course . . ."

Neoliberal Poverty Governance and the Adoption and Safe Families Act of 1997

STEPHANIE A. BRYSON

Part I: Irma Jo Bartlett's Children Are Removed Because the House Is Dirty

On June 1, 1998, one year after the Adoption and Safe Families Act was signed into law, twenty-six-year-old investigations caseworker Tammy Williams wrote,

> Child welfare received a call. Reporting party stated that the children's bedroom is filthy. There is dirty clothes trash and other objects on the bedroom floor. Mother's room is also filthy with various items on floor. Dishes are piled up in the sink. Cockroach eggs on counters near food items. Housing Authority does not allow the homes to be this filthy.
>
> Ms. Bartlett works 30 hrs. a week at Burger King. Housing Police have spotted 6 yr. old outside running the streets after 10 p.m. [The Department of Human Services] recommends that children be placed in DHS custody for 5 days pending investigation.[1]

Stapled alongside this report in an envelope marked "Bartlett" were Polaroid photos taken the day the report was filed.[2] In one photo, two blond boys, about ten and six years old, look startled by a camera flash. Both boys have dirty cheeks and short crew cuts. Both wear striped short-sleeved shirts, shorts, and cowboy boots. Under a section titled "Worker Observations," the investigations worker added,

> Worker observed Ms. Bartlett to become very emotional when officer and worker notified her that her children were being taken into protective

73

custody. She would have outbursts of crying and then stop. She had no explanation to why the rooms were as bad as they were except that she was tired and stressed out after working 30 hours a week.

She could not explain why the kids are out after dark unsupervised. Worker observed dirty dishes stacked up in the sink. The dishes still had food stuck to them. In the cabinets, worker found cockroaches and large cockroach eggs. There did appear to be plenty of food in the home. There was approximately three gallons of milk in the ice box. There was a bowl of spaghetti uncovered in the ice box. Around the base boards of the home was dirt and trash. . . . Ms. Bartlett appeared to be cognitively slow. Unknown if any mental illness. She is approximately 4′8″ tall. She has short blonde hair. She appeared to have dark circles under her eyes and several missing teeth. It is unknown at this time if she has the capacity to protect her children.

I read these words near the end of data collection on a policy implementation study of the Adoption and Safe Families Act, or ASFA. Supporters have called ASFA "the most sweeping change in federal child welfare law in nearly 20 years" (Spar 2004, summary), while critics have called it "the worst law affecting families ever enacted by Congress" (Guggenheim 2021, 711). Signed into law by President Clinton in 1997, ASFA (P.L. 105-89 [1997]) overturned a quarter century of child welfare doctrine by prioritizing adoptions over family preservation (Trivedi 2023). It did this in two main ways. First, it accelerated timelines for the termination of parental rights, mandating that once a child had been in foster care for fifteen of the most recent twenty-two months, the state must move to sever the legal relationship between parent and child.[3] Second, it actively promoted adoptions by authorizing payments to states for every adoption the state finalized above an established baseline (Stoltzfus 2013).[4] While ASFA continued to allocate funds for family reunification, its goal was to promote permanency through adoption rather than family preservation.

Congress passed ASFA a year after the Personal Responsibility and Work Opportunity Reconciliation Act (PRWORA), which imposed work requirements on and fundamentally dismantled cash assistance to poor families. Some child advocates and policy makers (Gelles 2003) heralded ASFA as a bill that would finally move half a million children out of foster care and into permanent homes. Detractors, however, argued that ASFA would have devastating consequences for communities of color that were already demonized by the War on Drugs, harshly punished by mass incarceration, and pushed further into poverty by welfare-to-work legislation (Roberts 2002).

Using the focus-group-tested keywords "safety, permanency, and well-being," ASFA passed with strong bipartisan support. In a prescient and powerful dissent on the floor of the House of Representatives on April 30, 1997, ASFA's only Democratic opponent, Patsy T. Mink (D-Hawaii), predicted that ASFA and PRWORA would combine to create even greater precarity for the United States' poor families (Raz 2022): "I cannot vote for a bill that takes welfare reform one step closer to the final penalty of poverty: The loss of one's children by edict of the Government. First you take their money away. Then you force them into desperate conditions of poverty. Then you deem them unfit to raise their children and you remove them from the home and place them in foster homes. Then after 18 months you put the children up for adoption. Whose family values do we stand for?"[5]

* * *

About five years after ASFA was enacted, I set out to conduct a mixed-methods study of its implementation. Since I was especially interested in how ASFA was affecting family reunification, I selected a Bible Belt state known for its pro-family values, demographic diversity, and Christian conservatism. Using national child welfare outcome measures, I selected four counties, two with optimal family reunification outcomes and two with less optimal outcomes. Within these demographically comparable counties, I conducted (n = 42) semistructured interviews with thirty caseworkers, seven supervisors, and five judges to understand how ASFA had changed adoption and family reunification practice. To triangulate data, I also observed eighteen family and drug court hearings and conducted twenty-three separate case-file reviews.

After two years immersed in routine practice under ASFA, I was still surprised by my reaction to Irma Jo Bartlett's "dirty house" case. In part, it was the *way* it was written—the grammatical errors that betrayed the educational proximity between worker and mother, the worker's effort to drive a wedge of professionalism into that narrow gap, and the nauseating combination of uncovered spaghetti and cockroach eggs in the same terse paragraph.

It was the not-so-subtle suggestion that working thirty hours a week in a notoriously demeaning and physically grueling fast-food job was an illegitimate claim to fatigue. It was the omission that Burger King aims to keep its employees part-time so it can avoid paying their health insurance.

It was the affective surveillance of Irma's emotion regulation: "She would have outbursts of crying and then stop"—as though the news of her children's removal might generate an unmitigated torrent of grief or, conversely, no torrent at all. Either might prove perilous, as Irma's grief could be a proxy of maternal fitness—or a confirmation of its absence.

It was Irma's inability to explain why her public housing unit was "filthy" and cockroach-ridden, as though she, alone, depressed the value of the property. It was the very existence of "Housing Police," an institutional reminder that poverty entrains personal surveillance *by police* while wealth buys property surveillance *from police.*

It was the low-fidelity professional euphemism "cognitively slow," followed by the stigmatizing stain of mental illness. Even without confirmation, the possibility of mental illness and intellectual disability cast a pall over Irma's maternal suitability.

Finally, it was the brusque description of Irma's missing teeth—missing, as it was, the structural context of health-care inequality, including dental care, which dramatically curtails the employment possibilities of poor people like Irma.

It would be difficult to find an individual child welfare case that more perfectly exemplifies Kerry Woodward's (2021) argument that the US child welfare system—now a sprawling $29 billion public-private conglomerate—is fundamentally a system of racialized and gendered poverty governance. To understand how this system has developed in the past twenty-five years, one must understand the outsized impact of ASFA, under which two million families have now been dissolved (Guggenheim 2021). As of this writing, a growing coalition of advocates, parents, and professionals is demanding ASFA's repeal (e.g., Roberts 2022; Trivedi 2023).

In this chapter, I analyze two examples of child welfare practice under ASFA: the family reunification case of Irma Jo Bartlett and the adoption decision-making phenomenon of Blond, Blue-Eyed Baby. In these archival practice snapshots, I suggest that ASFA was the perfect companion to PRWORA and other punitive neoliberal policies of the era. It encouraged caseworkers to enact classed, gendered, and racialized decisions in the service of producing good neoliberal citizen-parents. In discussing both case material and interviews, which mostly concern white children and families, I wish to underscore how gendered poverty governance operated alongside racial privilege. In the next section of the chapter, I briefly define neoliberal poverty governance. I then return to Irma Jo Bartlett's fateful involvement with what abolitionists are now calling a system of "child taking" (Briggs 2021), "family policing" (Roberts 2021), and "family regulation" (Polikoff and Spinak 2021) to show how ASFA encouraged market rationality in child welfare decision-making.

ASFA and Neoliberal Poverty Governance

The social welfare historians Frances Fox Piven and Richard Cloward (1971, xv) famously referred to the function of social welfare policy as "regulating the political and economic behavior of the poor." As they described it, in times of economic contraction, social welfare expands to contain social unrest. In times of economic expansion, it shrinks to force workers back to work. Joe Soss, Richard Fording, and Sanford Schram (2011) write that although contemporary poverty governance retains some historical features of social control used for centuries, it is different in two main ways: *paternalism* in managing the poor and *neoliberalism* in organizing society.

In practice, this means that systems like welfare, healthcare, education, and housing—systems that ostensibly exist to meet needs—have been privatized and reengineered by the neoliberal state as "behavior modification programs that regulate the people who rely on them" (Roberts 2019, 1700). The ultimate goal of this regulation is to produce "good neoliberal citizens" who endorse the promises and priorities of neoliberalism: "(1) self-sufficiency via hard work in the formal labor market; (2) rational thinking, planning, and decision-making; and (3) emotional regulation and strategic self-presentation" (Randles and Woodward 2018, 45). While it might be tempting to see neoliberalism as simply a by-product of late advanced capitalism, on the one hand, or of power/knowledge regimes on the other, Loïc Wacquant (2012) has argued that neoliberalism must be historicized so as not to be confused with simple materialism or, conversely, governmentality. In his words, what is "neo" about neoliberalism is the way the state operates in relation to the market and the polity. Wacquant proposes that neoliberalism represents a historically novel "articulation of state, market, and citizenship that harnesses the first to impose the stamp of the second onto the third" (2012, 71). According to Wacquant (2009, 2010, 2012), this novel articulation has created a "Centaur-state" in which the wealthy and powerful receive reward, while the "precariat," the class of people forced into a precarious existence at the margins of society, is punitively and paternalistically policed by law enforcement, medical professionals, judges, and caseworkers, among others.

A central feature of neoliberal poverty governance is its reliance on punitive means like mass incarceration to produce compliance within the precariat—especially in Black, Indigenous, and Latine communities. In the United States, carceral studies historians have begun to reveal the continuity of racist criminalization from the colonial era to the present. For example, Elizabeth Hinton and DeAnza Cook (2021, 263), in their overview of the mass criminalization of Black Americans, demonstrate how policing and criminalization "have worked in tandem historically to monitor and contain people of color and low-income groups within and beyond US borders." They argue that the state's use of policing, imprisonment, criminal law, and civil law to exert social control in Black communities is fundamentally constitutive of all American policy making—even contemporary policy making that might appear "race neutral."

Soss and colleagues (2011) also acknowledge the centrality of race in contemporary poverty governance. They write that "race-coded discourses provided essential resources for the political actors who drove the turn toward neoliberal paternalism." In this way, "race played a key role in shaping the governing arrangements that all poor Americans now confront" (Soss, Fording, and Schram 2011, 4). This context is important to consider as we examine ASFA, next, and later, as we return to the case of Irma Jo Bartlett, a white woman.

* * *

Just as PRWORA was an example of punitive, privatized, and paternalistic public-assistance policy, ASFA brought a similar neoliberal rationality to child welfare policy. This rationality elevated psychological parenting, the idea that children's developmental needs could be met by anyone, including adoptive or foster parents (Skolnick 1975)—and that a child might be harmed by remaining in relationship with a noncustodial parent. It did this at a time when the percentages of Black and Indigenous/Native American children in foster care had come under intense scrutiny and when many had been removed from single mothers.

In 2000, shortly after ASFA was passed, Black children under eighteen constituted 14.7 percent of the general population (O'Hare 2021) but 39 percent of the 552,000 children in foster care in the United States (USDHHS 2006). American Indian/Alaska Native children made up 0.9 percent of the general population (O'Hare 2021) but 2 percent of children in foster care (USDHHS 2006). Meanwhile, Asian, white, and Hispanic/Latine children were underrepresented among all children in foster care compared to their numbers in the total child population (O'Hare 2021; USDHHS 2006).

Between 1985 and 1999, the number of children and youths in foster care on a given day more than doubled—from 276,000 in 1985 to 587,000 in 1999 (US House of Representatives, Committee on Ways and Means 2012). When ASFA was passed, the bill's selling point was that it would deal with "foster care drift," the idea that half a million children were stranded, sometimes for the rest of their childhoods, in foster care. By shortening decision-making time frames and incentivizing adoption, ASFA promised to move children more quickly to "permanency." ASFA gained support, in part, because it prioritized children's *developmental needs* for safety, permanency, and well-being above the needs of their parents, who struggled to "turn their lives around" (Gelles 2003). To understand how this radical approach—the federal government mandating termination of parental rights within twenty-two months—gained widespread support in a country that has fiercely protected privacy and parents' rights (Raz 2022), one must understand the dominant narrative of how half a million children ended up in foster care in the first place.

The most common explanation in the social work and policy literature of the 1990s was that children in foster care were casualties of the AIDS and crack cocaine epidemics (CWLA 1996; USDHHS 1999), both highly stigmatized and racialized phenomena. However, the economists

Christopher Swann and Michelle Sheran Sylvester (2006) show in their analysis of foster care from this period that ballooning caseloads resulted from two demographic trends: (1) higher rates of female incarceration; and (2) significant decreases in welfare benefits. Both trends disproportionately affected women of color, contributing to the overrepresentation of children of color in foster care (Minoff and Citrin 2022).

In the ten years following the passage of the 1986 Anti-Drug Abuse Act, which shifted sentencing power from federal judges to prosecutors and imposed minimum sentences, the percentage of women incarcerated for drug offenses rose by 888 percent.[6] In this period, average prison terms for drug offenses also increased from sixty-two to seventy-four months, while actual time served increased from thirty to sixty-six months. Although incarceration rates of men during this period also doubled, women make up the vast majority of custodial caregivers, so when women go to prison, more children end up in foster care. Swann and Sylvester (2006) note that incarceration rates for women in their study predicted a 22.5 percent increase in the caseload rate, or 31.1 percent of the observed growth in foster care caseloads in the eleven years prior to ASFA.

Reductions in AFDC/TANF benefits were the second-largest contributor, predicting an 11.1 percent increase in foster care caseload rates during this period. Three things explain how welfare reform put more children in foster care. First, lower benefits reduced income, pushing families into poverty and increasing the likelihood that they would be charged with neglect and their children removed for inadequate housing, income, or nutrition. Second, since the relatives of child-welfare-involved parents are typically poor, kinship caregivers may have become formal foster parents to qualify for state assistance. Third, states may have treated foster care as a substitute for welfare (Swann and Sylvester 2006).

On this last point, Swann and Sylvester (2006) observed that the percentage of children covered by Title IV-E foster care increased dramatically immediately after passage of welfare reform. They speculated that states had significant incentive to shift children from TANF rolls to foster care when welfare reform changed from AFDC (a matching grant) to TANF (a block grant). In other words, states may have maximized federal reimbursements by (1) removing families from welfare rolls, (2) dissolving families and placing children in foster care, and (3) placing children with adoptive families, for which the state could then receive a financial bonus. In other words, just as Patsy Mink predicted, ASFA probably worked hand in hand with the Anti-Drug Act, PRWORA, and other punitive policies of the 1980s and '90s to systematically dismantle poor families, especially those from Black and Indigenous communities (Guggenheim 2021; Roberts 2002).

The law professor Martin Guggenheim (2021, 727) explains, "The racist stereotypes that fueled other social policies of the 1990s also fueled the idea that the state needed to intervene in Black families in order to save their children." He goes on to say that federal legislators who voted for ASFA were easily persuaded to embrace the idea that adoption by other/ wealthier families was preferable to returning children of color to their families. In hindsight, ASFA ushered in an unprecedented era in which one in one hundred US children by age eighteen will experience the loss of a parent through termination of parental rights (Wildeman, Edwards, and Wakefield 2020). In the pursuit of "freeing children for adoption," ASFA "created an unknown number of legal orphans" (Raz 2022).

Returning to Irma Jo Bartlett, we see how racial privilege intersected with gendered poverty governance to produce a questionable but probably different outcome than the outcome experienced by thousands of families of color under the reign of ASFA.

Part II: Irma Jo Bartlett's Children Are Placed in Kinship Care

After Irma Jo Bartlett's children were taken into protective custody, her child welfare caseworker allegedly taught her how to clean her public housing unit. When the worker returned a few days later, she reported that Irma "had only managed to clean her room and have the apartment sprayed for cockroaches." After several months of less-than-satisfactory efforts to keep her house clean, Irma's boys were placed in foster care. Although the caseworkers and judges I interviewed underscored the improbability of children being removed in a "dirty house" case, nationally, three in four children removed from their homes are removed for alleged neglect. Although the least well-defined type of maltreatment, neglect is highly correlated with poverty and consistently the most reported type of maltreatment in the United States (Annie E. Casey Foundation 2023a).

After the Bartlett boys were removed from their mother, both had stints in inpatient psychiatric facilities, which did not count toward their ASFA-stipulated cumulative fifteen months in foster care. Both then had multiple foster care placements. In May 2001, very close to the fifteen-month limit, the boys went to live with their maternal grandparents, after which they appeared to flourish, socially and academically. After the boys had been with their grandparents six months, a caseworker offered her gendered assessment of the grandfather's impact, which was not uncommon in the case files I read from this era of Republican-sponsored fatherhood initiatives (e.g., US House of Representatives 1998): "Since removal from their mother both boys have been inpatient at psychiatric facilities and placed in therapeutic foster care for a time. Yet, what they both really needed was the attention of a good male role model."

Before ASFA, the Bartlett family kinship placement might have continued as a long-term solution that enabled the boys to thrive in a two-parent home while maintaining connection to their mother. Indeed, one worker went out of the way to document the youngest boy's strong attachment to his mother and grandmother. However, under ASFA, child welfare workers were encouraged to facilitate "permanency" by terminating the rights of the custodial parent and by facilitating an adoption. In positing the grandfather as the catalyst of the boys' stability, the caseworker was doing two things: (1) establishing the paternal grandfather as a potential adoptive parent; and (2) building a narrative against Irma as a biologically and socioeconomically inadequate single mother—a familiar trope in an era of renewed enthusiasm for marriage rather than wage equity for single mothers.

In the judgment of the caseworker and the court, the boys' stabilization at their grandparents' house confirmed that Irma had indeed been the cause of substantiated neglect. This assessment was a decisive blow to Irma's perceived parental adequacy. While her boys were living with their grandparents, Irma did make progress on her case-plan goals, even paying child support to the state so it could pay her own parents to care for her boys. However, Irma was still judged inadequate. In a report to the court from late 2001, a newly assigned caseworker wrote,

> Irma Jo began working at Taco Bell on 9/11/01. Irma does not have a driver's license. She rides public transportation to work and walks home each day. Irma has a very difficult time providing for herself. Irma works 20–30 hrs. a week at $5.60 per hour. Child support automatically deducts $81.00 per week from her check. Irma lacks the necessary funds for food and utilities. Irma told worker she had no close friends and does not want to ask her parents for help. . . . Irma is a very warm and gentle person who is very likable; however she seems to lack the necessary motivation and assertiveness that is needed to provide a home for her children.

Throughout this case note are themes of neoliberal poverty governance: expectations of self-sufficiency, rational planning, and strategic presentation of self. Regarding self-sufficiency, we do not know if Irma was offered more than twenty to thirty hours a week at Taco Bell, but the fast-food industry has long been known as a "poverty employer" that keeps wages low and offers 75 percent of its employees only part-time work (Chang 2023). For Irma to support her family in the formal labor market, she would have needed at least two fast-food jobs. This would have meant paying for child care, asking her parents for help, or leaving her boys unattended.

Although Irma demonstrated many features of individual responsibility—refusing help, taking transit and walking home, trying to pay her bills while the state punitively deducted $81 of child support *per week* from her minimum-wage paycheck—she remained illegible as a good neoliberal citizen. While warmth, gentleness, and likability might register in some contexts as desirable parenting qualities, in the case note, these characteristics undermined Irma's strategic presentation of self. Indeed, the knockout punch to Irma's chance of reunifying with her boys was her lack of "motivation" and "assertiveness," two necessities in a neoliberal era that treats every person as an independent engine of gross domestic product and society as a federation of independent contractors.

* * *

Instead of investing in Irma's parenting capacity, instead of assisting Irma with food and utilities, the state removed her children and deducted more than 70 percent of her weekly take-home pay to cover the cost of foster care—essentially guaranteeing that Irma would go deeper into poverty and fail to reunify with her children. Based on a Reagan-era policy from 1984 (Child Support Enforcement Amendments of 1984, P.L. 98-378 [1984]) that led states to begin billing parents whose children were placed in federally subsidized foster care, this practice continued in all fifty states until 2022.[7] This policy underlines the paternalism of neoliberal policy, which seeks to punish rather than support single mothers—especially women of color.

In a study of child-welfare-involved mothers, Maureen Marcenko, Sandra Lyons, and Mark Courtney (2011) found that almost half of the 747 mothers in their sample had annual household incomes of less than $10,000, below poverty thresholds even for a single person. Mothers with a child or children in foster care experienced greater financial hardship than did mothers whose children remained at home (Marcenko, Lyons, and Courtney 2011, 435). The state's stinginess is difficult to understand when one considers data from an experimental study of 13,062 mothers receiving child support (Cancian, Yang, and Slack, 2013), which showed a decrease in maltreatment risk among mothers who received child support payments.

However, in a report on the relationship between racism and child neglect, Elisa Minoff and Alexandra Citrin (2022) argue that the stinginess of the child welfare system is structural, intentional, and rooted in racism. As mentioned, racism shapes the governing arrangements that poor, white families face, although differentially. Compounding centuries of racial discrimination in housing, health care, education, and employment, the racism within the child welfare system has, in the past one hundred years, created ever-harsher schemes of punishment and surveillance. This has had particularly devastating results for children and families of color. At each step of the harrowing and traumatic process—from investigations to reunification—children of color fare worse. They spend longer in foster care, reunify less with their families, and are most likely to age out of foster care as "legal orphans," putting them at higher risk for a host of poor outcomes in education, employment, and health over the long term. Minoff and Citrin (2022, 6) write, "It is long past time that we stop and ask ourselves why we approach neglect the way that we do. If we continue to turn to an intervening system that has been inextricably shaped by racism to solve a problem that racism has helped create, we will continue to see Black, Indigenous, and Latinx families separated due to circumstances related to poverty that could have been prevented in the first place with adequate supports and services."

This context is important to keep in mind as we discuss the resolution of Irma Jo Bartlett's case and the adoption case of Blond, Blue-Eyed Baby.

Part III: "'Oh, This One Has Money.' I Mean, of Course."

In mid-December 2001, just as Irma Jo Bartlett's case was careening toward an optimal ASFA outcome—"timely permanency" through adoption by the maternal grandparents, which could fetch the state a federal bonus of $6,000 per special-needs Bartlett boy—another caseworker "discovered" the biological father. In fact, Mr. Bartlett lived only an hour away.

Although Mr. Bartlett had not been involved in his boys' lives for the past seven years—he claimed that he could not locate them—he did pay child support the entire time. This fact, coupled with his job as a maintenance director at a large Baptist church, his combined income with his second wife of $50,000, and his apparent newfound eagerness to be a part of his children's lives, earned him an expedited home study.

Along with the number of bedrooms in the father and stepmother's house, its proximity to parks and recreational activities, and the parents' active life "centered around church, art, and sports," the home study worker recorded the following observations:

> Religion: The B's are members of the First Baptist Church. . . . Ms. B was a very devout Seventh Day Adventist . . . who was ultra-submissive in her previous . . . relationships. She was unable to be assertive. She and her children were victims of physical and emotional abuse by two men that she married. Her church family directed her to stay in these relationships until one of the fathers sexually abused her daughter.
>
> Attitudes toward Children: Mr. and Mrs. B seem to have realistic expectations of what parenting his sons will entail. It appears that Mr. B has been able to set limits with the boys when they recently had visits.

Physical Description and Personality: Mr. B is 6' tall and weighs 332 lbs. He has light brown hair and hazel eyes. He seems to be a happy, grateful, content person who enjoys people of all ages. He appears to be very dependable and hard working.

Marital Relationship: Although there is significant age difference between Mr. and Mrs. B (22 yrs) they describe their marriage as wonderful and healthy.

On the basis of this information, the home visit worker recommended immediate placement with the biological father, in the middle of the school year, with no typical family service requirements for new adoptive parents.

Irma Jo Bartlett appeared in court in January 2002 to contest the Department of Human Services' report. Her attorney argued that Irma's children were removed from her home "for having a dirty house," that Irma "has a job, a clean home, and parents that are willing to help her with the boys," that Irma's ex-husband "just appeared in these boys lives after a seven year absence" in which there were "no visits, cards, gifts or interaction between father and sons," and finally, that boys and birth father have "spent a total of three weekends together since the divorce." Irma's attorney concluded the "Objection to Placement" with the following pointed statements: "While movant has no reason to believe that the natural father is less than sincere in his desire to reunite with his boys, with which he had no contact for most of their lives, . . . Irma has completed her plan and stands ready to take the boys to her home. The test is not now, nor has it ever been, which parent can provide the most financial support to the children. It seems that the financial disparity plays a large role in the DHS recommendation."

The court did not agree to reconsider Irma Jo Bartlett for placement, but it did delay placement of the children with their biological father until the end of the school year, June 2002. Despite subsequent objections, Irma's parental rights were terminated, and custody was awarded to the biological father and his new wife in February 2003.

* * *

What distinguishes the case of Irma Jo Bartlett from the other twenty-three case files I read was the open allegation, by the mother's attorney, that DHS removed Irma's kids because Irma was poor. As a case of gendered poverty governance, the case is relatively straightforward. However, racial privilege also played a role. Given the absence of the father from the children's lives for seven years, the rush to placement and custody appears driven by worker and judicial predilection for the father's income, but it must be acknowledged that had the Bartletts been a family of color, the outcome might have been quite different.

On the basis of other case files I read and court hearings I observed, if Mr. Bartlett had been a father of color, his absence from his children's lives might not have been excused—even if he had been absent because he was incarcerated. Had the Bartlett children been children of color, they might have remained in revolving-door foster care placements before aging out, with no real family or permanency. If Irma and her parents had been Black, Indigenous, or Latine, it is uncertain that a kinship arrangement would have occurred at all. Though speculative, these outcomes are all too familiar for many families of color (Roberts 2022).

As it was, Mr. Bartlett's whiteness, marriage, church involvement, and steady employment firmly established him in the eyes of child welfare workers as the "unburdened embodiment of traditional American values" (Randles and Woodward 2018, 45). Mr. Bartlett was the good neoliberal citizen—an implicitly white, male, cisgender, straight, able-bodied, and financially stable ideal. Although he paid child support, Mr. Bartlett was literally unburdened from raising his children for the first years of their lives. Caring for them would probably have left Mr. Bartlett less financially stable than when caseworkers found him. In raising their children for the past seven years, Irma probably contributed to Mr. Bartlett's higher accrued assets and earning power. Since she needed to watch the kids *and* work, Irma did this at the expense of her own employability and, ultimately, her own parental rights.

In keeping with the leitmotif of mother-blame in Irma's case file notes, commentary about Mr. Bartlett's new wife was also gendered and harsh, reflecting the child welfare system's thoroughgoing need to construct a legally culpable party on which to blame maltreatment—even when the party is herself being abused by the church, the state, or a partner. In the same paragraph, the notes construct absent fathers like Mr. Bartlett as having unique agency in both regards. In their view, Mr. Bartlett was able to "set limits with the boys." He was able to earn an income of $50,000.

Never mind that he had been entirely absent as a father or that $50,000 was his *combined income with his new wife*, his willingness to assume parental responsibility meant that caseworkers could deposit all their fantasies about the Bartlett boys' future prosperity into a gendered and racialized conceptual repository of married dual-earner capital and presumed upward mobility. They went all in.

The Adoption Case of the Blond, Blue-Eyed Baby

If Mr. Bartlett was the ideal neoliberal citizen of family reunification practice, the Standard North American Family, or "SNAF" (D. Smith 1993), was ASFA's adoption ideal. Unmoored from reality or history, SNAF operates as ideological code: "It is a conception of a legally married couple sharing a household. The adult male is in paid employment; his earnings provide the economic basis of the family-household. The adult female may also earn an income; but her primary responsibility is to the care of husband, household, and children" (D. Smith 1993, 52).

In interviews with adoption rather than family reunification caseworkers, I observed that adoption workers sought to promote permanency by placing children in financially stable homes. On the rare occasion that they had scores of potential adoptive families, workers felt they could and should pick the "ideal" (read: SNAF) family. In the following extended interview vignette, Tracy, a thirty-three-year-old caseworker with six years of child welfare experience, provides an account of those factors that constitute good parents in the minds of child welfare workers in her county:

> S: If we got this group together and people could be brutally honest, if we did a hierarchy of families, how would it go?
>
> T: I absolutely think mother and father.
>
> S: Mother, father of any race? Presumably white?
>
> T: Presumably white, at least matching children. I would think that everybody would have the general conception that mom, dad, and matching children would be the most appropriate. . . .
>
> S: Okay, so . . . what about class? Do you think there's a sort of—
>
> T: [interrupts] Recently, a worker had a very young child up for adoption, and when the statewide staffing occurred, there was maybe

one hundred families interested in this little blond-haired, blue-eyed baby girl. So this worker got stacks and stacks of home studies to go through, and several of us had quite a good time reading them and trying to figure out which would be the best family, and we all gravitated toward, "Oh, this one has money." I mean, of course.

S: So the most resources—

T: The most resources, and a lot of times, it's just from the view that this child has never had anything, and wouldn't it be great for them to go into a home with a playground in the backyard and to have all the opportunity that's possible. . . . I think resources are very important. You don't necessarily want to place a child with a family that will have difficulty buying them clothes when you have the option of a different family that can buy them ten pairs of shoes. I think that definitely plays into what we think.

Other workers confirmed this general hierarchy, especially the worker whose task it was to pick the ideal family for the blond, blue-eyed baby girl in question. After deselecting those parents who already had children, Edward looked to see if parents indicated that they were Christian.[8] He then looked to resources:

E: Then my third [criterion] was money. Is this child going to have it made? And the family I decided on was a mother that was going to quit work as soon as she got a baby.

S: Would that have made a difference if the mom was going to keep working?

E: Yeah.

S: You would have wanted the mom at home.

E: That probably wouldn't have been the deciding factor. But she was. I wanted her to be provided for, and the dad made like $6,000 a month, and they lived in [midsize city]. That's a nice community. She's going to a private school. And that's stuff, you know, most kids don't get—period. And I think, well, if this is me, it's what *I* would like. And I don't know if that's right or not, but anyway . . .

Despite the religious convictions and avowed family values of the child welfare workers and judges I interviewed, they were organized by ASFA to make paternalistic and racialized decisions that skewed toward market rationality. In this way, child welfare practice under ASFA promoted a brutal three-pronged approach to neoliberal poverty governance. The act encouraged caseworkers to remove children from poor parents and to place them in foster care or institutional placements. It pushed poor parents deeper into poverty by requiring them to pay for the cost of foster care and other services. It systematically placed their children in wealthier families, more commonly white families than families of color. And among Black and Indigenous communities, it terminated parental rights at 2.4 times the rate of white families and created a group of legal orphans with no relationship to birth or adoptive parents (Wildeman, Edwards, and Wakefield 2020).

Conclusion

While everyone acknowledges that children must be protected from harm, evidence of the child welfare system's efficacy in this regard is hardly robust. A systematic review of health and well-being outcomes among children in out-of-home versus in-home care found limited evidence of better outcomes—and some evidence of worse outcomes associated with foster care (MacLean et al. 2016). Despite what caseworkers and courts may actually think about foster care, structurally, they place misguided confidence in the foster care system. This confidence is undermined by data showing a host of harms to children who are forcibly separated from their parents, including elevated cortisol and other hormone levels, depression and other mental health challenges, cognitive difficulties, and other physical and behavioral issues (Goudarzi 2018; Wan 2018).

ASFA has played a significant role in the family separations of the past quarter century. Summarizing its impact, Guggenheim writes, "It would be difficult to overstate how radical ASFA is, a law that no other nation in the world has come close to embracing. ASFA encourages states to permanently banish parents from the lives of their children, even when the parents never abused their children or harmed them in any way. It authorizes the destruction of familial relationships for no better reason than a parent, regardless of circumstances, being incapable of securing custody of her child from foster care within a fifteen-month period" (2021, 722).

A growing chorus of scholars and activists now impugn ASFA as a historical extension of colonial family eradication policies aimed at Indigenous and Black families (Alphonso 2021; Briggs 2021; Dettlaff 2023; Rocha Beardall and Edwards 2021). In a recent tweet, Dorothy Roberts refuted the idea that ASFA "freed" children for adoption by expediting permanent legal separation from their parents, calling this "a false market-based solution to foster care" that "supports the white savior narrative and masks the state neglect and violence that put children [in foster care]."[9] Long a reformer of the child welfare system, Roberts now calls for its abolition and urges the United States to build "a radically re-imagined way of caring for children and their families" (2021, 457).

* * *

Years ago, my colleagues and I, all child welfare researchers, won a very large federal grant ($13 million) to test permanency innovations in a five-year randomized controlled trial.[10] In good neoliberal fashion, we were required by federal funders to choose a target population and an evidence-informed intervention. Our target population was the group we knew the system failed most egregiously: children with psychiatric and intellectual disabilities who languished in inappropriate or inadequate placements; who were put on a polypharmacopia of psychotropic medications; who had disastrous, wrenching, and costly outcomes; and who were often from communities of color.

Before discussing our intervention with our five privatized child welfare agency partners, we conducted our research and chose a popular foster care intervention. It had good evidence, and we theorized that it would be most efficacious and easiest to implement. We got on the phone with representatives from our five privatized foster care agencies, who were guarded because they competed with one another for state foster care contracts. We told them our idea. Unanimously, they said, "We want to work with birth parents, not foster parents. There are no funds in this system to actually help families." Later, we called eminent researchers and prominent thought leaders to vet our choices for interventions. Again, to our surprise, they said, "Don't deliver a tertiary intervention. Give families money."

In a recent edition of the *Columbia Journal of Race and Law*, ASFA-affected mothers and abolition activists write, "Over the course of 20 years, the federal government . . . has spent tens of billions of dollars on paying other families to permanently raise our children and the children of the families we support. These numbers far outpace the money or energy that was invested in us, our families, our communities, and our advocacy. Can you imagine what we could be doing for our families if we had that type of investment?" (Albert et al. 2021, 877).

US social welfare policy can continue its punitive and paternalistic policing of families and communities. But it will do so, as in other eras, at the peril of the children it purports to protect. It is long past time for the United States to build a system of family support, not family policing. "Can you imagine what we could be doing for our families if we had that type of investment?" is the single best question we could hope to answer in the coming century.

NOTES

1 Bartlett case, verbatim transcript. Grammatical errors are original.

2 All dates and identities have been disguised.

3 Legal exceptions, which were not always implemented, included when children were in foster homes with biological relatives, when it was determined not in the child's best interest, and when the state failed to provide sufficient reunification services (P.L. 105-89 [1997]).

4 The original Adoption Incentives program created by ASFA authorized incentives to states of $4,000 per child; $6,000 per special needs child; and $8,000 for children nine years and older (Stoltzfus 2013).

5 105 Cong. Rec. H2023 (daily ed. April 30, 1997) (statement of Rep. Patsy Mink), www.congress.gov. This speech was specifically about the Adoption Incentives program that ASFA authorized.

6 This was compared to an only 129 percent increase in non-drug-related offenses during the same period (Mauer, Potler, and Wolf 1999, in Swann and Sylvester 2006).

7 In June 2022, the Children's Bureau acknowledged that it is "almost never in the child's best interest to collect child support from parents with family reunification goals" (US Children's Bureau 2022). It is unknown how many states are following this guidance.

8 This was a public child welfare agency in a Bible Belt state. While some workers I interviewed were careful to talk about leaving their values at the door of the DHS office, others were forthright about religious beliefs.

9 Dorothy Roberts (@DorothyERoberts), "The prioritization of adoption serves as a false market-based solution to foster care (eg, ASFA speeding up permanent legal separation to 'free' children for adoption)." Twitter, May 9, 2022, 6:11 a.m., https://twitter.com/dorothyeroberts/status/1523651807452737537.

10 This was a different study from the one described in this chapter.

4

"They Think They Can Punish You into Getting Sober"

Poverty, Drug "Crises," and the Foster Care System

TINA LEE

They think they can punish you into getting sober.
—Black mother of children in foster care in New York City

You can only do so many of these [parental rights termina-
tions]. You can only watch this happen so many times. . . .
Do they have the ability, most of them? Yep. Do they love
their children? Yep. But . . . their *years* of trauma, *years* of
drug use, *years* of struggling with mental health—you cannot possibly fix that in that amount of time [fifteen months
within a twenty-two-month period, the time a child can be
in foster care before a parental rights termination is to be
pursued].
—caseworker in Wisconsin

Recent critical scholarship on the child welfare system focuses largely
on urban areas, highlighting its punitive nature and role in governing
poor and marginalized populations in the contemporary United States
(e.g., Lee 2016; Reich 2005). Although there is a growing body of social
work literature about child welfare in rural, white communities, critical
scholarship in this context is still rare.[1] To begin to remedy this gap and
to better understand how the child welfare system governs poor populations in this context, this chapter takes an ethnographic approach,
presenting preliminary work in rural Wisconsin and comparing practices there to practices in New York City (NYC), focusing on cases
involving parental drug use. Research in Wisconsin is ongoing and has
included interviews with caseworkers and their supervisors (four, about

half of the staff), foster parents (two), and former foster youth (two); observations of permanency panel meetings; and analysis of standards for caseworker practice, statistics, news coverage, and reports. In NYC, I conducted fourteen months of fieldwork, which included observing family court, interviewing parents and following their cases, asking caseworkers for detailed descriptions of their work, and discussing cases with attorneys representing parents, children, and the child welfare agency (Lee 2016).

As one would imagine, these two locations are drastically different. NYC has one of the largest child welfare, or child protective services (CPS), systems in the nation, investigating approximately ninety thousand children each year (prior to the COVID-19 pandemic), with several thousand residing in foster care on any given day; an overwhelming majority of them are Black or Latine (New York City Administration for Children's Services, n.d.). In contrast, this Wisconsin county had a total population of 45,868 as of 2019 and was 94 percent white (US Census Bureau 2022c). This Wisconsin CPS agency serves a large geographic area (864 square miles) with a small staff of social workers, an institutional context quite different from the large and hierarchical system in NYC. In both locations, however, the child welfare system deals almost exclusively with poor families, as it does in the United States as a whole (Pelton 2015; Roberts 2002), and primarily with cases of child neglect, many involving parental drug use. In what follows, I demonstrate that rather than addressing the root causes of harm to children, many of which stem from poverty and lack of resources, child welfare systems take a punitive approach, often removing children and offering "services" that aim to create good parent-citizens through behavioral changes. These disciplinary practices are part of larger state poverty governance efforts across a variety of public and private institutions, including carceral and welfare agencies (Soss, Fording, and Schram 2011; Woodward 2021).

Child Welfare in Rural, White Communities

Social work literature on rural child welfare is largely descriptive, seeking to understand rates of maltreatment, identify risk factors, and discuss caseworker practice (Maguire-Jack and Kim 2021). The most recent national-level study found higher reporting rates in rural areas but did not find significant differences in substantiation rates or the provision of in-home services (Maguire-Jack and Kim 2021; but see also Maguire-Jack et al. 2020, which finds other studies that dispute this finding). Another study found that the relationship between higher rates of poverty and more CPS reports that has been documented in urban areas holds true in rural areas, except in majority-Black counties, where rates of reporting are lower (Smith et al. 2021). Although the authors were not able to explain these lower reporting rates, they suggest that this might reflect a lack of trust in authorities, a reluctance by professionals to file reports when services are not available, or norms that favor informal supports and community responses rather than state responses (Smith et al. 2021, 8).

This literature also notes that rural child welfare practice is made challenging by poverty, geographic distance and isolation, lack of resources and adequately trained staff, increasing rates of substance abuse, and a dearth of research on evidence-based practices (Belanger, Price-Mayo, and Espinosa 2008; Edwards, Torgerson, and Sattem 2009). The literature on rural casework practice with substance-using parents finds limited treatment options in rural areas, making it difficult for system-involved parents to comply with requirements for retaining or regaining custody of their children (Orsi et al. 2021; Sheridan 2014). At the same time, others have noted how the strengths of rural communities and their child welfare professionals help to overcome these challenges (Landsman 2002; Scales and Cooper 1999).

Unfortunately, this literature on child welfare casework in rural areas does not engage with the growing body of critical scholarship on the child welfare system. Although focusing on urban areas and Indian country, where most of the families involved are racial minorities, critical scholarship still provides key insights that can be applied to child welfare in rural, white areas.

First, the child welfare system, historically and today, deals with the effects of large-scale social inequalities, effects that are misunderstood as individual pathologies (see, for example, Gordon 1988; Roberts 2002). Despite the rhetoric of saving children from severe abuse, most cases involve poor families and issues of "neglect" that are closely related to poverty—drug use, domestic violence, and inadequate housing and food—that could be addressed with additional resources and services (Lee 2016; Reich 2005). The precise relationship between poverty and neglect is debated, with some scholars arguing that neglect and poverty are confused or are the same thing (Krane and Davies 2000; Swift 1995), others arguing that poverty creates conditions such as stress that lead to neglect (e.g., DePanfilis 2006), and yet others claiming that poor families' use of public programs makes them vulnerable to reports of suspected maltreatment (Edwards 2016; Roberts 2002).

Second, the child welfare system is a punitive one, tightly connected to other punitive systems such as welfare and policing. For system-involved families, its purported "services" are often mandatory and linked to the threat or reality of loss of child custody, with a focus on strict compliance for reunification rather than meeting families' needs. Requirements, such as parenting classes and substance abuse treatment, aim to change parents' behavior, based on the logic that their moral failings and poor choices are the main causes of their children's endangerment. Simultaneously, assistance meeting material needs is often nonexistent (Reich 2005; Woodward 2021). Thus, the child welfare system, embracing a neoliberal paternalist approach to poverty governance, manages rather than addresses poverty and seeks to turn poor people into responsible and self-sufficient citizens (Soss, Fording, and Schram 2011, 27).

Finally, this system disproportionately investigates and removes Black and Native American children (Dettlaff and Boyd 2020; M. Harris 2014), reinforcing racialized hierarchies, even, as I argue in this chapter, when it deals with white families.

Drug Cases in Rural Wisconsin and New York City

In both locations, drug use is a very prominent issue—methamphetamine in the Midwest and crack cocaine in NYC—and cases involving these drugs are very likely to end up with the parent losing custody of the child, at least temporarily but often permanently. Use of other substances, such as alcohol and marijuana, less commonly results in reports or child removals. In both places but at different times, reactions to drug "epidemics" have led to high caseloads and dramatic increases in foster care populations, outcomes that are seen as inevitable and thus unquestionable (Lee 2016; Witt 2019). When systems become over-whelmed, children are negatively affected—investigations are completed slowly, removals might be made with little investigation, and appropriate homes for children are difficult to find.[2] In Wisconsin, there has been a shortage of foster homes, and children are sometimes placed far from their families, making visits difficult. In NYC, during the height of the crack "epidemic," children sometimes slept in offices because there were not enough homes (Tobis 1989).

State standards in Wisconsin mandate either a safety plan or foster care placement when children are facing "present danger threats." Safety plans usually involve an alternative caretaker, which still amounts to an involuntary loss of custody. One definition of "present danger threats" is "parent is intoxicated now or is consistently under the influence." Use alone could thus justify a child removal, and caseworkers discussed re-movals as an almost automatic response to methamphetamine cases. When asked why removals are so common, they described these cases as all the same: extremely dirty and dangerous homes with dangerous people constantly in and out, children who are never supervised, parents who allow children to use with them, and sexual and physical abuse. The per-ception of a link between meth and sexual abuse was especially common among caseworkers, with the idea that meth causes parents not to care who is around their children or what they are exposed to, such as prosti-tution or pornography (for evidence of similar views among caseworkers in other parts of the country, see also Haight et al. 2005; Sheridan 2014). Caseworkers easily slipped from talking about a positive drug test to dis-cussing the worst cases they had seen, making it difficult to tell exactly how assessments are made and what levels of use and harm would cause a removal. The practice of removals in meth cases seems to be a statewide pattern, suggesting that state standards are a factor.

Although caseworkers also noted that poverty, a lack of safe and af-fordable housing, and lack of treatment services are a problem in this county, they attributed most of the child safety concerns they saw to drugs. Caseworkers also described methamphetamine as inherently more addictive and harder to manage than other drugs, leading them to see any use of meth as incompatible with good parenting. As one case-worker wrote, "drug use takes away a parent's ability to form a strong bond and maintain connections with their children" (Ader 2019, 21).

Another said of meth-using parents, "[Meth] is the only thing they think about, . . . and I think with other drugs, you have some ability to manage. We TPRed [termination of parental rights] a mom, . . . and she said, 'When you use meth, you don't even think about your child. You're not even a mom.'" When I asked that same caseworker to share a child welfare success story, she brought up a severe physical abuse case in which the "worker really wrapped services around them" and the family reunified. It is striking that physical abuse (a clear example of child harm and the reason, many people argue, that child protection systems are needed) was cited as a case in which services were successfully employed, while drug cases were seen as almost always leading to removals and often terminations of parental rights.

In NYC, a full third of the cases I observed involved drugs, and in most cases, children were in foster care until their parents engaged in treatment and consistently tested negative. In the cases I observed, this frequently took a year or more, even for motivated parents, given delays in referrals and caseworkers wanting a string of negative tests. Here, any illegal drug use could fit the legal definition of neglect, and many attorneys and parents stated that caseworkers did not distinguish between use and addiction; nor did they adequately evaluate how drugs were affecting parenting. Instead, a positive test or admission of use could easily lead to a removal (see Lee 2016). I asked a law guardian (attorney for the child in child welfare proceedings) and former caseworker and attorney for the city's child welfare agency if, legally, attorneys would have to show that drug use was affecting parenting, and she told me, "Technically, yes. What do we actually see? If a parent's using on a weekend, while their kid's being babysat by somebody else, like staying at Grandma's, I would hope they wouldn't bring that case in. Will they? If it's heroin, yeah, they will; if it's crack cocaine, yeah, they probably will. If it's marijuana, they probably won't; if it's alcohol, they pretty much can't" (Lee 2016, 109). Thus, crack was assumed to be automatically dangerous to children, and its use could result in a removal, even in the absence of evidence that children were unsafe. In observing court hearings, it was often difficult to tell exactly how drug use was affecting children or if the harms cited were primarily due to drug use or poverty. In many cases, positive drug tests were presented as the only evidence of maltreatment, and in others, concrete lapses in care, for example, inadequate food or lack of supervision, were attributed to a parent's drug abuse when lack of money or lack of child care was also a likely cause (Lee 2016).

In both locations, then, certain drugs were viewed as incompatible with safe parenting, and a lack of necessary resources was blamed on parental irresponsibility rather than poverty. Both meth and crack cocaine were discussed as more addictive and dangerous than other substances, while parents who use these drugs were described as monsters who forget their kids, use with them, and expose them to sexual abuse. These caseworker understandings of and responses to drug cases raise an important question about state intervention to protect children: Does the use of certain substances necessarily lead to addiction or behaviors that are inherently incompatible with minimally acceptable or safe parenting?

Race and Class in the Framing of Drug "Epidemics" and Their Harms

Beliefs about the harms of meth and crack are exaggerated in ways that reflect racial and class anxieties more than actual data. Race is crucial to understanding how and when drug use is framed as an epidemic and particularly dangerous and why state responses focus on policing and punishment. With crack cocaine, this framing came in the context of post-civil-rights-era backlash and fear of "inner-city crime," a discourse that focused on the supposed pathologies of poor, urban, Black people (see, for example, Mullings 2003; Sharff 1998). A decade later, methamphetamine became firmly linked to poor, rural, white people (Garriott 2013; Linnemann and Wall 2013), and fears about its dangers were linked to "a racial scare . . . of declining White status in the context of post-civil rights economic stratification" (Murakawa 2011, 220).

In the 1980s, the media and some researchers claimed that crack was more addictive than powder cocaine (Hart, Csete, and Habibi 2014) and extremely harmful to users and their children (Gomez 1997; Zerai and Banks 2002). Mothers who used crack were portrayed as monsters who were wholly irresponsible and unaware of their children's needs (Gubrium 2008). The discourse around crack has come to be seen as racist and classist (crack cocaine is far cheaper and thus more commonly used in low-income communities) exaggerations that led to dire consequences including increases in incarceration (Hart, Csete, and Habibi 2014) and in the number of children placed in foster care (Lee 2016). Despite evidence that the negative effects of crack cocaine were vastly inflated, caseworkers and attorneys I talked to still argued that drug use, especially crack, was inherently harmful (Lee 2016).

Discourse around meth today is similar. Under the heading "Meth-Using Parents Are More Likely to Abandon Their Children," one report stated, "Many law enforcement [officers] and social workers find some meth-using parents are either relieved or happy when social services removes children from the home as it allows the parents to continue using meth" (Wisconsin Statewide Intelligence Center et al. 2016, 33–34).[3] Here we see the unfounded idea that parents are so addicted that they are "happy" about child loss. Regarding the dangerousness of the drug, the same report declared, "parental meth use can lead to a lifetime of physical, social, or psychological issues in children" (Wisconsin Statewide Intelligence Center et al. 2016, 33). It is unclear, however, that a "lifetime" of issues is an automatic outcome or even what evidence is being used to support this claim. Nevertheless, this view is presented often to the public and in trainings for CPS workers, shaping their understandings and assessments of families where drug use is reported. Yet, just as with crack cocaine, research is mixed on the impact on children of parental methamphetamine use, and most research focuses on use while pregnant. Some reports have "suggested profound adverse effects on child development" of use during pregnancy, while subsequent longitudinal investigations found more subtle effects and factors that can "mitigate or intensify" effects, including more responsive home environments (Smith and Santos 2016, 142). It is thus unclear whether there is adequate evidence to support automatically removing children in cases in which meth *use* is discovered. This seemingly automatic response might be less about risk and more about a sense of moral panic.

Second, assessments of when drug use might be compatible with parenting are complicated by the role that resources play in parenting. Children not eating, not going to school or to the doctor, or not being properly supervised can be dangerous, depending on the severity and the age of the child. The issue, however, is where to assign blame for these conditions and how to address them. Any mother struggling with drug use might not be able to meet her children's needs, but, unlike a poor mother, a middle-class mother will be able to keep that child safe using other resources—a babysitter, money for food, treatment, and so on. While not discounting that drug use can be harmful for children, especially with regard to forming a quality relationship with them (Barnard and McKeganey 2004), the most common reasons caseworkers removed children in cases of parental drug use were related to a lack of resources or parents' inability to access treatment.[4] The decision to remove a poor child due to parental drug use, with inadequate assessment of actual harm and without providing the family with needed services (for information about service provision, see later in this chapter), is, in effect, a decision to place a child in foster care because the parent has insufficient resources. Thus, casework practice in drug cases is one way the state regulates and punishes poor parents.

Framing Drug Use and Child Harms as an Individual Problem

Caseworkers in both locations also see drug use as a purely individual problem, ignoring larger structural factors and instead focusing on reforming parents in the hopes of making them self-sufficient "neoliberal citizen-parents" (Woodward 2021). Although explicit references to race were not made by caseworkers in either location, descriptions of why parents struggled differ in racially coded ways. For example, when I asked caseworkers in Wisconsin why meth use is increasing, they were either unsure or pointed to individual-level factors: "I don't know. I think it's cheap. . . . I think there's a lot of hurting people in this world that just don't know how to begin to deal with their own traumas . . . so they numb. . . . and I think it starts younger and younger with these generational families that the parents haven't quite figured it out, so then they're allowing their kids to use with them."[5]

Although caseworkers expressed sympathy for parents and recognized individuals' trauma, they ignored larger structural inequalities, which are often the root causes of both individual and community traumas. Some caseworkers mentioned the lack of treatment, but none talked about structural issues like poverty and its association with violence and other traumatic experiences that might explain why drug use has increased or why some parents struggled. As another caseworker told me, "the macro piece of social work, I don't think any of us are ever involved enough in that" (Haight et al. 2005 describes similar views among Illinois professionals).

In NYC, explanations for drug use also focused on individual pathologies, but without the sympathy accorded to white parents in Wisconsin. Drug-using parents (especially mothers) were portrayed as completely focused on themselves and not caring at all about their children. More generally, women of color involved in the child welfare system were viewed as irresponsible, unable to learn from past mistakes, and unwilling to ever put their children's needs above their own. As one caseworker described her clients, "Well, it has to do with, I think, arrested development. A majority of people haven't grown up and still have a teenage mentality. . . . Most of the families that we service are a one-parent household and mostly women, . . . where the father may be incarcerated, out of the picture, don't know who the father is. It's very limited the support that they have. Unemployed, okay, no high school education . . . And if they didn't value education for themselves, they certainly don't value it for their children." These discourses hint at larger social structures (the educational system and job market) but blame parents' individual attitudes (lack of value placed on education), irresponsibility, and childish behavior for family problems and poverty. Caseworkers saw these poor Black and brown mothers as unacceptable risks to their children rather than struggling mothers who loved their kids but needed help. According to caseworkers, these mothers consistently made bad decisions, making constant, intrusive surveillance and foster care placement—rather than help meeting their material needs—necessary. Following these views, intensive surveillance of families, strict behavioral requirements (extending to whom mothers could let into their homes or have a sexual relationship with), and even child removals were deemed necessary (see Lee 2016).

In Wisconsin, then, despite being sympathetic, caseworkers discussed intergenerational poverty and trauma in ways that painted certain families and parents as irredeemable and living in separate cultures that embrace pathological behaviors. These stereotypes, not unlike culture of poverty stereotypes of poor people of color in urban areas, refer to those who have historically been deemed "white trash" (Hartigan 2005; Wray 2006). They also reflect the contemporary rhetoric of anti-meth campaigns (Linnemann and Wall 2013; Murakawa 2011). In NYC, discussions of irresponsibility, "arrested development," fatherlessness, and mothers self-ishly putting their own needs ahead of their children echo long-standing stereotypes of irresponsible Black mothers or "jezebels" (Collins 2000; Roberts 1997). In both cases, parents are racialized and seen as risks rather than potentially fit parents.

Despite these individual-level explanations, drug use is a symptom of structural inequalities (Garriott 2013; Mullings 2003). In NYC in the 1980s and 1990s, deindustrialization and increasing income inequality left many people in communities of color either without jobs or with only poorly paid service jobs; some turned to the drug trade to survive or to deal with despair. The rural Midwest has been hit hard in recent decades by the decline of family farming as a viable way to survive, and farmers (or youths who might become farmers) have been forced to find other income opportunities (Garriott 2013, 30–31). However, good jobs are hard to find without being willing and able to move to more urban areas, without reliable transportation, or without additional education. Meth use arose in this context since it could be produced locally from easily available household items and is useful "as a means of perfor-mance enhancement in the context of manual labor" (Garriott 2013, 27). It can help people work longer hours, can be manufactured and sold when jobs are unavailable, and can be used to self-medicate to deal with despair and trauma.

These links between poverty, economic changes, and drug use suggest that, if the goal is to protect children from harm, families need both ser-vices that focus on individual psychological or behavioral issues (coun-seling and drug treatment) and help escaping poverty (cash assistance, meaningful job training, and policy solutions such as living wage laws or universal basic income). In fact, research shows that increasing fam-ily incomes decreases child welfare reports and risks of maltreatment (see, for example, Cancian, Yang, and Slack 2013; Raissian and Bullinger 2017). However, rather than dealing with the root causes of negative out-comes for children (poverty and lack of resources), the system focuses on individual behaviors, attempting to change them through various forms of education, counseling, and supervision, all while "protecting" children by removing them from their families.

The irony of this response is that removal itself is harmful and state systems do not adequately care for children either. Emerging evidence shows that children facing similar risks who are not removed have better outcomes than those who are (Doyle 2007, 2008), that infants staying with mothers in treatment is better for both mothers and babies (Wobie et al. 1997), and that contact with child welfare does not improve child outcomes (Evangelist, Thomas, and Waldfogel 2023). The likely harms of foster care for children have also been well documented, including continued maltreatment, multiple placements, trauma related to the interruption of relationships, interruption of schooling, discrimination against LGBTQ foster children, and loss of ties to culture and community (see, for example, Finck et al. 2021; Trivedi 2019). The 1997 Adoption and Safe Families Act (ASFA) did cite harms from foster care as one rationale for time limits on foster care placements. However, it ignored the harms of removal and focused on adoption more than on reunification.[6] Finally, those who "age out" of foster care are also more likely to have a range of negative outcomes including early pregnancies, dropping out of school, and criminal justice involvement (Pecora et al. 2005). Given all that is known about the harms of removal and foster care, it seems reasonable to conclude that the child welfare system is not just (or even primarily) about protecting children but about disciplining and controlling poor families.

A Similarly Punitive System

Although caseworkers truly want to help families and do not see themselves as punishing or coercing, the system does operate in these ways. First, there are numerous parallels between policing and social work and even direct cooperation between the two (as Fong and Smith explain in chapter 9 of this volume), which can lead to coercion. In NYC, caseworkers discussed the difficulties of providing services because their policing role prevented or betrayed trust. One caseworker explained how, although she asks parents to be honest about their issues so she can assist them with services, service provision is difficult because parents do not trust her after she tells them that she might remove their children. Another one stated, "What was kind of hard for me sometimes is that . . . you had to develop a relationship with them to get the information, and then this is the information that I'm using against you. . . . And the agency, . . . they want you to be a social worker, but it's law enforcement that you're doing. I'm investigating as if I'm a detective, trying to gather information for a case that I might file against them."

Parents also told me that they did not trust caseworkers to help and instead felt they were judgmental and punitive. Attorneys explained that using the promise of services to get parents to disclose their issues also led to removals in low-risk cases, turning help into potential punishment. For example, if a parent admitted that they smoked marijuana (defined as lower risk), a caseworker would obtain a court order requiring the parent to stop using and "engage in" services to keep custody. If the parent later violated the court order, a removal would occur for that reason. Given data about the trauma of removal and the harms of foster care for children, this is a problematic outcome.

In Wisconsin, caseworkers similarly combine investigative and helping roles, and I suspect (but do not have data yet) that they face similar issues with regard to building trust with parents and families. In addition, there is direct collaboration between law enforcement and social workers here. Caseworkers praise their good relationships with police and regularly enlist their help in approaching families during investigations. This collaboration is probably related to the increase in drug testing that, according to caseworkers, had led to more removals over the past few years. As one state report notes, "Social services in western Wisconsin . . . noted a decrease in cooperation from meth-using parents which has led law enforcement and social service workers to make joint home visits. Law enforcement is more skilled than social service workers in identifying meth in the home, and therefore parents are unable to deny meth use or ignore the social service workers" (Wisconsin Statewide Intelligence Center et al. 2016, 33). It is unclear that law enforcement officers are, in fact, "more skilled" than social workers in spotting meth. Social workers get extensive training in this. Instead, this account can be read as law enforcement being used as a "stick" to get parents to cooperate and submit to testing.

Service provision is similarly punitive, but with key differences between the two sites. In Wisconsin, all caseworkers answered an emphatic "no" or "never" when asked if they had adequate services for parents. They also acknowledged that complying with court orders is difficult:

I don't know that I could complete and comply with the court order. . . .
I think when you take a parent who most likely is struggling with mental

health, they're struggling with AODA [alcohol and other drug abuse] issues, and we throw a list of conditions on them and things that they need to comply with. . . . If I were a single mom, and I was working full-time, how on earth am I gonna get to three AODA appointments in a week? How on earth am I going to get to my mental health appointments in a week? Then you don't have transportation. . . . There's probably three to four pages of conditions.

Note that, in this caseworker's account, sobriety and compliance, not child safety, drives decision-making after a child is removed, as is true in NYC as well (Lee 2016). Despite acknowledging these problems, caseworkers continue to write court orders in this way, probably because they show that the county has made "reasonable efforts" as required by law; these efforts can be used to show parental noncompliance to set up a case for termination of parental rights.

The practice in Wisconsin is also to strictly adhere to the 1997 ASFA rule that agencies should initiate termination of parental rights proceedings when children have been in foster care for fifteen of the previous twenty-two months. This contrasts with NYC, where children regularly stayed in foster care well past the ASFA timeline because either judges were supportive of delaying terminations or court calendars led to cases moving extremely slowly (Lee 2016). As a Wisconsin caseworker explained, because these timelines are too short given the realities of treating meth abuse, they have processed far more terminations of parental rights over the past several years:

We will tell our clients that relapses are expected. . . . But then we have the state, who says fifteen out of twenty-two months, and if you have a relapse at twelve months, what does that look like? In three months, I'm supposed to be filing TPR [a termination of parental rights]? But I haven't even given this parent a chance to come out of their relapse and get back into treatment. . . . It's super hard. . . . [Available treatment is] twenty-one days and you're out, or maybe thirty days and you're out. Uh-uh [no, laughs], like, we need long-term treatment. . . . Research tells us six months to a year is a critical time in a meth user's sobriety and whether they'll relapse or not, and we're sending them out after twenty-one days of sobriety? They're not sober!

The state is thus removing children and moving quickly toward terminating parental rights while caseworkers are very aware that they do not have services to help parents deal with their addiction and regain custody. These timelines also require caseworkers to begin planning for "permanency" outside of the parent's custody and discussing the possibility of losing parental rights very quickly.

Caseworkers describe the pain that these practices cause parents (leading, in some cases, to continued drug use or relapses), descriptions that contradict reports that meth-using parents "forget they are parents" or are "happy" to have their children removed. Although these timelines aim to facilitate permanency and protect children from the harms of extended foster care placements, removals are still traumatic, and permanency is not always achieved. For example, researchers estimate that anywhere from 3 percent to 47 percent of adoptions are disrupted (Coakley and Berrick 2008).[7] In addition, not all children end up being adopted at all. In Wisconsin, children "age out" of the foster care system at eighteen and face numerous issues, given the lack of support for the transition to independent living.[8]

In NYC, although more services were available, crushing caseloads meant that caseworkers often did not make referrals in a timely manner and services had long waitlists. Both factors regularly delayed service plans for months. In addition, I found that parents were required to comply with practically any service required by a caseworker, whether it met the family's needs or not. Service requirements could expand throughout a case and focus almost entirely on education and counseling that "attempt to resocialize parents to behave in ways that are seen as appropriately parental" (Reich 2005, 115). Noncompliance with service plans frequently led to removals, delayed reunification, or termination of parental rights. In many cases I observed, service plans became practically a full-time job, and it was very difficult to meet all requirements, given lack of transportation and other resources. Compliance with service plans could also lead to lost income and thus an inability to support the child, which could then be used to further delay reunification or to make a case to terminate parental rights (Lee 2016). Given how caseworkers in Wisconsin described court-ordered service plans, I strongly suspect that parents there have similar experiences, but research with parents is needed.

Again, these profound family disruptions are harmful not only to parents but also to children, who experience issues including trauma from removal, lengthy foster care placements, frequent placement changes, and difficulties aging out of the system. Although in New York children are entitled to remain in foster care until age twenty-one and to use educational and other supports to help them transition to independent living, many do not get this help. One attorney who represented these youths told me that "discharge to the homeless system" was a common plan. Thus, the system can often perpetuate the poverty that it deals with daily. Rather than supporting families or contributing to greater child well-being, it manages and punishes poor families.

Despite profound and troubling issues in both places, there are also some positive practices in Wisconsin. First, working in a smaller agency and in a rural area allowed caseworkers to be more creative in how they approach cases. Supervisors and the county board (which allocates local tax dollars and sets rules about how budgets can be spent) allow freedom in how caseworkers spend their funds. For example, they can buy household supplies or gift cards at a local Walmart; a story about finding money to help buy a trailer home was relayed to me multiple times. It is important to note, however, that these strategies are used to facilitate reunification rather than to prevent removals. These strategies are also probably related to the greater sympathy afforded white parents. In contrast, the extremely hierarchical and inflexible bureaucracy in NYC does not allow caseworkers to creatively meet material needs in these ways. Thus, white families in Wisconsin are afforded more support, in some cases, than Black and Latine families in NYC. Wisconsin caseworkers are also more creative in developing safety plans and more willing to find alternatives to a formal foster care placement (usually by finding family to care for a child informally, sometimes keeping the child in their normal residence). However, it should be noted that this still entails a loss of custody for the parent. In contrast, NYC caseworkers were more insistent about formal foster care placements (even with kin) because these allow them more power over the family with regard to monitoring and enforcing required service plans.

Another positive practice in Wisconsin involves efforts to allow birth parents to have contact with children after permanently losing custody. Caseworkers often work out informal contact agreements with adoptive parents; however, these cannot be enforced. I spoke with foster parents who had very negative views of birth parents and expressed not wanting to deal with them. Other research documents similar views and how they are related to limited contact between birth parents and their children (Hudson and Levasseur 2002; Sanchirico and Jablonka 2000). Thus, I would guess that many plans for contact do not materialize in practice. Efforts to facilitate contact post-termination were rare in NYC, a difference that probably stems from the sympathy afforded white parents as well as from the different institutional context.

The Role of Race and Class in CPS in Rural and Urban Communities

Findings in NYC and preliminary results in rural Wisconsin demonstrate the essentially punitive nature of the child welfare system and its role in poverty governance. In both locations, the root causes of parental drug use are almost entirely ignored. Connections between large-scale structural problems that leave some people vulnerable to poverty and traumas, on the one hand, and drug use (which, in the absence of social supports, can be a way to cope and self-medicate), on the other, are not made. Instead of support for vulnerable families, drug use is met with policing, child welfare reports, and, too often, child removal. Given ASFA timelines, scarcity of services, and continued poverty, parents are not always able to regain custody, while children often suffer in foster care or when they age out. Despite the similarities, there are also striking differences between the two sites. In contrast to NYC, Wisconsin caseworkers express more understanding of and sympathy for parents, and, in some cases, creatively work to support parents or try to ensure that parents can see their children if parental rights are terminated.

These similarities and differences are best analyzed in relation to the overall goals and function of the child welfare system as well as the different racial and institutional dynamics in each location. The similarly punitive nature of the child welfare system in both places is linked to the fact that it is, and has always been, a system that intervenes almost exclusively in the families of class and racial "others." It has always dealt with families through surveillance and the threat of child removals while failing to provide resources that would help families thrive, justifying these actions on the basis of the ideological presumption that it is necessary to protect children (Gordon 1988; Lash 2017). Rather than providing needed resources, most service plans require parents to participate in individualized services that aim to change behavior. Part of the argument that legislators made in support of ASFA was that (Black) parents were getting too many chances to regain custody, harming children who need permanent families quickly (Guggenheim 2021; Stein 2003). Thus, ASFA imposed strict timelines for reunification and incentivized adoptions. That relatively quick removals and inadequate reunification services occur in both locations is thus not surprising. At the same time, there are different racial dynamics at play in these two locations.

Paying closer attention to whiteness, without centering white experiences and losing sight of the disproportionate harms faced by families of color, can help to explain these dynamics. Rather than only discussing race in relation to disparities between whites and people of color (see, for example, Font, Berger, and Slack 2012; M. Harris 2014), whiteness must be analyzed not as an unmarked "norm" but as a racial category that includes class ideologies (e.g., the cultural assumption that being white implies being middle class) and is internally divided, with categories of marginally or "not quite" white within it (see, for example, Hartigan 2005; Wray and Newitz 1997). For example, the first agencies that removed children for "cruelty" and placed them in foster homes or orphanages in the urban Northeast mainly intervened in the families of recent eastern and southern European immigrants, who were seen as racially inferior and not-quite-white (Lee 2016). Thus, I contend that child welfare is about the governance of racialized poverty even when it is primarily dealing with poor, white communities.

I have found the scholarship around the category of "white trash" particularly helpful in thinking through the similarities and differences in these child welfare practices. Although white parents are, in some ways, viewed and treated more sympathetically and with more understanding, caseworkers do not simply decide that these parents are likely to be good parents because they are white. Their poverty and their drug use mark them as dangerous and make child removals seem necessary. Caseworkers demonize meth use, drawing on discourses that portray it as extremely addictive, dangerous, and in-compatible with parenting—just as similar beliefs around crack have led to punishing poor, Black mothers. These discourses are, in turn, related to fears about white status decline and anxieties about changes in rural areas (increasing poverty, uneven development, loss of farm-ing income, and increases in crime). As others have pointed out, the discourse surrounding meth marks users as "white trash" (Murakawa 2011), a "boundary term" or way to define who is fully white and who is not (Wray 2006).

The category of "white trash" is maintained (even if not directly named) through child welfare practices that punish some poor, white drug users and mark them as so undeserving that intense policing and child removals are necessary. Although the caseworkers I interviewed never referred to parents as "white trash," they did describe them in ways that echo other descriptions of white trash—as living in trailers; being dirty, poor, sexually promiscuous, and unable to hold jobs and function without state surveillance; and generally having intergen-erationally dysfunctional families. These white families are clearly set apart from the rest of the community, as people in positions of power draw boundaries between those who do and those who do not need intervention. When discourse about a meth "epidemic" that is suppos-edly extremely dangerous for children comes together with stereotypes about folks living in poverty, it is easy to see how child removals and state intervention are seen as necessary, despite expressions of sympa-thy and understanding, especially in this policy context. Much like the way the crack cocaine "epidemic" spurred the expansion of both polic-ing and child welfare interventions in urban areas in the 1980s to early 2000s, a meth epidemic has led to similar outcomes in rural areas today (Linnemann 2013). In both locations, these systems are fundamentally about how the state regulates poor communities and uses racialized ideas about certain presumably problematic behaviors to justify intense surveillance of families and the removal of children to foster care. Al-though the stated aim of this system is to protect children from harm, its failure to address the root causes of harm to children and its inabil-ity to provide better care mean that these children remain vulnerable to negative outcomes and the perpetuation of intergenerational harms. As recognition of these harms and of the deeply embedded racism and classism of this system spreads, more scholars and activists are calling for its abolition and for changes that will, in the long run, help to dismantle it (Lee 2022).

NOTES

1 There is critical scholarship about practice with Native American families in rural areas where the Indian Child Welfare Act applies (Bjorum 2014; Brown and Rieger 2001).

2 In this Wisconsin county, caseworkers responded within forty-eight hours in 33 percent of cases investigated between December 2017 and December 2018 and in only 18 percent of cases between October 2020 and October 2021 (Wisconsin Department of Children and Families 2024).

3 The report cites electronic communications from the FBI as the source of this information.

4 State guidelines about when a safety plan (usually removal of the child from the home but sometimes removal of the parent from the child) is required include "psychological torture" and "extreme emotional abuse," but I have not heard caseworkers reference cases like this.

5 Caseworkers did not present concrete examples of children using with their parents; it is unclear whether this is happening.

6 Part of the reason for this policy choice was that it aligned with the idea that poor and minority families were dangerous and got too much help. These arguments made foster care prevention seem risky for children while enabling parental unfitness.

7 The wide range in estimates is partly related to how disruption is defined. Some researchers count any time a child is not living with the adoptive parent(s) after the adoption is finalized, while others include only children returned to an agency prior to finalizing an adoption.

8 My university was a pioneer in assisting former foster youths' transition to college. The small program is largely supported by private donations.

The Child Welfare System and the Left Hand of the State

5

Surviving the "Child Welfare" System

How the Family Policing System Punishes and Controls Survivors of Violence

SHANTA TRIVEDI AND ERIN CARRINGTON SMITH

Sharwline Nicholson, a thirty-two-year-old, Black, single mother from New York who was working and putting herself through school, was attacked by the father of one of her children when she wanted to end their relationship. During the attack, Ms. Nicholson sustained a broken arm, fractured ribs, and head injuries. Before leaving for the hospital, Ms. Nicholson left her children with her neighbor, whom she had relied on for child care in the past. Despite making proper arrangements for her children's care, New York's Administration for Children's Services (ACS) went to her neighbor's home and removed her children. Although her children were asleep and unharmed during the attack, ACS alleged that the children were at "imminent risk if they remained in the care of Ms. Nicholson because she was not . . . able to protect herself nor her children because [her boyfriend] had viciously beaten her."[1] The removal of Ms. Nicholson's children was based on the troubling presumption that, by experiencing intimate partner violence (IPV), seemingly in the presence of her children, she had failed to protect them from exposure to that violence.

The "child welfare" system's goal is to protect children from harm (CWIG 2020b). It does this through state and federal law dictating when children should be removed from their homes to protect them from abuse or neglect. The Child Abuse Prevention and Treatment Reauthorization Act of 2010 (42 U.S.C. § 5106g [2010]) defines abuse and neglect as "any recent act or failure to act on the part of a parent or caretaker which results in death, serious physical or emotional harm, sexual abuse or exploitation or . . . an act or failure to act which presents an imminent risk of serious harm." At the state level, definitions and interpretations of IPV's relationship to child maltreatment vary; while two states consider exposure to IPV child maltreatment and can hold the survivor accountable, other states have specific protections to prevent survivors of IPV from being held responsible (Victor et al. 2021).

Because of mandated reporting laws in all fifty states requiring police, doctors, social workers, psychologists, and others to report suspected child maltreatment under threat of civil and criminal penalties (CWIG 2019a), many mothers who report violence to seek help instead become embroiled in the "child welfare" system (Fong 2020). This is a symptom of the increasing intersection between the "right hand" and the "left hand" of the state, whereby carceral and public welfare systems work in tandem as one poverty governance system (Brayne 2014).

For those who are trapped in this web and advocates who help low-income parents navigate this system, "child welfare" is a misnomer; it is more accurately dubbed the "family policing system," demonstrating how it was designed to surveil, control, and punish families (Roberts 2020). The way the family policing system interacts with IPV survivors and their families is perhaps the clearest example of this. Once enmeshed in the system, mothers who have experienced IPV are accused of "failing to protect" their children from the same violence they experienced themselves. Others who do not believe they are experiencing IPV must accept their status as "victims" and comply with unsolicited services, from counseling to parenting classes. Those who refuse may have their children removed because system actors believe they lack "insight" into their experiences as victims, thereby risking further violence at their children's expense (Dunlap 2004; Washington 2022).

Even when children remain at home, their mothers face intrusive surveillance and constant judgment through investigations and court-ordered supervision. In far too many cases, the harm of removing children from their mothers is overlooked or minimized. A particular harm associated with system involvement under these circumstances is that it makes IPV survivors less likely to seek help in the future. One study showed that a third of survivors who had family policing system involvement following an IPV report listed fear of having their children removed as a barrier to reporting future abuse (Ohio Domestic Violence Network 2022). As chapters by Brant (chapter 6) and Fong and

Smith (chapter 9) in this volume also show, there are negative effects of collaboration between welfare and carceral systems, specifically the increased existence of "system avoidance," for fear of government surveillance (Brayne 2014, 371).

This chapter explores how the family policing system harms both mothers and children by entangling survivors and suspected survivors of IPV—especially poor women of color—in a web of surveillance and punishment under threat of losing their children. It looks at both the unique harms of removing children from parents experiencing IPV and how the system exacerbates survivors' trauma. Finally, it recommends ways the family policing system can support rather than dismantle families in need. To do so, the system must acknowledge the harm of removal, the root causes of violence, and the part it plays in perpetuating cycles of trauma among low-income communities of color.

Race and Class Disparities in the Family Policing System

When it comes to family policing, "ideas about parental fitness are deeply intertwined with race, class, and family structure in ways that affect the likelihood of a maltreatment report" (Edwards 2019, 55). The perception of low-income, Black mothers as lesser parents than their middle-class and white counterparts is on full display in the family policing system (Neal 1995; Roberts 2022). Because neglect laws are written so broadly, caseworkers and police often rely on their own opinions and interpretations of what constitutes risk to children. "Conditions of poverty—lack of food, insecure housing, inadequate medical care"—are frequently seen "as evidence of parental unfitness" (Roberts 2022, 21), with "homes in Black communities" often perceived "as more hazardous for children, even when the alleged parental infraction—like allowing a toddler to momentarily stray away, or having bottles of alcohol in the house—happens in white affluent homes, too" (Roberts 2022, 22). Following removal, court opinions approving terminations of parental rights also cite conditions like poverty, housing insecurity, and substance use as broad indications of "bad" parenting, even absent indications of harm (Neal 1995). Although the existence of a "better" foster home in a "better" neighborhood should have no bearing on whether a parent's rights are terminated, too often such considerations enter the psyche of courts making these decisions (Neal 1995; see also Bryson, chapter 3 in this volume).

Compounding these issues is the fact that the family policing system is inextricably linked with the criminal legal system, which itself is infused with institutionalized racism. These systems work in concert to surveil families and ultimately tear them apart. Parental involvement with the criminal legal system, which has a long history of disproportionately stopping, investigating, and arresting Black people, often sparks family policing investigations that become the basis for separating Black families. Overpolicing in low-income neighborhoods helps create a police-to-foster-care pipeline in which police are almost twice as likely to report Black parents than white parents to the family policing system (Edwards 2019). Michelle Burrell (2019), a family defender in New York, has compared family policing system investigations to stop-and-frisk policies because of their similarly invasive and biased nature. Others have dubbed the phenomenon the "new Jane Crow"—a system that criminalizes the parenting choices of poor women of color (Clifford and Silver-Greenberg 2017).

Year after year, Black and brown children make up a disproportionate percentage of the foster care system population (USDHHS 2022a). Native American and Alaskan Native children, for example, are disproportionately represented at over two and a half times their proportion in the general population (NICWA 2021). One study in California showed that approximately half of all Black and Native children will experience family policing involvement before their eighteenth birthdays and, overall, experience system involvement more than twice as often as white children. The same study found that low-income children (those whose births were paid for by public insurance) were six times more likely than those with private insurance to have their parents' parental rights terminated (Putnam-Hornstein et al. 2021). As Dorothy Roberts (2002, 6) wrote in her seminal book *Shattered Bonds*, "If you came with no preconceptions about the purpose of the child welfare system, you would have to conclude that it is an institution designed to monitor, regulate, and punish poor Black families."

When the first author of this chapter represented parents accused of abuse and neglect in Brooklyn, she witnessed race and class disproportionality and bias firsthand. Other attorneys around the country confirm this experience. They have had clients judged solely for poverty and circumstance: keeping their clothes in trash bags after suffering water damage from a hurricane or having evidence of roaches or rats among their belongings in New York City homeless shelters. Criticism for parenting decisions can even extend to the mundane, from dirty dishes in the sink and laundry on the floor to what parents choose to feed their children. Parents are judged for giving their children juice or Chinese takeout (Gottlieb 2010) or feeding their babies culturally appropriate foods like rice and beans (Maddali 2014), choices that every parent in the United States makes every day but for which only some must face invasive interventions.

This bias extends to survivors of IPV, especially low-income women of color, who are more likely to be reported to the "child welfare" system when they seek help (Ohio Domestic Violence Network 2022). Once they are in the system, poverty remains a significant barrier to compliance with system-required services. "Failure to protect" laws that consider witnessing IPV a form of child neglect are a clear example of how the family policing system operates as a form of poverty governance, trapping poor women of color who seek help in a cycle that strips them of their autonomy, amplifies their existing struggles, and far too often finds that the only "solution" is to dismantle their families. This system ignores the actual needs of both IPV survivors and their children, to the detriment of the entire family.

The Harm of Child Removal in the Context of Intimate Partner Violence

Child removal from homes where IPV is known or suspected to have occurred is based on studies that show that a child's exposure to violence can have lasting adverse effects. There is evidence that children exposed to IPV may also be at risk of maltreatment by the person causing harm (Humphreys et al. 2018). Even absent physical harm, studies show that exposure to violence is harmful in and of itself (Howell et al. 2016; Lundy and Grossman 2005; Moylan et al. 2010). While the terms "exposure" and "witnessing" are often used interchangeably, "exposure" can refer to a wide range of situations, including seeing, hearing, experiencing, or witnessing the aftermath of violence (Dunlap 2004). Studies show that exposure to violence can lead to a wide range of emotional and behavioral impacts on children (Howell et al. 2016; Moylan et al. 2010), as well as negative impacts on their cognitive development (Howell et al. 2016; Koenen et al. 2003) and physical health (Howell et al. 2016).

However, the effects of exposure to IPV will vary depending on the circumstances of each case (Dunlap 2004, 571). The child's age and gender, whether the person accused of violence is the child's father versus the mother's new partner, and the frequency, severity, and nature of the violence all impact how IPV affects children (Weithorn 2001). Unfortunately, most state laws fail to reflect the intricacies of each family situation or consider that, in many cases, even when children do experience harm due to exposure to IPV, the level of harm does not necessitate removal (Dunlap 2004). For example, under Maryland law, neglect is defined as the "failure to give proper care and attention to a child by any parent . . . under circumstances that indicate: (1) that the child's health or welfare is harmed or placed at substantial risk of harm; or (2) that the child has suffered mental injury or been placed at substantial risk of mental injury."[2] Imagine a scenario in which a child is awakened by her parents arguing, comes into the room, and witnesses her father hit her mother. She is distraught as a result. The mother puts the child to bed, calms her down, and she falls asleep. The child continues to be traumatized by what she has witnessed. Did that mother "fail to give proper care and attention"? It seems likely that removing the child from that mother would be even more traumatic. Even more complicated is a scenario in which the father comforts the child, apologizes, and calms the child down. Did the father "fail to give proper care and attention"? Should the child be removed from the father?

Despite the obvious complexities of these scenarios, most courts continue to use a one-size-fits-all approach by erring on the side of removing children. The assumption in most of these cases is that the harm of staying in a home with violence is always worse than the harm of removal. However, children who are removed from their parents due to family policing system involvement experience intense trauma that manifests in anxiety, depression, posttraumatic stress disorder, and grief (Trivedi 2019). In fact, the Centers for Disease Control and Prevention (CDC) consider both exposure to IPV *and* family separation "adverse childhood experiences" (CDC 2023). Further, the American Academy of Pediatrics

(AAP) has warned that separating children from their parents "can cause irreparable harm, disrupting a child's brain architecture and affecting his or her short- and long-term health. This type of prolonged exposure to serious stress—known as toxic stress—can carry lifelong consequences for children" (Kraft 2018). Children removed from their parents often experience confusion and guilt about whether they or their parent did something wrong to precipitate their separation (Trivedi 2019). When IPV exists and the state removes children from their nonoffending parents, children's existing feelings of guilt are intensified, and they may blame themselves or their nonoffending parents for their removal.

While adverse circumstances and trauma leading up to the placement of children in foster care may contribute to some of these children's poor outcomes, studies across the country show that children placed into the foster care system face an increased risk of physical and sexual abuse and medical neglect, including a lack of access to mental health treatment or even routine medical care and immunizations (Myers et al. 2023; Pecora et al. 2005). According to the AAP, "Children and adolescents in foster care have a higher prevalence of physical, developmental, dental, and behavioral health conditions than any other group of children" (AAP 2005) and are less likely to graduate from high school or attend college than their peers (Courtney et al. 2010). The economist Joseph Doyle found that when these children "age out" because they are too old to receive foster care services from the government, they are more likely to experience poverty, be unhoused, and have legal system involvement (Doyle 2007). Other research shows that as these children become adults, they are more likely to require counseling for psychological or emotional problems and to attend substance abuse treatment programs (Courtney et al. 2010).

Children exposed to IPV are uniquely vulnerable to the harms of removal. This is because one of the most significant factors impacting how children process exposure to violence is their attachment to their nonoffending parent. Secure attachments are crucial to a child's development of resilience and competence (Howell et al. 2016). Further, when IPV is involved, it is critical the child sees that their nonoffending parent is protected and that the violence they witnessed has come to an end (Kaiser and Foley 2021). The child's relationship with their protective parent and a resolution to the turmoil in their home is vital to their development of resilience and the skills necessary to recover from exposure to violence. With regard to mitigating any traumatic impacts of exposure to violence, secure attachment to a parent (or other adult) is the child's "most important protective resource"; studies of children exposed to violence and war have found that separation from family is "one of the most potentially damaging consequences of war for children," while children cared for by their parents suffer far fewer adverse effects (Osofsky 1999, 38).

Experts believe that even when parents struggle to keep children safe, children still organize their behaviors and thinking around their relationship with their parents. When these relationships are broken, and no other adult can help the child make meaning of it, not only are children confused and scared, but they also may blame themselves for the loss of their parent (Eck 2018). Thus, in many situations, removal causes more harm to children than does leaving them with their mothers and, in some situations, with both parents, potentially depriving them of the restorative benefits of staying in their home after exposure to violence.

Even the family policing system acknowledges this harm. The US Department of Health and Human Services' Office of Child Abuse and Neglect's "user manual," titled *Child Protection in Families Experiencing Domestic Violence*, explicitly states, "While children's safety is the primary responsibility of [Child Protective Services] caseworkers, to prevent additional trauma every attempt should be made to maintain the child with the nonoffending parent if it is appropriate and possible." To do so, the manual states that children should only be removed from parents under certain conditions, including after "all other means of safety have been considered" and when the "victim" is unable to protect children and "unable . . . to accept services" (Selleck, Newman, and Gilmore 2018, 92). In reality, however, the family policing system defaults to separation from the father and leaves little leeway for mothers who push back against required services or simply cannot complete them, running contrary to its own admission that child removal is a traumatic event.

A "Failure to Protect" Families in Need

In Sharwline Nicholson's case, her children were placed in foster care even though several other less disruptive and traumatic placements were available. Ms. Nicholson first suggested placing her children with relatives in New Jersey, but her caseworker, Mr. Williams, refused to move them out of state because it required him to get a court order. She then suggested a cousin in the Bronx, but Mr. Williams declined, citing a lack of proper beds in the home. Instead, the state placed Ms. Nicholson's children with strangers. After removing the children, Mr. Williams waited several days to file the case in court. Revealing the intentional and coercive nature of this type of removal, Mr. Williams testified "that it is common in domestic violence cases for ACS to wait a few days before going to court after removing a child because, after a few days of the children being in the foster system, the mother will usually agree to ACS's conditions for their return without the matter ever going to court."[3] Mr. Williams's willingness to give such damning testimony suggests that this practice was so commonplace as to be unexceptional to him. Ms. Nicholson's children were eventually returned to her twenty-one days after they were removed. During this time, her son turned six years old, but Ms. Nicholson was unable to see or speak to him on his birthday. Further, while the children were in the foster care system, their foster mother slapped Ms. Nicholson's son, leaving him with a swollen eye, and her daughter returned with a rash on her face and "pus running from her nose."[4]

Ms. Nicholson and others who were similarly affected by ACS sued, and in 2004, the case went to the New York Court of Appeals. The court held that a parent being a victim of abuse and a child thereby being exposed to violence was not alone sufficient for a finding of neglect. In deciding whether a parent experiencing abuse who stayed with the person inflicting harm exercised a "minimum degree of care," the court determined that the many risks involved in leaving that situation—such as the risks and burden of relocating, seeking assistance, and pursuing criminal prosecution—must be considered. A court must also consider how frequent and severe the violence was and what resources and options were available to the mother. Further, in deciding whether to remove a child from their parent, a court cannot simply identify the risk of harm involved in remaining in the home. Instead, it must weigh whether that risk can be mitigated by reasonable efforts to prevent removal and then balance that risk against the harm of removal before deciding what is in the child's best interest.[5]

Although this decision was rightly lauded as a huge step in the right direction, in practice, this standard is not always applied. Post-*Nicholson*, mothers in New York have still been routinely charged with failure to protect their children from exposure to IPV (Perrone 2012). For example, in 2007—just three years after the *Nicholson* decision—the mother in *In re Angelique L.* was deemed neglectful after her boyfriend hit her in front of her children. On appeal, the court distinguished this case from *Nicholson* because here the mother's boyfriend had also hit the children in the past. Although the court correctly considered the children's special vulnerabilities, as directed by *Nicholson*, and noted that one child expressed a desire to stay with the foster parents, it failed to balance the risks of remaining in the home with the harm of removal. The court also failed to review what resources were available to the mother to help her improve her situation. Instead, there was only a cursory mention that the mother did not want her boyfriend to leave the home, partly because she was financially dependent on him (Perrone 2012). Although poverty was at the heart of the issue, the only solution the state offered was to remove the children.[6] It appears that the agency never considered providing the mother with material support, such as food or a voucher for housing or child care, that would have lightened her load and enabled her to be more financially independent.

Results like these further the conception that "good" mothers must do whatever it takes to protect their children, including somehow preventing their own abuse. They presume that "good" mothers would immediately leave abusive relationships because that is what is best for their children. In other contexts, people understand that survivors of violence may stay with their partners for a number of reasons: they still love their partners; they do not want to interact with the court system; they have nowhere else to go; they believe leaving would make them less safe; they are embarrassed; they believe their partners are good parents and do not want to deprive their children of contact; or, in many cases, they depend on their partners for financial support. In the family policing system, however, the only possibility is that the mother lacks insight into the severity of the situation and therefore is a bad and selfish mother, unworthy and incapable of protecting her children (Washington 2022).

To this end, once the family policing system suspects IPV in the home, it tends to require an order of protection against the person accused of violence as a condition of the children staying with their nonoffending parent. Judges often have absolute discretion to issue these orders, often without a hearing, arguably violating basic constitutional principles (Jaros 2010). If a mother states that she does not want an order of protection, she is accused of choosing her partner over her children. Once the order of protection is in place, even over the mother's objections, her failure to comply with the order (by, for example, letting the children see their father) is seen as further evidence of her incapacity (Washington 2022). In this way, family courts create their own evidence. The fact that the order of protection is in place means that the father is a danger to the children. A violation of the order is further evidence that the father poses a threat to his children and that he lacks respect for the court's authority. At the same time, the mother's involvement with the violation is used to show that she lacks insight into the severity of the situation and therefore cannot be trusted to parent her children.

In a recent analysis of state-level child welfare policies related to domestic violence, Bryan Victor et al. (2021) conclude that only four states offer survivors unconditional protection from this type of family policing system intervention: Iowa, New Hampshire, Oregon, and Wisconsin. The Iowa Department of Human Services, for example, includes a note in its guidelines explicitly designed to protect IPV survivors "from a founded or confirmed child abuse report for failure to protect children from exposure to or involvement in domestic violence." The note indicates that the statutory definitions of child maltreatment are not to be construed "to hold a victim responsible for failing to prevent a crime against the victim" (quoted in Victor et al. 2021, 458). Eleven states offer conditional protection whereby, for example, survivors will not be accused of neglect unless they fail to leave the person accused of violence.[7] One of these eleven states, Montana, includes in its Department of Public Health and Human Services manual that social workers should "ensure that the non-offending parent is not blamed for the abuse that occurred and its impact on the children." However, when the nonoffending parent "repeatedly returns to the offending parent w[ith] the children, social workers should consider whether she is failing to protect them" (quoted in Victor et al. 2021, 459).

The Supreme Court of North Carolina, a state where neither explicit nor conditional protections are provided, illuminated this point in 2020 when, in considering the appropriateness of terminating parental rights, it stated that "continued likelihood of future neglect is present when the parent continues to *participate in domestic violence*, fails to truly engage with her counseling or therapy requirements or fails to break off the relationship with the abusive partner."[8] This statement epitomizes the survivor's experience. She is painted as a participant in her own abuse, forced to comply and "truly engage" with counseling that she may not have asked for or felt necessary, and expected to leave her partner or risk losing her children permanently. Further, once she has suffered abuse, the system permanently views her judgment as impaired and thus assumes that there is a "likelihood of future neglect" because she may be subject to violence again.

Even when the mother wants to leave her partner, in accordance with the family policing system's preference, the state provides no resources or guidance to help her successfully separate (Cross 2018). For those survivors who want to leave, many end up in the same conditions as they were before leaving their abusive partner, or worse. Because survivors often lack meaningful support like housing and child care, they may risk family policing involvement anyway. For example, in *Adoption of Bernadette*, a mother and victim of IPV left the person who caused her harm and moved to Massachusetts.[9] As is often the case for survivors, she found herself unhoused and without alternatives. Eventually, she voluntarily relinquished custody of her children to the Department of Children and Families (DCF) to try to get back on her feet. Rather than assist in any productive way, DCF required that she somehow simultaneously find suitable housing, attend parenting classes, engage in therapy, maintain employment, attend meetings with DCF, and visit her children regularly.

Although the mother was still struggling, she managed to substantially comply with this plan by finding employment, visiting her children, attending therapy, and eventually moving into a trailer. Despite this, at a meeting that she was unable to attend, DCF changed the goal in her case from family reunification to adoption. Ultimately, the mother's parental rights were terminated. On appeal, DCF based its argument that she was an unfit mother on her failure to fully comply with services (even though she was in substantial compliance), her homelessness, her "unstable lifestyle," and her "strained relationship with DCF" after she had understandably become upset when she learned that a caseworker told her daughter that her mother should stop fighting the adoption.[10]

The appellate court raised several concerns about DCF's conduct, questioning why reunification efforts were abandoned after only ten months and why "DCF did not provide the mother with assistance in attempting to rectify her housing instability—the central issue that led to the children's removal—until after the children's permanency goal had changed to adoption."[11] Despite this, the court affirmed the termination of the mother's parental rights, finding that she had not obtained appropriate housing and had failed to engage with her service plan or ensure that the children received their own services to deal with their special needs. In this case, the mother left the person accused of harming her and voluntarily put her children in the foster care system so that she could improve her situation. Rather than give her material support like housing assistance that she desperately needed or assisting her with child care or transportation to help her get her children needed services, the agency created a list of hoops for her to jump through. As is often true, the case was no longer about her parenting but rather about how good she was at hoop-jumping (Stark 2005).

In addition to the many hurdles erected for nonoffending parents, the system also assumes that the person accused of violence is beyond repair. If we are serious about protecting children from harm, however, the knee-jerk reaction of removing the perpetrator must also be interrogated. While there are certainly benefits to this approach, there are also downsides if this person is a parent who shares a close bond with the child and if the mother does not support the approach (Stark 2008). The idea that the mother should, by default, be the primary caregiver and responsible for most household tasks and that fathers are unnecessary or useless is based on outdated stereotypes. These gendered stereotypes are compounded by stereotypes about low-income fathers and fathers of color being "absent." In reality, Black fathers are more likely than white and Hispanic fathers to be involved in the day-to-day care of their children, including feeding, bathing, helping them with homework, and taking them to activities (Jones and Mosher 2013).

As a practitioner, the first author represented parents in multiple cases in which previously intact families with active fathers were forcibly separated, leaving the mother with less income and increased caregiving responsibilities. In these cases, the mothers did not identify as "victims" of violence, did not want the fathers to be removed from the home, and wanted to maintain the family relationship. The state, however, required mothers to comply with orders of protection prohibiting the fathers from returning home (in many cases, making them homeless) or having any contact with their children. If they did not cooperate, they were threatened with losing custody themselves. When the first author requested hearings to challenge fathers' separation from their children, in many cases, these requests were denied because the judge concluded that there was no separation if the children had remained in the mothers' custody; this decision meant that the fathers had no ability to challenge the decision to limit their paternal contact to weekly supervised visits. Moreover, this is an example of how the father's role and relationship with his children were undervalued and the caregiving responsibilities presumed to be the mother's responsibility. Almost always, when the proceedings concluded, the family reunited, with the children and fathers having lost a year together—the duration of the unwanted order of protection.

Today, over two decades after Sharwline Nicholson fought to protect IPV survivors and their children from the family policing system, the law continues to offer only limited protections. The intersection of stringent mandated reporting requirements and vague abuse and neglect laws promotes a system through which women continue to be referred to the family policing system when they experience IPV. When a woman calls the police, receives medical treatment, or seeks refuge in a domestic violence shelter, many of the "helpers" she encounters are mandated by state law to refer her to the family policing system if they believe child maltreatment has occurred. If they fail to do this, they can face loss of their professional licenses, fines, or even misdemeanor or felony charges that can carry prison sentences of up to five years (CWIG 2019a). In this atmosphere, many mandated reporters believe that regardless of the particulars, if there is potentially violence in a home, they must report.

Although the fact that exposure to IPV can cause harm is not disputed, "failure to protect" laws and those that can otherwise be broadly interpreted to include survivors of IPV lead to misplaced blame on surviving mothers and exacerbate the harm to both mothers and children.

For instance, mothers who seek to escape IPV by entering domestic violence shelters are subjected to even more risk because they face ongoing "parenting surveillance" (Fauci and Goodman 2020). After being controlled and criticized by their former partners, many mothers are subjected to the same types of control when shelter staff judge their parenting styles and behaviors. One study showed that "most survivors described parental monitoring and control, in which staff set parenting rules and observed, judged, and intervened in their parenting" (Fauci and Goodman 2020, 250). The stress of this situation is compounded when women know that the staff around them are also mandated reporters whose assessments can have catastrophic consequences for their families. Many survivors therefore change their behavior around shelter staff to avoid being reported, an added burden while simultaneously dealing with the traumatic fallout of IPV (Fauci and Goodman 2020).

Recommendations

The irony of the family policing system's treatment of IPV survivors is that the state mimics the behavior it is trying to prevent. Its cycle of coercive control mirrors the hallmarks of domestic violence by surveilling survivors, forcing them to engage in certain behaviors to gain approval, limiting their autonomy, and subjecting them and their children to harm if they do not comply. Before children are removed, the state may threaten the mother with their removal to dominate her and force compliance. Once ensnared, she is dragged through the system repeatedly, while every perceived failure is examined and used as cause to remove her children and, often, terminate her parental rights. Rather than helping survivors, the state engages in a pattern of victimization, to the detriment of both the mother and her children.

In these cases, rather than exacerbating an IPV survivor's traumatic experience of coercive control, the family policing system should provide real help and cooperation in a manner that protects and empowers the mother to make choices about her family. Yet in 2022, the Violence Against Women Act (VAWA) allocated over $140 million to the criminal legal system's response to violence against women (and another $33 million for related responses in rural areas); yet only about $36 million was allocated to housing and related services (Office of Public Affairs,

USDOJ 2022). This was in spite of the fact that IPV is a significant risk factor for housing instability and homelessness among women and children (Aratani 2009) and the greatest need (after physical safety) identified by IPV survivors (Lyon, Lane, and Menard 2008). Housing is also a standard requirement for family reunification after child removal. Reallocating even a fraction of the VAWA money to housing assistance could make a considerable difference in survivors' ability to leave, if that is their goal. Child care is also a significant issue for most low-income families but can particularly impact survivors who seek to leave their partners (Futures Without Violence 2022). Providing opportunities for economic independence is crucial. This could involve increasing employment options through microfinancing for small businesses, establishing programs that provide a living wage, and offering opportunities for skill development (Goodmark 2018).

Additionally, mandated reporters should never report violence unless there is an imminent risk of harm to the child, as this is the legal standard in most states. If a mother is reported and does not want assistance, the system should respect her parental decision-making and autonomy and close its investigation unless there is evidence of direct harm to the children. If, and only if, the mother supports the removal of the person accused of violence, social workers should assist her in obtaining an order of protection or finding alternative safe, affordable housing if needed to extricate herself from the violent situation.

Given that orders of protection or criminal intervention are only temporary solutions to a situation the mother understands best, it is crucial that the mother lead the safety planning in collaboration with social workers. Forcing the mother into unnecessary services rather than crafting a collaborative safety plan is counterproductive and burdensome. Even worse, services, such as parenting classes, undermine and blame mothers when such services are infused with the assumption that being subjected to abuse renders them poor parents (Stark 2005). Experts consistently caution that each family needs to be assessed holistically for risk before drawing conclusions about harm levels and necessary interventions (Holt, Buckley, and Whelan 2008).

Rethinking how we assist families experiencing IPV means investing both time and money into giving survivors the specific material resources they need, understanding and addressing the root causes of violence, and working with people to minimize violence before it occurs or recurs. Ultimately, much violence is the result of our collective failure to meet basic human needs and ensure that people have access to food, shelter, clothing, and a living wage. Some people—especially men— who face the chronic stress of under- or unemployment and poverty are more likely to perpetrate violence. But to better serve families, we must cut violence off at its roots (Goodmark 2018). "We need to see that anti-poverty work is anti-violence work, that anti-racism work is anti-violence work, that mental health work is anti-violence work" (Goodmark 2022, 13). Programs that provide employment opportunities, job stability, and the ability to earn a living wage could significantly impact rates of violence (Goodmark 2018). Access to services within the community to address trauma, substance use, and mental health concerns in a nonpunitive way is crucial to violence prevention. The almost $10 billion federal budget for family policing currently allocates ten times more to foster care and adoption than to prevention and reunification (Brico 2019). If that budget were turned on its head, we could fund services that prevent harm, rather than paying foster parents to raise other people's children.

The family policing system also fails to properly address perpetrators of violence once it has occurred. Rather than addressing the root causes of violence, the system offers perpetrators only one option: batterer intervention programs (BIPs). Many such programs require fathers who are already struggling financially to admit that they are "batterers" and pay a fee to demonstrate accountability. This further reduces their income and increases their stigma, making violence more likely, not less (Shah 2017). In 2009, the National Institute of Justice met to evaluate these programs (see Carter 2010). Although some experts believed they had promise, even the programs' proponents admitted that lack of consistency and regulation across the country had produced unmeasurable results. Since then, more states across the country have implemented standards for BIPs, but with few substantive changes or means of measuring success. Today, forty-four states have established BIP standards, but 90.9 percent of these state standards fail to delineate any definition of what participant success looks like beyond simply completing the program, and 72.7 percent do not provide for any participant follow-up (Flasch et al. 2021).

Finally, to help the entire family to safely heal, there must be access to coparenting services that help parents learn how to work together in a collaborative, respectful, and safe manner that prioritizes their children's well-being. The parent who has caused harm should also be able to engage in supervised and therapeutic visitation in cases in which those restrictions on parental liberty are necessary for safety. Programs that serve the whole family and involve the person who causes harm, particularly when the survivor wants to keep the family intact, are crucial so the person who causes harm can understand their role in the process and the family (Shah 2017). Services also need to be free, accessible, and inclusive across cultures, language, family structures, ability, mental health status, and socioeconomic status, among other important considerations.

According to Leigh Goodmark, who has written extensively about the problems with carceral responses to IPV, "If people subjected to abuse are harmed rather than helped by turning to the legal system for assistance, it is not working well. When the justice needs of those the system was meant to benefit go unmet, a justice system is not fulfilling its purpose" (2018, 5). In the case of the "child welfare" system, neither the needs of children nor their mothers' needs are met, and in many cases, their families are in a worse position than if they had had no system involvement at all. Put simply, in the words of the parent advocate Joyce McMillan, "Help isn't help if it doesn't help." The current family policing system's response to IPV helps no one.

NOTES

1 Nicholson v. Williams, 203 F. Supp. 2d 153, 170 (E.D.N.Y. 2002).
2 Maryland Code, Courts and Judicial Proceedings § 3-801, https://mgaleg.maryland.gov.
3 *Nicholson*, 203 F. Supp. 2d at 170.
4 *Nicholson*, 203 F. Supp. 2d at 172.
5 Nicholson v. Scoppetta, 3 N.Y.3d 357, 820 N.E.2d 840 (2004).
6 In re Angelique L., 42 A.D. 3d 569 (2007).
7 The eleven states are Alaska, Florida, Kentucky, Maine, Michigan, Montana, Nevada, New Jersey, Texas, Washington, and West Virginia. The remaining thirty-five states vary significantly in how their abuse and neglect statutes address or remain silent on "failure to protect." Many states include language such as "emotional abuse," "risk of physical harm," or "mental or emotional injury," all of which

can and have been interpreted broadly to include a failure to protect children from exposure to IPV (Victor et al. 2021).

8 Matter of K.L.T., 374 N.C. 826, 846, 845 S.E.2d 28, 42 (2020) (emphasis added).

9 Adoption of Bernadette, 179 N.E.3d 1129 (Mass. App. Ct. 2021).

10 *Bernadette*, 179 N.E.3d 1129.

11 *Bernadette*, 179 N.E.3d 1129.

6

Avoiding Support, Avoiding Punishment

Fear of the Child Welfare System in the Opioid Era

KRISTINA P. BRANT

Between 2016 and 2022, I lived and worked in Appalachian Kentucky, examining the impact of the opioid crisis on rural communities. When I entered the field, I was immediately struck by the pervasive presence of the child welfare system in the lives of poor families navigating parental substance use. Yet over time, I witnessed the proliferation of substance use treatment services and the development of new initiatives aiming to support mothers who use drugs, as well as their children. Nonetheless, these new services did not seem to improve the lives of the mothers I met as intended. In this chapter, I draw on interviews with rural families and service providers to demonstrate how the long arm of the child welfare system constricts mothers' willingness to seek help—both for themselves and for their children.

Within the United States, both punitive and supportive institutions serve as instruments for poverty governance, allowing the state to manage poor people's lives through surveillance and regulation (Piven and Cloward 1971; Soss, Fording, and Schram 2011; Wacquant 2009). One such institution, the child welfare system, exists at the nexus of both punitive and supportive functions (Woodward 2021). The child welfare system aims to support and protect children yet simultaneously punishes parents through child removal, a process that ultimately harms many children as well (Roberts 2002). These contradictory roles have evolved from an entrenched stereotype about the deficiencies of nonwhite and poor mothers (Bridges 2017). If these mothers are depicted as incapable of raising their children, then state surveillance and regulation can be justified as necessary to protect their children.

In recent years, public attitudes regarding substance misuse have largely shifted from support for punitive to therapeutic responses (Kolodny et al. 2015). This shift is rooted in racism: while crack cocaine use among urban, Black populations in the 1980s and 1990s propelled mass incarceration, opioid misuse among rural, white populations in the first and second decades of the twenty-first century inspired a more compassionate, treatment-focused approach (Shachar et al. 2020). Yet this shift has not been evident within the child welfare system. Instead, amid the opioid crisis, child welfare involvement has accelerated (Ghertner, Waters, et al. 2018). And, reflecting the demographics of opioid misuse, this increased child welfare involvement has predominantly impacted rural white families (Meinhofer and Angleró-Díaz 2019).

These two seemingly disparate trends—a shift toward therapeutic responses to substance use and increased child welfare involvement for substance-using parents—are not at odds. *Poor,* white mothers, not white mothers generally, have borne the brunt of recent criminalization of maternal substance use (Bach 2022). As a political ideology, white supremacy is the belief that white people are superior to and should dominate people of other races; high rates of rural, white poverty and maternal substance use undercut these foundational ideas of white supremacist beliefs. Khiara Bridges (2020, 843) argues that punishing poor, white mothers who misuse opioids marks them as "a population of people who have been disloyal to their whiteness." These punishments signal that poor mothers who use drugs are "not quite white," thereby asserting that poverty and substance misuse are not characteristic of white motherhood. By investigating and punishing poor, white mothers who use drugs, then, the child welfare system redefines the boundary of whiteness to exclude these mothers. Paradoxically, increased child welfare involvement among poor, white mothers who use drugs protects the veil of white supremacy in the United States.

How does this threat of child welfare involvement impact rural, poor mothers who use drugs, and how does this threat affect their children? I find that the threat of child welfare involvement compels rural, poor mothers who use drugs to avoid social service and public health institutions. This fear can spill over to relatives helping to raise these mothers' children, who may also avoid supportive services to evade child welfare involvement. Providers recognize the fear that these mothers and relatives hold and seek to distance themselves from the child welfare system. However, these providers are deputized as mandated reporters; if they witness evidence of parental substance use, they must report it to the child welfare system. In doing so, providers risk losing contact with both the family in question and other families around them. The omnipresence of the child welfare system limits the efficacy of these supportive programs; families who need services the most learn that they must avoid support to avoid punishment.

In this chapter, I focus on three types of services that mothers learn to avoid: medical care, family support programs, and substance use treatment. Each of these services is intended to support children's healthy development and well-being. Medical care facilitates healthy fetal development and positive birth outcomes; family support programs provide early childhood developmental interventions and in-kind assistance like food and infant supplies; and substance use treatment programs focus on strengthening family relationships and building parenting skills. Therefore, when mothers are afraid to access these services, they are not the only ones who lose out on support. Ultimately, their children do not receive the early medical attention, developmental interventions, and material goods they need to thrive, and the stability of their home life remains tenuous. Paradoxically, while these services aim to aid child development and decrease child welfare involvement, their embeddedness in the child welfare system results in the further isolation of the most vulnerable families and exacerbates the very hardships they intend to address.

Poverty and Substance Use in the Child Welfare System

Since the inception of the child welfare system, it has disproportionately impacted families of color and poor families (Roberts 2002). Recent administrative data demonstrate that Black and Indigenous children are far more likely than children of other races and ethnicities to experience child welfare investigations, foster care placement, and permanent separation from their parents (Edwards et al. 2021; Wildeman, Edwards, and Wakefield 2020). While similar data are not collected on parents' income or poverty status, research has shown that contact with the child welfare system is widespread in poor neighborhoods (Fong 2019b;

Roberts 2002), and survey data show that material hardship predicts such contact (Thomas and Waldfogel 2022). Furthermore, the limited administrative evidence that does exist shows that families involved in the child welfare system are overwhelmingly poor (Kang et al. 2019).

Scholars have long explained the disproportionate involvement of poor families through the family stress model, which holds that economic insecurity places pressure on parents that can lead to maltreatment (Conrad-Hiebner and Byram 2020). Historically, some scholars have asserted that this model can also account for the disproportionate involvement of Black and Indigenous families, since Black and Indigenous populations in the United States face higher rates of poverty (Hill 2004). However, more recent research has pointed to the role of institutional racism in subjecting families of color to greater family surveillance and punishment (Dettlaff and Boyd 2021; Merritt 2021). Indeed, poor, Black children are still overrepresented in the child welfare system, in comparison to poor, white children (Briggs et al. 2022).

Similarly, there is evidence that the disproportionate involvement of poor families may be due not solely to increased risk but rather to class bias. Research has shown that both caseworkers and laypersons conflate poverty and neglect, leading to higher rates of investigations and substantiations among poor families (Dickerson, Lavoie, and Quas 2020; Lash 2017). Yet, even beyond individual-level bias, institutional definitions of neglect are conflated with conditions of poverty (Rose and Meezan 1993). In all states, the definition of neglect includes at least one poverty-related indicator, such as inadequate food, shelter, clothing, or supervision (Williams, Dalela, and Vandivere 2022). As of 2022, only twenty-seven states noted that parents should be exempt from accusations of neglect if such an indicator is present only because of their financial status (CWIG 2022a). Therefore, in the remaining half of the states, the symptoms of poverty alone can trigger child welfare involvement (Rebbe 2018). States' definitions of child neglect reflect the United States' broader approach to poverty governance: child welfare policy blames parents for their poverty rather than recognizing that society creates and perpetuates this poverty (Woodward 2021). The government utilizes its resources to surveil and police poor mothers rather than to promote their economic prosperity through aid and support (Roberts 2001, 2007).

Poor parents facing child welfare investigations indeed believe that poverty motivated their initial contact with the system (Fong 2017). Since the child welfare system is embedded in a larger web of social institutions that, in tandem, regulate the lives of the poor, reliance on social services can lead to system contact (Fong 2017; Paik 2021). Once poor families have an open case, compliance with the system's expectations may also prove impossible (Lee 2016).

Facing strict timelines, poor parents must transform their entire economic situation—securing housing, transportation, and child care while also working low-wage jobs (Doran and Roberts 2002). Therefore, just as poverty can precipitate contact with the child welfare system, it can also prolong child welfare involvement and ultimately lead to the permanent loss of parental rights (Eamon and Kopels 2004).

Among parents of color and poor parents, those who use drugs are particularly impacted by child welfare involvement, as the child welfare system treats parental substance use as an indicator of child neglect even without direct evidence of neglect (Harp and Bunting 2020; C. Henry et al. 2018). Even if parents purposefully use strategies to protect their children, for example, shielding their children from drug-related activities and keeping a safe home environment, simply testing positive for illicit or unprescribed substances or possessing drug paraphernalia can precipitate child removal (Richter and Bammer 2000). Unsurprisingly, then, scholars attribute rising child welfare cases during the ongoing opioid crisis to increased rates of substance use and overdose (Ghertner, Waters, et al. 2018). During my study, parental substance use directly contributed, indirectly contributed, or was a risk factor in 72.2 percent of the Kentucky cases in which children were removed from their parents and placed in out-of-home care (Kentucky Youth Advocates 2018).

Substance use is not unique to poor populations; amid the opioid crisis, higher-income groups have also experienced increases in opioid use disorders and opioid-related overdoses (Hansen 2017). Yet poor parents who use drugs are more likely to come into contact with the child welfare system compared to wealthier parents (Canfield et al. 2017). First, because the child welfare system disproportionately polices poor families, poor parents are more likely to face investigations that detect substance use and lead to child removal. Research shows, for example, that medical providers are more likely to randomly drug test pregnant patients who are Black and poor, as compared to those who are white and higher income (McCabe 2022). Second, higher-income parents have greater access to resources that can deflect the attention of the child welfare system. For example, utilizing child care or babysitting can allow higher-income parents to better shield their children from substance use, avoiding situations in which a police officer, mandated reporter, or other neighbor may contact the child welfare system (Pimentel 2019). In rural communities, higher-income families' personal and professional connections to judges, prosecutors, and case workers can also help parents avoid an investigation or removal even if the child welfare system is contacted (Brant 2022).

If child removal does occur, higher-income parents may also follow case plans more easily than poor parents do. Substance use treatment—especially long-term residential treatment and medications for opioid use disorder—can increase the odds of parental reunification (Grella et al. 2009; Hall et al. 2016). Higher-income parents with private health insurance or affluent family networks can not only secure necessities like housing and transportation but also afford drug screens and substance use treatment. In contrast, poor mothers are beholden to the meager support they receive through their local child welfare offices, which are often ill equipped to help parents navigating substance use disorder (Radel et al. 2018). In some states, poor parents also lose Medicaid when facing child removal, further restricting access to treatment (Buer 2020). Consequently, research shows that reunification is less likely among mothers who use drugs *and* face socioeconomic risk factors, as compared to those with more stable financial situations (Lloyd 2018).

Poor mothers who use drugs lie at the intersection of two highly surveilled populations. Because of their poverty and because of their substance use, they face higher risks of child welfare investigation, child removal, and termination of parental rights. Black and Indigenous mothers who are poor and use drugs lie at the intersection of *three* highly surveilled populations, leaving them even more vulnerable to child welfare involvement. What are the consequences of this heightened threat of child welfare involvement? In the remainder of the chapter, I consider how fear of child welfare involvement shapes poor mothers' willingness to seek help and providers' abilities to connect with them, ultimately limiting the support afforded to these mothers and their children. While my study focused on rural white families, I recognize that Black and Indigenous mothers probably face similar, if not heightened, levels of fear and distrust due to the even greater risks of child welfare involvement that they face.

Parental Substance Use in Rural Appalachia

My findings derive from fieldwork conducted in Appalachian Kentucky between 2016 and 2022. Since the start of the opioid crisis, this region has seen some of the largest increases in both substance use and child welfare system caseloads (Annie E. Casey Foundation 2023b, 2023c; Rigg, Monnat, and Chavez 2018). While the growing prevalence of substance use is a newer development, it is rooted in the region's vulnerability: Appalachian Kentucky has long been home to some of the most concentrated and persistent poverty in the country (Economic Research Service 2023). Most counties where I conducted fieldwork have poverty rates greater than 30 percent (US Census Bureau 2022b).

I focus on a subset of ethnographic interviews with fifty relatives raising children, twenty-five parents who use or used drugs, and sixty representatives from public, private, and nonprofit institutions that served these families. I first recruited parents and relatives by visiting substance use treatment programs and family support groups, respectively. I also recruited respondents through snowball sampling, allowing me to reach both relatives and parents who were not connected to such groups. Interviews ranged from forty-five minutes to three hours in length, focusing on respondents' family dynamics, substance use history, and interactions with local institutions. The relatives in my sample had various legal arrangements; some had adopted children, some served as foster parents, some possessed legal custody, some held guardianship, and some served as informal caregivers without any kind of legal recognition. All parents had experienced a period in which they did not physically live with their children, although four had never experienced child welfare involvement, as their family's caregiving shifts were entirely informal. Reflecting the demographics of the mostly racially homogeneous region, all parents and relatives in my sample were white; and reflecting the gender disparities of child welfare involvement, all but four parents were women. All parents in my sample struggled with financial insecurity. Relatives, however, possessed a range of socioeconomic statuses, from those who received only government assistance to those who worked as teachers and lawyers.

While conducting interviews with relatives and parents, I noted the different local institutions that respondents mentioned when recounting their experiences. I then deliberately recruited people from these institutions for interviews. These interviews ranged from thirty minutes to one hour in length, focusing on perceptions of families impacted by parental substance use. The resulting sample includes early childhood specialists, parenting class instructors, substance use counselors, harm reductionists, and government assistance caseworkers, among others.[1]

Navigating the Entanglement of Support and Punishment

In my earliest conversations with teachers, pastors, doctors, and other community leaders, I heard a recurring theme: concern for the growing number of children whose parents use drugs. Community members believed that local child welfare offices were becoming overwhelmed due to parental substance use, and signs on nearly every street corner advertised private foster care agencies seeking foster parents. Yet, over the course of my fieldwork, I noticed that the state was increasingly attempting to address parental substance use—and its impact on children—through multiple approaches. While the child welfare system investigated and removed children from parents who use drugs, a growing number of programs were seeking to reduce child welfare involvement through earlier intervention. I watched private treatment facilities proliferate, and I saw the state develop public health initiatives to support mothers who use drugs and to assist their children.

By expanding access to treatment and support, these new programs could both improve mothers' chances of recovery and support infant and early childhood development. However, I noticed that the threat of child welfare involvement was keeping poor mothers who use drugs from enrolling in such programs. Since the state deputizes service providers as mandated reporters and since evidence of substance use or drug paraphernalia can result in child removal, poor mothers who use drugs feared inviting any scrutiny into their lives. They learned that to avoid child welfare involvement, they must avoid even supportive services that claim to help them and their children. This fear was prevalent among mothers with substance use disorders and mothers who use drugs who do not have disorders—a distinction often ignored, as discussed in Lee's chapter 4 in this volume. Kelsey, a mother with opioid use disorder who lost custody of her four children, told me, "It's a Catch-22. You can't get help if you're still gonna be getting punished at the same time." In the following sections, I describe how poor mothers who use drugs learn to avoid three forms of supportive services: medical care, family support programs, and substance use treatment. I posit that such avoidance ultimately harms not only mothers but also their children.

Avoiding Medical Care

First, expectant and new mothers who use drugs may avoid medical institutions out of fear that seeking care could provoke child welfare involvement. Expectant mothers, for example, may avoid prenatal care, fearing that a positive drug test or admission of substance use could prompt doctors to contact the child welfare system. Bethany worked at one of the few residential treatment centers in the region that allow children to live with their mothers at the center. Upon starting this job, Bethany was shocked to find that many of her clients had not sought prenatal care for this very reason. She relayed,

> We've had several incidences where women have come into the program, and we've taken them to local hospitals for care, and as soon as they find out they're in treatment, they treat them like crap. They talk down to them. It's like their attitude completely changes, and it's like no wonder people don't want to come in and ask for help. . . . We've got several women who've come in at the end of their pregnancy, and they've not had any prenatal care for that very reason. They're afraid to go to the doctor because they're gonna lose their child.

Yet pregnant women may not only avoid seeking prenatal care; they may even avoid hospitals during labor and delivery. After three mothers explained this fear to me, I relayed this story to Judge Wilson, a family court judge, asking if their fear was justified. She replied, "If there's drugs in their system, they're gonna remove them. If you have kids at home, and you have one that's positive at the hospital, they'll remove the one at the hospital and the ones at home."

This fear can prompt expectant mothers to avoid certain doctors or hospitals that they believe may contact the child welfare system. Shannon, for example, left her home in Ohio to give birth in Kentucky; she feared that her local hospital would report her, as she had lost custody of her older children in the past. Yet when Shannon's baby tested positive for opioids in the hospital in Kentucky, she was removed anyway. Following this removal, Shannon had to manage the trauma of this separation without her support network. If she returned to Ohio, she would be four hours away from her child's new foster home.

Even more alarming than Shannon's experience was a new trend observed by both relative caregivers and mothers. Mothers who had experienced child removal at the hospital were now helping other mothers give birth at home to avoid removal themselves. While Shannon's own experience with the entanglement of medical care and the child welfare system led her to avoid her local hospital, information diffusion among mothers provoked these women's fear of hospital births. Home births without a licensed professional may be dangerous, yet these women were willing to risk both their and their infants' safety to avoid contact with the child welfare system.

The vulnerability evoked by medical institutions is particularly acute for poor mothers. Those from well-connected and higher-income families can wield greater agency in interactions with medical providers, whom they may even know personally. Margie's daughter, for example, entered a methadone clinic during her pregnancy to manage her opioid use disorder and facilitate healthy fetal development. When Margie's daughter gave birth, her infant tested positive for methadone, and a nurse contacted the child welfare system. Luckily, Margie held a respectable job with the state. When her daughter told her what was happening, Margie purposefully came to the hospital in her work uniform and asserted that her daughter was using methadone as prescribed. She convinced the investigator to leave without opening a case, and she reported the nurse's actions to hospital administration. Margie recalled, "I got that bitch fired. I'm sorry I said that in that way to you, but I got her fired, and I'm not sorry that that happened." While this incident could have led to more sustained child welfare involvement and even child removal for another mother, Margie's socioeconomic status and related sense of agency enabled her to protect her daughter's rights and keep her daughter and granddaughter together.

Ultimately, the proclivity for poor mothers who use drugs to avoid medical care during and after their pregnancies threatens to harm both themselves and their children. Without prenatal and postnatal care, expectant mothers may not catch complications that could threaten their own or their infants' lives. Such care is especially important for mothers who use drugs because of increased risks of such complications (Prasad and Jones 2019). Yet mothers are willing to take these health risks to avoid the more certain punishment they would face if medical providers were to initiate child welfare involvement. In many states, state law mandates that medical providers report prenatal or postnatal substance use to the child welfare system; in Kentucky, for example, such reporting is required if the provider believes prenatal or postnatal substance use may be or may become associated with child maltreatment (BJA 2023; see also CWIG 2019b). While these providers may contact the child welfare system believing they are operating in the best interest of the child, paradoxically, this practice places children at risk by discouraging expectant and new mothers who use drugs from seeking medical care.

Avoiding Family Support Programs

Fear of child welfare involvement may also lead mothers who use drugs to avoid family support programs, like early childhood care and parenting assistance. Such programs often provide in-home care, such as sending a specialist to meet with parents and children to conduct developmental assessments and provide interventions. Yet in forty-six states, including Kentucky, people in some or all such professions in which frequent contact with children is common are mandated reporters; they must report evidence of substance use or drug paraphernalia to the child welfare system. In the other four states, all people are mandated to report child maltreatment (CWIG 2023). When parents learn of this requirement or experience a report, they may exit these programs, even if they truly desire these services for their children.

Becky, a social worker in one early childhood education program, explained, "We have had to call CPS [Child Protective Services] on a few families, and most of the time, unfortunately, we do lose them, even though it's supposed to be confidential." While fear of child welfare involvement discourages program participation among low-income parents who use drugs, Becky noted that this is not common among low-income parents generally. She continued, "Normally they don't stop seeing us if we've called, like, due to the house being in disarray. CPS will usually just give them such and such time to clean it up. Those people don't usually quit the program. It's just if there's drugs involved." Because substance use is more likely to trigger removal than other poverty-related indicators of neglect, like housing conditions, contact with the child welfare system evokes greater anxiety among poor parents who use drugs than among poor parents who do not.

Poverty can, however, increase the chance that a parent who uses drugs will face an investigation. Mindy and Jim, for example, first experienced an investigation when a teacher contacted the child welfare system about their children's recurring bouts of lice. Lice can certainly affect children across income levels. However, within Eastern Kentucky, recurring lice is typically viewed as an indicator of child neglect, especially when coupled with other signals of poverty. Mindy and Jim had struggled to afford treatments to rid their trailer of nits, but this alone would not have triggered child removal. Nevertheless, once an investigation was open, they were drug tested, and their positive results sparked removal. Their poverty opened the door for a child welfare investigation, and their substance use solidified the outcome of removal.

Like Becky, Miranda, another social worker in an early childhood education program, had witnessed parents quit after her team reported signs of substance use. Yet Miranda noted that parents also avoid her program as they learn from one another's experiences. She explained, "We've had families call and say, 'We don't want you all back because we know you were the one that called [Child Protection Services].' . . . And then they share with somebody else, so sometimes for some people, there may be a perception of, 'Oh gosh, they reported my friend, yada, yada,' and that can change things."

Just as information spreads among expectant mothers to avoid giving birth at certain hospitals, information spreads among parents to avoid enrolling in certain family support programs where staff may contact the child welfare system. Because of this diffusion of information and fear, providers struggle to recruit poor parents who use drugs into their programs. Miranda explained, "Sometimes the more challenged families or most at-risk families aren't as open to having us there, and that's what's kind of scary sometimes. There's a lot of families out there that could really benefit from our services, but when there's bad things going on, you're not as willing and open to having people come into your home."

Yet home visits are not the only deterrent to participation. Brandi runs a program that provides prenatal support to poor expectant mothers who are at risk of substance use. While Becky and Miranda must conduct home visits, Brandi can meet mothers in other locales, like public health departments or public libraries. Yet Brandi has found that mothers are fearful of sharing any personal information, even on neutral grounds. She explained, "I've had expectant mothers sitting out in a hot truck waiting on her partner, who's getting services inside [the county health department], and I'm like, 'If you come in, I'll do a brief class with you, and you'll be back before he's out. I'll give you this. I'll give you that.' And nothing. . . . Our target audience is those higher-risk ones, but those higher-risk ones are the most reluctant even just to come to a general class." While Becky's, Miranda's, and Brandi's programs claim to serve families to minimize child welfare involvement, parents learn to avoid these programs, as providers may contact the child welfare system to report the very issues for which they are seeking help.

To overcome recruitment and retention barriers, many providers attempt to distance themselves from the child welfare system, at least in perception. Miranda, for example, does not call herself a "social worker" due to the conflation of this term with the child welfare system. She explained, "I do not present myself as a social worker, because just that name alone is very off-putting to our families. They see social workers as Child Protection: 'You're removing my child.'" Peggy, who runs a grassroots volunteer group that distributes Naloxone (a medication used to reverse opioid overdoses), explained that her team strategically times child welfare system reports so that the parents whom they serve will not grow suspicious of them. She said, "We had to have a couple of trap houses shut down. We had to keep that under wraps. But there was kids in there, and kids don't need to grow up in that. . . . I had to call the social worker we work with, and we had to act fast, and I had to stay out of it, because if word got out in the street, it would put me and my team at risk." Peggy knew that this association would cause parents to lose trust in her group, so she sought to uphold the illusion that her team would not contact the child welfare system.

Other providers not only sought to minimize the perception that they cooperate with the child welfare system but also actively tried to avoid doing so. Becky, for example, informed parents that she must report the presence of drug paraphernalia, trying to signal that they should conceal any evidence of substance use. Becky recognizes that parental substance use can have varying impacts on a child. She explained that seeing a packet of unprescribed buprenorphine would concern her far less than finding a mother unconscious while her infant lacks supervision. Yet reporting each scenario can produce similar consequences. Recognizing that reporting a more minor transgression can still result in child removal, Becky tries to reduce her chances of witnessing such an act. While she must report what she sees, she would rather continue helping families than lose them.

Fear of family support programs' connections to the child welfare system can even impact relatives who are caring for children due to parental substance use. Maureen, who leads a parenting group in her county, struggles to recruit relative caregivers to participate. She explained, "They don't want to put their lives out there for everybody else to know. . . . I'm sure in the past there have been people who have come to these and said, 'Oh guess what? So-and-so down the street does this and this. . . . She doesn't have her child because of such and such.' They worry about something like that. Especially in a small town."

Relatives who are caring for children informally have often stepped in to protect parents and avoid child welfare involvement. Yet if participating in support programs exposes their family's situation, leaders and other participants could still contact the child welfare system to provoke its involvement. Avoiding such programs, then, may seem like a necessary safeguard to keep one's caregiving role private and avoid child welfare involvement.

Relative caregivers may even avoid applying for government assistance for this reason. Elaine had recently taken in two grandchildren and was struggling to afford food, yet she was fearful of applying for SNAP (the Supplemental Nutrition Assistance Program, more colloquially known as "food stamps"). She worried that the Family Support office could alert the child welfare system if it learned of her caregiving role, leading to an investigation of her daughter. Elaine was instead relying on churches that do not require recipients to disclose information to access food, but this support was meager. The surveillance that poor families must endure across interconnected social institutions imposes a unique stressor. A wealthier relative may avoid disclosing their caregiving role without negative repercussions; but for Elaine, protecting her family from child welfare investigations came at the expense of fully providing for her grandchildren's needs.

Just as poor mothers' avoidance of medical care can impact both themselves and their children, poor mothers' and relative caregivers' avoidance of family support services can impact mothers, caregivers, and their children. The early childhood education programs that Becky and Miranda worked for aimed to address the very issues that the children of mothers who use drugs may experience, such as developmental delays or behavioral issues caused by prenatal exposure. The prenatal support program that Brandi worked for aimed to reduce the incidence of such issues among the children of expectant mothers who use drugs. For poor mothers and relative caregivers especially, government food assistance programs like SNAP can provide crucial nutritional support for children. When mothers and caregivers feel like they cannot enroll in such programs for fear of child removal, their children ultimately lose out on the educational services and material support that could have aided their healthy development. Because these supportive services serve as the long arm of a child welfare system that punishes parents for substance use, they fail to reach the children of parents who use drugs.

Avoiding Substance Use Treatment

Finally, mothers who use drugs may avoid seeking treatment for substance use disorder out of fear that doing so could provoke or prolong child welfare involvement. Bethany, the substance use treatment counselor introduced earlier, explained, "That's the biggest thing for women that keeps them out of treatment. They have kids and don't have anyone to watch them, so they can't go into treatment, so they lose them. Or they go into treatment, so they leave them with somebody, and their kids are taken. So, it's a Catch-22."

Seeking treatment may require a mother to leave her children with a relative or family friend. Feasibly, this caregiver could file for custody while the parent is away, or alternatively, the caregiver could attract the attention of the child welfare system themselves. Paradoxically, then, while seeking treatment and entering recovery could help mothers parent their children and decrease the risk of child welfare involvement in the long term, mothers may avoid seeking treatment if they fear that doing so could invite child welfare involvement in the short term.

For parents from wealthier families and parents in two-parent households, this fear may be minimal. Phil, for example, cared for his niece informally when his parents paid for his sister, a single mother, to attend residential treatment. Because Phil's family was upper middle class and well connected, they never feared that the child welfare system would intervene; caseworkers, service providers, and other mandated reporters knew that Phil's niece was safe with him. Yet unlike Phil's sister, a single parent from a poor family may worry that leaving their child with a relative could attract surveillance. Recall Elaine, who worried that alerting the Family Support office about her caregiving responsibilities could invite a child welfare investigation. Since Elaine was poor herself, there was no guarantee that a caseworker and judge would deem her a suitable caregiver for her grandchildren. While Elaine was willing to care for her grandchildren, doing so felt risky due to her poverty and lack of connections.

Elaine's fear arose from the child welfare system's surveillance that poor people endure. Yet parents may also fear that a caregiver themselves could spark a more permanent custody change. This fear was a barrier for Brooke, a poor mother of five who had considered seeking residential treatment for opioid use disorder. A pastor at a nearby church offered to drive Brooke to treatment and keep her children while she was there. Yet Brooke could not trust that she would get her children back; she worried that the pastor could petition for emergency custody while she was away, claiming that Brooke had abandoned her children. This fear propelled Brooke to decline the offer. She prioritized keeping her children with her in the present, even if her longer-term stability would remain precarious.

Phil's, Elaine's, and Brooke's situations involved informal caregiving arrangements without present child welfare involvement. Some parents, however, must weigh attending treatment once child welfare cases are already open. Allan, a public defender, explained that case timelines could pose a barrier to seeking treatment. Speaking about his clients, Allan said, "They don't want to go to treatment 'cause they gotta leave their kids for six months. . . . That means they have got to basically abandon their children for six months. And a lot of times, those kids are in the system, and if you abandon your kids in the system for six months, when you get out, you won't have kids, because they will start the process of terminating your parental rights." Allan's clients would prefer to serve probation or a short-term jail sentence, rather than receiving a diversion to residential treatment, as a shorter separation from one's children has a lower chance of being made permanent.

The fear that Allan described is not unfounded. Nicole, a child welfare system case manager, acknowledged that this scenario had happened recently to a father in her caseload. She recalled, "I had a dad who fought very hard, voluntarily went into the [treatment] program, and came out losing his kids, because he chose the ninety days—he chose a longer-term program—and by the time it was all over, the judge had decided the kids were in a good place, and they just needed to stay there." While poor parents like Brooke may fear that seeking treatment could provoke child welfare system contact, those with existing cases like Allan's clients may fear that seeking treatment could prolong their existing cases and even lead to a permanent loss of parental rights.

Fear of child welfare involvement may also motivate parents to avoid other types of substance use services outside of residential treatment. As Margie's story demonstrated earlier, some actors in the child welfare system have not embraced medications for opioid use disorder (MOUD) like buprenorphine and methadone. If MOUD use does not fit a case-worker's or judge's standards of "sobriety," then MOUD use can diminish a parent's chances of reunification. Therefore, while MOUD can improve a parent's chances of recovery in the long term, paradoxically, choosing to use MOUD could hurt their child welfare case in the short term. Jerrica, who works at an MOUD clinic, relayed how some child welfare system caseworkers view MOUD use as incompatible with parents' case plans: "Actually, just this morning, I was consulting with someone at one of our other treatment centers, and she called, and she said, 'What can we do?' Because a neighbor had called Social Services on one of their patients, and now Social Services is telling them they have to quit because they're not 'clean.' That varies county by county and sometimes social worker by social worker."

Teri, who worked in legal aid, reported seeing similar resistance to MOUD among judges in court. She explained, "A prior user can hardly ever convince the court, 'I am clean now. I'm not gonna go back,' because their position is the harm is done. 'You did this. You weren't with your kids for this long period of time. It's not in their best interest to re-establish a relationship with you.' I've had them treat Suboxone [a brand of buprenorphine] just like it's another drug. They're like, 'I want to see your Suboxone levels come down. This isn't something that you should be on long term. It should be helping you to become completely drug free.'" Hearing of such occurrences, parents may fear that using MOUD can deepen child welfare involvement and thus choose to avoid these resources to appease the system.

If we believe that parental substance use can be detrimental for children's well-being, then our goal should be to make recovery as feasible as possible for parents to achieve. Longer-term residential treatment and MOUD have been proven to improve the recovery outcomes for people with opioid use disorder (Blanco and Volkow 2019; Greenfield et al. 2009). Receiving parent education at residential treatment can even facilitate the development of positive parenting skills (Camp and Finkelstein 1997). Yet, if poor mothers fear attending long-term residential treatment or utilizing MOUD, then recovery becomes harder to achieve. Consequently, these mothers' substance use disorders may progress, and any negative child impacts of parental substance use disorder will persist or even worsen. Without the ability to seek treatment while avoiding child removal, mothers become unable to help themselves and their children by working toward recovery.

Conclusion

A growing literature documents how the threat of contact with the child welfare system structures parents' decisions and actions across social spaces. Leslie Paik (2021) details in her ethnography of poor families' interactions with social institutions how parents recognize that seemingly independent institutions—hospitals, schools, social support agencies, and child welfare offices—are, in practice, integrated into a larger system; consequently, parents see these institutions as one and the same. Through interviews with poor mothers, Kelley Fong (2019a) found that fear of child welfare involvement can encourage poor parents to alter their behavior with these other institutions; while mothers do not avoid these institutions entirely, they do conceal their hardships, home life, and parenting behaviors from providers.

Yet, in the case of poor mothers who use drugs, I find that fear of contact with the child welfare system *can* encourage wholesale institutional avoidance. Because evidence of parental substance use can precipitate child removal, mothers who use drugs learn to avoid educational, medical, and other social service providers who may witness such evidence. The expansion of services for parents who use drugs has not necessarily encouraged help seeking; rather, it has extended the reach of the child welfare system. The understanding that interactions with these providers can lead to child welfare involvement may come from one's past experiences or through word of mouth from others. This proclivity to avoid supportive services can even spill over to poor relatives who are helping raise these mothers' children.

Public and private funds continue to funnel into programs aimed at reducing the impacts of the opioid crisis. There is particular interest in expanding services for children impacted by parental substance use. How can we ensure that these interventions reach families who need them the most? Poor mothers who use drugs fear seeking help, as supportive services are embedded in a child welfare system that surveils poor families and treats parental substance use punitively. A focus on family-based intervention—treating family units rather than treating parents and children separately—could alleviate such fear and encourage participation. If more treatment programs welcomed co-residing children, not only might parents feel more comfortable seeking treatment, but facilities could also address children's needs concurrently. Family-based intervention strategies would not punish parents who come in the door but instead would escalate families' care as needed. Providers could respond to a relapse, for example, by further wrapping services around a family or increasing treatment level, rather than initiating child removal. Ultimately, such a model would not only facilitate parents' recovery but also detect and meet children's needs at earlier stages.

Recall Brooke, who wanted to pursue residential treatment but was anxious about family separation. While there are a few treatment facilities in Kentucky that serve families, Brooke's children were too old and too many in number to meet these facilities' requirements. If Brooke had access to treatment options that fit her needs as a mother and were accessible without significant financial resources, she may have received the services she desired. Ultimately, if parents feel comfortable seeking help, then supportive services will reach parents at earlier stages in their substance use disorder and in their children's development. If we threaten to punish parents for seeking help, we only further isolate those families who need support the most, allowing their challenges to escalate.

NOTES

1 Harm reductionists are volunteers and professionals who seek to reduce the negative social and physical consequences associated with substance use by providing information, tools like Naloxone, and service referrals in a nonjudgmental manner.

7

Navigating the Crossroads of Child Welfare Involvement and Housing Insecurity

Reimagining Support for Vulnerable Families

CYLESTE C. COLLINS AND RONG BAI

Housing insecurity and child welfare system involvement, while independent risk markers of children's well-being, interact in significant ways. In this chapter, we discuss the relationship between the two and how neoliberal ideology and social policy affect families' outcomes. We discuss interventions that seek to provide housing quickly to assist families with child welfare system involvement and conclude that housing as a primary intervention is essential but insufficient for resolving child welfare cases; the most vulnerable families need additional support and advocacy. Finally, we discuss the practical and policy implications of fully supporting families with various needs who are also involved in multiple social service systems, including the housing, child welfare, and public assistance systems.

Housing Insecurity and Child Welfare Involvement

Considered separately, housing insecurity and child welfare system involvement can have tremendous impacts on children's health, sense of safety, and educational achievement (Fowler and Farrell 2017; Fowler and Schoeny 2017). A significant subset of families, however, experience both housing insecurity and child welfare involvement, which exacerbates risks to children's well-being. A growing body of research demonstrates that families who are involved with either housing assistance or child welfare have a higher risk of being involved with both systems; housing insecurity often precedes child welfare system involvement, which for children is associated with future housing insecurity (Fowler et al. 2020; Park et al. 2004).

In 2021, approximately three million children were reported and assessed for maltreatment in the United States; approximately 600,000 of those cases were substantiated, and about 113,000 children were placed into the foster care system (USDHHS 2023). There are substantial racial disparities in child welfare involvement. Black and American Indian children—especially those from low-income backgrounds residing in impoverished neighborhoods where child removal is more prevalent due, in part, to heightened child welfare system surveillance—are disproportionately represented in the child welfare system (Annie E. Casey Foundation 2020; Fong 2017; Roberts 2022). Black children are more likely to be reported as maltreated, taken from their parents, and placed in foster care than white children are; they are also less likely to reunify or achieve permanency in foster care (Dettlaff and Boyd 2020; Harp and Bunting 2020). Such disparities underscore the importance of approaching these issues using an intersectional perspective (Roberts 2022; Woodward 2021). While the scope of family housing insecurity is difficult to assess, the Annual Homelessness Report to Congress (AHAR) consistently estimates that about one-third of people experiencing homelessness live in a family with a child under age eighteen (M. Henry et al. 2021, 2022). In January 2020, the single-night estimate of unhoused people living in families was 171,575 (53,739 households), 90 percent of whom were sheltered (versus unsheltered) (M. Henry et al. 2021, 2022). Measuring homelessness—especially family homelessness—is challenging, however, because of the array of living situations families may navigate. Thus, homelessness estimates are conservative; they do not account for people living in unstable or temporary housing situations, including those doubled up or staying in motels or those experiencing other forms of housing insecurity, such as those threatened with or experiencing eviction and/or those forced to move frequently (Sullivan 2022). In this chapter, our discussion of housing-insecure families thus refers to those in shelters or other facilities as well as those in other unstable or temporary living situations.

Overall, housing-insecure families are more likely than securely housed families to interact with an array of social service systems, mandated reporters, neighbors, and others (e.g., people they encounter in shelters or motels) who may report them to the child welfare system (Fong 2019a). As such, they are more likely to be investigated by the child welfare system and are also more likely to have substantiated child welfare cases compared to low-income, stably housed families (Bai et al. 2020; Dworsky 2014). However, the child welfare system is not equipped to address housing issues directly but instead refers families to housing assistance services. When child welfare agencies and homeless services neither collaborate nor coordinate, housing-insecure families may not receive adequate or timely housing assistance (Cunningham et al. 2015; Fowler et al. 2017), which can result in child removal or delayed reunification. In turn, children in housing-insecure families are more likely than housing-secure children to be separated from their families (Dotson 2011; Shinn, Brown, and Gubits 2017). In some US states, child welfare workers cite housing insecurity or housing inadequacy as a factor in foster care placement; in fact, 9 percent of foster care cases nationally are reported as related to inadequate housing (USDHHS 2022a), even though housing insecurity is a symptom of severe poverty, not bad parenting (Culhane et al. 2003). Severe family poverty and the resulting housing insecurity typically stem from a combination of complex, interrelated individual and societal factors. These include mental health issues, domestic violence, unemployment, increasing housing costs, and inadequate access to essential resources and support systems to assist with these challenges (Byrne et al. 2021; Shelton et al. 2009). Families of color and families headed by women are overrepresented among both those experiencing homelessness and those involved with the child welfare system (M. Henry et al. 2022; Olivet et al. 2021;); this is especially true for Black, single mothers (Human Rights Watch 2022).

In addition to homelessness, unstable housing and housing that is deemed to have too few bedrooms based on family size can both be reasons for child removal and/or can prevent reunification (Fowler et al. 2013). For example, parents who receive housing vouchers or reside in public housing may lose their housing assistance due to child endangerment charges or custody loss. They may then face difficulties reunifying with their children because they no longer qualify for the same number of bedrooms they needed when their children were in their care. Whatever the reason, the absence of a stable living environment—and one large enough for their children—presents substantial obstacles for parents seeking reunification, who must proactively execute their child welfare case plan, which inevitably requires them to have a stable place to live.

Poor mothers, and especially poor mothers of color, face particular scrutiny and surveillance by mandated reporters and the child welfare system; for mothers staying in homeless shelters, this scrutiny is exacerbated. Mothers living in shelters describe facing stigmatization and being overlooked, marginalized, and/or perceived as aberrant, incompetent parents (Cosgrove and Flynn 2005). Even when sheltered with their children, mothers are often unable to fulfill their roles as mothers while in the "physically restrictive environment" of a shelter (Azim, MacGillivray, and Heise 2019). For women who have lost custody of their children, staying in a shelter might represent a step toward fulfilling their case plan and moving toward reunification; at the same time, they are under constant surveillance there and must prove to system actors that they are fully committed to their children (Barrow and Laborde 2008). Young parents and fathers—who may not even be recognized as parents if they are sheltered without their children—may have even less access to the services needed to find stable housing and reunify with their children.

Experiences of the nearly twenty thousand young people who age out of foster care each year (USDHHS 2022a) illustrate some of the negative impacts of the child welfare system with regard to perpetuating housing insecurity. Under the Federal Fostering Connections to Success and Increasing Adoptions Act of 2008, youth in foster care in approximately forty-eight states are permitted to remain in care beyond their eighteenth birthday (CWIG 2022b). This provision allows them to continue receiving services to help them develop their independent living skills and transition successfully to adulthood. Despite these efforts, these young individuals face numerous challenges, making self-sufficiency an unrealistic goal for many (Greeson et al. 2020; Rome and Raskin 2019). Aged-out youth often have no support systems and tend to struggle with mental health problems, substance abuse, low educational attainment, homelessness, and unemployment (Kelly 2020). Their use of positive parenting practices may be limited by their experiences of trauma and maltreatment and their lack of positive parenting role models (Dworsky 2015; Rouse et al. 2021). In line with these challenges, aging-out parents are more likely to be housing insecure and investigated for child maltreatment (Font et al. 2020).

Navigating Neoliberal Systems

Neoliberal poverty governance, which prioritizes economic market rationality and emphasizes work and individual responsibility, is rooted in an understanding of the poor as inadequate and in need of state surveillance and management (Roberts 2014; Soss, Fording, and Schram 2011). Neoliberal policies aimed at providing assistance exclude those who cannot participate in the market yet also fail to support efforts to provide workers with a living wage (Mays 2021; Roberts 2014). Neoliberalism has shaped the design and implementation of state programs such as the housing assistance and child welfare systems, deprioritizing the funding of safety nets and setting the stage for formal and informal state surveillance of poor families, leading to maltreatment reports and investigations (Fong 2020; Soss, Fording, and Schram 2011).

While the housing assistance and child welfare systems' purported goals are to help children and their families access services to achieve children's well-being, safety, and stability, US child welfare system policies focus on parents' individual actions rather than "the systemic injustices creating the conditions for maltreatment" (Fong 2020, 631). This approach is consistent with neoliberalism's focus on ensuring that people—often poor people of color—take personal responsibility for "poor choices" (Schram 2018). The complex interweaving of systemic and individual issues, including the structural inequities associated with race, class, and gender and the ways these inequities shape childhood trauma, mental health issues, and substance abuse, are largely ignored. Black mothers, disproportionately represented in the child welfare system, are repeatedly framed as inadequate mothers undeserving of assistance, usually with little recognition of the long history of racist policies that have shaped the conditions in which they must mother (Neubeck and Cazenave 2001; Roberts 2022), including, in many cases, housing insecurity.

Requirements that families involved in both the homeless services and child welfare systems must meet as preconditions to reunification reflect neoliberal principles of self-reliance and personal accountability.

Parents are often expected to obtain housing; attend educational ses-sions, mental health treatment, substance abuse treatment, and/or parenting classes; and seek employment, all from different providers. Research has found that parents with children in foster care must attend an average of eight service events per week and that about one-third of parents were assigned services that were not appropriate to their needs (D'Andrade and Chambers 2012). Families are also penalized for con-flicts or purported missteps, for example, attending visitation but miss-ing another appointment (Barrow and Laborde 2008). Yet, when parents do not have some of their most basic needs met, such as having a stable living environment, it can be challenging for them to attend all required services even when they are highly motivated to work on their child welfare case plans.

The concept of cumulative disadvantage is useful for understanding how poverty is often cyclical and why simply obtaining housing is in-sufficient to break child welfare involvement cycles among those who are experiencing housing insecurity. Cumulative disadvantage reflects how systemic and societal structures contribute to differences between people's economic states; those who experience early disadvantages will be more likely to continue to experience disadvantages, which accumu-late, making climbing out of persistent poverty especially difficult (Melo, Guedes, and Mendes 2019). Severe deprivation—acute, compounded, and persistent economic hardship—of which housing insecurity is a marker, is one of the most devastating outcomes of cumulative disad-vantage (Desmond 2015). Structural racism, a core cause of cumulative disadvantage, significantly shapes who experiences severe deprivation, while gender, race, and sexual orientation intersect in ways that make it much harder for some to escape that cycle of deprivation (Collins and Chepp 2013; Melo, Guedes, and Mendes 2019). If we are to be effective in breaking cycles of cumulative disadvantage, interventions that address people's intersectional statuses and complex needs are necessary.

Interventions Addressing Housing Insecurity and Child Welfare Involvement

Many recent interventions for addressing housing insecurity follow the successful Housing First model, which was originally designed for chronically homeless single men experiencing homelessness and struggling with substance abuse and/or mental health issues. Housing First provides permanent housing without a prerequisite of enrolling in treatment, employment, or other programs (Padgett, Henwood, and Tsemberis 2016). In this way, the original Housing First premise runs decidedly counter to neoliberal thinking. In the Housing First model, permanent housing provides an important foundation for addressing people's other needs (e.g., substance abuse and/or mental health treatment). As applied to families who are housing insecure and involved in the child welfare system, the literature suggests that ensuring housing security is necessary before families' other needs can be addressed (e.g., mental health treatment and parenting skills education) (Collins et al. 2022; Fowler et al. 2017). A number of Housing First–focused interventions for families have been implemented and studied to assess how ensuring stable housing impacts families with child welfare involvement. We discuss several of these in the following sections.

The Family Unification Program

The Family Unification Program (FUP), a US Department of Housing and Urban Development (HUD) initiative, has served more than three hundred communities across the United States since its inception in 1990 (USHUD 2022). FUP provides Housing Choice Vouchers—federal subsidies to offset the cost of private market rent (also known as Section 8)—to very low-income child-welfare-involved populations. The first group consists of families for whom housing insecurity is a primary factor in the children's foster care placement or has delayed the child's reunification; the second group comprises foster care youth who have aged out of the system and are experiencing homelessness or risk of homelessness (USHUD 2022). Families with Housing Choice Vouchers can search for housing and use their voucher as payment, or partial payment, for the rent. This allows families flexibility in selecting housing where they want to live, with the hope that their housing will be stable. However, the program's challenges include the limited supply of both housing units and landlords willing to accept the vouchers; in addition, many of the available units are lower quality and in undesirable neighborhoods (Fowler and Schoeny 2015). Unlike the original Housing First approach, the use of vouchers relies on the private housing market while embracing the neoliberal tenet of "consumer choice" regarding where to live (Oudshoorn et al. 2023); families' housing choices are often constrained by the options available.

FUP, despite its challenges, has shown positive effects by both reducing homelessness and preventing foster care placement (Fowler and Schoeny 2015, 2017; Fowler et al. 2018; Pergamit, Cunningham, and Hanson 2017). At a thirty-six-month follow-up after the investigated families had received housing assistance, the FUP showed decreased rates of foster care placement, compared to similar families who did not receive housing assistance. While positive, the FUP's impact on foster care placement is relatively small (Fowler et al. 2018), and it has had no or minimal effects on family reunification (Pergamit, Cunningham, and Hanson 2017). This finding was consistent with other studies showing that housing programs did not result in changes in child maltreatment rates and patterns (Gubits et al. 2015, 2016).

The Family Options Study

The Family Options Study (FOS) represents the most recent large-scale effort of the homeless service system to address family homelessness. In this study, over twenty thousand homeless families from twelve US communities were randomly assigned to different housing interventions, including emergency shelters, rapid rehousing (quickly housing people currently experiencing homelessness and providing rental assistance for up to eighteen months with housing-focused services), transitional housing (providing up to twenty-four months of on-site housing with on-site support services), and permanent housing vouchers (providing subsidized rent without support services) (Gubits et al. 2015). The FOS's rigorous design allowed researchers to disentangle the effects of various types of housing interventions on families experiencing homelessness. Researchers found that permanent housing vouchers reduced the possibility of foster care placement at the beginning (one and a half years after the intervention began), but those effects diminished over time (thirty-six months after intervention). There were no differences in family reunification at follow-up between housing intervention groups (i.e., permanent housing subsidy, rapid rehousing, transitional housing). A thirty-seven-month

follow-up found that rates of child removal were not significantly different between families in the housing intervention group and those in the
control group receiving usual services (traditional shelter and housing services without priority access) (Fowler 2017; Gubits et al. 2016). Permanent
housing subsidies, however, reduced new parent-child separations compared with homeless services, and rehousing generally helped some, but
not all, homeless families reunify (Gubits et al. 2015). Similarly, although
the study found that housing subsidies reduced housing instability and
food insecurity and improved children's and adults' well-being, there were
no significant differences in reunification rates (Gubits et al. 2015, 2016).
Housing subsidies temporarily reduced the possibility of child removal
but were insufficient in helping families reunify. This is probably because
housing is only one of many factors affecting child removal and reunification (Fowler 2017).

Partnering for Family Success

Partnering for Family Success (PFS), in Cuyahoga County, Ohio,
was a randomized control trial (RCT) examining the effectiveness of
quickly housing child-welfare-involved housing-unstable families (following the Housing First model).[1] The program provided intensive
trauma-informed case management to families whose children were
in out-of-home placement (OHP). Adapting critical time intervention,
an evidence-based practice that strengthens vulnerable people's ties to
their communities and families during periods of transition, the program aimed to reduce the number of days children spent in OHP by
25 percent. Although the intervention did not reach this goal, a qualitative analysis found that clients and child welfare workers greatly valued
the program, especially the PFS service providers. These findings suggest that professionals from outside the child welfare system can provide
strong support for struggling families while at the same time being helpful to overburdened child welfare workers (Bai et al. 2019).

In PFS, parents (mostly mothers) felt the PFS providers cared about
them, advocated for them, and gave them hope of resolving their child
welfare cases. Assisting clients in securing housing, developing essential
skills (for interactions with landlords, their children, and others), and
facilitating their access to therapy and community resources contributed

to family stabilization and improved clients' ability to navigate their child welfare cases (Bai et al. 2019). Because PFS providers got to know the families well, child welfare workers also viewed PFS providers as trusted professionals who gave honest assessments of the parents' progress, advocating for the family and helping to move cases forward toward reunification when things were going well. Child welfare workers said the program was especially unique in helping families obtain housing quickly.

The PFS program experienced several challenges, however. Because participating families were often in deep poverty, even after obtaining housing, maintaining the household was often challenging. Families had trouble obtaining various basic material needs for their families (e.g., diapers, clothing) and/or did not have skills to care for their housing (i.e., cleaning, household maintenance, and/or repair) (Collins et al. 2016). Parents also struggled to find employment that paid them enough so they could afford even the nonsubsidized portion of their rent, child care, necessary furnishings, food, and supplies to care for their children. This was especially true for large families. However, overall, families were grateful for their housing assistance, tailored support, and their relationships with their PFS workers, who, for some, were their only source of social support.

From our interviews with PFS workers, we gained particular insights into some of the inequities within the child welfare system. One surprising PFS study finding was that Black children were more likely than white children to reunify with their parents (Collins et al. 2022); this is counter to decades' worth of national statistics showing racial disparities in reunification rates and timelines. In a qualitative follow-up study, we interviewed PFS staff, child welfare workers, and families about their program experiences, asking specifically why they thought Black children were more likely to reunify. PFS program workers hypothesized that white families' less severe cases of maltreatment were probably screened out and/or closed at earlier stages before child removal and that among white parents, only those with the most serious cases had their children removed, while a wider range of maltreatment severity probably led to child removal in Black families. PFS workers believed that due to racial bias, Black families might have had their children removed for less severe instances of maltreatment, making their cases easier to address and facilitating faster reunification once they had housing support. For neglect cases, they said Black families' cases were often more overtly poverty and/or housing related, making them more responsive to housing support, enabling faster stabilization and reunification. PFS workers acknowledged how systemic racism and trauma affected the families with whom they worked and discussed how they helped families move toward reunification (Collins et al. 2022).

The PFS study also found that state and judicial system representatives, including guardians ad litem (GALs, appointed by the court in abuse and neglect cases to protect children's best interests), judges, and magistrates, frequently disregarded mothers' case progress. Child welfare and PFS workers reported that these system actors often prejudged their clients based on initial child removal reasons. For example, some GALs indicated that they would be unwilling to return children to mothers who had used drugs, regardless of their case-plan progress. Other qualitative research on service providers (e.g., child welfare caseworkers, landlords, and even their own staff) who work with chronically homeless families found that providers had substantial prejudices against very poor families, especially those who experience overlapping issues such as mental health issues and/or substance abuse (Collins et al. 2016).

In interviews, PFS parents described how punitive the child welfare system could be and how they felt that their child welfare caseworkers were carefully watching and waiting for them to make a mistake; this is similar to the fears of surveillance found by others (Fong 2019a; see also Brant, chapter 6 in this volume). PFS clients described visitation as a double-edged sword, as they both looked forward to seeing their children and found the supervised visits stressful due to the surveillance, restrictions, and potentially punitive outcomes (see also Lockwood 2018). One of the greatest challenges for PFS clients was the expectation by child welfare workers that clients could not be late to or miss visits. PFS clients reported that child welfare workers changed visitation schedules to fit their own schedules without regard for the mothers', resulting in clients having to cancel other appointments necessary for their case plans, something also found in past research (Barrow and Laborde 2008). In one situation, a child was in foster care more than two hours away, and the mother did not have transportation to attend the visit. The client said that her child welfare worker judged her as insufficiently dedicated to reunification and out of compliance with her case plan rather than acknowledging the mother's poverty and lack of resources, experiences reported in the literature as well (Barrow and Laborde 2008; Fong 2023). Such messages aimed at mothers who have already experienced trauma by having their children taken from them—and having experienced multiple other issues such as substance abuse, domestic violence, and childhood trauma—only compound the difficulty of their situations.

In one of our projects that was a precursor to PFS—a pilot Housing First project serving chronically homeless young adults and families struggling with mental health and/or substance abuse—the funder's goal was for clients to become "self-sufficient" (Collins et al. 2016, 2019). This embrace of the neoliberal logic of self-sufficiency by agencies charged with helping families—including child welfare, mental health, and housing assistance organizations—created more barriers for them. In interviews with service agency staff, however, we learned that the staff recognized that clients not only struggled to achieve self-sufficiency but also generally viewed "self-sufficiency" as unrealistic and reliance on others as necessary to get through life (Collins et al. 2019). Despite receiving different types of public assistance, very few families received cash aid through Temporary Assistance for Needy Families (TANF) or income through employment. "Zero-income" families faced particular challenges in maintaining their housing situations, and case managers were often limited in how to help them (Collins et al. 2019). Even with housing assistance, myriad personal and structural barriers made "self-sufficiency" challenging for very poor families. Rather than programs aimed at self-sufficiency, more substantial and individualized support is needed to keep families together or reunite them (Lyon-Callo 2004; Schram 2018).

Policy and Practice Recommendations

While perhaps an instrument of wealth accumulation for the affluent, housing is a basic human need and a social justice issue (Mays 2021). Our most ambitious desire is for large structural and policy changes that ensure no one goes without affordable housing. To address housing issues most effectively, it is essential to acknowledge the constraints that neoliberal ideals place on policy makers' views and then promote a shift in attitudes. Within the context of neoliberalism, adopting a "radically incremental" approach involves a gradual strengthening of social protections, thereby helping families avoid poverty, regardless of their participation in the labor market (Schram 2018).

Some scholars see the child welfare system as intractably broken and call for its wholesale abolition because it was created to police Black families and has a net negative effect on society (Dettlaff et al. 2020; Roberts 2022), while others argue that it needs to be reformed (Barth et al. 2020). We advocate for a pragmatic approach that seeks comprehensive reform and a reshaping of the child welfare system to address systemic issues, promote equity, and prioritize the well-being of children and families. We are also open to abolition if there is a pragmatic way to accomplish that. This would include exploring innovative solutions that address the underlying social determinants contributing to family involvement in the child welfare system, including poverty and housing instability, and developing alternative guidelines for assessing and intervening in poverty-related neglect cases. It is crucial to work toward a society that not only protects children but also addresses the social and economic factors that lead to child welfare involvement. The goal should be to create a system that genuinely serves the best interests of children and families and is more responsive, just, and supportive. We also believe major cultural shifts are necessary that work toward valuing Black motherhood and promoting positive public images of pregnant Black women and Black mothers to counter narratives that Black families are weak and/or fragmented (Alphonso 2021; Morgan 2018). Efforts to reshape federal social policy to be explicitly antiracist are also needed.

At this writing, the current political environment in the United States seems especially hostile toward supporting families facing severe deprivation. Recent policy efforts to whitewash US history (Wong 2021) will ensure that any attempts at radical or redistributive strategies fail. Instead, encouraging policy makers to prioritize affordable housing and increase the availability of housing vouchers is crucial (Cosgrove and Flynn 2005). Solutions to severe deprivation and associated hardships require complex, cross-system collaboration, a departure from policy makers' usual approaches (Barrow and Laborde 2008; Desmond 2015). Housing and child welfare issues cannot be approached as silos. As we have argued, the issues are interconnected, and problems in these areas co-occur; policies and programs must not only recognize this but pro-actively plan for multipronged, tailored approaches to assist families.

In PFS, trauma-informed professional advocates who were intimately familiar with families and who also worked productively with child welfare workers were invaluable; both families and child welfare workers saw them as partners. Models such as this offer promise and hope for vulnerable families as they resist the expectation of self-sufficiency inherent in neoliberal values, approach families with compassion and understanding, and emphasize strengths-based approaches that empower families while helping them navigate multiple, complex systems (Azim, MacGillivray, and Heise 2019; Harp and Bunting 2020). Advocates who are knowledgeable about—but work outside—the housing and child welfare systems and who understand structural racism and how poor families experience discrimination hold the most promise for helping families. By being flexible and understanding the substantial barriers parents face, advocates can do the frontline work of walking hand in hand with families. By challenging the victim/pathology model supported by neoliberalism, advocates center families' resilience and consider how behaviors may be adaptive for families' life circumstances (Cosgrove and Flynn 2005). Advocates who can bridge communication (and trust) gaps between child welfare workers and their clients can create opportunities to empower and show care and respect for families' strengths and abilities to persevere in difficult conditions.

Reforming the culture of child welfare must include moving away from a punitive approach toward an understanding of the importance of strengthening families and understanding that most children are better off with their parents. Consciously and proactively shifting away from language that describes families in "us" versus "them" or "worthy" versus "unworthy" terms (Kingfisher 2012) may also be helpful. Child welfare practice should adopt more compassionate responses toward struggling families by including current and/or former clients as important stakeholders who contribute to key decision-making and whose views and expertise are valued. Forming such alliances has advantages over maintaining adversarial relationships with families. However, a shift away from neoliberal values would be required. If neoliberal values continue to dominate child welfare services, manifesting in individualized case plans focused on penalizing families viewed as insufficiently responsible and self-sufficient, shifting child welfare models away from punitive models may be extremely difficult, time-consuming, and/or ineffective.

In addition to providing housing-unstable families with advocates who can help improve their experiences with the child welfare system, it is important to consider the feasibility of implementing longer-term strategies rather than relatively short-term ones (Barrow and Laborde 2008). Most programs and funding working to help families obtain housing have been relatively short term, ranging from a few months to about two years. Programs offering impoverished families housing, essential material supplies, and even intensive therapeutic and case-management support for limited periods are important for establishing a strong foundation on which families can build (Fowler et al. 2018). Yet such programs tend to focus on the short rather than the long term and provide no ladder for increasing families' economic mobility. While the neoliberal focus on "self-sufficiency" expects families to quickly attain economic and housing stability, few programs explore the extent to which longer-term investments in education and employment would help families reunify and ultimately climb out of poverty. In PFS, many client interviewees wished the program could have been longer, even forever. More work is needed to determine the program duration needed for long-term, sustainable improvements in clients' situations, which may require permanent housing for some, in direct contrast to neoliberal thinking.

The research tells us that housing is not a quick fix for most families who find themselves at the nexus of housing insecurity and child welfare involvement. Focusing on housing, without addressing the deeper social and economic issues clients face, will never be adequate for long-term stabilization. Further, social services infused with neoliberal values focused on self-sufficiency and personal responsibility are not effective. Concentrating on long-term stabilization among families with cumulative disadvantages and addressing those multiple layers of disadvantage including trauma will not be possible through short-term efforts and will not produce quick payoffs. We believe there is great promise in coupling housing interventions with long-term trauma-informed intensive case management and advocacy, which could help resolve both housing insecurity and child welfare involvement and be an important step in helping pull families out of poverty.

Conclusion

In the United States, the child welfare and housing assistance systems are key neoliberal poverty governance institutions that both aid and discipline poor families. While it is necessary to recognize that affordable housing is foundational to disrupting cycles of cumulative disadvantage, it is only one piece of the puzzle. A central feature of child welfare and housing assistance systems is monitoring families—particularly those headed by Black mothers—under the guise of protecting children but without regard for the harm that such "protection" causes. In the long term, it may be necessary, as some scholars argue, to abolish the child welfare system (Dettlaff et al. 2020; Roberts 2022). In the meantime, we urge service providers and policy makers to consider approaches that guide families through these systems using advocates trained in intersectional trauma-informed care who know the challenges that housing-unstable, child-welfare-involved families face. Programs like PFS that engage professionally trained advocates with small caseloads and that provide resources can incite hope and might help stabilize families. Ultimately, however, funders and policy makers must invest in tailored, supportive, longer-term programs that include wraparound services to help families truly thrive, rather than expecting them to become economically "self-sufficient" through more responsible choices. To do so, policy makers and program service providers will need to examine and adjust their adherence to neoliberal ideology and commit to helping the most vulnerable families in our society not just to survive but, ultimately, to flourish.

NOTE

1 This was the first county-wide Pay for Success study. Pay for Success is a funding model in which investors pay for testing an intervention. If the intervention's goals are met, the local funders, in this case the county, pay the initial investors back (see Fischer and Richter 2017).

PART IV

The Child Welfare System and the Right Hand of the State

8

Family, Interrupted

Children's Exposure to Therapeutic Governance and State Surveillance in Family Drug Treatment Courts

LAURA TACH, ELIZABETH DAY, AND
BRITTANY MIHALEC-ADKINS

Family drug treatment courts (FDTCs) are an increasingly popular alternative to traditional child welfare and criminal justice system interventions for parents struggling with substance use disorders. FDTCs aim to provide a suite of services to support recovery and family reunification, but in exchange, low-income caregivers and children are subjected to intense state scrutiny of their personal behaviors, recovery, and sobriety. Despite the increasing use of FDTCs across the United States, we know little about children's experiences of these courts or the consequences of FDTC participation for family dynamics. In this chapter, we address these gaps in the literature by exploring children's experiences of poverty governance and therapeutic surveillance within FDTCs. Drawing on in-depth interviews with twenty-one current and former participants in an FDTC in the rural Northeast, we find that children are liminal participants in the FDTC system, existing at the periphery of FDTCs yet exposed to a range of unfamiliar and intrusive state systems as their parents engage in an intensive process of mandated self-transformation and self-reliance.

Although FDTCs' stated goal is to protect children, the requirements placed on parents—most often low-income mothers—tend to be experienced vicariously by children in ways that cause trauma by placing them in unfamiliar environments that they perceive as threatening and by undermining family relationships. We conclude by discussing ways in which the dual poverty governance and therapeutic surveillance mandates of FDTCs could be adapted to better attend to the needs and well-being of disadvantaged youth.

Child Welfare and Poverty Governance

The child welfare system represents a classic example of poverty governance in the United States—a system that does not aim to end poverty per se but to "manage low-income populations and transform them into cooperative subjects of the market and polity" (Soss, Fording, and Schram 2011, 2). Scholars and critics of the child welfare system have argued that many cases of child maltreatment should be understood as symptoms of poverty and social marginality rather than the individual moral failings of parents (Roberts 2002; Woodward 2021). The primary objective of child protective intervention is to ensure child safety, with the well-being of parents as a secondary consideration in service of the first goal (Reich 2005). To achieve these goals, the child welfare system couples assistance with coercive governance, blending the punitive and supportive roles of the state (Woodward 2021).

The child welfare system has enormous power to govern the inner workings of family life, particularly for families living in poverty: it has the authority both to remove children from their parents and to decide whether and when they can be reunified. Prior research has shown that parents must demonstrate their rehabilitation in a variety of ways in order to gain back custody of their children, which requires them to open up their home life and interactions with children to intensive state surveillance and reform (Reich 2005). For example, they must address other material, social, economic, and health-related conditions—often themselves by-products of poverty and social marginality—determined by the state to be barriers to creating a safe and stable home environment for their children. To yield the most favorable results for their families, parents must show deference to caseworkers who make the decisions about their families' futures (Lee 2016; Sykes 2011). However, Jennifer Reich (2005, 159) and others have shown that despite parents' attempts to demonstrate good-enough parenting, caseworkers continue to value and institutionalize specific cultural definitions of "good parenting" that have been "widely criticized as overly reliant on images of white and middle-class women."

The intervention process is daunting for children, just as it is for parents. A recent systematic review of children's experiences of child protective interventions found that children felt afraid, overlooked, confused, uninformed, and worried about their families (Wilson et al. 2020). Children described experiencing significant disruptions to nearly all aspects of their lives, including changes in close relationships and the introduction of many new state actors, institutions, and systems of surveillance. Because low-income, Black, and American Indian children are considerably more likely to have contact with child protective services, these state-induced family disruptions are raced and classed experiences in the United States; and because low-income women are disproportionately custodial parents, they too are overrepresented in the child welfare system and face heightened scrutiny of their mothering (Reich 2005; Roberts 2002; Woodward 2021).

Drug Courts and Therapeutic Governance

Parental substance use disorders are a contributing factor in a large and growing number of child protection cases (Sepulveda and Williams 2019). Family drug treatment courts are one strategy for addressing child protection cases in which parental substance use was determined to be a contributing factor in the alleged maltreatment. As of 2019, there were an estimated five hundred FDTCs currently operating in counties across the United States (OJJDP 2021). Located within civil courts, FDTCs are a collaboration between family courts with jurisdiction over child protective proceedings, child protective services (CPS) departments, and local drug treatment and recovery services. Specific approaches of FDTCs vary across the country, but they share the common goal of offering families additional supports and services that are not always provided by traditional CPS interventions, such as drug treatment and mental health services, family preservation efforts, and peer coaches/mentors.

FDTCs are modeled after criminal drug courts, with components adapted to address the unique needs of parents and children in a civil court setting. Rather than incarcerate those who are charged with drug-related criminal offenses, drug courts provide mandatory treatment services coupled with intensive judicial supervision. Drug courts are part of the larger "problem-solving" court movement, in which courts are used to address social problems like addiction, domestic violence, and mental illness (Moore 2011). The model of therapeutic jurisprudence utilized by drug courts is framed as nonadversarial—assistance rather than punishment, helping rather than disciplining—although it remains coercive in that the alternative to participation is incarceration.

Although drug courts have been lauded as less punitive alternatives to traditional criminal justice involvement, their racial and economic disparities have come under scrutiny. White offenders are more likely to be diverted to drug courts than are their Black counterparts (Lilley, DeVall, and Tucker-Gail 2019; Sheeran and Heideman 2021); for those diverted to drug court, Black participants are less likely than white participants to complete the terms of their court supervision, probably due to Black participants' greater experiences of economic and social marginality.[1] Participants of color are also subjected to harsher sanctions for noncompliance (O'Hear 2009). Similar racial disproportionalities exist within FDTCs, with white families overrepresented and Black families underrepresented relative to the overall child welfare population (Breitenbucher et al. 2018).

Because low-income individuals who use drugs are less likely to have access to private (and costly) therapeutic and recovery services, drug courts and FDTCs have become primary sites of drug rehabilitation for the poor (Gowan and Whetstone 2012). As such, drug courts and FDTCs are examples of therapeutic governance—medicalized approaches to managing the psychology and behavior of marginalized populations in ways that align with the normative expectations of the state (Polsky 1991). This constitutes a substantial expansion of the purview and institutional power of the courts. Rather than simply determining punishment for past behavior, drug courts support and coerce individuals toward recovery. This affords the courts much greater surveillance and judgment of personal lives, including actions and thoughts that are not necessarily illegal but that the court may deem relevant to a person's recovery (Tiger 2011). In particular, they engage in what Nikolas Rose (2000) has called "responsibilization"—interventions that compel self-regulation and self-reliance of the poor. Responsibilization interventions are classic examples of neoliberal social policies that promote "personal responsibility" and "self-sufficiency" in the realms of work and family, with the goal of turning participants into "good neoliberal citizens" (Randles and Woodward 2018). Through intensive interpersonal relationships with counselors, caseworkers, and other social service professionals, judges adjudicate the degree to which an individual has internalized the messages from recovery and taken responsibility for their actions. A key part of treatment and therapy involves disclosing personal, often traumatic life events and engaging in deep reflection, introspection, and emotional confession (Best et al. 2016). As with child welfare caseworkers, the fates of defendants in drug courts are largely determined by counselors' and court actors' assessments of whether they have "truly" completed this process of self-transformation versus "going through the motions," which ultimately determines who completes the terms of their court supervision successfully (Burns and Peyrot 2003).

One consequence of this intensely internal focus on recovery and self-transformation within drug courts and FDTCs is that it obscures the broader structural conditions of social and economic marginality. These conditions, which include poverty, racism, and sexism, can lead to self-medication and drug use, reduced access to private forms of therapy that can help parents avoid child removal, and racialized stigmas surrounding drug use (Gowan, Whetstone, and Andic 2012; Kenny and Barrington 2018; Netherland and Hansen 2017). Another consequence of intensive FDTC surveillance is that there are more opportunities for the parent to be observed making mistakes or failing to meet expectations and thus more opportunities for sanctions and punishment (Fong 2020). For example, most upper- and middle-class parents who see a private psychiatrist can be assured that what they disclose will be held in confidence, but FDTC clients can be sanctioned by the court for failing to fully commit to their therapy and treatment program or for disclosing substance use to these professionals. The regulation of FDTC clients' bodies and demands for complete sobriety mean that those who fail a urinalysis drug test or who protest their mandated treatment plan can be punished by having contact with their children taken away or progress on their cases undone. For this reason, court-mandated treatment in drug courts has been called the "fuzzy edge" of the criminal justice system (Gowan and Whetstone 2012, 87).

FDTCs represent a case of extreme state surveillance, one that merges the therapeutic governance of drug courts with the poverty governance of the child welfare system. To receive the services and supports of

FDTCs, low-income parents must subject themselves to highly intensive and intrusive forms of supervision and control in exchange for subsidized treatment, economic supports and social services, and the possibility to reunify with their children. What little research there is about experiences with FDTCs focuses on parents (Moreno and Curti 2012), so we know little about the experiences of children within the FDTC systems and how these experiences affect family relationships. We explore parents' descriptions of their children's experiences in this chapter, conceptualizing children as liminal participants in the FDTC system as their parents engage in an intensive process of mandated parenting reform, sobriety, and self-transformation.

Documenting Parent and Child Experiences in Treatment Court

Our study focuses on FDTC participants in a Rust Belt county that includes a small city and its rural surroundings. The process for receiving FDTC services commences automatically when any petition of child neglect filed with the court includes an allegation of caregiver substance misuse. While participation in FDTCs is described as voluntary, declining to participate results in parents receiving a permanent charge of child neglect, and successful participation in FDTC waives this consequence. A large majority of FDTC participants who are parents have their children removed from their custody and placed with foster families or kin caregivers. After consenting to participate, the caregiver begins moving through three phases of programming that take approximately twelve to eighteen months on average. During that time, participants interact with a range of child welfare, mental health, legal, and social services professionals during in-patient or out-patient treatment, weekly court hearings, periodic home visits, regular drug screenings, and a suite of other services determined by the FDTC.

We recruited twenty-one former FDTC participants for this study through several methods, including by mailing study fliers, by attending drop-in office hours at the child welfare agency office, and via referrals from other participants. The in-depth interviews were semistructured and open-ended. Because the average age of children was just eight years old, we did not interview children directly but instead asked parents to reflect on what the FDTC experience was like for their children and how it affected their family dynamics. The sample of former program participants interviewed consisted of sixteen women and five men in their twenties and thirties, reflecting the gendered nature of the child welfare system, in which mothers are overrepresented. At the time of the interview, one-quarter (five) of parents were single, 14 percent (three) were married, and 62 percent (thirteen) were unmarried but in romantic relationships. Participants had two children on average.

Reflecting the demographics of the county and the racial disproportionalities found in other family treatment courts, a majority (eighteen) of respondents were white. Underscoring the central role that the child welfare system plays in poverty governance, most respondents reported incomes of less than $10,000 in the previous year, partly a function of barriers to employment while in FDTC and recovery and low levels of public assistance, especially direct cash aid. Opioids were the most common substances that respondents reported using; other common substances included marijuana, cocaine, and alcohol.

"I Was All He Had": Trauma Associated with Removal, Separation, and Visitation

Nearly all parents interviewed for this study described both the initial removal of their children and the prolonged separation from them as being among the most traumatic and impactful elements of FDTC. Lisa, a mother of one teenage son, grew up in a single-wide trailer, where she was sexually abused and recalled learning to fend for herself at an early age.[2] She described the experience of her son's removal by saying, "It's the worst fucking feeling in the world. It's awful. It feels like somebody ripped your soul out and was holding it hostage." Importantly, parents described their children's removal and subsequent separation as traumatic not only for themselves but also for their children. Lauren, a mother of three who grew up with parents who were "severe alcoholics," recalled that while her children were out of her custody, it was "hard": "because, you know, looking at them and seeing the sadness on their face every time we had to leave, or you know, seeing the sadness on their face when they knew time was—like, the time was up to see each other, you know? They would be like, 'Oh, time's up,' and they— you know, they start crying."

In addition to parents missing and wanting to see their children more often, they worried about the impact of disruptions to parent-child bonds for their children's well-being. Erica, a mother of six who experienced chronic housing insecurity, recalled that even though they had had unstable housing, her kids were always with her, and CPS ruptured those close bonds: "I was allowed to see my kids once every other week. And my—like, for my son, he was four years old at the time and had been with me every day of his life. . . . Even when I was going to school, he went to school with me. Um, so it really messed with him. And then, so for him to see me once every other week even though I was clean, . . . it really pissed me off."

Ashley, who described a "rough childhood" that involved her mother's rotating cast of abusive boyfriends, further described her concern about the lingering effects of this state-mandated separation on her own child and how she was left to cope with his trauma from FDTC involvement on her own:

> At first, they just took everything away from me. You know, they took the child, and then I wasn't able to see [the child] for a good month. And then the visits were so short. That's trauma on him—you know, not just trauma on me. That's trauma on him. He's—he's only allowed to see his parents for what, two, three hours, two times a week it was? And then he's crying at the fricking door. . . . And that's trauma on him. He remembers that. So, you know, I'm gonna have to explain that to him. [FDTC] don't. I have to.

Many parents had themselves dealt with caregivers who were absent due to drugs or unstable family relationships, and they recognized the long-term trauma that such fractured bonds had caused them. They were heartbroken that the state had now forced their children to go through a similar experience—an experience to which low-income families are more likely to be subjected given their overrepresentation in the child welfare system. These stories reveal the visceral trauma that results from state-sanctioned poverty governance administered by the child welfare system, which disproportionately surveils and disciplines low-income families by design (Woodward 2021). Due to the limited resources of families with low incomes, they come into greater contact with public

systems than do their middle-class counterparts, and these public systems in turn have strong, long-standing ties to the child welfare and
court systems (Fong 2017, 2020; Katz 1996; Lee 2016). Limited financial resources also funneled the low-income parents in this study to the
child welfare and court systems, as they were not able to use private
resources to manage challenges that arose with their mental health or
home environments (Reich 2005; Sykes 2011). Furthermore, because
women are more likely to be custodial parents—both nationally and
in this sample—the experiences of trauma associated with removal
and separation are also disproportionately borne by women. A majority of parents in the sample worried about how the lingering trauma
associated with removal and separation would continue to impact their
children in the future. The loss of custody and separation was perhaps
even more restricted and enduring for parents in FDTC than for the
average CPS case because it was accompanied by mandated inpatient or
outpatient substance-use-related treatment, during which visitation was
supervised and very limited.

"My Parental Rights Were Gone": Diminished Authority to Monitor and Advocate

Parents felt they had little power when it came to making decisions
about their children's lives and well-being, even after they were making progress toward FDTC milestones and demonstrating their sobriety.
Instead, they felt that foster and kinship caregivers, and ultimately the
court, held all the power and did not take their concerns seriously. The
involvement of multiple caregivers and conflicts over parental authority had negative consequences for children, such as uncertain routines
and schedules, conflicting expectations among different caregivers, and
a lack of secure and stable relationships with the adults in their lives.
Some parents attributed their disempowerment to the stigma of their
prior substance use, which they felt made state actors and other caregivers treat them as though their parental rights did not count for anything.
This is a prime example of how neoliberal child welfare agencies and
treatment courts individualize blame and stigma as a means to promote
personal responsibility among parents under state supervision. The
focus on the personal and moral failings of individual parents obscures

the broader roots of social and economic marginality that contributed to their FDTC involvement.

For example, Lauren felt angered that her child's foster caregivers and CPS caseworkers seemed to wield all the power—so much so that her son had a dental procedure without her knowledge or consent, even though she had been "clean" for six months. Lauren further explained that she was frustrated with the power of the court to make decisions about her child's health and safety without her input: "I was pissed that day in court. I was like, 'You know, I do everything you guys ask me to do. I've done it for a whole year. I'm here. I'm willing to do the work. I see my kids consistently. I go to school functions. I do everything. Why was I not informed that my son was having a two-and-a-half-hour surgery on his teeth?' And they did not have answers for me." Parents perceived that foster families, and especially those providing kinship or relative care, had a great deal of discretion and power in deciding when to allow or curtail access to their children. This was further exacerbated by different standards and expectations regarding parenting across households, which parents felt caused their children confusion and hindered their ability to set stable parenting expectations and routines. While Rachel's son was in her mother's custody, she recalled, "He had to listen to their [FDTC's] rules, my mom's rules, and my rules. So that—you know, that's crazy for a kid. But they [FDTC] didn't care. That was the one thing where, like, it didn't matter who I told. It really did confuse him. And everybody struggled with it. He didn't want to be there, so he was mad at them the whole time, you know, at my brother's. He was just—he was mad at the world, so. He didn't understand what was going on."

Many parents told us that conflicts with their children's foster families (including kinship care) led to confusion for the children. They also felt that state actors viewed them as inferior caregivers because of the stigma tied to their previous substance use, even after they were in recovery. Additionally, many women in this sample felt that their parenting was scrutinized more than that of fathers and that caseworkers were less forgiving or willing to make accommodations for them than they were for the fathers in the sample—illustrating the gendered expectations of the treatment court (Tach et al. 2022). It is also notable that the parents in this mostly white sample perceived high levels of stigma surrounding their substance use; these experiences would probably be even more acute for racial-ethnic minority populations, for whom drug use has more severe racialized meanings and consequences (Ezell et al. 2021; Netherland and Hansen 2017; O'Hear 2009).

Trusting "Adults with Authority": Children's Experiences of Systems Involvement

Following the disruption of removal from their parents' care, the low-income children in this sample had a slew of new adults and institutions enter their lives, even more than do children involved in traditional child welfare services. New adults included foster caregivers, CPS investigators, social workers, court-appointed guardians, lawyers, the family court judge, courtroom officers, the FDTC coordinator, home visitation professionals, parenting educators, and treatment providers. New institutional environments included foster home placements, supervised visitation settings, Department of Social Services offices and waiting rooms, the FDTC courtroom, new schools and childcare settings, and other venues used for service provision and parenting education. Prior research has shown that children's contact with such systems shapes their own legal socialization; children who have harsh or unfair experiences with legal systems perceive state actors as less legitimate and, perversely, are more likely to become involved with the criminal justice system later on (Fagan and Tyler 2005; Kolivoski et al. 2016).

The addition of new adults and institutions also came with major changes to routines and schedules. Parents described a range of consequences for children that they attributed to this extensive new network of people and experiences in their children's lives, most notably uncertainty, fear, and discomfort. The unpredictability and instability of contact with various unfamiliar adults was not conducive to children's development of secure attachment relationships. Furthermore, in some of these settings, professionals shared details with children regarding their parents' drug use and other familial hardships without parental consent. As Adam—who was a father of one eight-year-old and who grew up middle class until his battle with addiction took him on a downward economic spiral—described when asked what the experience of FDTC was like for his son: "Overwhelming at first. 'Cause obviously you had to meet so many new people. . . . At first, you know, he's like going to all these new transitional things. Like I said, he had transitional problems. So he went from, okay, seeing Dad to not seeing Dad all of a sudden. And then meeting all these new faces. And then, oh, [lawyer]'s gonna pick you up every Tuesday and Thursday to go see Dad. And then oh, Dad's not showing up, so then [lawyer] would have to sit and play with him."

Several parents also described strong negative reactions toward their caseworkers, emphasizing a trickle-down effect on their kids' interactions with those professionals. As Erica, a mother of six who works as a home health aide, described about her family's caseworker, "She's a cunt. She didn't involve me in anything. . . . She had stopped my visitation over that [drug] test without waiting for it to be sent out. She would call and say things—my kids didn't even like her. She would walk in my friend's house, and my son would go hide under a bed until she left." Allison, a mother of two who received public assistance while attending community college before her drug use led to an arrest for shoplifting, echoed this sentiment regarding her children's guardian ad litem. She described not only immediate discomfort with that individual but also the negative feelings this engendered toward other services and adults in her life:

> I know my kids weren't comfortable with the law guardians 'cause they made them feel like they wanted [them] to be taken away. So now my kids have a hard time trusting adults. It's taken me forever to convince my daughter to go to therapy because I know it will be good for her, I know that she needs it, and I know that therapy helps me. So I'm like, "I'm all for it. Whatever you need to do." She has refused, and that's in the documentation that she has, and everybody's pushed her to try to get therapy, but she refuses. . . . It took me a long time to get them to trust adults with authority, I think is more the word—not adults but adults with authority. They felt like anytime they would go to an adult or say something bad about, you know, a parent or anything, that it would be like they were gonna get taken away again.

Importantly, few of the FDTC experiences to which children were exposed were designed *for* the child; the focus of the FDTC intervention is, primarily, on the parents' recovery and self-sufficiency. Therefore, these experiences were not always developmentally appropriate for children, and parents described their children's fear and uncertainty in reaction to meeting so many new people and being in so many new institutional settings. Many parents described long-lasting struggles their children would face, including trusting adults, developing secure relationships, and seeking help from social and mental health services that they had come to mistrust through their involvement with FDTCs. As a result, children experienced adverse collateral consequences from the systems of poverty governance and therapeutic governance to which their parents were subjected as conditions of their reunification.

"I Will Always Have Guilt": Changes to Parent-Child Relationships

Compared to traditional child welfare services, FDTCs provided parents and children with clearer state-mandated messages regarding drugs (Day et al. 2023). Like the child welfare system more broadly, these messages often conformed to middle-class notions of acceptable parenting, including middle-class norms around the extent and nature of supervision and interaction with one's children (Lareau 2011; Soss, Fording, and Schram 2011; Woodward 2021). As a result, most parents described a change in their mind-set regarding the compatibility of drugs with parenting, coming into alignment with the messaging of the state. As described by Briana, a mother of one who described money as tight growing up while her own mother struggled with a crack addiction,

> I didn't realize what they meant by "neglect." I was like, "What do you mean 'neglect'? Do you see this home?" You know, "I got a home. I got food in the fridge. . . . I smoke, but it's only, you know, at my friend's house. I don't smoke around my son." . . . It took months for me to realize that that's not what they mean by "neglect." You can't be impaired and tend to—fully tend to his needs, you know what I mean? Because kids, they want structure. . . . You can't provide structure to somebody if you don't got structure. And that's neglect.

Briana's narrative reveals how she slowly adopted the state's messaging around what counts as neglect and the level of engagement and "structure" that she was told her child needed in order for her to be deemed an acceptable parent and regain custody.

Daniel, a father of three who now works full-time at a fast-food restaurant, also described a shift in his mind-set that impacted how he parented his children. He reflected, "I just fully became a better dad just all around. . . . My mind is always on my kids. There's no distractions. So it feels good. [Prior to FDTC] I just didn't care. I didn't care if one shot of heroin was gonna kill me that day. Now it's a million times different." He also described how this led to concrete changes to his parenting behaviors that were "definitely a lot more positive": "You know, hands-on, more in control. And I try to bring as much intelligence and learning into what I'm doing. Like, if I'm gonna tell my kid to do something, I'm also gonna explain it to him, like, so he understands it." Like Briana, Daniel's description illustrates how his parenting behaviors were shaped to meet the middle-class expectations of the state regarding how "hands-on" and "in control" he was with his children.

Despite the alignment of parenting and sobriety that many parents felt they had achieved, many also reported major challenges to reestablishing close and trusting relationships with their children following the trauma of removal and separation that accompanied FDTC. For instance, multiple parents described the struggle they faced to regain their children's trust after reunification. Maria explained the impact: "I mean, it definitely was hard on them because they weren't with their parents. I still feel bad about that, but I can't—I don't know. I feel bad about, you know, losing them, but I know getting them back don't make it all alright, you know? Like I said, it's something that's got to be built up over time, that trust, you know. . . . I know they felt awful a lot of long nights without their mom and dad. And we were a very tight-knit family before they got taken."

Maria's story highlights the negative consequences of the state-required separation, combined with insufficient care and resources provided by the state to help heal these fractured bonds. Notably, she internalizes this guilt ("I feel bad about that"), rather than blaming the state for its role in fracturing her once "tight-knit" family. This internalization of blame is one hallmark of the neoliberal welfare state (Rose 2000).

Other parents shared that they too struggled with lingering guilt about how FDTC participation had affected their parenting behaviors and relationships with their children. This theme of personal guilt provides additional examples of how participants internalized the state's normative expectation for personal responsibility. Lauren, the mother of three, told us, "In the beginning, when I first got them back, um, they were just given anything they wanted because we had that guilt. And now I'm trying to get back to the stricter me that was—the 'If you want this, you had to do this.' But um, it's hard." She further elaborated, "I will always have guilt for what I had to put them through, um, because I have been in a foster home, and I know how bad it is, and I know the pain of not wanting to be there. So I would, you know—and I do blame—I have to blame myself for it, because I made the choice to use drugs, and they blame me, and I could tell that they do." Lauren's quote reveals just how strongly parents internalized the messages of responsibilization and self-transformation dictated by the state, as she fully took on the blame for her "choice" to use drugs. These accounts of guilt and shame were especially pronounced among the mothers in our sample, revealing how gender shapes the state's expectations and shaming around what it means to be a "good mother" as well as the gendered disparities in how that shame was internalized by participants.

One specific consequence of FDTC participation and its model of therapeutic surveillance is that parents and children are confronted with state-sanctioned messages and education around addiction, drugs, and alcohol. In particular, low-income parents attended mandated parenting classes, while their children attended separate classes; during one module of the course, they—and their children—were told about the biological and social bases of addiction, its heritability, and the importance of sobriety. Parents described discomfort about their children being exposed to this information but also appreciated the opportunity it afforded for open and frank lines of communication. For example, Maria, who had a twelve-year-old and a nine-year-old, described her reactions to the course, saying, "They talk to the kids about drugs. . . . The only thing I liked about that part, which I really was very uneasy about in the beginning, was that it opened up mine and my youngest daughter's relationship more, because she was more understanding of what was going on. And now that—now she can tell, like—you know, she is aware of that kind of thing now."

For other parents, the sentiment leaned more toward frustration around their child being privy to information about drugs that they otherwise wouldn't have shared. As Emma described, "I felt like that subject [drug use] should be parents talking about it with their kids instead of, like, other people during a program." Unlike middle-class families, who typically are able to determine the messaging and timetable they deem appropriate for talking to their children about drugs, low-income children involved with FDTCs were exposed to state-sanctioned messaging around drug use and addiction regardless of their parents' own preferences or beliefs.

Considerations for Policy and Practice

Many aspects of children's experiences in FDTC were more intense versions of what children experience in traditional CPS involvement. Like the families in our study, children describe initial contacts with CPS as emotionally and psychologically stressful (Wilson et al. 2020); they feel frightened and lack a clear understanding of what is happening to them and describe their removal as a traumatic experience (Bell 2002; Mitchell and Kuczynski 2010). Additionally, children placed in out-of-home care often find it hard to follow different rules and routines across different homes and caregivers (Mitchell and Kuczynski 2010; Rauktis et al. 2011). Finally, children involved with CPS typically face great uncertainty about their futures, which can cause anxiety and result in emotional detachment as a protective response (Hyde and Kammerer 2009; Mateos et al. 2017). These adverse consequences of CPS involvement for children illustrate how CPS not only is a system of poverty governance but also actively *creates* new forms of trauma for children, which can in turn contribute to the intergenerational reproduction of poverty and drug use.

Several aspects of the FDTC experience are unique for families relative to traditional child welfare interventions. First and foremost, parents must commit to recovery from substance misuse, and their recovery and sobriety are intensively monitored during in- or outpatient treatment, while their children are placed into foster or kinship care. As a result, parent-child separation is more pronounced, ubiquitous, and enduring for those who become involved with the child welfare system for reasons related to substance use compared to other reasons for involvement (Ghertner, Baldwin, et al. 2018). Additionally, parents in FDTCs may face more diminished respect from authorities and find it even more challenging to advocate for their children, due to the stigma associated with their drug use (Kenny and Barrington 2018; Nieweglowski et al. 2018; Sykes 2011). Because white families like those in this study are overrepresented in therapeutic alternatives like FDTCs and drug courts, the experiences documented here are probably even harsher for families of color, who face racialized stigma and criminalized consequences for drug use within the traditional CPS system (Ezell et al. 2021; Netherland and Hansen 2017; Woodward 2021).

A second distinct aspect of FDTCs is that children are exposed to even more adults in positions of authority and even more systems of supervision and care. Children involved with the child welfare system alone have reported that the large array of new actors and institutions introduced into their lives leave them feeling confused, lonely, and like their voice is not heard (Wilson et al. 2020). In FDTCs, these new experiences extend beyond caseworkers and foster homes to include the FDTC judge and all other members of the FDTC coalition, whom parents described as hard to trust and scary for their children. Prior studies have found that children's stress associated with parent-child separation and challenges to forming secure relational attachment is similar to that experienced by children while their parents are incarcerated (Poehlmann 2005). Furthermore, many aspects of FDTCs, such as observing one's parent be subjected to drug screening by an armed officer or reprimanded publicly for a relapse in open court, are decidedly *not* child-friendly experiences. These experiences likely will have adverse long-run consequences, as prior research has shown that children's contact with unsupportive criminal justice and child welfare systems can lead simultaneously to greater mistrust of the legal system and greater entanglement with such systems (Fagan and Tyler 2005; Kolivoski et al. 2016).

A final distinct aspect of FDTCs is the mandated, state-sanctioned messaging around substance use and addiction, a defining feature of the therapeutic state. FDTCs require low-income parents and children to confront these topics during a period of family instability and to do so on the terms of the state, whether or not parents endorse the messages or feel their children are ready to receive them. By contrast, middle-class families have greater access to private addiction treatment on their own terms and without having their children removed. In FDTCs, parents' access to their children was conditioned on demonstrated sobriety and conformity to state-mandated values and beliefs related to the incompatibility of parenting and drug use. This expectation of responsibilization and self-control is the hallmark of the individualized approaches of neoliberal poverty governance and medicalized approaches of therapeutic governance (Rose 2000; Soss, Fording, and Schram 2011), both of which place blame, stigma, and responsibility for treatment on the individual rather than addressing systems of economic and social marginality that funnel families into both drug use and FDTC involvement. These expectations were gendered as well: we found that mothers in particular described internalizing guilt and shame around failing to meet the state's expectations for performance of the mothering role.

We wish to note several limitations of this study, which also suggest avenues for future research. First, our interviews were conducted with parents, not with children directly (though children were often present during interviews and sometimes chimed in), so we were not able to gather children's firsthand experiences and perceptions. It is possible that parents' perceptions do not align with those of their children or that other important aspects of children's experiences were missed, particularly during the period when parents and children were not in close, regular contact. A second limitation of this study is that it was focused on a community that was largely white, with little racial or ethnic diversity, and that had a disproportionate number of cases in which parents were misusing opioids compared with other substances. Given the racialized dynamics of child welfare systems, as well as the increased tendency to medicalize rather than criminalize white people's substance use (Netherland and Hansen 2017), future research on more diverse FDTC systems that include more minority families is warranted to understand which aspects of the experiences we describe here are unique to white families compared with families of color or are unique to families affected by the misuse of opioids relative to other substances.

Despite these limitations, this work suggests concrete recommendations for FDTC policy and practice. First and foremost, agencies and courts should reconsider the practice of child removal. Although agencies' reasons for recommending child removal are related to safety concerns, parents and children generally do not view removal as a protective measure but rather experience the action as traumatic—in ways that affect well-being and relationships long after cases are closed. However well intentioned, separating parents from children in the early stages of FDTC involvement to "allow" parents to focus on sobriety and recovery could, perversely, make recovery and family reunification more difficult. There are several promising approaches that policy makers and practitioners can consider as alternatives to child removal. First, differential or alternative response models have been adopted in some states to connect "low-risk" families to needed resources and services instead of requiring traditional child welfare system involvement in order to access services. Second, federal guidelines have also expanded to allow states access to federal funding that was previously only accessible after child removals, making in-home interventions more feasible. Third, state and federal policy makers can revise statutes so that parents with substance use disorders are not automatically designated as "high-risk," which could allow them to access needed resources and services through differential/alternative responses that do not require separation from their children. Finally, policy makers and agencies can prioritize funding for treatment models that keep families together, such as family-based residential treatment programs that offer safe housing arrangements for parents and children to live together while receiving comprehensive services to promote family well-being and prevent child maltreatment (Rivera and Sullivan 2015).

Additionally, child protection agencies and family courts must address the pervasive stigma that parents and children experience around substance use. Parents reported many instances in which they felt that court and social service professionals stigmatized, judged, and excluded them from decisions regarding their children due to their past or present substance use. These encounters had lasting adverse consequences for their feelings of self-worth, trust, and engagement with FDTCs—and for their parenting self-efficacy and parent-child relationships.

Implementing trauma-informed models of care is one potential avenue for educating service providers about stigma and adapting organizational and interpersonal practices to avoid stigmatization. Although implementation varies across agencies, the common underlying goals of trauma-informed care are to foster safe environments, transparency and trust, choice and empowerment, collaboration and mutuality, peer support, and responsiveness to culture and historical trauma (Harris and Fallot 2001). Although organizations are increasingly adopting trauma-informed care trainings and practices, we caution that such efforts are not sufficient on their own to counteract the deeply entrenched societal stigmas held against people who use drugs, even among well-intentioned service providers (Tach et al. 2022).

More broadly, this research highlights that the web of supervision and services that families must navigate via FDTCs constitutes an extreme form of poverty governance and state surveillance. For some, the program provides a mechanism for parents to reclaim their sobriety as well as their dignity as caregivers and providers. For others, however, the experience is coercive, with access to children tied to demonstrated sobriety, acknowledgment of personal shortcomings, and performance of behaviors that conform to the expectations of the state.

Viewed in this way, FDTCs magnify both the policing and providing aspects of involvement with traditional child welfare interventions as they manage the behavior and sobriety of low-income caregivers.

NOTES

1 The studies summarized in this paragraph measured the racial category "white" as non-Hispanic white individuals and the racial category "Black" as non-Hispanic Black individuals.

2 All names used are pseudonyms to protect respondents' confidentiality.

9

"We're All Working Together"

Interinstitutional Collaborations between Police and Child Protective Services

KELLEY FONG AND ASHLEE SMITH

Eleven-year-old Ricky and eight-year-old Amira had recently moved from the Dominican Republic to New Haven, Connecticut, where they attended the same K–8 school. One April day after school, they were pulled into a school meeting room across from the nurse's office to talk with a man they had never met. Ricky, a small boy, wore a Red Sox hoodie. Amira had her hair up in braids. They sat silently at the table without fidgeting.

With the school's assistant principal translating into Spanish, the man asked how they were doing and tried to engage them in conversation, with little success. Through the assistant principal, the man explained that they were not in trouble—the school just wanted to make sure everything was all right. He told them he would talk to their mom, then talk to each of them and go see their house. He assured them that he was not police; he was "just a social worker."

Indeed, the man was a Child Protective Services (CPS) investigator, called after the school felt that Ricky and Amira's mother had neglected their medical needs. Graciela, their mother, was in the middle of her fast-food shift when the school called saying that Amira had strep throat.

Graciela could not be on her phone at work, so she hung up, planning to return the call during her break. But by then, CPS had already been notified—exemplifying the US tendency to call on child protection authorities to manage marginalized families (Fong 2023).

As the investigator indicated to Ricky and Amira, CPS deploys social workers, rather than enforcement officers. He did not arrive at the school with lights and sirens; he did not wear a uniform or carry a gun.

And yet, scholars and activists underscore the similarities between CPS and police, referring to CPS as the "family policing system," given its reliance on surveillance and punishment (Rise 2021; Roberts 2020, 2022; upEND, n.d.). Low-income families of color like Graciela's are swept up into a system that investigates them and even separates them.

This chapter draws on fieldwork in Connecticut with families like Graciela's and the CPS staff who investigated them as a case study to elaborate entanglements between CPS and police. We show how these two institutions operate not only in parallel but in tandem. Beyond relying on similar logics to regulate marginalized populations, they also directly collaborate as each does its work, with CPS assisting and supporting police in carrying out policing efforts and vice versa.

Cogovernance

Scholars have long traced connections between child welfare and criminal legal systems. Dorothy Roberts wrote in 2002 that the two "institutions serve a similar social function. Both use blame and punishment to address the problems of the populations under their control" (2002, 206). At a macro level, both systems constitute part of a broader social policy regime that structures state responses to social problems and marginalized groups (Edwards 2016, 2019). They are central systems of poverty governance that primarily intervene with families and communities marginalized by race and/or class, especially Black and Native American families.

The child welfare and criminal legal systems operate under similar logics of governance, responding to social insecurity and poverty "by disciplining and shaping the behavior of a racialized and gendered poor population" (Woodward 2021, 430). Through paternalistic and punitive social control tactics, these systems endeavor to transform deviants—those who are deemed criminals or "bad" parents—into rational, responsible "good citizens" (Woodward 2021). In doing so, CPS operates akin to police. Legal scholars document parallels between CPS investigations and stop-and-frisk policing (Burrell 2019) and show how CPS investigators essentially perform law enforcement work (Ismail 2023).

Both systems also intervene in the very same families. As Roberts (2012) argues, prison and foster care overlap in the lives of poor mothers of color and their children. A considerable share of CPS-impacted children is also affected by parental incarceration, with Lawrence Berger and colleagues (2016) finding that 28 percent of Wisconsin children subject to a CPS report had a parent incarcerated in state prison or Milwaukee County Jail in the same month or the eleven months following the report. Nationally representative data show that among children who were subject to a CPS investigation and living at home, 30 percent lived with a primary caregiver who had been arrested (Phillips and Dettlaff 2009). Black children are especially likely to see their families entangled in both systems.

The two systems are gendered as well, drawing on notions of normative masculinity, femininity, motherhood, and fatherhood to identify, assess, and respond to those who are deemed in need of intervention (Woodward 2021). With policing largely focused on men and CPS sweeping up women in the same families and communities, it might seem reasonable to understand these systems as working in parallel, in a sort of poverty governance division of labor. We follow Dorothy Roberts (2022) in arguing that CPS and law enforcement not only work alongside each other, doing similar work in the same communities, but collaborate. As Roberts writes, "CPS staff not only act like police officers; they also work hand-in-hand with police officers" (2022, 191). Formal US child protection efforts originated with reformers coordinating closely with local law enforcement (Myers 2006). The most recent "best practice" guidelines continue to advise CPS staff to work with police (DePanfilis 2018). The ideal of interinstitutional, multidisciplinary collaboration is often taken for granted, with scholars and practitioners seeking to strengthen these partnerships (Casey Family Programs 2019; Newman and Dannenfelser 2005).

Law enforcement and CPS define some of the same situations as within their purview, inviting collaboration. For example, as Trivedi and Smith discuss in chapter 5 of this volume, states are increasingly constructing children's exposure to domestic violence as child maltreatment, following research documenting the adverse effects of this exposure on children's emotional, behavioral, and physical health (Henry 2017). Simultaneously, domestic violence is considered a criminal act that can prompt intervention by law enforcement (Fagan 1996).

Substance use, mental health needs, homelessness, and other adverse situations frequently draw the attention of both child welfare and policing authorities as well. Moreover, allegations of child physical and sexual abuse often fall under the jurisdiction of law enforcement, as severe forms of child maltreatment are considered criminal acts. Such situations may indeed have important implications for children's well-being, a topic that child maltreatment researchers have studied extensively (e.g., Gilbert et al. 2009).

This chapter focuses on tracing the collaborative practices that emerge across criminal legal and child welfare authorities. These practices, too, matter for children's well-being. A growing literature examines the negative consequences of police exposure for children and youth (Legewie and Fagan 2019; Rios 2011; Shedd 2015), as police have woven their way into the neighborhoods, schools, and community centers of children in marginalized communities. To the extent that CPS is another key institution working in tandem with police, children's experiences with CPS expand and intensify their families' exposure to policing. And, conversely, families' experiences with police expand and intensify their children's exposure to CPS.

Susan Phillips and colleagues (2010) identify multiple ways criminal legal and child welfare institutions intersect by analyzing case records of children removed from their homes. First, CPS sometimes became involved because parents were arrested or incarcerated; in other cases, CPS investigations exposed parents to arrests, including arrests on outstanding warrants. Second, caseworkers used criminal records to make claims about the threats parents posed and/or to evaluate relatives for custody placement. These important findings invite a broader examination beyond what we might see in case records. What do these relationships look like on the ground? Might CPS expose children and families to police beyond cases in which police make arrests and beyond cases in which children are removed? This chapter considers the wider scope of police-CPS entanglements.

Studying Police-CPS Collaborations in Connecticut

In 2018, the first author conducted fieldwork in two field offices of the Connecticut Department of Children and Families: one covering the city of New Haven and another covering a set of small towns in northeastern Connecticut. In New Haven, nearly all families involved with

CPS are Black or Latine; the northeastern office primarily intervenes with white families, with some Latine families as well, mirroring the racial/ethnic composition of the region.

Although there is no "typical" child welfare system, CPS in Connecticut operates similarly to agencies around the country. Reports of child abuse and neglect come into a central state hotline, where staff screen calls and route them to field offices. Field offices then assign caseworkers to assess the allegations, via either a "family assessment response" or a traditional investigation. Investigators have about six weeks to decide whether to substantiate the allegations and whether to keep the case open for ongoing CPS oversight. If the agency deems children unsafe at home, it can remove children from parents' custody. Connecticut receives approximately thirty thousand child maltreatment reports each year (authors' calculations), most of which allege neglect rather than abuse, in line with national data. Also consistent with patterns nationwide, Connecticut families' exposure to CPS varies substantially by race and class: families of color, especially Black families, are disproportionately reported, and reports are concentrated in poor neighborhoods and neighborhoods of color (Fong 2019b; USDHHS 2021). A national study of families involved in the child welfare system shows that well over half are below the poverty threshold, and the vast majority are low income (Dolan et al. 2011). In Connecticut, although family-level income data are not available, most CPS reports involve children living in neighborhoods with at least 10 percent of families below the federal poverty line, even though only 28 percent of Connecticut children reside in such areas (Fong 2019b).

To illuminate interinstitutional collaborations in practice, this chapter primarily draws on observations of CPS investigative work as well as nine interviews with law enforcement personnel (patrol officers, detectives, and a supervisor) in both areas, four in New Haven and five in northeastern Connecticut. These law enforcement interviews are part of a larger set of interviews with local professionals who are legally mandated to report suspected child abuse or neglect to CPS.[1] The interviews focused on interviewees' experiences reporting to CPS, as well as their relationships with, perceptions of, and recommendations for the agency. CPS observations involved shadowing investigators as they visited families as well as participating in other office activities, including staff meetings and training sessions. For this chapter, the first author reviewed all nine law enforcement interviews and all data excerpts (from other interviews and ethnographic field notes) mentioning police or law enforcement to inductively identify ways police and child protection work intersects at CPS's front door. We detail five key ways police and CPS are interwoven.

Police Trigger CPS Investigations

First, and most directly, police route families to CPS by filing reports of child abuse and neglect. In all fifty states, police are legally required to report suspected abuse and neglect to child protection authorities. They receive training on these reporting responsibilities and are subject to legal and financial penalties if they fail to report maltreatment.[2] Law enforcement professionals are consistently among the most frequent CPS reporters. In federal fiscal year 2019, they made nearly half a million reports—19 percent of all reports, eclipsed only by education personnel at 21 percent (USDHHS 2021). Police are thus a major entry point into CPS. Families' police interactions can trigger CPS interactions—probably more intensive ones—given higher substantiation rates among police-initiated reports (Edwards 2019).

In interviews, police officers shared how readily they turned to CPS, generally saying they did not hesitate to call. As an officer in a small town in northeast Connecticut shared, "If you have any questions, just make a referral." Whereas school personnel could be "gun shy," this officer explained that he preferred to make the CPS referral and let someone else decide. "If you think about CPS, then just call them," echoed a patrol officer in New Haven.[3] Even when patrol officers declined to call CPS—for instance, when they were called out for domestic violence but did not see children exposed to this violence—they said their supervisors sometimes had them file reports anyway, perhaps due to concerns about liability if the police department failed to report.

In line with CPS reporting more generally, police report Black families at higher rates than other families. Research documents racially biased decision-making among police officers—for instance, in deciding whether to stop and search someone (Gelman, Fagan, and Kiss 2007). This bias probably affects CPS reporting as well, channeling Black families, in particular, to CPS. In 2015, police reported approximately 1 percent of Black children nationwide to CPS authorities, nearly double the rate of white children (Edwards 2019).

Moreover, police are increasingly calling CPS. In recent years, CPS reports from police—especially reports of Black families—have risen, and, in turn, a growing share of CPS reports originate from police. Between 2002 and 2015, the proportion of children who experienced a police-initiated CPS report increased 60 percent among Black children, 39 percent among white children, and 23 percent among Latine children (Edwards 2019).

In a national study, Frank Edwards (2019) connects the spatial distribution of policing to unequal exposure to CPS. In counties with higher arrest rates, police report a greater share of families to CPS, accounting for county demographic and other characteristics.[4] The racialized geography of policing thus seeds a racialized geography of CPS exposure. Where police play a larger role in governing marginalized populations, police interventions spill over to give CPS a greater reach as well (see also Edwards 2016).

CPS is not just a passive receptacle for reports from police but can actively encourage these reports. Across the country, police, like other mandated reporters, receive training on their reporting responsibilities that urges them to report any and all suspicions of abuse and neglect, no matter how slight. CPS agencies may also facilitate police reports in particular. In Connecticut, police officers appreciated not having to call the public hotline number to make a report; they enjoyed a direct law enforcement line to expedite their reporting. "[CPS] stepped up when they got us a dedicated law enforcement line," remarked a patrol supervisor. "That's big for us as far as [helping with] time constraints."

Furthermore, police greatly appreciate having CPS as an option to call on. In interviews, police described how calling CPS helped alleviate their own workloads. A state trooper in northeastern Connecticut explained that his office struggled with persistent staff shortages, saying, "It's frustrating, because they want more and more from us, and there's less and less of us. That's why I said I worked fifteen hundred hours of overtime [last year]. Because there's no one to work." As such, he was relieved to be able to pass off families to CPS. If CPS could focus on children's needs, he said, "that's great, 'cause I don't have—and I know it's gonna come out wrong—I don't have the time." Likewise, police sometimes turned to CPS in part for practical reasons. For example, one case involved a toddler found unattended. "Obviously, we can't babysit her and can't expect the people who found her to babysit her," said the New Haven patrol officer called out to the case. "We're not set up for that. That's CPS. They're set up to do that." Police viewed CPS as compensating for some of their own limitations; in their view, CPS offered expertise, skills, and resources they lacked. Police thus help to determine the scope of child welfare interventions, a process that funnels many families, especially Black families and low-income families, to CPS in addition to facilitating police officers' own work.

Police Provide Backup Support in CPS Investigations

In addition to serving as a source of referrals to CPS, police also support the ensuing CPS investigations in multiple ways. For instance, CPS investigators rely on police—or the threat of police—to back them up when investigating families and removing children. On multiple occasions during the fieldwork, the researcher saw police accompany CPS to investigations and/or removals. This exposes children to police officers who come to their homes and schools to question their parents or stand guard with CPS social workers, which may make children apprehensive and anxious. In contexts of criminalization and injustice, police presence conveys a sense of exclusion, rather than safety, to marginalized youth (Bell 2017; Shedd 2015). Even as CPS may profess to want to help families rather than to police or punish them, their (real or potential) copresence with law enforcement to carry out investigative work belies this supportive aim.

Police assistance, or the possibility thereof, facilitates CPS's work in two ways. First, CPS sees calling on police as helpful in ensuring investigators' safety. Investigators in Connecticut articulated the personal risks involved in their work. One investigator described walking alone up back staircases to find families and said he often thought about how no one would find him if something happened. Investigators knew of CPS staff who had been assaulted on the job, and some had received detailed death threats against themselves and their families. They shared news stories about CPS workers in other states who had been severely hurt or even killed by parents who were frustrated with the agency.

In this context, Connecticut investigators appreciated the sense of security they felt police could provide. Connecticut CPS policy guidance notes that CPS may contact law enforcement when "the safety of a person, including the [investigator], may be at risk during the field response." A New Haven patrol officer explained her role with CPS: "You're just pretty much there a lot of times just to make sure nothing happens to them, 'cause we're talking about—people don't like CPS coming. . . . I'm glad we work together when necessary."

Even if, as observed in the research, police mostly stood around in the background, their presence provided reassurance to CPS workers. One removal observed during research involved a white family in the northeastern region living in public housing and involved with CPS due to poor housing conditions. The parents were upset but did not make any threats; the two uniformed police officers stood back without intervening. Even so, the investigator mused lightheartedly afterward that it was a good thing the police were there, or she "could have been punched and gone on medical leave." In an informal professional development session, a social worker in training expressed interest in investigations work but worried about her safety in such cases. The veteran investigator leading the session assured her that CPS staff generally knew which cases required additional caution. "Those are the referrals. Your supervisor says, 'Go with the police, or take a coworker,'" she said.

In particular, when removing children, CPS staff sought out police accompaniment. In a different informal professional development session a month prior, another experienced investigator advised a group of new social workers, "Don't ever do a removal without the police." As she explained, "you can't predict how people will respond," so police will make sure "we're safe." The investigator recalled one removal case in which the mother hit the investigator as the investigator was putting the child in her car. "She was then tackled by police, arrested for assault, . . . and they took her away." Though this investigator then articulated that instances of CPS staff's safety being threatened are rare, CPS investigators found uniformed police a reassuring presence when removing children.

CPS also relies on police when parents do not comply with CPS requests. CPS policy in Connecticut states, "If parents refuse entry into the home and there is reasonable cause to suspect that the child is at imminent risk of harm, [the investigator] shall contact the police and request assistance." In an informal professional development session, the group was discussing a hypothetical "dirty house" report. A new CPS social worker asked what to do if the parent refused to let them in. Both of the veteran investigators leading the session said they would call the police. One recalled a recent case in which this occurred: "We have the police out there, . . . so she let me in the house." (Police may not have warrants to enter homes, but their law enforcement authority may increase pressure on parents to comply with CPS.) In the fieldwork, reports regarding conditions of the home typically involved parents under stress, with limited social and economic support. Moreover, due to class and race biases, the "dirty houses" of privileged families may never come to CPS's attention. Thus, as we see, CPS can invoke police to investigate issues related to poverty. Likewise, in a training for prospective investigators, the trainer advised the group that if parents are refusing access to the child—for example, in a hypothetical case involving parents not taking children to medical care, another situation potentially related to resource constraints—investigators could have the police do a well-being check and respond together. "Police, sometimes their presence alone is enough to have parents say, 'Oh, okay, we'll go to the doctor.' Sometimes them just standing there can garner cooperation."

As this trainer recognized, police are a threatening presence that can pressure parents to acquiesce to CPS. Even if police are not physically copresent, CPS can invoke the possibility of police intervention to support the agency's directives. As an investigator emphatically directed a mother regarding her partner accused of domestic violence, "He better leave, or I'm calling [town] PD [police department]." And CPS does not even need to specifically threaten police intervention, because parents know it is a possibility. A mother under investigation explained that she allowed the CPS investigator into her home because she knew "what could happen: She could sit right at the bottom of that driveway . . . until the police officer comes. . . . They can sit right there until they have cause to take your children." Thus, whether explicitly stated or implicitly understood, police accompaniment facilitates CPS investigative work. Precisely because police represent coercive power, police presence helps CPS staff to feel safer and to cultivate compliance from parents.

Police Supply Information for CPS Investigations

CPS's investigative work also depends on police because of the information police provide. When conducting investigations, CPS relies on—and privileges—information from police. A key part of CPS investigations involves gathering information from "collateral contacts." In Connecticut's CPS policy, law enforcement stands atop the list of contacts, followed by schools, childcare providers, pediatricians, and others. Likewise, in an interview, a Massachusetts CPS investigator described her agency's typical response to a newborn with a positive toxicology screen: regarding collateral contacts, she explained in a matter-of-fact tone, "We would check how many times the police had been to the home or if there had been any police involvement. We'd want background checks, things like that—just pretty basic, standard stuff." Trainings for frontline CPS staff in Connecticut repeatedly reiterated the importance of requesting information from police. "You get so much information" from police reports, a trainer emphasized. In cases in which investigators thought the family might have had related police contact, such as domestic violence cases and cases involving medical or mental health crises, investigators tried to obtain police reports before visiting, if possible. In this way, police accounts can frame investigators' perceptions from the outset.

Police accounts are just that—accounts, subject to biases and misinformation—and low-income communities of color are especially exposed to police. CPS nevertheless sees police as a trusted information source and reviews police accounts uncritically. In a training session for new investigators, the trainer urged attendees to use critical thinking skills to assess parents' accounts. "Does this jibe with the police report?" he asked. "Is the family saying there's no substance use or family violence, and then you do an address search and find the police were called a lot for the parents being drunk?" As these comments indicate, police records are held up as objective accounts against which others can be compared.

During the fieldwork, the researcher never heard CPS staff question information contained in police reports. Information from police checks and police reports was highly regarded, seen as absolute truth. In one case, the investigator was not sure what to make of domestic violence allegations upon meeting with the mother. Later, the investigator came by to tell the researcher that she had just received the police reports on the case: "four within a month!" She had an exaggerated, expressive reaction to this information. The investigator presented the police reports, which were quite lengthy, with a page or more of small text detailing each situation. With these reports, the investigator's uncertainty vanished: she relayed that the mother was afraid of CPS, "for good reason." This mother might indeed have been subjected to serious domestic violence and in need of support; the point here is to highlight how influential police reports are in CPS's assessments. To the agency, police reports become concrete evidence justifying CPS's oversight. This evidence builds a narrative of deficient parenting—in the case of domestic violence, a narrative of a mother's supposed "failure to protect" her children from exposure to domestic violence, which can prompt child removal.

To CPS, police contact crystallizes conditions that CPS may find difficult to nail down. For instance, one investigator explained, "It's hard to gauge drinking, outside of an incident coming to the home from the police or something like that, where the police report [that] Mom was intoxicated during a domestic fight or something like that." Likewise, in the domestic violence case mentioned earlier, the mother did not want to acknowledge domestic violence to the investigator. The investigator explained that she would request police records as part of CPS's process; if police reports revealed a domestic violence incident, "that's kinda some confirmation." When CPS questioned parents about domestic violence or arguments, they often asked whether anyone had been arrested or whether the police had been called. In marginalized communities, residents may call on police to resolve interpersonal disputes or obtain services (Bell 2017; Goffman 2014). Yet, despite the unequal racial and spatial distribution of policing, CPS views conditions that come to the attention of police as more serious, necessitating more intensive CPS intervention. This intervention, in turn, can end up penalizing parents in highly policed communities by responding to the challenges they face with scrutiny and child removal rather than resources and assistance.

Police decisions carry considerable weight and can shape CPS cases. In one case involving a child found unattended outside, the investigator initially reserved judgment on the situation. "I'm waiting to see the police report," she said, adding, "I like to go out with the police report, because it usually has more information in it regarding what people said or what happened. . . . That will be more telling." But, she reasoned, "the police not charging [the mother] goes a long way." In a different case involving another child found unattended, CPS decided to substantiate the allegations. The investigator explained that they go by the police's "risk of injury" charge, and in this case, the caregiver was arrested.

Police records also inform the options families have when CPS investigates. In some cases, CPS institutes "safety plans"—often, short-term informal custody arrangements after CPS identifies conditions it deems unsafe. When devising these plans, CPS conducts criminal background checks on those whom the agency might ask to care for the children temporarily. A pattern of "continuous criminal justice contact," a trainer explained, would raise flags, consistent with the findings of Phillips and colleagues (2010). "Make sure you're doing your due diligence. Check police and CPS records before you're partnering with people." In one case, a mother had a twin sister who wanted to care for the baby. The CPS supervisor pointed out that the sister had multiple domestic violence incidents involving the police. The sister replied that that was several years ago and that she had left that partner completely. The supervisor said that, nevertheless, it had happened multiple times and domestic violence was "not a one-time thing." As such, CPS did not pursue the sister as a potential caregiver for the baby. Of course, not all families' domestic violence incidents come to the attention of the police—for example, those in single-family homes with spacious yards may not have neighbors close enough to overhear, and some social service providers and/or social networks may have resources to respond to domestic violence without involving the police. Here, too, we see how policing as a means of governing marginality opens up additional spheres of surveillance and reshapes family life unequally along lines of race, class, and gender.

Police and CPS Formally Collaborate, Blurring Interorganizational Boundaries

Not only do CPS and police collaborate out of habit or chance, but formal organizational structures support their teamwork (see also Roberts 2022). Such arrangements, heralded as a way to break down silos between agencies, can take several forms. First, CPS may designate liaisons to the local police and may even colocate staff. The offices where the researcher conducted fieldwork placed frontline investigative staff within local police departments, where they could serve as resources for police and CPS alike. These "outposted" workers could help police with situations and questions related to children; they could also use their police department access to pull police reports more expeditiously for their CPS colleagues. A police detective reflected on the CPS investigator housed in his office, whose desk was right next to his: "I like having [her] in. It's nice to be able to bounce questions back and forth. If I need something, she's here." As he explained, "Something pops up, we can just hit the ground running. She'll drop whatever she's doing at that point. We'll go out and address it just immediate. It's nice to be in my position, where I can have a lot of those contacts, where I can make phone calls to people, where you can talk to some of the girls on the road [i.e., CPS investigators]." As we see, police and CPS are explicitly overlapping—rather than separate—entities, fostering close working relationships.

Second, police and CPS work on cases together. Sometimes this involves direct collaboration on individual investigations. A detective explained regarding cases in which her office and CPS are both investigating, "Instead of interviewing everybody separately, we do it as a joint investigation. I do that quite frequently with CPS, and it always works." More generally, "multidisciplinary teams," a common practice around the country, aim to facilitate information sharing and interagency coordination in sexual abuse cases, severe physical abuse cases, and other complex cases in which CPS and law enforcement are involved (Herbert and Bromfield 2019). In Connecticut, these multidisciplinary teams are written into state statute (Conn. Gen. Stat. § 17a-106a [2018]). In regular meetings, the Connecticut multidisciplinary teams convened people from the state attorney's office, hospital child-abuse specialists, and others, as well as police and CPS. In a training session for new

CPS investigators, a trainer explained that these teams provide an opportunity to share information and get updates; they do not need parents to sign an information release allowing CPS and other members of the interdisciplinary team to share information across agencies, as would be needed in other information-sharing efforts. Beyond these multidisciplinary teams, New Haven also has a widely praised Child Development–Community Policing program in which police, CPS, mental health providers, and others meet weekly to review and coordinate on cases. The program embraces police partnerships as a means of addressing children's exposure to violence, suggesting that police can "capitaliz[e] on their roles as representatives of control and authority in the face of violent and traumatic events" (Yale Child Study Center, n.d.).

Third, "child advocacy centers" across the country serve children who may have experienced sexual or severe physical abuse (National Children's Alliance, n.d.). At these centers, children participate in forensic interviews so they do not have to recount their experience multiple times. CPS, law enforcement, and others view the live interview feed together, a physical copresence that encourages collaboration. In observations, they treated one another collegially as teammates, each sharing information and looking to make the other's job easier. For example, one case involved possible touching of a young girl by a neighbor. As we waited for the forensic interview to begin, the detective introduced herself to the CPS investigator, sharing that the police knew the neighbor well. The detective noted that the neighbor had no history of anything like this and was "very drunk." "Early in the morning? And he was already wasted?" the CPS investigator asked. "Yeah, he's always wasted," the detective replied.

The CPS investigator then said that she had investigated the girl's family recently because the home was "really gross"; she advised the detective not to go in. The CPS investigator closed the door, presumably to talk candidly about the case. They exchanged information about the case at hand, with each sharing what she had heard from various parties about the incident under investigation. Beyond that incident, the CPS investigator also gave the detective her take on the girl's mother, who was not under criminal investigation. The CPS investigator said that she had made referrals to assist the mother with hygiene and resources. The mother, she noted, was "lacking in a lot of resources," and CPS had "a lot of concerns." The CPS investigator reiterated her distaste for the family's home, which she said had a foul odor and sticky floors: "I leave, and I smell. It's gross." After the forensic interview, the detective and the CPS investigator swapped contact information. The researcher stepped out to speak with the mother and returned to see the detective and CPS investigator talking together in hushed tones. The detective told the CPS investigator to just call if she needed anything.

As we see, this forensic interview brought CPS and the police together to build a collegial, collaborative relationship. Formal structures enable informal conversations about families. In one view, doing so breaks down silos; in another, it enables one agency's judgments about a family or situation to ripple out to affect another's. CPS and the police join forces to govern poverty. Their paychecks may come from different arms of the state, but interagency boundaries are blurred when they work in the same offices and attend the same meetings. Together, they figure out what to do with families. CPS may aspire to present a softer side of the state, but the agency's formal collaborations align it squarely with law enforcement. They are, quite literally, side by side, a unified front in their engagement with marginalized families.

CPS Expands the Reach of Policing and Criminal Legal Intervention

In a final mechanism of collaboration, just as police call on and provide information to CPS, CPS does the same for police and other representatives of the penal state, in ways that can trigger or exacerbate criminal legal entanglements. CPS sharing parents' (or others') disclosures with police may be especially concerning because, with broad data-sharing agreements and releases of information, parents may not know CPS will pass along their statements to police. Police, in turn, can use the information in ways that parents neither anticipate nor want. The social work scholar Alan Dettlaff recalled that during his years as a CPS investigator in Texas, "the police routinely asked me to interview parents, specifically because I did not have to provide Miranda warnings. Then they would use their data sharing agreement to access everything the parents said [and] use it against them."[5] Parents may share information with CPS in an effort to cooperate with them or because CPS offers the promise of assistance. But as we see, any support CPS may offer comes hand in hand with the possibility of punishment—and not only within the child welfare system. CPS and police are so tightly intertwined that parents' disclosures can enable further surveillance and criminalization by law enforcement authorities.

In a Connecticut case, a mother's boyfriend signed a release of information allowing the CPS investigator to speak with his probation officer. But this release of information did not specify what CPS could or could not share. The investigator called the probation officer, first asking whether the boyfriend was from another state (as a search of CPS records in Connecticut had not yielded anything) and whether he was "okay around a four-year-old." Then, unprompted, the investigator shared the name of the motel where the family was staying, adding the room number: "in case you need it." She mentioned to the probation officer that the boyfriend asked her not to tell the probation officer that he was at the motel, as he wanted to share this himself. This investigator aligned herself with the probation officer rather than with the family who had confided in her. In informing the probation officer about the boyfriend's whereabouts, she facilitated the criminal legal system's surveillance.

CPS can also expand and deepen criminal legal system involvement by calling on—and urging others to call on—law enforcement. CPS encourages parents themselves to turn to the police in domestic violence and other situations, then rewards those who do as exhibiting an "appropriate" response, even as some parents may have (justified) concerns about summoning armed officers to their homes. While visiting one mother in a domestic violence case, for example, the investigator devised a safety plan with her. The plan stated that she would abide by the protective order and call the police if her partner came to her home. He added that it "might not be the worst idea" to have the police come over and take a report after he left. "The second I step out the door, call," he advised. The mother said that her children would be scared if they arrived home from school to find the police there; the investigator replied that that was better than the children being scared that she was hurt. The investigator gave her the phone numbers of a domestic violence hotline and the police, advising her on what she might say to the police. Here CPS encouraged not only social services uptake but also police uptake, even as parents attuned to their children's well-being—especially Black parents like this mother—might have understandable hesitations about involving police and might prefer to address situations like domestic violence through other means (see also Goodmark 2011). In this investigator's view, ensuring the family's safety necessitated law enforcement intervention, exemplifying CPS's active role in policing families.

CPS staff members can also reach out to police themselves in ways that implicate (often, marginalized) people and subject them to further criminalization and punishment. For instance, the researcher observed how CPS's outreach to police, probation officers, and others led domestic violence perpetrators (fathers or mothers' boyfriends) to be arrested or rearrested, against mothers' wishes. In one such case, the investigator called the parole officer of the mother's boyfriend and informed the parole officer about a recent police contact at the family's home, of which the officer had not been aware. "My question to you: Is there a way you can get him out of the house?" the investigator asked. After hanging up, the investigator noted that he hoped to get the boyfriend locked up again, and indeed, the boyfriend was incarcerated within weeks, on the basis of the information CPS provided his parole officer. The mother was upset with CPS's response, which disrupted her own plans and did not address the longer-term situation. But she could not stop its course. Once her situation came to CPS's attention, CPS alerted the parole officer, and her boyfriend was swiftly taken back to jail. "I was already taking steps on figuring out what I need to do for me and my kids," she said afterward, reflecting that CPS's involvement "just made it worse."

In another example of CPS expanding criminalization, the parents of a newborn baby became upset after the CPS investigator visited them at the hospital. (The researcher did not observe these interactions but heard the staff involved in the case recounting them shortly thereafter.) Due to the parents' distress, the investigator suggested that the hospital have security around. The police came and ran the parents' names through their computer system while milling about. Upon doing so, they realized the mother had an outstanding warrant for failure to appear on a marijuana charge and took her in. CPS thus channeled the mother back to the criminal legal system, the intervention of which—jailing and perhaps fining her—would probably only impede her ability to care for her newborn. The criminal legal contact then opened up further surveillance by CPS, as CPS staff mentioned this warrant at the meeting where they ultimately decided to remove the baby from the parents' custody.

Thus, CPS and police jointly surveil and govern marginalized populations: Police alert CPS. CPS alerts the police. CPS relies on information and backup from police. CPS, in turn, offers interventions and information that bolster police efforts. And on and on—all of this collaboration supported by formal and informal structures. Police and CPS agencies have made considerable efforts to break down silos. Indeed, for marginalized families in particular, getting caught up in one system makes one visible and vulnerable to the other.

Conclusion

You'll have the ones where . . . hospital makes a referral to
CPS. Then CPS has to come and check the home, see how
they're living, and they'll call us to come to the house. CPS is
a service. Police is a service. Fire is a service. Everybody is a
service, and we're all working together to serve a community.
—police officer in New Haven

Examining the entanglements of two supposedly distinct systems of poverty governance—police and CPS—we show how they are not ultimately that different or separate. CPS investigative practices are intertwined in multiple ways with policing. Each relies on and feeds the other, facilitating each system's work. Referrals, information, and support flow from one to the next and back again. These practices are deeply entrenched, woven into routine patterns of activity (Roberts 2022).

As scholars have emphasized, racialized poverty governance occurs in interactions across, and in relationships between, supposedly distinct agencies, organizations, and systems (Lara-Millán 2017; Paik 2021; Seim 2020). In the case of police and CPS, we see how cross-institutional collaborations create "feedback loops" (Haney 2018) that expand and deepen marginalized families' exposure to systems of social control. Police and CPS shuttle families—and their personal information—back and forth; sometimes they even show up together. Encountering one system makes a family vulnerable to the other.

Researchers and practitioners have typically focused on identifying and removing barriers to police-CPS collaboration, advocating for more seamless coordination across systems (Cross, Finkelhor, and Ormrod 2005; Newman and Dannenfelser 2005). Thus, this interinstitutional collaboration is not incidental but intentional, undertaken with an aim of breaking down silos. But breaking down silos, in another light, means more centralized and expansive social control of marginalized populations; misunderstandings involving one's children can lead to law enforcement involvement, and gratuitous police stops can put one at risk of forcible family separation. Given the trauma of police and CPS encounters alike, we should be moving to shrink, rather than expand, the reach of these systems into people's lives. Doing so will require attention not only to each system individually but also to their points of connection, to the ways each system bolsters the other.

As we saw with Ricky and Amira's investigator, CPS likes to distinguish itself from police. But upon closer examination, CPS's work is deeply entangled with policing. As such, CPS cannot separate itself from the punitive, carceral state; it is part and parcel of it, a willing and even eager participant. The two systems are tied together in a symbiotic relationship.

NOTES

1   For more details on the larger research project, which also included interviews with investigated mothers and CPS investigators, see Fong 2020, 2023.

2   In Connecticut, mandated reporters' failure to report constitutes a misdemeanor and, in more extreme cases, a felony, carrying a penalty of up to one year in prison and/or up to a $2,000 fine (Callahan 2020). For a national summary, see CWIG 2019a.

3   For consistency, this chapter substitutes "CPS" for interviewees' references to the Connecticut Department of Children and Families.

4   Within-county increases in arrest rates are also associated with increases in police-initiated CPS reports, although the magnitude of these predicted increases is smaller.

5   Alan Dettlaff (@AlanDettlaff), "When I was a CPS worker, the police routinely asked me to interview parents, specifically because I did not have to provide Miranda warnings." Twitter, June 7, 2001, 6:03 a.m., https://twitter.com/AlanDettlaff/status/1401887590807126024.

10

Under Surveillance

Immigrant Children and Families Caught between the Child
Welfare and Immigration Enforcement Systems

KRISTINA K. LOVATO

As a single undocumented mother trying to make ends meet following a partnership destroyed by intimate partner violence, Maria lived in
a small apartment in New York City and worked as a nanny. One eve-
ning, a neighbor called 911 to report what sounded like violence in the
home. The police arrested both Maria and her partner. Child Protective
Services (CPS) placed Lola, three years old, into temporary foster care
with strangers. Maria was charged with emotional abuse. At the time of
booking, Maria's fingerprints were automatically sent to Immigration and
Customs Enforcement (ICE) and checked against the Criminal Apprehension Program—formerly known as Secure Communities—a data-sharing
program that gathers information about people who have been arrested
and sends the information both to the FBI and to the US Department of
Health and Human Services (DHHS) to flag for potential immigration
violations. ICE flagged Maria for deportation and issued a hold.

Within thirty days, Maria was sent to an immigration detention center two hundred miles away. Her court-appointed attorney was unable
to locate her, and she missed her initial dependency court hearing. The
court kept Lola in foster care. Two months later, Maria's attorney located
her and informed her of her next hearing, but ICE refused to trans-
port her. After significant effort, Maria arranged to call the court, and
Child Protective Services presented a reunification plan that included
mandatory parenting classes, domestic violence support, finding secure
housing, and parent-child visits. ICE detention prevented Maria from
complying with any part of this case plan. CPS developed the permanency plan with two possible outcomes: (1) if Maria was released from

ICE detention, CPS would attempt to reunify her with her daughter as long as she was not living with the formerly abusive partner; or (2) Maria's parental rights would be terminated if she was not released from ICE custody and/or was deported and could not meet the case-plan requirements. Lola would then be placed for adoption.

Nine months after separation, Lola turned four years old and was still in foster care. She had lost her ability to speak Spanish. After eleven months in detention, Maria was deported to her home country of Honduras. CPS did not know how or where to find her and did not contact the Honduran consulate for assistance. Maria moved in with relatives in Honduras. She contacted the US child welfare worker to request that Lola be relocated to live with her. CPS confirmed that it would not consider reunification in Honduras until Maria arranged a home study, completed a domestic violence support group and parenting classes, and secured employment. Within seventeen months, Maria was close to completing the service plan, but CPS petitioned to terminate her parental rights, as the federal deadline of twenty-two months was near. Lola continued to live with her foster parents in New York City and experienced ongoing nightmares, sadness, crying bouts, anxiety, longing for her mother, and a lost connection to her cultural heritage.[1]

＊ ＊ ＊

During the Trump administration, the Department of Homeland Security (DHS) used family separation as a weapon to deter migration to the United States. Images of migrant children being separated from their parents and detained in crowded cages flooded the media, evoking widespread condemnation of the inhumane family-separation policy (Dickerson 2022). ICE collaborated with local child welfare agencies throughout the United States not only to police parents but also to deport them. The separation and incarceration of poor immigrant families of color reflect the punitive functions of ICE, DHHS, and CPS.

As Maria and Lola's story highlights, undocumented families face additional risks around child welfare involvement because of the possibility of detention and deportation. Detentions and deportations have largely targeted Latine migrants from Mexico and Central America, primarily El Salvador, Guatemala, and Honduras (Ryo and Peacock 2018). Many immigrant families, especially poor and/or undocumented ones, are at greater risk of child welfare system involvement compared to middle-class, white families, who typically have more resources and are less likely to be suspected of child maltreatment. Lower socioeconomic status often leads to increased surveillance by mandated reporters in social service settings that many immigrants use to meet their health and educational needs (Fong 2020; Lee 2016; Roberts 2002). This chapter is about undocumented families whose experiences of being involved in the child welfare system are shaped by their "illegality" and their social position as mostly low-income individuals of color. Focusing on the parents and children who are caught at the intersections of immigration and child welfare, I argue that the marginalized race, class, and gender statuses of many immigrants intersect to place them in danger of child welfare system involvement and thus put their children at risk of separation and the resulting trauma that can affect long-term health and development (AIC 2021).

Immigration Policy Landscape

The United States has a history of exclusionary immigration policies, obstruction of citizenship, and deportation of people of color. It has historically excluded immigrants who are not racialized as "white," adopting policies such as the 1790 Uniform Rule of Naturalization Act and the 1882 Chinese Exclusion Act (Kanstroom 2010). More recently, the Illegal Immigration Reform and Immigrant Responsibility Act (1996) dramatically limited the rights of noncitizens facing deportation, expanded the types of offenses marked for deportation, and permitted retroactive deportation. The USA PATRIOT Act of 2001 also implemented broader immigration enforcement, making it more difficult for immigrants to obtain legal permanent residence or to access social services (Brabeck and Xu 2010; Hagan, Rodriguez, and Castro 2011).

During the George W. Bush and Obama administrations (2000–2016), deportations from the United States reached historically high levels, without explicit priorities in place for arrest and removal. The Trump administration's 2018 Zero Tolerance policy for people entering the country without authorization reestablished restrictive enforcement practices, which dramatically expanded the categories of individuals classified as "priorities for removal" and made nonviolent infractions, including unlawful entry, deportable offenses (Greenberg et al. 2019; Pierce and Bolter 2020). Before this, immigrant children were sometimes separated from their families at the border, but not as explicit federal policy. According to DHS (USDHS 2023b), the Trump administration systematically separated over four thousand children from their parents at the US southwestern border—including children and parents who were exercising their legal right to seek asylum; this was the shocking culmination of a series of policy decisions by successive administrations targeting Latine immigrants for separation, detention, and deportation. As of September 2023, over one thousand children were still waiting to be reunified with their families nearly five years after the implementation of Trump's Zero Tolerance policy (USDHS 2023b).

According to US Immigration and Customs Enforcement (2021), official deportations of members of family units spiked to approximately 14,500 in 2020 and diminished during the pandemic, as Title 42, an emergency health order, prevented asylum seekers from entering the United States in the first place. After a federal judge blocked the use of Title 42 on children, thousands of children who were sent back to Mexico with their parents/guardians reentered the United States unaccompanied in order to escape dangerous border camps, where families who were unable to enter were waiting. While forced family separations diminished under President Biden, US authorities reported at least 142 children separated from their families in fiscal year 2022 (USDHS 2023a). While separating far fewer families, the Biden administration largely chose to maintain or enact policies that harm asylum-seeking families, such as by creating a dedicated immigration court to adjudicate and expedite family cases at the southwestern border. In addition, during spring 2023, ICE created the punitive Family Expedited Removal Management (FERM) program, which places parents and children apprehended at the US border into a rapid screening process to identify asylum claims; this has essentially become a policy of rapid removal. Families who are admitted to await a court hearing are kept under heavy surveillance (National Immigrant Justice Center 2023). Altogether, the apprehension, detention, and removal of immigrants continue to be significant stressors for Latine communities in the United States.

Beyond separating the families of asylum seekers, the Trump administration also sought to make it more difficult for low-income immigrants to enter the United States through legal channels. In 2019, the Trump administration amended the Public Charge Ground of Inadmissibility rule, making it more difficult for immigrants to obtain permanent residency or earn a visa if an applicant was dependent on—or seemed likely to become dependent on—government aid, such as Medicaid, which was formerly not included in public charge determinations (USCIS 2019). Even before this proposed rule was implemented, it led many immigrant families, often including citizen children, to avoid seeking assistance, including health-care coverage and other aid for which they were eligible (Bernstein et al. 2019). In December 2022, the much-anticipated Biden administration public charge regulations rolled back Trump's amendment to public charge determinations and provided clarifications about which immigrants are exempt and when the receipt of public benefits will be considered in a public charge determination. Once again, Medicaid, the Supplemental Nutrition Assistance Program (SNAP), housing assistance, and other noncash benefits are exempt from public charge determinations (National Immigration Law Center 2022; USDHS 2022).

The Challenges Faced by Immigrant Families

Poverty puts families at risk of surveillance and accusations of neglect; most families in the child welfare system are poor. Thus, higher rates of poverty among immigrants, and especially undocumented immigrants, increase their risk of child welfare system involvement (Dettlaff 2012). As of 2021, 27 percent of children in immigrant families were reportedly living in low-income households with at least one working parent, compared to 18 percent of children in US-born families (Annie E. Casey Foundation 2021). In addition, many immigrant families face language barriers, low levels of formal education, and—in the case of undocumented immigrants—legal barriers to formal employment. Twenty percent of children in immigrant families lack a parent with a high school diploma, leading to limited parental employment opportunities and low economic earning power (Anderson and Hemez 2022). Children of immigrants are also more likely to live in overcrowded housing, defined by the US Census Bureau as more than two people per bedroom, and are at greater risk of inadequate nutrition than are children of US-born parents (Dettlaff and Fong 2016). Yet, immigrant families are less likely to receive public benefits (e.g., Temporary Assistance for Needy Families [TANF] and SNAP; see Chaudry and Fortuny 2010) and have health insurance (KFF 2023).

Since the mid-1990s, policies targeting immigrant families have exacerbated economic disparities by restricting immigrants' access to services and programs while limiting their rights. The 1996 Personal Responsibility and Work Opportunity Reconciliation Act (PRWORA) enacted the five-year bar, which requires even lawful permanent residents who arrived in the United States after 1996 to wait five years before they can enroll in federally funded programs such as Medicaid, SNAP, TANF, and Supplemental Security Income (SSI) (Harrington 2020). As a result, PRWORA changed documented immigrants' access to public health insurance in two ways: directly, by denying Medicaid benefits for five years, and indirectly, by denying or limiting immigrants' participation in TANF, which is an important entry point into accessing Medicaid.

This rule exacerbated economic and racial inequities and harmed children and families. Immigrants' use of these means-tested programs fell sharply after the passage of the federal law (Fix 2009), raising concerns that the fear or stigma associated with PRWORA may have led even those immigrants who were eligible for benefits to avoid applying. Further, undocumented immigrants, regardless of when they arrived, remain ineligible for nearly all public aid.

For undocumented families, in addition to risks associated with poverty come the risks of detention and deportation, which further enhance their vulnerability to child welfare system involvement (Dettlaff and Fong 2016). Despite these risks, there is little data on how many children are in state care because of deportations. Over a decade ago, Seth Wessler (2011) identified at least fifty-one hundred children in foster care in the United States resulting from immigration enforcement. Projections from the same study placed the number of children of immigrants in foster care at fifteen thousand by 2016. In 2019, ICE deported 27,980 people who claimed to have at least one US-born child (AIC 2021). While many children of deported parents do not end up in the child welfare system, as they may be cared for by their other parent or by family members, more deportations inevitably mean more children of immigrants entering foster care. These forced family separations have important consequences for family economic security and cohesion and for the mental health and well-being of children (Greenberg et al. 2019).

Surveillance under the Neoliberal Therapeutic State

During the late twentieth century, an intellectual and economic movement known as "neoliberalism" emerged, joining forces with right-wing religious interests and imposing paternalistic governance on those who were poor, treating them like children who "[lack] the capacity to know what is in [their] best interest and [have] yet to develop the self-discipline needed to act effectively on such knowledge" (Soss, Fording, and Schram 2011, 23). This approach to governance leads institutions working with poor families, including child welfare agencies, to presume that poor individuals require "personal and family transformation" to comply with expectations of economic self-sufficiency and middle-class notions of good parenting. The power that the child welfare system wields can be used to punish these families if they do not demonstrate the behavioral changes that the "therapeutic state" seeks (Polsky 1991, 3–4).

Once families enter the child welfare system because of supposed maltreatment, the state expects parents who are deemed unfit to engage in therapy and parenting education so that they may become "responsible parents," and family courts enforce strict compliance (Lee 2016). The modern therapeutic state requires knowledge of participants' intimate and personal lives (Fong 2023; Polsky 1991). For many low-income immigrant families, engaging in social support services leads to distressing and coercive surveillance. For example, everyday behaviors—like going for a doctor's visit or a child going to school—involve observation and tracking by mandated reporters, including health professionals, educational personnel, and law enforcement officers, making immigrant families hypervisible and vulnerable to the state. In essence, human service and helping institutions, such as schools and health-care settings, become part of state policing and control efforts.

However, surveillance is not only a tool of punishment; it is sometimes a conduit for support as well (Lyon 2002). These dual qualities—the possibility of obtaining needed material or therapeutic support, such as housing and mental health services, alongside the threat of forcible intervention—shape the child welfare system. In turn, the system widely investigates family and domestic life by drawing referrals from social services, community-based agencies, and health-care, educational, and law enforcement organizations (Fong 2020; Lee 2016). For immigrant families who may avoid accessing services because of a fear of detention and deportation, the dual feature of surveillance as a means of identifying needs for support and controlling marginalized populations creates a complex tension. The fear of child welfare involvement and the fear of immigration enforcement are thus intertwined.

Forced Family Separations

In addition to the scrutiny experienced by many poor families of color, undocumented parents of color also face immigration-related surveillance by police and immigration enforcement systems, which adds to their risk of child welfare involvement. In Wessler's (2011) pivotal report on undocumented children and the child welfare system, he discusses three ways the immigration enforcement and child welfare systems intersect. First, in many cases, immigrant children enter foster care because of their parents' arrest or detention, as illustrated in Maria and Lola's story (Wessler 2011). Mass incarceration has resulted in the disproportionate imprisonment not only of African Americans but also of Latines, Native Americans, and some Asian Americans. In fact, the Hispanic incarceration rate—including immigration-related detentions—is between two and three times higher than that of non-Hispanic whites (Carson 2022). Disproportionate imprisonment rates are not explained by disproportionate rates of criminal activity but rather result from discriminatory practices and decisions at every stage of the law enforcement and criminal justice systems (Alexander 2010). Undocumented residents may be detained by ICE directly or arrested by police and then issued an ICE hold, which could result in CPS taking custody of their child(ren) (Wessler 2011). Even when family members are available to care for the children—and despite laws that privilege kinship placement over foster care with nonrelatives—many states prevent the placement of children with undocumented residents, or in some cases, even authorized noncitizens, despite kinship ties (Ayón, Aisenberg, and Cimino 2013; Greenberg et al. 2019).

The second way a child of undocumented parents may enter the child welfare system is when a case entails an allegation of child maltreatment that brings a family to the attention of both CPS and ICE simultaneously (Wessler 2011). As we saw with Maria and Lola, when immigration enforcement is involved in CPS investigations, what might have been a clear case resulting in prompt reunification will often result in an ICE hold, detention, and forced family separation when parents are undocumented. In many cases, ICE arrests are solely because of a parent's immigration status and not connected to child-welfare-related issues (such as abuse or neglect). Once parents are detained, they are denied the due process right to advocate for themselves in juvenile court, where child welfare custody cases are heard (Wessler 2011).

The third path to forced family separation for undocumented parents and their children, according to Wessler (2011), may begin with a substantiated child maltreatment situation that is then exacerbated by a parent's detention, interrupting reunification efforts. Regardless of the path into the child welfare system, having a child removed from the home is a devastating experience for parents, one that is made much more difficult for those like Maria who are at risk of detention and deportation. Forced family separations are also likely to be experienced as traumatic by children like Lola, who suffer the deleterious effects at the intersection of immigration enforcement and child welfare involvement. The detention and removal of a parent may also have serious implications for family economic security, cohesion, and mental health (Dettlaff and Fong 2016; Lovato 2019). Deportation-related family separations may involve multiple trauma-inducing experiences for youth, who may witness the forcible removal of a parent, resulting in the sudden loss of a caregiver and/or the abrupt loss of their family home environment. Such traumatic events may cause significant psychological and emotional consequences for deportees and their family members, including increased risk for mental health problems such as psychological distress, anxiety, depression, insomnia, fear, and worry (See, for example, Allen, Cisneros, and Tellez 2015; Lovato and Abrams 2021; Zayas et al. 2015).

Required Services and Family Reunification

Parents who are involved with the child welfare system are required to complete long and often complicated service plans to reunify with their children, typically consisting of both therapeutic and economic elements. Parents must address their problems and fulfill requirements quickly, often with little to no assistance. In 1997, the enactment of the Adoption and Safe Families Act (ASFA; P.L. 105-89 [1997]) accelerated the timeline for parents to complete their service plan, as states are expected to move toward terminating parental rights after a child has been in foster care for fifteen of the past twenty-two months. Service-plan expectations that might be possible for middle-class families may be unattainable for the low-income families who constitute the overwhelming majority of child welfare clients, especially for low-income immigrants and parents of color (Lee 2016). Caseworkers generally develop a case plan addressing why the family entered the system and requiring parents to complete services within a six- to twelve-month time frame. For example, a parent might be required to attend a parenting or anger-management class, complete mental health and/or substance use treatment, and/or secure housing. Parents must attend meetings and appointments, often requiring additional hours of waiting and commuting time. Appointments for services are often available only within normal working hours, which may pose problems for working parents without access to flexible schedules or paid time off. Also, services that are on a sliding scale or accessible to low-income people often have long wait lists (Lee 2016).

Attending to these case-plan requirements may be even more complicated for immigrant and especially undocumented families than for other poor families. Difficulties completing requirements quicky due to an overburdened system and barriers of poverty are further compounded by legal status, detention, and deportation, thus increasing immigrant parents' risk of having their parental rights terminated (Ayón 2009; Wessler 2011). Immigrant families who lack legal authorization may also experience barriers to fulfilling their reunification-plan obligations because of a lack of bilingual and culturally competent services (Dettlaff and Fong 2016). In addition, parents who are fearful of or unfamiliar with therapy or distrustful of state involvement because of the

restrictive immigration-enforcement climate or experiences in their former countries of residence may also experience difficulty in complying
(Fong 2020).

In addition to the services required of most parents seeking reunification, there are also expectations of financial self-sufficiency. While difficult for all poor families, these expectations are particularly difficult for
immigrant families, who are often ineligible for vital supportive services,
such as housing and cash aid, which are essential for them to regain
custody of their children. In addition, immigrant parents' legal statuses
may prevent them from obtaining employment or meeting other requirements that could facilitate reunification (Dettlaff and Fong 2016).

Children may also be thwarted from reunifying with parents because
of the lack of coordination between the immigration and child welfare
systems, which may prevent immigrant parents from attending their
children's court hearings. Biases or misinterpretations of agency policy
among staff often prevent reunification with undocumented parents,
parents who do not speak English, and parents living outside the United
States; thus, parents who have been deported for no reason other than
their immigration status are frequently blocked from reunifying with
their children (Casey Family Programs 2020).

Once parents are detained and their children are in CPS custody, parents are separated from their children and prevented from participating in case plans and advocating for their families. Communication and
visitation can be challenging when immigrant parents are transported
to detention far from where they were apprehended. These issues can
be further exacerbated by other factors, such as strict visitation rules or
the high cost of telephone calls from within detention centers, where
incarcerated people and their families pay an average of five dollars
for a thirty-minute call, which can add up quickly (AIC 2020; Rascoe
2022). As depicted in Maria and Lola's experience, the termination of
parental rights and permanency timelines move forward, while detained
parents are largely powerless to complete their case plans, revealing a
complex tension. Even when courts recognize the significant barriers
facing detained parents and do not find the parents to be noncompliant, courts will rarely slow the ASFA reunification clock or wait to move
forward with a permanency plan to account for the needs of families
when parents are detained (AIC 2021). The lack of coordination and

communication means that one hand is creating a reunification plan and the other is forbidding parents from complying with it (Wessler 2011). This systemic contradiction often fast-tracks the children of immigrant parents to adoption. Parental deportation too often eliminates the possibility of family unity when children are in the child welfare system, as child welfare departments and courts often move to terminate the parental rights of mothers and fathers who have been deported (Dettlaff and Finno-Velasquez 2013).

Family reunification has long been a goal of both federal immigration law and child welfare policy. The central value of keeping families together is also at the core of international agreements on human rights, including the Universal Declaration of Human Rights and the International Covenant on Civil and Political Rights (United Nations 1990). However, US law and practice threaten family integrity and undermine the best interests of children whose immigrant families may be dealing with urgent economic and social needs yet may also be unable to access valuable support, such as SNAP and Medicaid. Although research shows that outcomes for children are ultimately better when they are reunified with their own parents or placed with relatives, children of deported parents and adult family members who are undocumented face barriers to this end.

Key Policy Recommendations: Advocacy and Future Directions

The child welfare system must be significantly reformed and reduced in its scope. Its ties to immigration enforcement must be severed to reduce intergenerational harms that have been perpetuated by structural racism, classism, and anti-immigrant policies (Fong 2020). The failure of the system to address the root causes of harm to children and its inability to provide responsible care mean that children in mixed-status or undocumented immigrant families remain susceptible to high rates of posttraumatic stress disorder, anxiety, depression, suicidal ideation, and loss of cultural connection across generations (Dreby 2012; Lovato and Abrams 2021; Zayas et al. 2015). Restrictive immigration policies and practices negatively impact the well-being of immigrant families and should be changed. I find the most compelling path forward to be instituting significant immigration-related and child welfare reforms—at the federal, state, and local levels—aimed at keeping families together and creating a parallel community response that promotes immigrant access to financial and social services, which could eventually eliminate the need for a child welfare system response altogether. We need policies at all levels that promote the inclusion and well-being of immigrant families.

Policies to reduce poverty among children in immigrant families are also needed to further prevent child welfare involvement. Children in immigrant families are becoming a larger share of all US children; they are disproportionately poor, and they and their families often have restricted access to the social safety net. Social assistance, such as SNAP or subsidized housing, should be provided to all US residents as a human right, irrespective of legal status. This prioritizes individuals' health and welfare before state-imposed legal categories. State and local governments should further develop innovative policies to address economic disparities that disproportionately affect people of color and immigrant families, increasing their vulnerability to child welfare system involvement.

Child Welfare System Policy and Practice Reforms

In the short term, state, county, and city governments should be more attentive and responsive to the needs of immigrant families, at both the administrative and legislative levels. All states' child welfare systems are responsible for compliance with both federal and state requirements; while most are state administered, they are county administered in nine states, and two states have state-county hybrid administrations (CWIG 2018). Therefore, the following recommendations require implementation at all levels. Policies informing the child welfare system must be reenvisioned from the perspective of families so that parents' roles are valued and families can remain together whenever safe and possible. Child welfare services must implement policies that will eliminate family separations except in cases of actual or imminent physical harm. Child welfare systems should also establish clear policies supporting undocumented parents and families in the child welfare system, including transparency about the rights of undocumented parents and extended families to be treated equitably as viable caregivers for children.

At the organizational level, child welfare agencies should develop specialized staffing to serve children and families more effectively (Lovato et al. 2024). New York City, Los Angeles, San Francisco, and several other cities and states have dedicated offices and/or liaisons whose primary role is to support child welfare agencies on immigration-related issues and provide resources to caseworkers who work with immigrant families to expand their capacity for serving diverse families (Greenberg et al. 2019; for example, see Finno-Velasquez and Sepp 2022). This awareness of and responsiveness to immigrant needs should be implemented everywhere. In 2012, California enacted distinct legislation, the Reuniting Immigrant Families Act (SB 1064), that addresses parental and family rights and enables detained parents to take steps to place their children with family members before removal. To do so, it has extended the period within which reunification can occur and made it easier for children to be placed with a qualified caregiver regardless of their immigration status. A law of this kind should be adopted federally to benefit immigrant families.

As noted in the case of Maria and Lola, when a parent is detained or deported by ICE, various barriers to family reunification can arise. For example, their detention or deportation may make it incredibly difficult to participate in child welfare proceedings or comply with family reunification services. After the Trump administration had instituted a more punitive policy, President Biden restored and updated a 2013 ICE policy that has become a vital tool for assisting child welfare agencies in addressing challenges for detained or deported parents. The Interests of Noncitizen Parents and Legal Guardians of Minor Children or Incapacitated Adults (Parental Interests Directive [PID]) policy states that ICE's immigration enforcement activities should not unnecessarily act as a barrier to the parental or guardianship rights of noncitizen parents or legal guardians. On the basis of this policy, ICE should allow parents/guardians to make alternative care arrangements for their children in the case that a parent has been detained/deported. The policy also states that (1) detained parents should be geographically located near their children for ease during visits; (2) parental participation in child welfare proceedings, services, and programs should be facilitated; (3) visitation between children and parents should be coordinated regularly;

and (4) parents/guardians who are removed from the United States can be granted parole so they can return to participate in a Termination of Parental Rights hearing (Immigrant Legal Resource Center 2022). The existence of this policy, however, does not guarantee that ICE and child welfare agencies will follow it. Yet, these are standards that all child welfare agencies should adhere to in order to decrease barriers to reunification for parents who are detained or deported.

Relatedly, all caseworkers, supervisors, attorneys, and judges who practice in dependency court should be required to participate in trainings on immigration law and current enforcement policies. Within child welfare departments, confidentiality policies should be reviewed to ensure that they explicitly limit information sharing with federal immigration authorities, and child welfare workers should be given guidance about talking with families about their rights regarding confidentiality. When the separation of families is unavoidable in either the immigration or child welfare system, policy should ensure that parents can maintain frequent contact with their children to maintain and strengthen these relationships. Child welfare agencies and detention facilities should better assist families in maintaining contact by making it less costly for detained parents to contact children and ensuring that ICE detains parents close to where their children live. Further, child welfare agencies should establish memoranda of understanding (MOUs) with consulates across Latin America and, in particular, Mexico's federal child welfare agency, Dessarollo Integral de la Familia (DIF), to ensure visitation when the child is in the United States and the parent is in Mexico.

Child welfare agencies should also refer youth and families to community-based legal services as needed, as well as to trusted immigrant-serving organizations and/or other trusted community partners who have long-standing relationships with immigrant communities (Lovato and Ramirez 2022). In addition to potentially securing the release of detained parents and thus facilitating family reunification, these agencies can offer social support groups, "Know Your Rights" workshops, and other advocacy-based trainings that help immigrant families feel safe in their respective communities. Child welfare professionals should also advocate for systemic change for immigrant children and families.

Immigration Policy Recommendations

In the long term, the federal government must halt all family-separation practices and implement policies that will ensure that family separation will not be reinstated in the future. ICE should be bound to act in the best interest of children, just as family courts are supposed to do. Unique policies are needed for enforcing immigration law among people with children in the United States, regardless of the immigration/citizenship status of the children.

The federal government must cease practices pertaining to the criminalization and separation of immigrant families and ensure that if there is a situation in which a parent is detained, immigrant children are placed in the least restrictive setting, such as with another family member, regardless of legal status. Further, policy makers must implement safety measures to ensure that family separation does not occur again under future administrations. Immigration reform must eliminate mandatory deportation laws that needlessly separate families.

We must also look at humane pathways so that people who are undocumented or in a legally precarious status can work toward becoming citizens, making employment and accessing public benefits easier. Federal reforms should offer a path to legal citizenship for unauthorized immigrants so that deportation is no longer a default and so that parents can have security for themselves and their families. In the criminal and immigration systems, centering policy on the needs of families requires reducing incarceration, deportations, and detentions according to the risks—if any—individuals pose to society. Relatedly, immigration reform must address systemic due process problems with detention and deportation procedures.

US responses to child maltreatment primarily focus on individual parents' behaviors rather than the systemic injustices creating the conditions for maltreatment. An increasing body of literature suggests that community-level strategies (Daro and Dodge 2009) and broad-scale antipoverty policies (Berger et al. 2017; Yang et al. 2019) show potential for addressing child welfare involvement among disenfranchised communities of color and immigrant communities. Shifting power to families and communities ensures that they have the resources to prevent harm from taking place and to address harm when it occurs (Dettlaff 2023).

In addition, there are growing community-level approaches that center mutual aid, which has been defined as the "collective coordination to meet each other's needs, usually from an awareness that the systems we have in place are not going to meet them" (Spade 2020, 7). These approaches are separate from child welfare agencies and based within community models, where trusted organizations, networks, and groups provide care to one another. Mutual-aid programs meet basic needs while also operating as activist organizations that dismantle oppressive and restrictive systems.

In summary, we must envision approaches that promote equity, compassion, and inclusion within the broader context of immigration law. Policy makers and practitioners should consider other policies, including mass legalization (Song and Bloemraad 2022), universal health care for all (Onarheim et al. 2018), and programs establishing community-focused integration (Bloemraad 2006) that promote the welfare and adjustment of immigrant communities across the United States. Lastly, we must also address the weakening of the US social safety net alongside its increasingly punitive approach. The safety net combines vital assistance with coercive surveillance of intimate family life, which causes further social stratification and negative child and family outcomes for poor immigrant families.

These policy recommendations are extensive, but enacting any one, few, or several of them would be highly impactful on the lives of immigrant parents, children, and the communities where they live. As depicted through Maria and Lola's experiences at the start of this chapter, undocumented families are at significant risk of child welfare involvement due to experiencing high levels of poverty and risk of surveillance. Ultimately, the child welfare system's methods of supervision, control, and forced separation of immigrant families must be amended to center a common mission to meet human needs, prevent violence, maintain permanency, and care for all children, families, and communities.

NOTE

1 Lola's story is a composite of case studies (see Duffy 2010) from the experiences of undocumented immigrant families with whom the author worked as a former caseworker.

11

Cages and Foster Homes

Racialized Poverty Governance Regimes and Family Separation across US States

FRANK EDWARDS

US criminal justice is deeply racialized (Murakawa and Beckett 2010). Anti-Black politics and ideologies were central to the early development of US systems of policing and incarceration (Muhammad 2011) and were critical in the dramatic expansion of the carceral state (Hinton 2016; Murakawa 2014) that has institutionalized coercive confinement as a default solution to social problems (Gilmore 2007). Notwithstanding the central role that criminal justice plays in US racial stratification (Pettit 2012), police and corrections are not the only sets of agencies that constitute contemporary systems of social control. Poor families and families of color encounter a battery of state and private agencies tasked with monitoring and regulating their behavior (Paik 2021). Child protection agencies are one such state system that engages in coercive social control (Roberts 2012, 2022). These agencies hold one of the more extreme powers of the state: determining when to separate children from their families. Child protection services (CPS) agencies coordinate the surveillance of children and youth for signs of abuse and neglect and make decisions about when it is appropriate to remove children from their homes and place them into foster care. Forced separation has profound personal, psychological, and social consequences for children, parents, families, and communities.

On an average day, there are more than four hundred thousand children in foster care in the United States (USDHHS 2022a), about 1 in every 185 children. Nearly all of these children were removed from families living in or near poverty. In an average day, there are about 1.8 million adults incarcerated in the United States (Kang-Brown, Montagnet, and Heiss 2021), about 1 in every 184 adults. Nearly all of these adults were poor at the time of their arrest (Rabuy and Kopf 2015). These two systems are deeply intertwined, representing central components of the carceral systems that routinely disrupt the lives of poor people in the United States. As in US prisons and jails, children and families drawn into child protection systems are overwhelmingly poor (Fong 2017) and disproportionately Black and Indigenous (Dettlaff and Boyd 2020). These two systems jointly manage and reproduce racialized poverty in the United States. This system of racialized poverty governance is directly linked to historical and contemporary policy efforts to commodify, denigrate, and regulate Black women's reproduction (Roberts 1997, 2002). Contemporary poverty governance is also a product of efforts to advance settler colonialism through the elimination of Indigenous nations and assimilation of Native children (Haight et al. 2018; Wolfe 2006).

We can see how anti-Black racism and settler colonialism work in tandem by observing how policy systems are linked together. Because similar political, social, and economic forces are at play in the design and implementation of policy across domains, states tend to develop relatively stable "policy regimes," packages of policy that broadly share ideological underpinnings and practical orientations. This chapter shows that racial inequalities in two formally distinct (but practically intertwined) social policy domains are deeply connected and argues that state social policy regimes tend toward similar levels of racial inequality across formally separate but institutionally linked policy systems. As Fong and Smith described in chapter 9, though formally separate, processes and outcomes in criminal justice and child protection are tightly linked at the place level. Social policy regimes (May and Jochim 2013) share similarities in both the kind and intensity of social policies that exist across organizational boundaries at the place level. They reflect diverse political preferences and institutional configurations that help to explain variation in a wide variety of domains including criminal justice (Barker 2009; Sutton 2013), child protection (Edwards 2016), and social welfare policy (Esping-Andersen 1990; Orloff 1993; Soss, Fording, and Schram 2011).

This chapter presents two key sets of findings that show how racial inequalities in coercive social control are tightly correlated across policy domains at the place level. First, I show that states that disproportionately incarcerate Black people are also likely to (1) disproportionately place Black children into foster care, (2) have a disproportionately high number of Black children in foster care caseloads, and (3) exhibit inequity in the rates at which Black children are reunified with their families. Second, I find that states with unequal rates of American Indian and Alaska Native (AIAN) incarceration are likely to have high levels of inequality in the rates at which AIAN children enter and remain in foster care. State social policy outcomes are systematically unequal across domains, and similar mechanisms simultaneously account for the multiple kinds of coercive interventions by government agencies that are experienced by poor families. When a state incarcerates more Black or Native adults, that same state will put more Black or Native children in foster care.

Racial Inequalities in Child Protection and Criminal Justice

The US child protection system, like the US criminal justice system (Lee et al. 2015; Pettit 2012), is characterized by significant and durable patterns of racial inequality and the overwhelming poverty of its subject population (Jacobs 2014; Roberts 2002, 2022). Child welfare systems routinely fail to track the poverty status of involved families, but administrative and qualitative data show that the overwhelming majority of system-involved children are poor (Fong 2017, 2020). Poverty and racism play key roles in selecting children for investigation and in adjudicating maltreatment cases. Black and Native adults are incarcerated in prisons at very similar rates to which Black and Native children are in foster care. Data from 2014, the last year included in this analysis, showed that Black children were 2.6 times more likely to be in foster care than white children, and AIAN children were 5.5 times more likely to be in foster care than white children (author's calculations).

Racial inequalities in criminal justice outcomes are a function of structural racism (Peterson and Krivo 2010; R. Sampson 2012), the unequal treatment of people of color by criminal legal system actors (Harris, Evans, and Beckett 2011), and differential racialization of local policy systems (Harris 2016). The sources of child protection disparities have received far less attention from sociologists and are subject to substantial debate. Quantitative investigations of the relationship between race and child welfare outcomes generally focus on evaluating whether a racial gap exists between so-called risk factors for child abuse and neglect, like poverty, and inequalities in child welfare system outcomes (Drake et al. 2011). This body of research generally suggests that this gap between maltreatment risk and inequalities in system outcomes—described as the contribution of system bias to child protection outcomes—is small and that racial inequalities in child protection are primarily a function of racial differences in child abuse and neglect. However, this research typically fails to acknowledge that structural racism directly causes child poverty through pathways including residential segregation, labor-market discrimination, environmental racism, punitive welfare policy, and historical and intergenerational trauma. Many child welfare scholars also treat family separation as a primary and appropriate policy response to family poverty and instability, despite the trauma caused by family separation and evidence that other interventions can address root causes of family crisis without coercion (Pac et al. 2023).

At the same time, ethnographic, historical, and legal studies illustrate that interactions between the child protection system and poor mothers of color are routinely racist, paternalistic, and coercive (Fong 2020; Lee 2016). Biases among street-level bureaucrats toward families of color may lead to higher levels of scrutiny by the state and higher levels of disruptive intervention from child protection agencies when families become subject to investigation (Roberts 2002). Historical institutional processes, such as the tight connection between family court proceedings for juvenile delinquency and those for suspected child abuse and neglect, have also locked in punitive and racialized approaches to child welfare and family crises (Simmons 2020). This body of literature shows that child protection, like other systems engaged in regulating and punishing the poor, prioritizes punishment over aid and surveillance over support. This style of intervention is historically contingent, reflecting US and local political interests in managing poverty through racist modes of punishment and control.

Racialized Poverty Governance Regimes

State social policy systems can be characterized as regimes when government agencies that are formally separate pursue goals that share the same set of priorities and follow the same set of logics. In the context of settler colonialism and racial politics, social policy regimes can advance racist agendas through the design and targeting of policy interventions (Omi and Winant 1994; Wolfe 2006). A diverse set of policy institutions in one place may take on the same basic shape, as similar sets of policy feedbacks (the effects of policy itself on the policy process), political pressures, and rules and procedures lead to common styles and patterns of intervention. Because child welfare systems and criminal justice systems operate subject to similar racialized political pressures, share government infrastructure, and engage in similar projects of managing poor people who are typically confined to particular neighborhoods and places, they are very likely to exhibit similar styles of work and magnitudes of racism in their operations. Scholars who study institutions often refer to processes like this as "institutional isomorphism," a process by which organizations become increasingly similar to each other over time. This process of isomorphic convergence across policy systems means that communities of color that are subject to high levels of surveillance and coercive intervention in one policy domain are very likely to exhibit high levels of inequality in other neighboring policy domains. The regulatory, supportive, and coercive actions of these state agencies overlap to create complex and oppressive policy environments in which low-income families of color both depend on and are subject to the onerous demands of multiple state agencies (Paik 2021).

While poverty governance literature has compellingly described the relationships between poor families and the state, the ongoing efforts of the US government to eliminate Indigenous peoples has received relatively less attention in explaining the contemporary model of US poverty governance. Settler colonialism has deeply structured US social policy systems like child welfare and education (Jacobs 2014; Ross 1998). AIAN communities are also subject to disproportionately high levels of incarceration and criminal victimization (Rolnick 2016).

Boarding schools, the primary intent of which was to eliminate Native nations by aggressively assimilating AIAN and Native Hawaiian children to white values and practices (Newland 2022), played a powerful role in establishing an especially coercive strand of child and family policy in state and federal systems that has an enduring legacy in child welfare today (Crofoot and Harris 2012). Despite the protections of the

Indian Child Welfare Act of 1978 (discussed in some detail by Hontalas in chapter 2 of this volume), which includes mechanisms to reduce the extreme rates at which AIAN children were separated from their families and communities, vast inequalities in rates of child welfare system involvement persist for AIAN children and youth (Rocha Beardall and Edwards 2021), a result of the resistance of street-level bureaucrats and state and federal court actors to fully implementing ICWA's protections (Brown 2020).

Analysis

This chapter evaluates whether state policy regimes display coherent patterns of racialization across formally distinct but practically intertwined policy domains. I construct a series of models to evaluate whether disparities in criminal justice system outcomes for Black and AIAN people relative to whites predict disparities in foster care entries, caseloads, and family reunification exits from the foster care system. This panel of outcomes allows for a general evaluation of how racial inequalities in policy outcomes are structured by both family inequality and institutional processes. Levels of inequality in the criminal justice system and child welfare systems vary tremendously across states (see figure 11.1). Place plays a powerful role in structuring how families live, how institutions work, and how social meanings of race shape public policy. Foster care systems have dynamic populations as children enter, exit, or remain in care.

Single point-in-time measures may fail to capture the breadth of a system's reach or miss important features of the flow of children into and out of the system. To capture inequality at multiple stages of foster care, this study evaluates three foster care system outcomes: entries into foster care, reunification exits from foster care, and foster care caseloads. Entries capture the flow of children into the system, while caseloads (all children in the system in a reporting year) are additionally sensitive to children who remain in foster care for longer periods of time. Children exit foster care through reunification when a parent, kin caregiver, or prior legal guardian regains custody of a child; this is often the preferred outcome for children if the risk for future maltreatment is low.

I construct a series of regression models to explore the relationships between unequal criminal justice and unequal child protection after controlling for levels of inequality in family disadvantage, family structure, socioeconomic status, crime, or political contexts. I estimate these relationships with multilevel models that adjust for time-stable differences across states. The results of these models allow us to evaluate whether policy inequality in one domain is a useful predictor of policy inequality in another domain.

This analysis primarily relies on data from the Adoption and Foster Care Analysis and Reporting System (AFCARS), the National Prisoner Statistics (NPS), and the American Community Survey (ACS). I join these data sets to construct a state-year panel for the years 2000–2014. I construct counts of all children entering foster care by race (entries), all children in foster care for any length of time during an annual reporting period (caseloads), and all children exiting foster care to reunite with a parent, family member, or legal guardian (reunification exits). I also construct annual measures of Black and AIAN incarceration per capita.

I include a series of controls to adjust for population risk of child maltreatment. Child poverty, a single-parent family structure, parental unemployment, and low parental educational attainment are well-established predictors of child welfare system involvement, and so I include measures that describe racial inequalities in these outcomes as controls in the models. Because local politics probably affect policy design and implementation, I also include a control for the political ideology of a state's legislature (Berry et al. 1998). To account for other key policy contexts, I include measures for local crime and policing from the Uniform Crime Reports and details on the operation of core welfare programs like Temporary Assistance for Needy Families (TANF), the Supplemental Nutrition Assistance Program (SNAP), and Medicaid as statistical controls.

Findings

States with high levels of racial inequality in incarceration tend to also have high levels of inequality in foster care for both Black and Native children. Unequal incarceration rates are a powerful predictor of unequal foster care entries and unequal foster care caseloads. Racially unequal incarceration accounts for far more variation in levels of inequality in state foster care entries and caseloads for Black and AIAN children than do racial differences in common measures of maltreatment risk, like child poverty. These results demonstrate that racial inequalities in levels of formal social control (e.g., incarceration) are strongly correlated at the place level, after controlling for local inequalities in social disadvantage. In other words, states systematically vary in the degree to which their social policy systems are racialized. High levels of racial inequality in one domain (e.g., incarceration) are strongly predictive of high levels of racial inequality in neighboring domains (e.g., child welfare system involvement).

Rates at which children and families of color experience foster care vary dramatically across states. About 0.5 percent of the US child population was in foster care in 2014. The annual proportion of Black children experiencing foster care varied during this period from a maximum of over 8 percent in Wyoming and Oregon to a minimum of 0.8 percent of the Black child population in Mississippi (state averages for 2000–2014).[1] The percentage of AIAN children in foster care varied from a maximum average of over 12 percent in Nebraska, Minnesota, and Hawaii to a minimum of 0.4 percent of the AIAN child population in Virginia and Mississippi, with a state median of 2 percent of AIAN children experiencing foster care annually. Consistent with prior research, these data show that the risk for experiencing foster care is very pronounced for AIAN and Black children.

The distribution of foster care caseload and incarceration disparities for Black and AIAN children in 2014 is displayed in figure 11.1. These maps demonstrate how racial inequalities in both foster care and incarceration vary across states. Darker colors on the map indicate higher levels of inequality for Black and Native communities, and lighter colors indicate lower levels of inequality relative to white rates. In an average state, Black children were about four times more likely to be in foster care than their white peers were, and AIAN children were about three times more likely to be in foster care than white children were. In an average state, Black adults were about seven times more likely to be incarcerated than white adults were. AIAN adults were three times more likely to be incarcerated than white adults were.

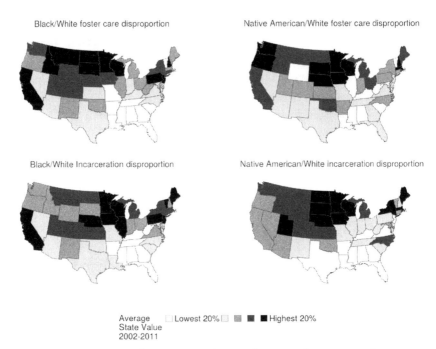

Figure 11.1. Foster care and incarceration disparity by race and state, 2014 values in quantiles. (Note: Although Alaska and Hawaii are not included in the figure, they are included in the analysis.)

States in the Midwest and Mountain West generally have very high rates of both incarceration and foster care for Black and AIAN children and adults. For example, South Dakota had the highest level of Black/white inequality in foster care during this period, as well as an above-average disparity in incarceration rates. There were about ten times more Black children in foster care than there were white children in foster care. Similarly, AIAN children in Minnesota were about twenty-four times more likely to be in foster care than white children were; Minnesota also had among the highest rates of racial inequality in incarceration rates. Unlike Midwest and Mountain West states, states in the South generally have low rates of racial disparity in incarceration—despite high rates of incarceration across racial groups—and have relatively lower rates of foster care for Black and AIAN children. Mississippi, for example, had the lowest average levels of Black/white inequality in foster care. Black children in Mississippi were only 1.2 times more likely to be in foster care than their white peers were.

Southern states' low levels of racial disparities in foster care are probably related to the weak and narrow set of welfare institutions in these states. The social policy systems of Jim Crow in the US South were designed to ensure that Black workers remained dependent on white elites for wages by categorically excluding Black people from eligibility for social programs and dramatically limiting the availability of social supports funded by government in general (Quadagno 1994). These low levels of funding for social services, education, and public health have led to lower levels of maltreatment surveillance and lower levels of investment in the kinds of institutions that generate high levels of child welfare system contact. The relatively sparse and underfunded set of welfare state institutions that exist today in the US South are especially pronounced in those parts of the South that have the largest Black populations (Baker 2022). This link between racist politics and social policy systems has led to low levels of both state supports for many Black families in the South and relatively lower levels of paternalistic and coercive family surveillance and policing in the South (Wulczyn et al. 2023).

The geography of the dispossession of Indigenous peoples also plays a role in explaining the racial geography of foster care and incarceration today. While many AIAN nations (with notable exceptions) were forcibly removed from the US South before the US Civil War, a large number of AIAN nations remained in open conflict with the US government until the late nineteenth century. Tribes in the Midwest, West, Great Plains, and Alaska experienced significant US government efforts to forcefully assimilate AIAN children through institutions like Indian boarding schools. These practices over time transformed into the mass removal of Native children into foster care (Jacobs 2014). While the Indian Child Welfare Act of 1978 provides protections against many of the worst practices from earlier periods of Native family separation, levels of AIAN foster care and incarceration remain incredibly high today in places where genocidal family separation policies were most active (Rocha Beardall and Edwards 2021).

To illustrate the relationships between unequal incarceration and unequal foster care outcomes for Black and AIAN children, I estimate the predicted relationship between unequal incarceration and unequal foster care on the basis of model results, displayed in figure 11.2. To estimate these predicted values, I hold all predictors (e.g., poverty, racial

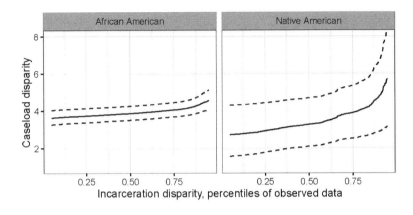

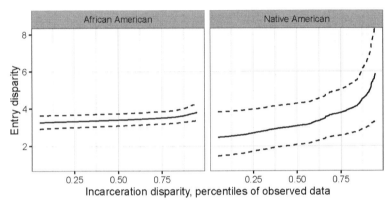

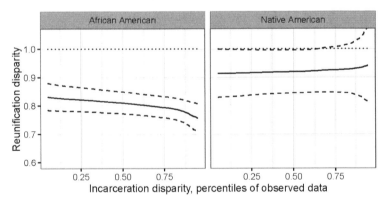

Figure 11.2. Predicted foster care inequality (caseload, entry, and reunification) between white and Black children and between white and AIAN children. Point estimates (solid) and 95 percent prediction interval (dashed). The dotted line (at 1) indicates equity with whites (curves not crossing 1 are statistically significant).

composition, political alignment of state legislature) constant except for incarceration inequality. I then systematically vary incarceration inequality from a relatively low value to a relatively high value and compute the model prediction for child welfare inequalities (with uncertainty) for each hypothetical value of incarceration inequality.

Figure 11.2 shows the expected levels of inequality in foster care after adjusting for inequality in other socioeconomic conditions and state political and policy contexts. States with higher levels of Black/white inequality in incarceration tend to have higher levels of Black/white inequality in foster care entries. Child poverty inequality is the strongest correlate of reunification inequality. In places where there is deep racial inequality in poverty, Black children are less likely to be reunified with their families than white children are, further evidence that child protection systems are tightly linked with broader systems of racialized poverty governance. As for Black children, inequality in AIAN child welfare outcomes is also well explained by inequality in incarceration.

Figure 11.2 shows a clear positive relationship between the unequal incarceration of both Black and AIAN adults and the unequal placement of Black and AIAN children into foster care. For states with higher levels of racial inequality in incarceration, these models predict higher levels of racial inequality in the number of children entering foster care and the number of children remaining in foster care year to year and *lower* rates of Black family reunification exits from foster care compared to white families' rates of reunification. That is, as incarceration inequality increases, Black children are less likely than white children to be reunified with their families after entering foster care. These models do not show a clear relationship between AIAN incarceration and reunification.

The Implications of Links between Racialized Systems of Poverty Governance

The criminal justice and child welfare systems are tightly linked. They share organizational ties, have similar adversarial legal procedures, and are subject to the same cultural and political forces that routinize suspicion of Black and Indigenous peoples. Given how overlapping contact with criminal justice and child welfare systems within families is common, criminal justice and child welfare agencies tend to be particularly active in the surveillance and policing of residents in poor communities, especially poor Black and AIAN communities. Many families in these neighborhoods therefore have overlapping contact with both systems (Berger et al. 2016; Roberts 2012). Such overlaps provide evidence that poverty governance regimes in the United States are racialized in regionally specific patterns.

This study provides strong evidence that racial inequalities in the experience of formal social control co-occur within states. Neither policing nor child welfare casework happens in a vacuum. Social control is deeply embedded in politics, policy systems, and community and interagency relationships. The social conditions and structural inequalities encountered by frontline workers from one domain are often identical to those encountered from another. Police, caseworkers, and judicial actors routinely intervene in the same communities and families, are subject to similar sets of pressures and incentives, and operate within similar cultural fields that couple ascribed race with presumptions of dangerousness. While this study cannot isolate the causes of the place-based links between unequal criminal justice and unequal child protection, it does provide strong evidence that the often-extreme racialization in a state's efforts to police crime, control the poor, and regulate parenting is tightly linked and not well explained by racial inequality in the incidence of socioeconomic disadvantage (e.g., higher rates of poverty among Black and AIAN families).

Racial politics structure the distributions of state coercive and redistributive interventions (Fox 2010; Soss, Fording, and Schram 2011). Policy makers and street-level bureaucrats select where to concentrate resources or target coercive social control on the basis, in part, of three things: implicit or explicit motivations (such as white backlash to Civil Rights Movement gains for Black Americans) for hoarding resources among favored groups (Quadagno 1994); liberal racial paternalism that led to a stronger federal prison system (Murakawa 2014); and the targeting of groups (i.e., people of color) perceived by powerful constituencies to threaten white political and economic dominance (Jacobs and Tope 2007). These maldistributions are a function of the deep structural inequalities that characterize many Black and AIAN communities at the same time as they become mechanisms through which social inequality is reproduced (Pettit 2012; Roberts 2012).

The tight links between inequalities in criminal justice and in child welfare strongly suggest that racism drives the approaches policy makers take toward the poor across a wide range of policy systems. While both policing and child protection are very efficient at subjecting large numbers of poor people to surveillance and coercive intervention, they do a poor job at addressing a fundamental cause of family crisis and instability: poverty. Echoing calls to defund police and adequately fund robust social and community infrastructure, a number of families, lawyers, and scholars are demanding the abolition of the child welfare system as we know it (Dettlaff et al. 2020; Roberts 2022). The overwhelming majority of CPS cases are directly related to the negative impacts of poverty on children and families. Housing instability, inadequate medical care, lack of child care during work hours, and parental stress driven by financial precarity all can clearly harm children. But directing resources to public goods that solve these underlying problems does much more to improve safety for children than policing and punishing parents does. A number of cities and states are experimenting with guaranteed incomes, universal preschool, and expanded social housing as alternatives to continuing to expand criminal justice and child protection systems. These efforts are laying the groundwork for a new vision for child welfare, in which the actual welfare of children and families takes priority over the policing and surveillance of low-income parents.

NOTE

1 State-level rates of entry and disproportion reported in text are 2007–14 average values calculated from AFCARS foster care caseloads and ACS child population estimates. AFCARS data available by request at www.ndacan.acf.hhs.gov/datasets/datasets-list-afcars-foster-care.cfm. American Community Survey accessed through IPUMS—USA: https://usa.ipums.org/usa.

PART V

Future Directions for Child and Family Well-Being

12

How Reforms Stabilize Policing, Surveillance, and Terror

The Case for Abolition of the Child Welfare System

ALAN J. DETTLAFF AND MAYA PENDLETON

The child welfare system, more accurately called the family policing system, is predicated on the subjugation, surveillance, control, and punishment of mostly poor and disproportionately Black and Native children and families. The system benefits from the widely held perspective that the family policing system is a legitimate, supportive helping system, a system that protects the safety and well-being of children through necessary state-sanctioned interventions. Yet the history and reality of the system's impact on the lives of children, families, and communities underscore how the system functions to maintain poverty, anti-Blackness, white supremacy, racial capitalism, and settler colonialism.

The destruction of Black and Native families is foundational to the United States. Both Black and Native communities experienced displacement and significant domination under the grips of slavery and settler colonialism. Slave owners separated families for myriad reasons—to pay off debt, as punishment, for profit—all of which had the effect of asserting and maintaining oppression. While the Thirteenth Amendment ended the system of chattel slavery, family separations continued through forced apprenticeships of Black children established under the Black Codes. This history of family separation both during and after slavery created the foundation for the state's contemporary practice of family separation (Dettlaff 2023). The making of what we now know of as the United States also required the attempted elimination and dispossession of Native communities, which necessitated children being torn from their families (Estes 2016). This history of harming and separating Black and Native families is directly reflected in the organization of current systems impacting Black and Native communities; history is repeated through today's system of family policing.

Today, more than half of all Black children in the United States are investigated by child welfare authorities (Kim et al. 2017). Native children are removed from their families at a rate nearly three times greater than their proportion in the overall population (Puzzanchera et al. 2023). Most of these families are also poor. The harm that results from family policing intervention is also well documented. Stories detailing the abuse and neglect of children while in foster care are routinely reported by journalists (e.g., Asgarian 2020). The harm and trauma of state-sanctioned separation of children from their families—whether at the United States–Mexico border, through incarceration, or by way of family policing—are also widely known (Dreby 2012; Johnson and Easterling 2012; Trivedi 2019).

Despite these facts, calls to address harms perpetuated by the family policing system remain focused on fixing the system through reforms that seek to increase racial equity, tweak how decisions are made about removal, provide preventative services, and implement better training for family policing agents. These reforms beg the family policing system to do the impossible: to perform family policing in ways that shrink the scale of family policing and give the appearance of making forced separation kinder and more acceptable. Reforms therefore fundamentally, and at times intentionally, misdiagnose the problem of family policing. In doing so, reforms uphold and support the further expansion of racism and economic inequality. The problem is not that we need a family well-being system instead of a child welfare system or that child welfare agencies lack a multicultural workforce and need access to better training. The problem is that the system itself is built to harm and oppress marginalized children and families and excels at doing so.

This chapter details how reformers continue to locate racial disproportionality and disparities as the key problems plaguing child welfare systems while ignoring how the system's presence cements racial and economic inequities. In outlining the failure of popular child welfare reforms, the chapter underscores how reforms further entrench a harmful system while failing to build alternatives that actually support the well-being and ultimately the liberation of children and families from oppressive systems. In response to the endless cycle of popular but failed reforms, the chapter offers the abolition of family policing as a path forward. To build a society where children, families, and communities are safe from harm—both harm that might occur within homes and harm that results from state violence—carceral systems, including the family policing system, must be abolished. Abolition offers space that reform confines—space to actively work toward a world where children, families, and communities are safe and, most importantly, free from oppression.

Racial Disproportionality in the Family Policing System

While the practice of separating Black children from their parents originated with chattel slavery, the use of family separations to maintain the oppression of Black families through the modern family policing system was first brought to national attention by Andrew Billingsley and Jeanne Giovannoni (1972) in their seminal publication *Children of the Storm: Black Children and American Child Welfare*. Prior to the 1960s, Black children were largely excluded from family policing systems, as the bulk of "child welfare" services were intended to provide aid to white families experiencing extreme economic hardship primarily due to the death or disability of the father. As these poverty-relief efforts were expanded throughout the mid-1900s and more Black families became eligible for poverty-relief services, racist policies in the form of morality tests were established to limit their eligibility for these services, such as "home suitability clauses," "man-in-the-house rules," and "illegitimate child clauses." These policies, combined with a shift in the focus of child welfare services from poverty relief to "child protection" in the 1960s—including mandatory reporting laws and an emphasis on family separation as a response to "neglect"—resulted in a rapid increase in Black children placed in foster care (Dettlaff 2023).

By the end of the 1970s, it was well documented that Black children had become significantly overrepresented in this system (e.g., Magura 1979; Shyne and Schroeder 1978). By 2000, Black children represented 38 percent of children in foster care, a rate more than double their proportion among the general child population (Ganasarajah, Siegel, and Sickmund 2017). This phenomenon of racial oppression by the family policing system later became known as "racial disproportionality," a term that originated from efforts in the juvenile punishment system to measure and understand disproportionate minority contact. As of 2021, Black children remain nearly one quarter (22.8 percent) of all children forcibly separated from their parents and placed into foster care, although they represent only 13.8 percent of children in the general population (Puzzanchera et al. 2023).

Just as the family policing system has systematically separated Black children from their families at astounding rates, Native families have been decimated by family policing. As settlers sought to gain control over Native lands to form the United States, they also sought to eliminate and replace Native cultures; this led to the forcible placement of Native children in violent, white supremacist Indian boarding schools. Thus, assimilation became a key component of settler colonialism in the United States' historical context. Although specific estimates are difficult to obtain, conservative estimates suggest that over one hundred thousand Native children were placed in Indian boarding schools by the 1970s (National Native American Boarding School Healing Coalition, n.d.). This history of destroying Native families and communities directly informs how the family policing system treats Native families today. The national Indian Child Welfare Act (ICWA) of 1978 intended to reform the system and was established in recognition that family policing disproportionally impacts Native children, yet Native children are still nearly three times as likely to be removed from their homes and placed in foster care compared to their white counterparts (Puzzanchera et al. 2023).

Since racial disproportionality was first documented, researchers have debated its causes and whether it results from racial biases within family policing systems or from what some have called "disproportionate need" among Black families due to their higher rates of poverty and related risks for maltreatment. Yet this debate was largely created as a means of distracting from the real problem that both created and perpetuates disproportionality. Racial disproportionality in the family policing system exists because of racism. This racism is present both within family policing systems and within broader society.

Research has documented the presence of racial biases within the family policing system that result in racial disproportionality (e.g.,

Dettlaff et al. 2011; Rivaux et al. 2008). This occurs not only in the form of explicit and implicit biases among decision-makers but also through implementation and enforcement of decades of policies that largely reflect a white, middle-class parenting standard. In addition, Black children and families are more likely to experience poverty and related risk factors, which may be associated with greater risk of maltreatment and make Black families more vulnerable to contact with family policing systems. Yet this "disproportionate need" is the result of centuries of structural and institutional racism that began with the forced enslavement and dehumanization of Black people (Dettlaff and Boyd 2020) and continues today through a government-maintained system of racialized poverty. From the Black Codes that followed the abolition of human chattel slavery to the Jim Crow laws that were deemed constitutional through 1964, the enduring consequences of these racist laws and policies include racial residential segregation, the increasing wealth gap, unequal access to quality education and health care, and inequities in housing and employment that each act to maintain the "disproportionate need" experienced by Black families. These issues of "disproportionate need" are then compounded by the surveillance and disproportionate reporting of Black families to family policing systems, which trigger their involvement in a system governed by racist policies.

Thus, what has long been referred to as "racial disproportionality" or "racial disparities" is better described as "racist inequities," as this term more accurately captures the underlying role of racism in contributing to long-standing inequities. Terms such as "racial disproportionality" obscure the role of racism in contributing to this problem (Kaba 2021), suggesting that the inequities in family policing systems exist through an unknown, passive cause that disproportionately impacts Black children. Rather, "racial disproportionality" exists because of racism that is actively inflicted on Black children and families, both within society through an array of government policies and systems that directly and deliberately established and maintain racialized poverty and, specifically, within the family policing system. "Racist inequities" maintains the focus on the active racism that perpetuates the inequities in this system.

What "Racial Disproportionality" Obscures

Over the past several decades, child welfare systems have identified and implemented many reforms in attempts to address "racial dispropor- tionality," although the intended goal of these reforms has been debated among scholars. Those who have supported theories of "disproportion- ate need" and criticized efforts to lessen disproportionality argue that since involvement in the family policing system is based on need, "pro- portional" representation should not be the desired goal. Rather, these scholars argue that Black children should be disproportionately involved in this system due to "disproportionate need" and thus that they should be forcibly separated from their families at greater rates than white chil- dren are (e.g., Bartholet 2009; Bartholet et al. 2011).

Despite the racism embedded within these critiques, these views in- fluenced many of the family policing system's efforts to address racist inequities throughout the 2010s. The debate that emerged regarding the causes of racist inequities, and the subsequent critiques of efforts to ad- dress disproportionality through antiracism training or other efforts to address racial bias (e.g., Drake et al. 2011), left many people in family po- licing systems unsure of how to proceed. This resulted in many systems discontinuing their efforts to address racial disproportionality, while many funders also discontinued their support of efforts to decrease dis- proportionality through antibias training and other efforts to target bi- ases in decision-making.

Yet, after nearly a decade of inattention, this stalled response dra- matically changed following the murder of George Floyd in May 2020. As awareness of the vast harms inflicted on Black Americans by the police and policing grew, activists and scholars began to draw parallels between the harms of policing and the harms caused by the family po- licing system (Dettlaff et al. 2020; Fitzgerald 2020; Roberts 2022), with several calling for full abolition of the family policing system as a means of ending these harms. Since that time, "racial equity" has emerged as the goal to address the racist inequities of the family policing system. Building from President Joe Biden's Executive Order 13985, "Advancing Racial Equity and Support for Underserved Communities through the Federal Government," Associate Commissioner of the Children's Bureau Aysha Schomburg (2021b) wrote to "child welfare leaders" across the country, stating, "Historically, the child welfare system has not served all people equitably," and asserting, "The federal government as a whole, and the Children's Bureau specifically, is committed . . . to advancing equity through our work at the federal level and through our work with states, territories, tribes, and all other grantees." Schomburg (2021a) affirmed this message in a subsequent blog post for the *Children's Bureau Express* titled "Equity Is a Right," in which she stated, "At the federal level, we are scrutinizing our current policies, we're having tough conversations, and we're identifying policies that exacerbate inequity and we are prioritizing them for change."

The logic of racial equity as a goal makes sense on its surface. The existence of racial disproportionality has long been understood as a problem because Black children are disproportionately overrepresented among children in foster care compared to their proportion in the general population. So the logical solution to this problem would be proportional representation, meaning that Black children are represented among children in foster care at a rate equivalent to their proportion in the population.

Yet this logic obscures what efforts to address racial disproportionality have attempted to hide for decades. The family policing system is not a benevolent helping system, and racial disproportionality is not a problem because of disproportionate representation. Racial disproportionality is a problem because of the racist abuse and harm inflicted on Black Americans by family policing intervention. Although enormous gaps exist in current safety-net services such as Temporary Assistance for Needy Families (TANF), Supplemental Nutrition Assistance Program (SNAP), Children's Health Insurance Program (CHIP), and others, these services are designed to provide essential resources for children and families in need. In contrast, the interventions used by the family policing system do not provide any direct, material assistance and are by no means benign interventions. Research consistently demonstrates that forcible family separation is a source of significant and lifelong trauma, regardless of how long this separation lasts (e.g., Mitchell and Kuczynski 2010; Sankaran, Church, and Mitchell 2019). Beyond this initial trauma, decades of research have documented that children who are subjected to placement in foster care are at risk for a host of adverse outcomes as adults, including poverty, low educational attainment, homelessness, unemployment, mental health disorders, and incarceration by the criminal punishment system (Courtney et al. 2011; Doyle 2007, 2008; Lowenstein 2018).

While family policing intervention harms children of all races, particularly poor children, the harm that is inflicted on poor, Black children is exacerbated by the racism and abuse already inflicted on them by US society. Black families and communities are disproportionally torn apart by other carceral systems such as the criminal punishment system, which is now a primary mechanism of racialized family separation, with one in nine Black children impacted by parental incarceration (Murphey and Cooper 2015). Because of racism and the racialized poverty that results from economic oppression, Black children in the United States face the threats of poverty, poor health, incarceration, emotional distress, and suicidal ideation (e.g., Hanks, Solomon, and Weller 2018; Hope, Hoggard, and Thomas 2015). For Black children who experience the additional trauma of family separation and foster care, these risks are exponentially exacerbated. Even in cases in which some form of intervention may be necessary, the negative outcomes associated with child welfare intervention only serve to further disadvantage Black youth. Thus, the child welfare system acts as an agent of racial oppression by knowingly and purposely perpetuating the conditions that facilitate this oppression: poverty, homelessness, joblessness, and other forms of disadvantage.

Further, for Black families and communities who are disproportionately torn apart by this system, the resulting harm and disintegration further weakens their ability to overcome the disadvantages that the child welfare system imposes on them. The surveillance and disproportionate separation inflicted on Black families and communities by the child welfare system have led to decades of intergenerational trauma and harm that act to maintain their disadvantage. This disproportionate interference also reinforces negative stereotypes that Black families are incapable of caring for themselves without government assistance and supervision (Roberts 2002).

Finally, given that the involuntary separation of children through foster care is not the first form of family separation to disproportionately impact Black families in the United States, it must be understood that for Black families, the trauma of involuntary removal is heightened by the legacy of forced family separation that was integral to slavery. The practice of forcibly and involuntarily separating Black children from their families must be understood through the history from which it came and recognized for the egregious trauma it continues to produce.

Thus, efforts to address "racial disproportionality" with a goal of racial equity obscure the harm inherent in family policing intervention and the oppression that this intervention produces for Black children and families. Simply producing "equity" in a system responsible for harm, racism, and oppression fundamentally misunderstands the problem it intends to address. And equitably distributing harm will still disproportionately impact Black children and families because of the racism and oppression they already face. Ultimately, goals of "racial equity" within the child welfare system obscure and ignore the real harm the child welfare system produces. Equitable harm is still harm, and thus, racial equity cannot be the goal for the family policing system.

The Limits of Child Welfare Reform

Training

Because of the enduring repercussions that decisions made by individuals working with and within the family policing system can have for families, including whether families enter the system at all, calls to make the family policing system more equitable are often accompanied by proposals to increase training. Specifically, reform efforts have focused on implementing an array of trainings on implicit bias, cultural competency, and antiracism more broadly for family policing agents. These trainings may address how parenting styles differ across cultures to help agents assess what is and is not abuse and neglect. Some trainings focus on giving family policing agents the tools to differentiate between poverty and neglect; for example, children often lack their own bedroom when families cannot afford to obtain housing with multiple bedrooms due to rising housing costs and low wages, not parental neglect. Agents might learn how to slow down their decision-making to mitigate unconscious racial biases that can impact how they interact with families of a race that is different from their own. They also might learn about the history of racism in the United States and how structural racism has created racial disparities that bring Black families and other families of color into the family policing system at higher rates. Regardless of the specific subject matter of these trainings, the undergirding logic of training as a reform strategy relies on the presupposition that if agents address their own biases and grasp an understanding of the larger economic and social context that families face, they might make better, more accurate decisions about when and if a child faces danger in their home.

The efficacy of these trainings, to the extent that they hold the capacity to create changes that lessen the harms of structural racism and poverty, continues to be dubious (Hanna 2021). Their inefficacy is at least in part due to a misunderstanding of the cause of racial disparities in the family policing system. Individual actors within the system do have the ability to make important decisions about the trajectory of families' lives. However, because family policing interventions are fundamentally harmful and built around a white, middle-class standard by which all other parents are judged, even tremendous shifts in individual behavior and biases cannot structurally reform a system predicated on oppression. Offering more training as an answer to racism within the family policing system fallaciously assumes that the daily actions of the system—surveillance and the separation of children from their families—can be done in ways that are not harmful.

The argument for better training also assumes that the family policing system is organized to solve problems that families face. When children are removed from their families and placed into foster care, foster families receive monthly payments in order to care for additional children in their home. Yet struggling families do not receive payments from the family policing system to better care for their children and avoid removal. When children are deemed "unsafe" in their families' homes due to poverty, the system provides no support to end financial precarity. Conversely, parents and guardians are often required to attend programs such as parenting classes, counseling, and other services that require them to miss work (and wages) and use transportation they may or may not have access to, all while undergoing the emotional toll of being under family policing surveillance (see, for example, Lee's chapter 4 in this volume). If training is intended to combat the reasons why families enter the family policing system, the effectiveness remains to be seen. Training efforts, as a solution to the system's failure, provide family policing systems cover while creating negligible benefits to children, families, and communities who must navigate family policing and surveillance. Training presents a misalignment between the problem and solution. If racism is systemic, then individual actors cannot loosen the grip of racism within the system. If poverty, not neglect, overwhelmingly leads families into the system, then solutions that fail to locate capitalism and capitalist exploitation as drivers of poverty and financial precarity fall short of providing any concrete material change to families and communities.

Diversity

Nationally, family policing agencies struggle to maintain racially diverse workforces (Lawrence et al. 2020). Like many sectors, the family policing workforce often does not match the communities that agencies interact with, which may contribute to racial biases that lead to disparate outcomes for Black families involved in family policing systems. It is common for institutions to respond to accusations of racism, violence, and harm with diversity and inclusion efforts. The idea is that, if there is increased workforce diversity, families will have better outcomes within the system due to decreased experiences of racism. If the agencies do better at recruiting and retaining a diverse workforce, then over time, child welfare agencies will see better outcomes for Black families.

Similar to the inefficacy of training that reduces individual-level biases, increasing workforce diversity overestimates the power of individual actors to transform a system's functioning. Lessons learned from police reform efforts, for example, underscore this point. Black, Latine, and Asian police officers are generally no less violent toward Black communities than white police officers are (Menifield, Shin, and Strother 2019). In addition, research shows that police officers of color often harbor the same negative feelings about Black communities as white police officers do. Within the family policing system, studies have shown that cases involving Black children are more likely to be confirmed for maltreatment regardless of the race of the caseworker (Rolock and Testa 2005). Moreover, Black caseworkers assess Black families at greater levels of harm than do white caseworkers (Font, Berger, and Slack 2012), further demonstrating that increasing

diversity within the family policing workforce will do little to minimize the disparities that Black families experience.

Ultimately, increasing diversity provides oppressive systems with
the optics of progress that lend them greater legitimacy while failing to
change the underlying oppressive structures. Changing the makeup of
the family policing workforce does not change the system's oppressive
power to surveil, police, and separate families. Individual actors can do
little to lessen the impact of structural racism when their job requires
them to perform activities and duties that systematically oppress predominantly poor Black, Native, and Latine communities.

Decision-Making

With only limited time and resources, family policing agents make
life-altering decisions about families whom they investigate. Research
has also shown that agents make decisions that follow faulty decision-
making logic, often resting on emotions or little information to make
key decisions (Munro 2019). Workers frequently rely on personal discretion when making decisions about child safety (Graham et al. 2015).
Thus, shifting the way decisions are made about families has been
another key area of reform. In an attempt to eliminate individual bias,
decision-making processes have changed to involve multiple reviews
before decisions are made and to require families' involvement in decisions made about the future of their cases.

STRUCTURED DECISION-MAKING

Structured decision-making (SDM) is an approach that employs defined
decision-making criteria at each stage: screening for investigation, determining response priority, identifying immediate threatened harm, and
estimating the risk of future abuse and neglect. SDM uses a framework
that analyzes risk at several decision-making points: the initial phone
call, the first contact with the child/family, the initial investigation, the
case-plan requirements, the decisions made about removal, and the case
closure. Risk-assessment tools, described as the cornerstone of SDM,
are used at these various decision points, purportedly to ensure that
accurate, unbiased decisions are made about families and child safety
(Schwartz et al. 2017). SDM was introduced with the understanding

that agents' decisions are often impacted by their own biases, as well as by their moods and emotions, in hopes of lessening bias and bringing greater equity into how decisions about families are made (Park 2015).

However, despite intentions to produce less bias, the actuarial assessment technology used in SDM models is often riddled with the racism and bias it intends to remove. Research has shown that racism is built into these technologies; Black people are more likely to be categorized as having "higher risk" because individual bias is built into algorithms despite their being computer generated (Angwin and Larson 2016; Roberts 2019). Recent attempts to implement algorithms in the criminal legal system, for example, reveal that algorithms overpredict the risk that Black, Hispanic, and Asian individuals will commit crimes (Johnson 2022). Risk assessments used by the family policing system often identify prior system involvement as a predictor for removal and placement into foster care, creating a perpetual cycle of family surveillance and policing for families who are already exposed to the system's harm (Abdurahman 2021). Risk assessments also rely on normative, predetermined standards of risk and safety. This raises the question of who has the power to determine what is unsafe and what is safe. After safety is determined, who has the power to decide what course of actions need to be taken to maintain safety? In a family policing context, families do not have substantial power to determine what safety looks like to them. Moreover, even if SDM could deliver unbiased decisions, the reform fails to contend with the harm of family separation and leaves the underlying oppressive family policing interventions in place.

BLIND REMOVALS

Like SDM, blind removals are another reform that targets how decisions are made in hopes of ridding bias from decisions. Blind removals follow a simple concept. If agents normally present case findings to a panel of supervisors and managers and include information about the family's race, in blind removals, agents present the same information to the same panel of people while excluding information about the family's race, ethnicity, and other identifiers like names. Blind removals try to remove the ability of racism to influence the decisions made about families.

Blind removals were first piloted in Nassau County, New York, a county with racial demographics similar to those in the United States overall; initial reports showed that blind removals decreased the percentage of children removed from their homes who were Black from 57 to 21 percent (Pryce 2018). The accuracy of these data was debunked by researchers who showed that the percentage of Nassau County children placed into foster care who were Black has vacillated over the years—back to 52.5 percent as recently as 2019 (Loudenback 2021). Thus, the idea of blind removals as an answer to racism within the family policing system relies on faulty logic. While blind removals might lend the system greater credibility by being able to claim that racism does not impact the removal of children from their homes, the process does nothing to end the harm and trauma that accompany a family policing investigation and family separation. Blind removals as a reform leave family separation firmly intact while doing nothing to eliminate the carceral logics of invading families' homes, surveilling and regulating their behavior, and ultimately separating children from their families.

FAMILY DECISION-MAKING

The implementation of family decision-making through what is often called "family team meetings" also attempts to shift how decisions are made about families (Crampton and Jackson 2007). Whereas families are often handed down decisions about their lives, family policing agencies use family team meetings as a mechanism through which families presumably have more power over their case plans. Family team meetings normally involve multiple parties who might be relevant to a family's life and case plan: lawyers, extended family members, social workers, and other individuals who play a significant role in families' lives. By involving several different perspectives, the intent of family team meetings is to arrive at decisions about the future of families that involve all relevant parties, create comprehensive service plans and accountability mechanisms, and leave families feeling as though they have made decisions about their lives. While the implementation of family team meetings seeks to reform how decisions are made about families, beyond optics, they do little to alter the power dynamic at play between families and family policing systems. What mechanisms do families have at their disposal to refuse family team meetings without the threat of family separation? If the child welfare agency offers families support through services, how do these services contribute to the ongoing surveillance and policing of families? If the plans made for "child safety" go awry after the family team meeting, how do families ensure that child separation does not occur or that reunification remains an option in their case plan? In other words, family team meetings add the feeling and appearance of greater power and control for families over their lives, while ultimately continuing to concede power over their futures to the family policing agency.

Alternative Responses

There has long been criticism that family policing systems fail to offer adequate prevention services to support family preservation. Instead of offering families services and supports to keep families together, advocates argue that the system too often removes children from their homes when supportive services should have been considered. An analysis by Rosinsky and colleagues (2023) of family policing expenditures supports this claim, showing that family policing agencies tend to spend far more on out-of-home placement than on prevention services. As a solution to the lack of investment in prevention services, reforms have focused on increasing the availability of in-home services to families. This focus has led to the creation of alternative response systems. Generally, alternative responses assign families whose safety risk is identified as low or moderate to a less intensive case plan in hopes of strengthening the family and preventing future harm. The focus on prevention has also led to changes to financing streams that more easily allow for states to claim federal dollars for prevention services. The logic behind these reforms frames the family policing agency as a benign helping agency that, with the right investments and focus, can offer children, families, and communities the supports and services they need to be safe, healthy, and happy.

Kelley Fong (2020, 2023) details some of the key concerns with prevention services that are administered through the family policing system. Fong traces how the coercive power of child protective services can cause stress and strain in families' lives and even exacerbate social stratification, as many of the families who are subject to investigations are poor Black, Native, and Latine families. Because government entities have the power to remove children from homes, the services and supports they offer tend to create stress for families, even when services might be of use to them. When families receive prevention services that are administered by family policing agencies, they are also subject to monitoring by the agency while receiving those services. This monitoring creates scrutiny over many areas of families' lives. Families' lives become monitored by government agencies, unleashing a greater potential for future system involvement.

Further, families often lack the ability to make decisions about what services are best suited for them. Most families are mandated to comply with services as suggested by a caseworker, regardless of whether those services are of particular use to the family. In addition, services that agencies offer are normally rendered through private organizations that contract with the state. This means that families are only offered services that are approved for funding by official, state-sanctioned bodies like the Title IV-E Prevention Services Clearinghouse, which was established and is maintained by the federal government and has been sharply criticized for screening out programs that provide culturally and linguistically competent services (e.g., Wilson 2021). Services that are not already preapproved are not eligible for federal funding and therefore not offered to families, even if families would find those services helpful, such as services offered by their faith community or other community-based organizations.

While increasing prevention services appears to offer families greater supports, true support cannot be offered by family policing agencies when the support is coupled with increased monitoring, regulation of families' lives, and the threat of child removal if families do not engage in services in ways that are deemed acceptable by the state. Services rendered by family policing agencies also stymie children's, families', and communities' abilities to determine what care, healing, and support look like for them. Prevention cannot occur within an oppressive framework of surveillance and punishment, and reforms that advocate for prevention further legitimize the narrative that the family policing system is a helping system rather than a system of policing.

Abolition Is the Only Solution

The racist inequities that exist in the family policing system, and the harm and oppression that result, have been known for decades. Despite decades of reforms to address these issues, these reforms—as well as the current goals of racial equity—fundamentally misunderstand and misdiagnose the problem they seek to address. Reforms have failed to result in meaningful change because they have focused primarily on system improvements, while the foundational intervention on which child welfare systems are built—the forcible and involuntary separation of children from their parents—has remained unchanged. Reforms also fail to address the root causes for why families come into contact with the family policing system. Instead of mitigating the likelihood that children and families experience harm, the family policing system inflicts more harm in responding to hardships that families face. In other words, these efforts have failed because they have focused on improving a harmful system rather than eliminating harm.

Thus, the vision for the future of the family policing system must be a vision of abolition. The racist origins of family separation and the racist intent on which the system is built are so deeply rooted in its policies and structures that they cannot simply be revised or reformed. Reforms rely on mechanisms that seek to change how and to what degree children, families, and communities are oppressed and harmed, but they do not seek to end oppression and harm.

Reforms also fail to address how structural forces like poverty and racism shape families' experiences and interactions with each other. Abolition, on the other hand, involves simultaneously ending the racist structures that produce harm and building resources and supports designed by families and communities that promote the safety and well-being of children in their homes. This does not mean the creation of a stronger welfare state—this means the creation of a new society where the concept of "welfare" does not exist because all families have what they need. In this way, abolition is not about simply ending the family policing system; it is about creating a new society where the need for a family policing system is obsolete.

While this idea may initially appear radical, it is intended to be. Abolition of harmful systems that perpetuate racist inequities is the only way forward if we are to truly achieve a just and healthy society. For the family policing system, this work can begin by recognizing the misconception of family policing intervention as a "helpful service" provided to "vulnerable" families. Now is the time to critically reevaluate the use of forced family separation as an intervention for families who must navigate a society inundated with racism, discrimination, and unequal access to resources and opportunities. As the previous sections have addressed, forced family separation has its roots in the dehumanizing system of human chattel slavery as a means of maintaining dominance and control over Black families. Today, dominance and control are maintained through the systemic surveillance and overinvolvement of Black families in the family policing system and the harmful outcomes that result.

This harm will persist if we continue to surveil and separate families who are already impacted by racist policies that have segregated them into communities characterized by inadequate access to housing, health care, employment, education, and economic opportunities. However, the development of alternative responses continues to be stifled by entrenchment in and justification of the current model. These justifications often point to success stories or certain protective factors that may be achieved through foster care, such as a greater likelihood of graduating high school or enrolling in college (Font et al. 2018). Yet these and other perceived or actual benefits of foster care can be achieved through alternative means such as quality public education, free public college, or guaranteed incomes that do not inherently impart harm. By applying a strengths-based perspective in place of the existing deficit lens, we can begin to identify and amplify the strengths of families and communities and then use those to develop proactive and restorative courses of action. These can be used as the basis for redirecting funds that are currently used to maintain a massive system of foster care and instead begin the process of divesting from a harmful and oppressive system and investing in the safety and well-being of children, families, and communities.

In addition to direct material supports—including a universal basic income, permanent child allowances, and other direct cash transfers—we also advocate for broader structural changes necessary to end poverty and advance the safety and well-being of all children, including a housing guarantee, access to quality food, free public transportation, and free and accessible child care, health care, and mental health care. Each of these will require significant policy changes, but these are policy changes that are needed if we are to truly become a society that cares for the well-being of children. And these are policy solutions that are possible in the near term and have been shown to significantly reduce contact with family policing systems (Berger et al. 2017; Cancian, Yang, and Slack 2013). It is within the power of the government to significantly reduce, if not eliminate, poverty.

The Child Abuse Prevention and Treatment Act (CAPTA) is a key mechanism of poverty governance. CAPTA sets general guidelines about what child maltreatment looks like and serves as the federal standard for child maltreatment. CAPTA requires individual states to set definitions and standards for child abuse and neglect and requires states to adopt mandatory reporting procedures. Mandated reporting requires professionals—doctors, teachers, therapists, and other service providers—who come into contact with families and their children to report suspected abuse or neglect to a hotline. However, neglect is a broadly defined category that is often conflated with conditions of poverty, such as inadequate housing, inadequate supervision, lack of food in the home, and/or visibly worn or tattered clothes. Moreover, research reveals that "all states include at least one broad income-related factor in their definitions of maltreatment" (Williams, Dalela, and Vandivere 2022). In practice, this means that families can be reported to a child-abuse hotline and experience an investigation for factors directly related to poverty.

Poverty is detrimental to children's and families' well-being, but poverty is not the fault of individual parents. It is a systemic issue that can only be solved on a wide scale by systemic solutions. Thus, we can significantly reduce family separations that result from poverty governance by recognizing that neglect standards and definitions unfairly punish parents for the social and economic conditions they face while working to end poverty and the conditions that harm children and their families in the first place. The family policing system does not provide resources to remedy poverty, and as such, state-sanctioned separation of children from their parents should not be a response to families living in poverty.

We also seek to build on the strengths of families by shifting power away from state-sponsored interventions that are coercive and harmful and, rather, shifting power to families and communities and ensuring they have the resources necessary to promote healing, address harm when harm occurs, and be responsible to each other. Services should be available to families outside of carceral systems in ways that meet their holistic needs and account for the larger systemic issues, including societal racism and oppression, that serve as barriers to achieving their desired goals. Communities should have the responsibility for working with families to identify the services and supports that will best meet families' needs. Ultimately, what families need to thrive should be the standard used to determine the appropriateness of the services and supports they are able to access.

In calling for abolition, we recognize that there are extreme cases of abuse and neglect that occur in society. We also recognize that family policing agencies have often been unable to prevent harm to children— even with their coercive power of family separation—and often this harm occurs to children under their supervision. In this recognition, we seek to understand why we live in a society where such harm occurs and how we can support the creation of a society where such harm does not occur—this is the work of abolition. Abolition does not mean abandoning the need to protect children. It means building new ways of protecting and supporting families that also eliminate coercive systems of surveillance and punishment. When harm does occur, we seek solutions for harm that are noncarceral and do not rely on state-sanctioned family separation as a means of addressing harm. We seek to build mechanisms of support that do not cause further harm by separating families and fragmenting communities but, rather, mechanisms that support families in autonomously identifying what is needed for healing, for safety, and for preventing future harm.

Abolition is not intended to dismantle the child welfare system and leave nothing in its place. We are arguing the opposite. Abolition, as Mariame Kaba (2020) describes, is a positive vision in which we work toward building (not simply tearing down) the supports that communities need to truly thrive. Our vision for abolition includes communities having access to mental health services, jobs that pay living wages, well-funded public schools, health care, housing, child care, and community-based interventions to prevent harm from occurring in the first place. In some cases, communities will need to work intensely, invest heavily, and collaborate creatively to ensure that children are safe and that families stay together. In this way, we seek to render the use of state surveillance and separation obsolete because in its place, we have collectively created the conditions for all children, youth, and families to truly thrive.

Ultimately, we envision a society in which the idea of a government system that forcibly separates children from their parents would never be brought into existence because the idea is so repellant. We acknowledge that many of the specific strategies needed to achieve this vision are beyond what we have yet imagined. However, we assert that the supposed need to identify these specific strategies now is rooted in a culture of white supremacy that demands a solution before we can begin to explore what is possible. We also acknowledge that white supremacist culture seeks to control the solution and define whose expertise is centered in identifying that solution. In pursuing abolition, we understand that there is not one right way to achieve this—there are many paths, many futures, and many communities already innovating and building these alternatives—and we can continue to build.

Finally, in acknowledging the need for abolition, it is important to acknowledge that the family policing system is just one part of the carceral web. From incarceration to immigration detention to family policing, we oppose the surveillance and state-sanctioned separation of children from their families in all forms. We build on the work of reproductive justice, which centers bodily autonomy and asserts that parents should have the power to make decisions about how and when they will parent and the ability to raise their families in conditions that are free of oppression. We also recognize that reparations are key to abolition; beyond necessary monetary payment, we believe that true reparations require the dismantling of the structures that produce harm: racial capitalism, imperialism, colonialism, white supremacy, patriarchy, ageism, adultism, and anti-Blackness. In other words, we seek to build a world where the care, support, and well-being of children, families, and communities are fully realized.

13

Reimagining Child Welfare

A Social-Justice-Oriented System of Poverty-Related Family Support and Enhanced Reunification Services

DEE WILSON AND ERIN J. MAHER

Dissatisfaction with the US child welfare system has been widespread for decades and has reached a fever pitch during recent years. Some critics want to abolish the entire system. Others want a less extreme reorientation of child welfare policy and practice that goes beyond piecemeal reforms. Concrete proposals for a comprehensive reorientation of child welfare are few and far between, but there is a widely shared belief that the mission of child welfare must be reimagined with fundamentally different values and policy goals. This chapter is intended to contribute to the reimagining of child welfare, while retaining a strong commitment to the protection of children from child maltreatment, including neglect.

We validate many of the positions of other authors in this volume about the nature and extent of child welfare involvement among poor and low-income children and families and the disproportionate representation of Black and American Indian/Alaskan Native children. We acknowledge that the child welfare system functions as a form of poverty governance, given that most families who are reported and investigated for child abuse and neglect are impoverished, often severely so. This disparate representation increases as the level of (mostly coercive) interventions becomes more disruptive to family life, that is, when children are removed from their homes and placed in foster care. The institutional and policy structures of the child welfare system reflect race, gender, and class inequalities, particularly as they pertain to single, poor women of color, revealing unwritten social norms regarding what constitutes adequate parenting and child maltreatment (Lee 2016; Reich 2005). We share some of these critiques with upEND (2022) and other critics who seek to abolish the child welfare system (see Dettlaff and Pendleton, chapter 12 in this volume). However, we criticize their lack of acknowledgment of, and thus absence of plans to address, the devastating effect of chronic maltreatment on children, particularly chronic and pervasive neglect, the impact of which is often underestimated. In addition, we believe it is dangerous to abolish the child welfare system without offering concrete alternatives to respond to child maltreatment, which we lay out in detail in this chapter.

Extensive research on child-welfare-involved families has illuminated the intersection of parental poverty with trauma histories, substance use disorders (SUDs), domestic violence, and mental illness that can result in both serious physical and emotional harm to children (Fong 2017; Jonson-Reid et al. 2010; Loman 2006). In addition, the disproportionate involvement of Black and American Indian families in child welfare systems creates another racialized dimension to policy governance and social control of parenting practices. Whether this disproportionality stems from differences in poverty rates and/or institutional racism within the child welfare system (that is, racism rooted in social structures, policies, and decision-making practices) has been the subject of lengthy, ongoing debates (Dettlaff and Boyd 2020), including discussions about the overuse of mandatory reporting laws to surveil or "police" low-income communities of color (Roberts 2021, 2022). However, poverty and structural racism are not mutually exclusive explanations for racial disproportionality. Poverty rates, especially rates of extreme poverty among Black and American Indian families, are a major factor in racial disproportionality at the front end of child protection systems, while institutional racism and disdain for poor parents contribute to the most punitive intervention possible: the permanent loss of children through termination of parental rights.

We argue that child welfare systems should explicitly take on issues of community disadvantage and family poverty, both in early intervention family support services and in foster care and reunification services. Revision of statutes and policies will be required for this redirection of resources. A strong focus on child safety should permeate all reforms. If we address the economic survival and security needs of parents with child welfare involvement, families of all races/ethnicities will be better served, and racial disproportionality in child welfare outcomes will be reduced, though not eliminated. Child protective services (CPS) interventions will be viewed as less threatening, with large potential benefits to families rather than as a family misfortune. In addition, child welfare policy and practice should be reoriented to less frequent use of coercion, including court involvement, and greater reliance on voluntary service plans. Reversal of the preference in public policy for adoption over reunification is needed. Parents undergoing reunification with their legally dependent children should also receive the same economic support for a period of at least two years as parents who adopt children from foster care.

These goals can only be met through significant investments in concrete services that reduce material hardship in low-income families and safety-oriented services, rather than through persistent attacks on the child welfare system without practical, comprehensive solutions. At the same time, a system that fails to address underlying inequalities (both racial/ethnic and economic), provides insufficient supports to families, and quickly defaults to coercion is understandably vulnerable to such critiques. For example, qualitative studies of parents' experiences have found that child welfare involvement often does little to improve parental functioning and may drive families further into poverty, despair, and marginalization, leaving children in harm's way (Fong 2020).

Prevalence and Profile of Child Maltreatment and CPS Investigations

CPS is not a small program that touches a small percentage of marginalized families and vulnerable children; rather, CPS is present at some point in the lives of more than a third of low-income children and about half of Black and American Indian children (Kim et al. 2017; Putnam-Hornstein et al. 2021). Furthermore, severe poverty (income less than half the federal poverty level) is associated both with elevated rates of child maltreatment and with CPS involvement, including foster care. Black and American Indian families are three times more likely to be severely poor than are white families (Annie E. Casey Foundation 2024). A large survey of open child welfare cases in Washington State found that almost half of these system-involved parents were living in deep poverty, with an annual income of less than $10,000, and one-fifth did not have any income from either employment or welfare and were not living with someone whose annual income exceeded $20,000 (Marcenko, Lyons, and Courtney 2011).

CPS operates as a wide-net surveillance system, which is largely directed at low-income families who are also disproportionately Black and American Indian. Qualitative research has documented that the social service agencies that disadvantaged families rely on often make CPS reports in the hope that CPS may be able to help the struggling parents when their own agencies do not have the resources to do so (Fong 2017). Poverty has a large influence on the likelihood that families will be reported and investigated for child maltreatment; the system is structured toward surveillance. As noted by some scholars, "Child protection records reflect a system designed—through regulation, statutes, and policies—to do exactly what the numbers reflect: surveil and investigate large numbers of children and families even though only a small number will ultimately receive services. Unfortunately, the limited specificity with which CPS surveillance operates is disproportionately borne by low-income families and families of color" (Putnam-Hornstein et al. 2021, 1162). The idea that a higher screening rate is better than a lower one assumes that surveillance of marginalized communities, in and of itself, has a positive benefit for child protection, when in fact the opposite is the case. Lower screening rates are vital in reducing unmanageable workload pressures and, in so doing, improving the quality of CPS investigations and services.

Poverty-Related Services to Support Families as a Goal of Child Welfare

Child neglect is deeply enmeshed with poverty. Nationally, three-quarters of child maltreatment victims are substantiated for neglect, far outnumbering substantiated victims of physical abuse (17 percent) or sexual abuse (9 percent) (USDHHS 2022b). The *Fourth National Incidence Study of Child Abuse and Neglect* found that children in families earning less than $15,000 a year and/or with other markers of low socioeconomic status were seven times more likely to experience neglect than were other children (Sedlak et al. 2010). Given the profile of reported child maltreatment, predominantly neglect, and the strong (sometimes causal) association between neglect and poverty, one might assume that public child welfare systems make large investments in poverty-related services, such as funding for food, housing, clothing, transportation, medical and dental care, and child care. This assumption would be naïve. Some state child welfare systems have little or no poverty-related services, while most have modest and time-limited funds for concrete services. Only about 60 percent of families with a substantiated report of child abuse or neglect receive any post-investigation services (including in-home services and foster care). Less than a third of families with unsubstantiated CPS reports receive any post-response services (USD-HHS 2022b).

The services that families receive through CPS involvement do not usually address their concrete, basic needs. CPS agencies prioritize investigations and assessments, not the provision of family support services. We concur with Leroy Pelton (2015, 31) that "any strategy aimed at greatly reducing the incidence of child abuse and neglect must centrally address this bedrock context [poverty] in which severe harm to children thrives. Without a key focus on material hardship, other additionally desirable approaches will not succeed in significantly reducing the incidence and severity of child abuse and neglect within our nation."

Definitions of "Neglect"

Definitions of "neglect" in state statutes, as summarized by the Child Welfare Information Gateway (CWIG 2022a), reflect assumptions regarding parental responsibility that are rarely discussed or questioned. Depending on the state, "neglect" is defined as "failure," "refusal," or "inability" of parents, guardians, or custodians to provide "minimal," "essential," "necessary," or "adequate" care in providing for children's basic needs. Most state statutes provide a brief concrete list of basic needs such as food, shelter, clothing, supervision, and medical care. In a few states (e.g., Washington), "neglect" is defined abstractly as "negligent treatment or maltreatment," a fill-in-the-blanks definition. Educational neglect, failure to provide education as required by law, is included in many state statutes, though in some states (e.g., Washington and Oregon), a stand-alone allegation of educational neglect is not grounds for a CPS investigation. While most state statutes agree on a short list of children's basic needs, there are also large differences in states' definitions of other types of alleged neglect (e.g., parental use of illegal substances during pregnancy or a child witnessing domestic violence). A few states refer to a "pattern of inadequate or negligent care" in their neglect statutes, which is a rare attempt to address chronic neglect in law.

The emphasis on parental responsibility for the provision of adequate care of children is so ubiquitous in state statutes that it is easy to overlook. Just over half of states and the District of Columbia have an exception for acts of omission of care due to poverty or financial inability to provide (CWIG 2022a). For example, Wisconsin law defines "neglect" as a parent's "refusal, failure or inability" to provide necessary care "for reasons other than poverty." Although CPS is involved largely with indigent families, child protection is organized around investigations of parental wrongdoing. The services that child welfare agencies offer (or pressure parents to accept) are largely of a therapeutic and educational nature, designed to develop parenting skills or address parents' behavioral health needs, rather than concrete services intended to reduce material hardship resulting from poverty.

Currently, not a single state statute contains any language following the poverty exception with a requirement that the child welfare agency assist a family in obtaining the necessary resources to meet a child's basic needs or (even more strongly), if no such resources are available in the community, a requirement that the public agency fund or provide essential resources. State statutes are silent regarding the child welfare agency's responsibility, or the juvenile court's authority, to assist caregivers in meeting their parental responsibilities when lack of economic resources prevents them from providing adequate care. Policy makers in the United States have been careful to separate legal definitions of "neglect" from any legal requirement of public agency responsibility to meet children's basic needs when parents have inadequate financial resources. Defining "neglect" in terms of parental fault or failure to provide for children's basic needs rather than the inability to meet those needs (for whatever reason) leads to punitive policies and practices, such as ignoring families' homelessness or food insecurity while holding parents accountable for not caring for their children's basic needs. Revising state statutes and federal law to make the adequate care of children a joint parental and public agency responsibility is the first necessary step to reorient child protection programs around the needs of neglected children rather than around far-less-frequent reports of physical and sexual abuse. This one change in state and federal law, along with the funding to implement it, would lead to a dramatic change in how low-income parents react to CPS interventions, especially when such interventions address food insecurity, family homelessness or inadequate housing, lack of medical and dental care, and childcare needs. This change in law would diminish the absurdity of investigating allegations of neglect while allowing almost one-quarter of Black and American Indian families to live with chronic food insecurity (Haider and Roque 2021) and allowing families with children to live in cardboard boxes under freeways or in dangerous homeless encampments without offering concrete assistance to change these circumstances.

The Imperative to Reduce Coercion in Child Welfare

The goal of child protection reform should be to substantially increase benefits to families to ensure that all children receive a minimal standard of care, while reducing the use of coercion to the extent possible, without compromising child safety. Many scholars have pointed out the conflicting role of child welfare between coercion and social control, on the one hand, and assistance and support, on the other (Fong 2020; Woodward 2021)—what Fong describes as dual capacities for care and coercion. Currently, child protection in most public agencies involves a large element of coercion, with limited, if any, services and resources parents want and need.

Perhaps the lack of supportive services is one reason why child welfare services have been ineffective at preventing maltreatment recurrence (Fuller and Nieto 2014). For example, in Washington State, maltreatment recurrence ranges from 21 to 27 percent within twelve months, depending on service track (WSDCYF 2021). Strikingly, an analysis of a birth cohort in California found that 60 percent of infants who remained at home following a CPS investigation were the subject of another report within five years, and most of these parents had not received services at the time of the initial report (Putnam-Hornstein et al. 2015).

The association of foster care with the coercive removal of children from parents due to abuse and/or neglect is taken for granted in current policy discussions, but this association does not reflect the early history of foster care in the United States. In *Raising Government Children*, Catherine Rymph (2017) points out that most children in foster care during the mid-twentieth century were there due to parental request. She asserts, "Voluntarism was what made foster care benign. It helped families stay together instead of tearing them apart. Foster care did not really become a 'system' until it came to emphasize the element of coercion, which occurred with the decline of voluntary placement" (2017, 168). Foster care can frequently be used as a family support service, but not when it must be accompanied by legal system involvement and persistent threat of permanent separation. Many families experience crises that render them temporarily unable to adequately parent due to economic misfortune, escalation of interpersonal conflict, or a mental health emergency. It is not useful or necessary to bring all families whose children need foster care into the legal system and start a clock ticking toward termination of parental rights.

Parents in communities or neighborhoods with high levels of CPS involvement are acutely aware that a CPS investigation can lead to the temporary or permanent loss of their child; CPS is thus commonly viewed as an intrusion and misfortune. CPS should increase the benefits available to families and communities while reducing the threat of involuntary child removal. This alternative way of responding to families in crisis would effectively shift resources and power back to disadvantaged communities and families (Fong 2023). These goals can be achieved only with a large infusion of resources for families screened in for further investigation by CPS and through early intervention prior to and during a CPS investigation or assessment.

The likely objection that it would be prohibitively expensive to require public agencies to fund necessary poverty-related services for families with open CPS cases is mistaken. In fiscal year 2020, nationwide child welfare expenditures were about $31.4 billion, just over half of which was from state and local sources. Federal funding—which accounts for less than half of national expenditures on the child welfare system—has remained relatively stable in recent years (Rosinsky, Fischer, and Hass 2023). The federal government could easily double its investment in child welfare if policy makers were serious about child welfare system reform. Nothing is fiscally prohibitive about doubling federal support for child welfare in a country that spent trillions of dollars on pandemic relief in 2020–21 and has since had an annual federal budget of almost $7 trillion, at least one-fifth of which is discretionary spending (Congressional Budget Office 2023).

It is apparent from natural experiments of COVID-19 pandemic-relief policies that providing economic benefits to families works quickly and effectively to move children out of poverty. For example, the child tax credit authorized by the American Rescue Plan led to a 40 percent reduction in child poverty, which allowed those families to pay for essential needs (Wise and Chamberlain 2022). Other quasi-experimental studies have demonstrated that modest economic interventions reduce child maltreatment, especially reports of child neglect (Bywaters et al. 2016). A recent study (Johnson-Motoyama et al. 2022) found a strong relationship between more generous Supplemental Nutrition Assistance Program state policies and reductions in CPS reports, substantiated investigations (especially for neglect), and foster care placements.

It is not the cost of the reforms proposed in this chapter that stand in the way of their enactment. Rather, it is the values they embody: a shared public/parental responsibility for the welfare of low-income, disproportionately Black and American Indian children reported to CPS, mostly for alleged neglect. Furthermore, a large increase in poverty-related services provided to families at the time of the first or second maltreatment report, whether or not substantiated, has the potential to prevent situational and sporadic neglect from developing into chronic neglect, which over time may become coupled with physical, sexual, and emotional abuse. Research on chronically referring families has consistently found that allegations of multiple types of child maltreatment become more common as the number of subsequent reports increases (Jonson-Reid et al. 2003; Loman 2006).

Chronic Neglect as a Unique Manifestation of Child Maltreatment

Chronic neglect is a caregiver's "ongoing, serious pattern of deprivation of a child's basic physical, developmental, or emotional needs" (Kaplan et al. 2009, 2) and is distinct from situational or sporadic neglect, which is more common, intermittent, infrequent, and less severe in its impact on children's development. Both neglect and chronic neglect can have physical, supervisory, and/or emotional elements. Sarah Font and Kathryn Maguire-Jack (2020) point to a large body of research that has described the association of neglect with parental substance abuse and mental illness (often co-occurring) as well as domestic violence. They also document that the impact of neglect and abuse is different from and more detrimental than poverty alone. Chronic neglect generally has multiple causes (Jonson-Reid 2010; Kaplan et al. 2009; Loman 2006), only one of which is material hardship, and to equate neglect, and especially chronic neglect, with "just poverty" is dangerously misleading. Chronic neglect in early life can have lifelong negative effects on physical and mental health, including early mortality, and can result in the emergence of antisocial or violent behavior (National Scientific Council on the Developing Child 2012; Schuck and Widom 2021).

The etiology among poverty, substance abuse, mental health conditions, and domestic violence in child-welfare-involved families is not well understood or clearly articulated in child welfare research. A plausible hypothesis is that the combination of material hardship and psychological afflictions undermines self-efficacy, the ability of a parent to take reasonable actions on behalf of themselves and their children. CPS interventions in chronically neglecting families are often too little, too late. Ideally, CPS should never be the first or only contact a public agency has with a troubled parent. Voluntary services and supports need to be available to parents struggling with SUDs or with chronic mental health conditions before—not after—a CPS report is made. A strong, well-financed public health system could reach out to parents receiving publicly funded treatment for SUDs or severe mental health conditions, without the use of coercion and with offers of a wide range of parenting supports, including child care, respite care, and concrete assistance for material hardships. A model of shared expertise across the public health, child welfare, and behavioral and mental health systems could guarantee that parents have the financial resources to meet the basic needs of their children, including housing, food, transportation, and dental care. In addition, safety-oriented services such as child care, respite care, and in-home assistance for the care of disabled and chronically ill children are needed to protect children who present complex childcare challenges.

Such efforts will require ample resources from blended financing streams. Interventions will need to be delivered through strong interagency collaborations that include child welfare caseworkers, substance abuse treatment specialists, mental health therapists, public health nurses, and parent advocates. These case-management teams would ideally be colocated in family support centers. Finally, parental engagement and empowerment models should be embedded within the service-delivery framework to provide parents with an active voice in their treatment plans, which is an ethical imperative and an essential element of trauma-informed practice (Corwin 2012). These interventions need to be evaluated, sustained, and institutionalized as part of normal practice, rather than coming and going through temporary initiatives or pilot programs. The current child protection model for intervening in chronic neglect is a proven failure.

Research has shown high rates of burnout among child welfare workers generally due to the nature of the work (Pharris, Munoz, and Hellman 2022). These experiences are exacerbated when working with families who repeatedly come back into the system and whose well-being does not improve regardless of services. A CPS caseworker is assigned responsibility for a family with seemingly therapeutically intractable complex problems, with many (sometimes dozens) of previous CPS reports for a combination of types of child abuse, a multitude of service episodes, and a resistance to ongoing engagement (Chaffin et al. 2011; Corwin et al. 2014; Loman 2006). These families take up a disproportionate amount of child welfare resources (Loman 2006). One of the few studies to focus on the experience of workers dedicated to families experiencing chronic neglect found that caseworkers reported a desire for training in secondary trauma, the strain of emotionally difficult work, the need for more professional support, the potential for burnout, and the importance of self-care and maintaining hope (Corwin et al. 2014). CPS caseworkers also face the challenge of not always being able to provide the types of resources these families need, such as services for co-occurring SUDs and mental health disorders, domestic violence services, poverty-related services, early-intervention child development services, and therapeutic child care (Corwin et al. 2014).

Furthermore, the prevention of all-cause mortality from unintentional injuries and medical causes should be a case-planning goal in cases of chronic neglect and chronic maltreatment. The Child Abuse Prevention and Treatment Act (42 U.S.C.A. § 5106g) defines "child maltreatment" narrowly, as "parent or caregiver actions or failure to act resulting in imminent risk of serious harm to children." Such narrow definitions at the state and federal level reflect a dangerous mischaracterization of safety issues in chronic maltreatment, in which children experience cumulative developmental and emotional harm across multiple childcare domains (Wilson and Horner 2005).

Strengthening, Not Dismantling, Foster Care for Vulnerable Children

Over a quarter of children in US foster care are two years old or younger at the time of placement, and approximately half are under six years old (USDHHS 2022a). Proposals to eliminate involuntary foster care, even for highly vulnerable neglected infants and toddlers, have become common in publications by child welfare abolitionists. Most young children in foster care are placed there due to neglect and/or parental SUDs (Williams and Sepulveda 2019). In many of these cases, foster care or kinship care is the only safe alternative, especially in the absence of strong preventative, collaborative child welfare responses among public agencies as described previously. While children in foster care have higher rates of all-cause mortality than does the general child population (Chaiyachati et al. 2020), evidence indicates that foster care reduces all-cause mortality among very young children with reports of child maltreatment (Schneiderman, Prindle, and Putnam-Hornstein 2021; Segal et al. 2021). Foster care with legal involvement (that is, involuntary foster care) is necessary to ensure child safety in some circumstances and when adoption is the only good outcome for a young child (e.g., child abandonment). However, legal involvement is often used as a matter of course when voluntary service plans could be safely employed. US child welfare agencies need to relearn how to use voluntary foster care when no good purpose is served by making children legally dependent. We can learn from foster care programs in various European countries that are more family-support centered and characterized by voluntary partnerships with parents (Gilbert, Parton, and Skivenes 2011).

It is essential that foster care systems be strengthened and reconfigured rather than dismantled. While US foster care systems are often beneficial for infants and other preschool children, they often do more harm than good for school-age children and youth who have challenging emotional and behavioral disorders. Children with behavior problems are less likely to reunify with parents than are youths with few behavior problems (Akin 2011). These youths are often "bounced" from home to home, prescribed cocktails of psychotropic drugs, bullied by stronger peers in residential care settings, and sometimes abused by caregivers. Considerable evidence exists that US foster care systems, overall, are not therapeutic for youths with emotional and behavioral problems and are frequently unsafe (Katz, Courtney, and Novotny 2017), as reported by foster care alumni themselves (Havlicek and Courtney 2016). This disgraceful situation is the result of many policy makers' and child advocates' unwillingness to invest in transforming foster care into a therapeutic system with the goal of developmental repair from trauma, along with their unrealistic ideas about the immediate availability of evidence-based prevention programs that can be funded under the Family First Prevention Services Act of 2018 (FFPSA; P.L. 115-123 [2018]). As of yet, few children have received services under this new legislation, which was designed to promote evidence-based programs to prevent the need for foster care (Hughes and Riley 2023).

Many advocates, policy makers, and child welfare leaders view reductions in foster care as virtually identical to child welfare reform and prioritize the use of nonkin foster care. However, kin caregivers are generally no more prepared and able to care for youth with emotional and behavioral challenges than are nonkin foster parents, and recent research suggests that they are less likely to take in children with clinical levels of externalizing behavior (Ferraro, Maher, and Grinnell-Davis 2022). Efforts to reduce foster care placement, and especially nonkin placement, have strengthened resistance to investments in foster care systems and led to a stubborn refusal in some states to consider development of a cadre of professional foster parents to care for youths with emotional and behavioral disorders. In addition, persistent efforts embodied in the FFPSA are designed to greatly reduce or eliminate group residential care. Consistent disinvestment in foster care has resulted in a public policy debacle in many states, where child welfare agencies have been forced to use hotel placements, office placements, twenty-four-hour placements, emergency rooms, and jails—placements that can be characterized as systemic abuse of youths in need of a stable foster placement (Hughes and Riley 2023; Whitehead 2022).

The reality is that almost four hundred thousand children and youths are in foster care on any one day (USDHHS 2022a), and anywhere from 39 to 63 percent of children in foster care have clinically significant emotional or behavioral problems (Burns et al. 2004). FFPSA allows states to receive federal matching funds for in-home foster-care-prevention services that meet a high standard of evidence of effectiveness, referred to as "evidence-based." However, as mentioned earlier, few children are receiving these programs or services, and most are not targeted toward young, chronically maltreated children. Furthermore, evidence-based placement-prevention programs among children who are vaguely defined as "candidates for foster care" have not been established with clear evidence. For example, randomized control trials of family-preservation services from past decades found that a large percentage of children in the control condition (those not receiving family-preservation services) identified by caseworkers as at risk of imminent harm were not actually placed in foster care. In other words, these programs were often not accurately targeting a group of children "at risk" for foster care (O'Reilly et al. 2010; Schuerman, Rzepnicki, and Littell 1994). Expectations that FFPSA will safely reduce the number of children in foster care by funding services for a vaguely defined group of "candidates for foster care" has yet to be demonstrated.

The US child welfare system relies on legal structure, that is, making children legally dependent and limiting parental choice to an extreme degree, another example of the default to coercion embedded in US child welfare policy (Reich 2005). The consequence is that families with urgent needs rarely trust child welfare agencies to help them, preferring to seek other kinds of informal and formal support that put them at risk of being reported to the agency they hope to avoid. Parents with problematic substance use and/or chronic mental illness need to be able to place their children in foster care temporarily while accessing high-quality services to address their complex needs without endangering their parental rights.

Child welfare systems that aspire to safely reduce the use of foster care must increase the availability of safety-oriented services that include therapeutic child care (designed to address the needs of children who have experienced early trauma) and respite care (planned or emergency short-term care). They must also make large investments in improved in-home safety planning, in other words, agreements between the child protective services agency and parents regarding actions to mitigate safety threats when a child remains in the home after a child maltreatment investigation. Safety planning is arguably the weakest part of US child protection programs. Currently, little extant research guides in-home safety planning, which consequently is reliant on dubious practice wisdom.

Reversing Policy Priorities from Adoption to Reunification

The 1997 Adoption and Safe Families Act (ASFA; Public Law 105-89) was signed into law following a near doubling of the number of children in the US foster care system from 1986 to 1998 (US House of Representatives, Committee on Ways and Means 2018). ASFA was intended to substantially increase the number of adoptions from foster care, a trend that had begun before the law's passage. The law provided adoption incentives to states on the basis of the number of completed adoptions over a baseline, but it provided no incentives for reunification. ASFA limited timelines for reunification by requiring states to file for termination of parental rights when a child has been in foster care for fifteen of the past twenty-two months (absent compelling reasons to forgo termination action). In 1998, 15 percent of exits from foster care were to adoption, and 60 percent of exits were to reunification, compared to 25 percent and 47 percent, respectively, in 2021 (USDHHS 2006, 2022a).

States have been slow to make investments in innovative reunification practices models, despite much supportive rhetoric for family preservation. Brief stays in foster care are associated with increased likelihood of reunification (Akin 2011); however, the median time children spend in foster care has increased since 2011, and reunification rates have decreased in the past two decades (Annie E. Casey Foundation 2022). The law accomplished what it was designed to do—increase timely adoptions—though it is unclear whether ASFA developers envisioned a reduction in reunifications.

Changes in permanency outcomes of this magnitude over a couple of decades stem from more than a change in law. Statutory changes rarely have major impacts on outcomes unless public agency staff at all levels embrace the new law and implement it with strong commitment. Public agencies have embraced the ASFA goal of increased adoptions. In *Take Me Home*, Jill Berrick (2009) describes reunification as a lonely, compliance-driven process for low-income parents struggling with substance abuse and mental health issues. Berrick's stories of women who regained custody of their children describe caseworkers missing in action or making token efforts to support mothers in an uphill reunification effort. These stories reflect child welfare system values as embodied in caseworker practice, not just a policy preference for adoption.

Adoption has, until recently, been widely viewed as the most realistic and best permanent plan for children (especially young children) who cannot be safely reunified with parents, particularly when substance abuse is an issue. Former Health and Human Services secretary Alex Azar asserted, "Since the President [Trump] took office, we have focused on prioritizing adoption unlike any previous administration, and we have begun to see results" (ACF 2020).

Understandably, social-justice-oriented critiques of the child welfare system have led to fierce criticism of ASFA's goals and timelines as reflective of structural racism due to its role in permanently disrupting poor and Black families. In 2021, the percentage of exits from foster care to adoption, guardianship, living with other relatives, or aging out without permanence exceeded the percentage of exits to reunification. Currently, just under half of youths exit foster care to reunification (USDHHS 2022a). Furthermore, one study found that reentry into foster care is common, with about 27 percent of children experiencing reentry (Wulczyn et al. 2020). One-sixth of teenagers in foster care were initially placed in foster care before age five (Zulliger et al. 2015). The magnitude of foster care reentry rates is not inevitable; it reflects a lack of investment in stable and safe reunifications. Children who reenter foster care often spend much of their childhood in unstable foster care placements or group and residential care facilities—a hard road for youths with multiple early adversities.

These statistics reflect an alarmingly high and increasing rate of foster children who experience permanent legal separation from their birth parents. Experiences of permanent family separation are not borne equally. A recent study found that parents whose children were covered by public health insurance (i.e., low-income families) were six times more likely to have their parental rights terminated (TPR) than were parents with private insurance (Putnam-Hornstein et al. 2021). While racial disproportionality of Black and American Indian children in foster care is explained to a large extent (but not wholly) by the disproportionate percentage of Black and American Indian families in poverty and severe poverty, disproportionately high rates of TPRs for Black children (Wildeman, Edwards, and Wakefield 2020) reflect an implicit acceptance of permanent low-income and Black family separation.

In addition, the ASFA policy preference for adoption is influenced by the large number of infants who enter foster care. Infants are almost three times more likely to be placed in foster care than any other age group (USDHHS 2022a), and TPR rates are much higher for children who enter foster care as infants or toddlers (Wildeman, Edwards, and Wakefield 2020). Black and American Indian infants are two to three times more likely to enter care than are white infants (Wulczyn, Chen, and Courtney 2011). Consequently, the ASFA preference for adoption has an outsized effect on Black families, though not as great on American Indian families due to the Indian Child Welfare Act and ongoing resistance to TPR by tribes. For this reason, safely reducing TPR rates requires large investments in enhanced services for children from birth to age three and their parents and in reunification and post-reunification services, as outlined in this chapter. However, ASFA requirements do not vary by age of child or other characteristics of the child and parents. It is one size fits all, which is not defensible public policy.

Adoption assistance is a costly federal and state program that supports families who have adopted a child from foster care until they reach the age of majority, as long as the child meets eligibility criteria, regardless of the adoptive parents' income (CWIG 2020a). Over half of children adopted from foster care live in families with household incomes more than 200 percent of the federal poverty guideline (Vandivere, Malm, and

Radel 2009). Yet the costs of adoption support are rarely discussed due to widespread support for adoption across the political spectrum. However, the possibility of providing post-reunification support payments to parents is seldom considered, even though income support for low-income parents reunified with their child would probably reduce reentry into foster care rates. ASFA incentives reflect social values favoring adoption by middle- and upper-class families, while turning a blind eye to the possibility of safely increasing stable reunification rates. ASFA embodies social values that give little or no weight to the permanent separation of children from birth parents, despite the disproportionate effect on Black families.

* * *

Many studies on reunification during the past few decades highlight best practices for reunification (Luu, Collings, and Wright 2022; Ogbonnaya and Keeney 2018). We build on these and recommend the following: (a) use of multidisciplinary care teams for all children embedded within juvenile courts to address families' complex needs; (b) support of foster parent–birth parent alliances for mentoring and visitation; (c) post-reunification services, including reunification support payments of the same amount as adoption support for two years following reunification; (d) extension of ASFA timelines for six to twelve months, depending on the age of the child, to allow greater use of voluntary foster care agreements; (e) therapeutic foster care for at least twenty hours per week for preschool children following reunification to address childhood trauma and provide parent support; (f) use of reunification incentives to states to reverse the ASFA policy preference for adoption, and (g) major investments in housing services and other poverty-related services for parents who enter and complete substance use disorder treatment programs.

Conclusion

Our position is that US child welfare systems need to be reorganized and repurposed to respond more effectively to child neglect, by far the most common type of child maltreatment reported to child protection systems. This restructuring will require a large infusion of funding for poverty-related services and a revision of statutes to require that child welfare agencies provide resources and assist parents in meeting the basic needs of children. Providing for children's basic needs should be redefined in legal statutes as a joint parental and public responsibility.

We take neglect seriously. We do not agree with views expressed in some recent abolitionist critiques of child welfare systems that minimize the safety threats and developmental impact of neglect, especially chronic neglect, on children, by referring only to "extreme cases of abuse and severe neglect" as necessary for government intervention (Center for the Study of Social Policy 2020) and by conflating neglect with "just poverty." We advocate for an administrative restructuring of how public agencies respond to chronically reported families, most of whom are initially reported to CPS for alleged neglect and who (with rare exceptions) involve a parent with one or more chronically relapsing conditions (i.e., substance abuse, mood disorders, and/or domestic violence, and often other challenges as well) (Jonson-Reid et al. 2010; Loman 2006).

Foster care systems are vitally important to the health and safety of chronically neglected young children and should be strengthened rather than dismantled. At the same time, we strongly support use of less coercive child welfare practices, including more frequent use of voluntary service plans rather than out-of-home care regulated by federal and state law. Even when legal structure is necessary to protect children—and it sometimes is—we advocate for use of family empowerment models that give parents a greater say in case planning. We also advocate for revising ASFA to prioritize reunification over adoption, with the goal of increasing rates of safe and stable reunification.

We believe the current child welfare paradigm should be turned upside down, from a coercive system with a thin array of family supports to a family support system that uses coercion as a last resort. At the same time, a focus on child safety and the prevention of child maltreatment is paramount, as severe and/or chronic maltreatment has devastating (potentially lifelong) effects on children's health and well-being. Effective child protection systems cannot ignore or minimize the developmental damage resulting from chronic neglect and its frequent co-occurrence with other types of maltreatment.

Low-income families with child welfare involvement have been subject to an unnecessary degree of coercion and held exclusively accountable for meeting the basic needs of their children, despite severe poverty.

Policies and practices that permanently sever parent-child relationships have been prioritized, with little or no concern regarding the effects on parents who lose their parental rights. These policies are not necessary for child safety; rather, they reflect a set of social values in which low-income parents, particularly those who are Black and American Indian, are treated like a lower caste whose suffering, needs, and interests can be ignored. A humane and socially just child welfare system cannot operate in this fashion.

Conclusion

Toward a Society That Truly Supports Children and Families

JENNIFER RANDLES AND KERRY WOODWARD

Our primary goal for this volume was to bring together historical perspectives and empirical research on how the US child welfare system, or more aptly, the *family policing system*, operates as a form of gendered and racialized poverty governance. We have learned from the preceding chapters how the system surveils, controls, and punishes families, especially poor and low-income families of color, under the guise of protecting children from maltreatment.

Rather than providing the support families need to thrive, the system instead polices families on the basis of the presumption that when children lack a safe and secure home where their physical and emotional needs are met—what the system often defines as *child maltreatment*—it is the result of pathological parenting, rather than vast and deeply entrenched structural inequalities. As Lichtenstein showed (chapter 1), "unseeing" the gendered and racialized poverty at the root of the system was foundational to the professionalization of the child welfare field during the twentieth century.

Part 2 included chapters discussing key policies from historical and contemporary perspectives, addressing ongoing battles over the Indian Child Welfare Act (Hontalas, chapter 2) and implementation of the Adoption and Safe Families Act (ASFA) (Bryson, chapter 3). By comparing child welfare systems in New York City and rural Wisconsin, Lee (chapter 4) showed how geographic context and local racial dynamics shape child welfare practices. Part 3 addressed the left hand of the state and how even services intended to support families are often either insufficient or downright detrimental. For victims of intimate partner violence, calls for help often lead to family separation when mothers are blamed for "failing to protect" their children (Trivedi and Smith, chapter 5). Other parents—mostly mothers—enter the child welfare system when they seek addiction recovery services or prenatal and delivery medical care (Brant, chapter 6). Collins and Bai (chapter 7) showed that housing interventions for deeply poor families, while necessary, are insufficient for keeping those with the most extensive needs safely together.

Part 4 examined interactions between the right, or punitive, hand of the state and the child welfare system, specifically how child welfare and carceral systems collaborate to surveil poor families, especially poor families of color, using punitive tactics to police the boundaries of acceptable parenting. Chapters addressed the coercive impact of family drug treatment courts (Tach, Day, and Mihalec-Adkins, chapter 8), cooperation between police and child protective services (Fong and Smith, chapter 9), and the effects of immigration enforcement on families with undocumented members (Lovato, chapter 10). Finally, Edwards (chapter 11) analyzed how seemingly separate state social policy regimes—namely, child welfare and criminal justice systems—are racialized in similar ways, producing regional patterns of coercive intervention for poor and low-income families of color.

Given the many ways that the family policing system governs family poverty through disciplinary measures and partnerships with other punitive systems, what should be done? Arguing for abolition of the child welfare system, Dettlaff and Pendleton (chapter 12) reasoned that a system built on and rife with race and class oppression can never be reformed but must be eradicated in favor of building a new society where all families and children have what they need to thrive. Advocating for a major reform, Wilson and Maher (chapter 13) instead proposed a series of significant system improvements, including supporting foster parent–birth parent alliances, post-reunification services, and therapeutic foster care; extending ASFA timelines; and guaranteeing financial assistance for struggling families while also ensuring that the system protects children from chronic neglect.

Still, there are many critical issues—including challenges faced by groups uniquely impacted by the family policing system—that individual chapters did not discuss in detail. Some omissions were due to a lack of space or availability of relevant scholars. But often the research in these areas is new and sparse. We highlight in the following sections areas for future critical analysis, including the decentralized and privatized nature of child welfare and the impacts of mandated reporting policies. We then briefly discuss what is currently known about the experiences of fathers, parents with disabilities, and LGBTQ+ youth and families who have contact with the system. These groups have important stakes in how the child welfare system operates—often intersecting with ableist, heteronormative, and cissexist tendencies—as a form of gendered and racialized poverty governance. Next, we discuss how lessons learned from government responses to the COVID-19 pandemic provide further support for dismantling the family policing system and replacing it with a broader system of assistive policies that truly promote child welfare. We conclude by reflecting on abolitionist and reformist approaches to creating a society that provides for and protects rather than polices and punishes poor families.

A Decentralized and Privatized Surveillance System

Like other state systems—including those on the right (punitive) and left (assistive) hands of the state—the US child welfare system is decentralized, with most control resting within individual states and counties, leading to significant differences in policy and practices from one location to another. This decentralized structure helps to explain the wide variation in states' rates of child welfare involvement, children in foster care, and racial disproportionality. While there are comprehensive data about some state-level differences, one key metric is notably missing: poverty rates or socioeconomic level of system-involved families. Unlike racial data, the socioeconomic status of families involved in the system is not recorded. Despite this absence, state-level differences in racial disproportionality and rates of children entering the system due to neglect and housing issues—both tightly associated with poverty—are dramatic. For example, although Black youth are somewhat overrepresented in the Georgia foster care system (constituting 34 percent of the state's youth population but 39 percent of its foster care population), they are dramatically overrepresented in California's foster care population (constituting 5 percent of the state's child population yet 18 percent of the foster care population). Interestingly, despite Georgia's lower rate of foster care placement due to neglect (49 percent compared to 64 percent nationally), in 2021, 20 percent of children in Georgia's foster care system were removed due at least partly to inadequate housing (more than double the national rate of 9 percent). California, on the other hand, cited neglect as a cause of child removal in an astounding 86 percent of cases, but only 3 percent of cases cited inadequate housing (Williams, Rosenberg, and Martinez 2023).

While some of these differences may be due to how states record and calculate causes of child removal, state disparities call for much greater analysis; yet only a few scholars have critically examined their reasons or implications. For example, Carly Hayden Foster (2012) found that states with larger Black populations had far lower levels of racial disproportionality in foster care, raising questions about bias and how family separation decisions are made. Edwards's (2016) previous research revealed that children are more likely to be removed from their families and placed in foster care—and institutional state care—in states with weak, punitive welfare programs and large, punitive criminal justice systems. Additionally, Donna Ginther and Michelle Johnson-Motoyama (2022) demonstrated that when states implement restrictive policies that reduce welfare (TANF) caseloads, the number of children placed in foster care for neglect increases. We need more studies like these to inform national debates and policy.

Along with decentralization, privatization is a central tenet of neoliberalism. Before there were any federal child welfare laws, there were local private agencies that attended to issues of children's well-being, including child maltreatment. However, the past several decades of neoliberal governance have involved a growing number of government contracts with private organizations that are paid to perform government-mandated operations, especially foster care placement and oversight. Some states have embraced not only private, nonprofit agencies but also for-profit companies, raising questions about child safety and government oversight, as well as concerns about surveillance and governance of poor families with a profit motive.

Much like other private, for-profit institutions with government contracts—such as private prisons (USDOJ 2016)—many private, and especially for-profit, child welfare agencies are poorly regulated and often dangerous (US Senate, Committee on Finance 2017). Yet the research on privatized child welfare agencies remains thin and reveals mixed findings (Elgin and Carter 2020; Huggins-Hoyt et al. 2019). Despite the dearth of research, the US Senate Finance Committee issued a scathing 2017 bipartisan report on the privatization of foster care services—particularly for-profit ones. The report acknowledged insufficient data about privatized services nationally but found that states failed to adequately oversee agencies with which they contracted, claiming that children receiving services from for-profit agencies "have been abused, neglected, and denied services" (US Senate, Committee on Finance 2017, 2).

Investigative journalists have also raised serious concerns about privatized foster care. A *Los Angeles Times* analysis found that compared with foster care overseen by public agencies, California youth in privatized foster care were a third more likely to die because of abuse or neglect in foster homes (Therolf 2013). *USA Today* reporters analyzed a decade's worth of Florida records, finding widespread misplacement of children in foster homes where previous evidence of abuse, among other issues, existed. The US Department of Children and Families acknowledged the significant role of privatization in these egregious problems (Beall, Chen, and Salman 2020). By 2022, Nebraska—well-known for its privatization efforts—had ended privatized foster care due to ongoing problems (Loudenback 2022). These findings point to the need for more research on the extent of privatization and how it exacerbates the harms of the child welfare system.

As with privatization, the expansion of mandated reporting requirements has also led to the proliferation of agencies and people involved in poor families' lives. The 1974 Child Abuse Prevention and Treatment Act (CAPTA) required states to implement mandatory reporting of abuse and neglect in order to receive federal funds (Raz 2020). In the past decade, at least thirty-six states have increased reporting requirements, often by expanding the categories of professionals who are mandated to report suspicions of child maltreatment or by increasing the penalties for failing to report (Hixenbaugh, Khimm, and Philip 2022). Significant increases in the number of children reported for suspected maltreatment have resulted. By 2020, professionals were submitting two-thirds of the nearly four million reports of suspected child abuse and neglect in the United States; police officers and other legal/law enforcement personnel (20.9 percent), teachers and other education personnel (17.2 percent), and doctors and other medical personnel (11.6 percent) were the most frequent reporters (USDHHS 2022b).

Mandated reporting laws turn police, doctors, teachers, and others into the "eyes and ears" of the state in a multiorganizational system of maltreatment surveillance (Edwards 2019; Greenberg 2021). While more mandated reporting requirements lead to more investigations, there is no evidence that children are safer (for example, see City Council of Philadelphia 2022). Instead, as chapters in this volume show, mandated reporting often prevents parents from seeking assistance due to fear. Fong and Smith (chapter 9) illuminated how law enforcement personnel and CPS staff cooperate in ways often known to parents, who may avoid contacting police because they are afraid of child welfare system involvement. This is especially true for low-income parents of color, who are targeted for policing. Similarly, Brant's chapter 6 showed how this fear of being reported can lead families to forgo medical attention and economic and social supports to avoid those who might identify and report issues—such as mental health and substance abuse problems—to the family policing system.

While not addressed in this volume, the role of teachers and other school personnel as mandated reporters has fundamentally shaped the family-school relationship for marginalized families, causing them to experience school not as a great equalizer, provider of opportunity for upward mobility, or safe space but rather as another arm of the carceral family policing system. Although reasons are unclear, child maltreatment allegations from teachers, especially those involving Black children, are less likely to be substantiated than those by law enforcement and medical personnel (Harvey, Gupta-Kagan, and Church 2021; Kesner and Robinson 2002). Given the importance of trust between parents and educators and the risk of breaching trust, especially in unsubstantiated cases, many teachers do not believe they should be legally required to report (Hupe and Stevenson 2019). Some educators feel that schools would better serve children if they could refer families directly to food, housing, health, legal, and other services, instead of educational professionals being required to report suspected child maltreatment, which could include poverty-related hardships (Harvey, Gupta-Kagan, and Church 2021). More research is needed on the harms of mandated reporting, which instills fear that prevents parents from reaching out for help and turns families in need of support over to punitive authorities who may separate children from their parents rather than providing needed support. Moreover, we need to eradicate or overhaul mandated reporting requirements so that professionals who interact most with children report parents not to the family policing system but rather to a system of services and supports that will truly enhance children's health and educational well-being.

System-Impacted People Often Neglected in Research and Policy Discussions

Men's Involvement in the Child Welfare / Family Policing System

As many preceding chapters described, the US child welfare system disproportionately surveils, controls, and punishes mothers, who are the primary caregivers for most children living in poverty. Thus, women bear the brunt of the system's gendered poverty governance. However, fathers also potentially play an important, if often overlooked, role in promoting family reunification and child well-being among system-involved families. Compared to children without consistent contact with their fathers, system-involved children with engaged fathers have fewer and shorter foster care placements and experience more stability while in foster care (Coakley 2013). Children are also more likely to be reunified with their families when fathers are identified and spend more time with their children while the children are in foster care (Burrus et al. 2012). Yet children in foster care are significantly less likely than children in the general population to have had recent contact with their fathers (Malm 2003).

Although the child welfare system is under federal mandate to engage fathers and preserve family relationships, the system often falls short on both counts (Gordon et al. 2012). In over half of cases, fathers are never contacted during case planning for removal and foster placement (Coakley 2013). Caseworkers often cease early efforts to identify, locate, and engage fathers due to mothers' requests related to unhealthy coparenting relationships, unresolved custody and visitation disputes, and concerns about substance use, mental health problems, and paternal disengagement (Campbell et al. 2015). Research also reveals that child welfare workers feel less capable of working with men and tend to view men negatively, either because they assume that men lack or will not offer the additional resources families need or because they perceive men as too "risky" for women and children (Maxwell et al. 2012). Even in the absence of a criminal record or suspected violence, caseworkers tend to scrutinize fathers more than mothers when considering them as possible sources of child placement (O'Donnell et al. 2005).

Consequently, when fathers and other men caregivers are not involved in permanency planning, the child welfare system deems them noncompliant, uninterested, or unsuitable as a permanent placement option (Malm, Zielewski, and Chen 2008). Being deemed "risky" or irrelevant to children by either child welfare workers or family members can exacerbate low paternal involvement when men sense that others consider them harmful or ineffectual.

Publicly funded fatherhood programs have emerged in recent decades to provide employment and educational opportunities, parenting and relationship skills training, and connections to child support enforcement and child welfare systems (Randles 2020). Yet the same social problems that prevent many marginalized men from being involved fathers generally—poverty, unemployment, and strained relationships with children's mothers—also inhibit fathers' involvement during child welfare system processes. Punitive child support enforcement policies depict "good" dads as those who are gainfully employed and directly involved as financial providers in their children's lives. But these expectations exist in a social context characterized by economic precarity, unrelenting debt, the retrenchment of public assistance, and mass incarceration of the most socially vulnerable fathers (Black and Keyes 2021). A tight labor market often pushes marginalized men into non-unionized, low-paying, contingent jobs, making informal work, often illegal and dangerous, necessary for economic survival. In the 1990s, neoliberal capitalism collided with moralistic welfare reform and child support enforcement legislation that rescinded safety-net supports for poor families while penalizing poor fathers for not providing money they did not have (Haney 2022). Unfortunately, policies targeting low-income fathers have done little to funnel support to the mothers and children they were intended to serve.

As with mothers, fathers seeking reunification are expected to meet numerous conditions including attending agency meetings and parenting classes, keeping a job and making child support payments, finding and maintaining adequate housing, addressing alcohol and substance use issues, and visiting children regularly. Especially within a short time frame—generally a year or less—meeting any one of these conditions, much less all of them, can be prohibitively difficult for men in poverty (Coakley 2013), just as it is for women.

Future research must address how fathers and other men caregivers can be crucial sources of emotional, instrumental, and financial support to children and families and how policies and child welfare practices can better acknowledge, engage with, and support them. Policies that assist marginalized fathers with living wages, health care, and affordable housing are especially important for Black, Latine, and Native American fathers, who are more likely to struggle with limited education, poor health, substandard housing, incarceration, unemployment, and low wages, all of which undermine paternal involvement (Black and Keyes 2021).

Parents and Children with Disabilities

Parents labeled as disabled face additional challenges in the child welfare system, as "disability or diagnosis itself can be seen as synonymous with the inability to parent," based on prejudicial ideologies of a "normal" body and mind (Lorr and Frunel 2022, 478). This understudied group of parents—especially those with severe disabilities—is disproportionately Black and poor or low-income and suffers myriad economic hardships. These parents are also more likely to receive public benefits (Sonik et al. 2018), thus bringing them into contact with state surveillance and putting them at greater risk of family policing.

Thirty-five states include disability among the reasons that justify termination of parental rights (NRCPD 2022). In these states, child welfare and custody cases often focus not on actual signs of neglect or abuse but rather on how a parent's (usually mother's) disability poses potential parenting deficiencies. As Angela Frederick (2014, 34) has argued, "disability is one of the few instances in which parental rights can be terminated on the basis of parents' identity status rather than their actions," despite disability being a poor predictor of child maltreatment. As a result, parents labeled as disabled are more likely than those without disabilities to be separated from their children and less likely to be reunited, reflecting deeply rooted ableism—and a dearth of resources that would assist parents with disabilities—inherent in the punitive family policing system. Once parents with disabilities are separated from their children, they receive little support, as child welfare agencies rarely help parents meet basic needs such as housing and transportation or obtain the adaptive equipment or training that could help them care for children. Future research and advocacy must focus on how the system can instead provide parents with disabilities and the children they are often highly capable of parenting with the resources and support they need and deserve.

Children and youth with disabilities are also overrepresented in the child welfare system; they make up a third of the foster care population, are more likely to have been previously adopted, and are significantly less likely to have lived in kinship foster care (Slayter 2016). Children with disabilities are at greater risk of maltreatment, largely because their families and caregivers lack sufficient emotional and financial support to care for children who may require more extensive physical care, behavioral intervention, and financial resources, leading to parental stress and social isolation. Once involved in the child welfare system, children with disabilities tend to receive lower-quality services and are less likely to be reunified with their parents (Lightfoot 2014). More research, advocacy, and support regarding children with disabilities and their experiences in the child welfare system are necessary to fully understand their unique needs and concerns and to ensure that they and their families can access appropriate interventions, including respite care and other specialized supports.

LGBTQ+ Parents and Children

Like disabled parents, LGBTQ+ parents—who are also more likely to be poor and of color compared to parents overall—also experience disproportionately high rates of child welfare system involvement (Joslin and Sakimura 2022). Single LGBTQ+ parents are three times as likely to be near the poverty threshold as non-LGBTQ+ single parents. Further, lesbian mothers, who are disproportionately of color, poor, and disabled, are more likely to be surveilled and otherwise impacted by the family policing system (Polikoff 2018). More research is needed on the reasons LGBTQ+ parents have high rates of child welfare system involvement; possible bias among child welfare professionals must be explored, as well as the role of increased economic and mental health challenges experienced by LGBTQ+ parents.

More commonly discussed, LGBTQ+ youth are also significantly overrepresented in the system and have high rates of aging out of the system without a permanent legal attachment. According to a 2014 Los Angeles County study, LGBTQ+ youth accounted for 6 to 8 percent of the US population under the age of eighteen but 19 percent of children and youth in congregate or foster care (Wilson and Kastanis 2015). LGBTQ+ youth involved with the foster care system are also disproportionately youth of color (Erney and Weber 2018). Reasons for high rates of LGBTQ+ youth in the system are understudied, but two factors are known. First, LGBTQ+ youth are often rejected by their families, which may lead to higher rates of admittance into the system. Second, LGBTQ+ youth tend to remain in the system longer than heterosexual and cisgender youth do, finding fewer paths forward to permanency (Fish et al. 2019).

LGBTQ+ youth, especially youth of color, also face racist, heteronormative, and cissexist treatment in foster care and the child welfare system (Nourie 2022). Foster parents often promote heterosexuality as the normal, preferred sexual orientation, causing tension, isolation, shame, and bullying directed at LGBTQ+ youth in foster families (Robinson 2018). With relatively fewer options for safe gender- and sexuality-affirming foster or group home placements, LGBTQ+ youth experience more instability and less permanency (Scannapieco, Painter, and Blau 2018), increasing chances for substance use, psychiatric hospitalizations, and suicide attempts among LGBTQ+ youth in the foster system (Zaza, Kann, and Barrios 2016). Despite federally protected rights to safety, protection from abuse and harm, and equal treatment for all youth in state custody, not all states require that youth be treated according to their self-identified gender while in out-of-home care (Robinson 2018). That the system itself can inflict additional trauma on LGBTQ+ youth suggests that how we understand being at "risk" for maltreatment and even what constitutes maltreatment must be interrogated.

With many state lawmakers opposing gender-affirming care for trans youth, new risks of child welfare involvement have emerged. In early 2022, Governor Greg Abbot of Texas issued a directive calling medical treatment for gender "dysphoria" a form of child abuse, meaning trans youth could be separated from supportive parents for seeking care. The growing number of states passing antitrans legislation (see Trans Legislation Tracker, n.d.) presage greater risks of surveillance and punitive treatment by the family policing system for families who do not meet middle-class, white, able-bodied, neurotypical, heterosexual, and cisgender norms.

Lessons Learned from Recent Supportive Policies for Parents

As several chapters in this volume show, the shrinking social safety net, specifically the 1996 elimination of Aid to Families with Dependent Children and replacement with Temporary Assistance for Needy Families (TANF), has significantly shaped the contours of today's child welfare system. Since 1996, states have had wide discretion and flexibility under TANF to divert funding away from income support for families and toward other services, including child welfare/family policing services. This has resulted in two profound and negative shifts. First, states now only spend about one-fifth of their total federal and state TANF dollars on direct basic assistance for families with children, and only about one in five poor families receives any TANF assistance, down from almost seven in ten poor families in 1996 (Azevedo-McCaffrey and Safawi 2022). Although Black children are twice as likely to live in poverty as white children, they are less likely to live in states that offer more generous TANF benefits (Hahn et al. 2017). The loss of cash aid as an entitlement, restrictive policies adopted by many states further limiting access to aid, and related decline in cash aid amounts—all of which have disproportionately affected Black families—have led to more children entering the child welfare system (Ginther and Johnson-Motoyama 2022; Paxson and Waldfogel 2002).

Second, federal and state governments have shifted funding from cash aid (TANF) to the family policing system. In 2018, states spent about

$33 billion total on the child welfare system (Congressional Research Service 2023) but only about $7 billion in direct cash assistance to poor families (ACF 2019). Approximately 8 percent of TANF funds go to child welfare agencies annually, amounting to $2.6 billion in federal and state TANF funds used for child welfare programs in 2020 (Azevedo-McCaffrey and Safawi 2022). Meanwhile, the family policing system—unlike poor families—has numerous other funding streams, most significantly Title IV-E of the Social Security Act, along with at least seven other government programs (Jordan and Connelly 2016). Yet virtually none of the funds go directly to struggling families who need support to retain safe care of their children. Instead, much funding goes to foster families to provide for children who have been removed from their families and to agencies with which states contract to provide privatized "child welfare services."

In a particularly ironic turn, the family policing system has one additional source of funding: child support payments. Parents whose children are removed and placed in foster care must often pay to offset foster care costs, despite economic hardship being pervasive among most system-involved families. Most states' child welfare agencies refer all children placed in foster care to state child support enforcement agencies that can issue collection orders for parents whose children have been removed but who remain financially responsible for their children's care (Azevedo-McCaffrey 2022). If a nation's spending reflects its priorities, this is yet more evidence that we value the policing of poor families over their actual well-being.

COVID-19 and the resultant economic and social crises triggered reconsideration of these priorities. Child maltreatment rates tend to rise during periods of financial and family distress; many observers thus feared that economic and social challenges brought on by the pandemic would increase child abuse and neglect. Early on, child welfare workers noted concerns about unreported child maltreatment as children had less contact with mandated reporters when schools and medical offices closed and transitioned to virtual services, thereby curtailing direct surveillance of families (USGAO 2021). Moreover, much of the child welfare system, including caseworkers and courts, ceased regular operations. Yet, as the pandemic and shutdowns unfolded, the United States did something truly exceptional to support struggling families, including those most likely to become involved with the child welfare system. As part of a 2020 stimulus package passed via the Coronavirus Aid, Relief, and Economic Security (CARES) Act, heads of households making up to $112,500 and couples making up to $150,000 annually received $1,200 payments for each adult and $500 for each child younger than seventeen. Those who lost jobs were also eligible for $600 in weekly unemployment benefits. Eligible families then received subsequent stimulus payments totaling $2,000 in December 2020 and March 2021. As part of the largest distribution of direct cash aid to families in US history, the money was sent directly to parents without strings attached. Then, during the latter half of 2021, the federal government expanded the Child Tax Credit (CTC), disseminating monthly payments of $250 to $300 per child to thirty-seven million households with more than sixty-one million children (Cox, Jacoby, and Marr 2022).

Notwithstanding the stress of widespread job loss and school closures amid a global health crisis, we saw what some scholars have described as the "pandemic paradox" of child maltreatment: there was no evidence that child abuse maltreatment increased. Child welfare reports, emergency department visits, and hospital admissions for abusive head trauma all dropped during 2020, while hospitalizations related to child maltreatment were stable (Sege and Stephens 2022), despite greater economic and family risk factors, such as reduced work hours and layoffs. This is yet another example of what many child welfare experts have known for a long time: more public supports for families are associated with fewer cases of child maltreatment (Klevens et al. 2016; Kovski et al. 2022). The short-term policies implemented during the pandemic were highly successful in reducing childhood poverty—and child maltreatment, in particular (Bullinger and Boy 2023). Although many parents lost work and earnings, they had unprecedented public resources to buffer them from financial distress, including eviction moratoriums, increased food stamp benefits, utility assistance, and pauses on student loan debt payments.

Families who received the expanded CTC were more food and housing secure, ate more healthy foods, invested in child care and education, and experienced fewer financial crises (Hamilton et al. 2022). By offering unrestricted cash aid, tax credits and stimulus payments enabled parents to direct money where they knew it was needed. This starkly contrasts with most government assistance, which largely consists of services, in-kind goods, and restricted transfers, such as food programs that allow only for the purchase of certain food items (Azevedo-McCaffrey and Safawi 2022). After payments went out, more parents accessed basic necessities and experienced lower stress levels (Hamilton et al. 2022), which probably led to less child maltreatment and, in turn, fewer child maltreatment reports.

Social service providers also expanded services to families, especially immediate needs assistance such as rent, food, formula, and diapers, using CARES and other COVID-related funding. The pandemic brought into sharp relief how structural factors, such as job loss, lost wages, and racial inequities in health and health care, affect family dynamics and how more basic needs assistance can help. Governmental responses to the pandemic resulted in more resources for—and less direct surveillance of—poor and low-income families. The resulting lower rates of poverty and child maltreatment suggest that more support through unrestricted public assistance, not family policing, protects children from abuse and neglect.

Unfortunately, Congress's failure to permanently expand child tax credits led to a sharp spike in child poverty rates—from a low of 5.2 percent in 2021 back to near the pre-pandemic rate of 12.4 percent in 2022—which meant about five million more children living in poverty (Shrider and Creamer 2023) and consequently at higher risk for maltreatment, surveillance, and family policing system involvement. Even without expanded federal child tax credits, if all US states had public assistance programs similar to those of the most generous and inclusive states, around five and a half million fewer US children would live in poverty (Pac et al. 2020).

Despite relatively robust pandemic aid, racially disparate hardships continued, including higher poverty rates for Black and Latine children compared to white children. Moreover, Black workers who lost their jobs were less likely than white workers to receive unemployment compensation (Couch, Fairlie, and Xu 2020), while undocumented immigrants, many of whom are Latine, were unable to receive economic stimulus checks (Parolin, Curran, and Wimer 2020). Thus, even amid the pandemic paradox, racism and anti-immigrant policies shaped economic outcomes, which in turn shaped child welfare outcomes.

Reconsidering "Risk"

As we worked on this collection, Dorothy Roberts's path-breaking book *Shattered Bonds: The Color of Child Welfare* celebrated its twentieth anniversary, and she published *Torn Apart: How the Child Welfare System Destroys Black Families—and How Abolition Can Build a Safer World. Shattered Bonds* (2022). *Shattered Bonds* was a searing account of the racial and gender politics of the US child welfare system that tied the origins of "racial disproportionality in foster care" to a long national history of racial injustice. Roberts drew crucial attention to the deliberate political choice to police and punish poor Black parents for supposed individual failures to provide for and protect their children rather than address the systemic origins of racialized and feminized poverty. In the ensuing decades, Roberts was central to reformist efforts to overhaul the family policing system into a humane family support system.

Two decades later, however, Roberts sees no hope of reforming a system rooted in race, class, and gender injustices, particularly the separation and dehumanization of poor Black mothers and their children, into a system that truly protects and promotes child welfare. In *Torn Apart*, she argues that a carceral system designed to surveil, control, and oppress Black, brown, and Indigenous families cannot be "reformed" into a supportive system that prevents more harm than it perpetuates. She identifies two fundamentally faulty premises that undergird the system: that parental pathologies cause poverty and related hardships faced by children and families and that surveillance and family policing prevent child maltreatment (Roberts 2021, 2022). Roberts joins other scholars and activists working to abolish the system, including Dettlaff and Pendleton (chapter 12). Movements like upEND are committed to abolishing a system that maintains white supremacy, racial capitalism, patriarchy, and colonialism. More generally, abolitionists seek to make state surveillance and family separation obsolete by upending the systems and structures that harm families and creating a new society where children and families can thrive (Dettlaff 2023).

Alternatively, critical reformists such as Wilson and Maher (chapter 13) argue that, rather than abolishing the system entirely, the child welfare system should instead redirect its focus to combat community disadvantage and family poverty by making significant investments in concrete, noncoercive services that reduce material hardships among poor and low-income families. They also advocate for more robust reunification efforts, in part by offering reunifying families the same economic support as those who adopt children from foster care. A reformist perspective sees children as autonomous subjects with rights to sustenance, safety, and security that exist independently of their relationships to family members and generally assumes that child maltreatment will not end entirely, even with extensive public supports. Through the child welfare system, reformists claim, the state must guarantee these fundamental rights, even if it entails family separation.

We believe that ridding the child welfare system of its racist, colonialist, capitalist underpinnings would require abolition. However, we also recognize that until we have the world we desire, some children will still need care outside their families. Yet, instead of focusing on improving the child welfare system, which we are not hopeful can be fixed, we believe we must prioritize efforts to build a society where all children and families are fully supported—a society without poverty or vast inequality and one where communities provide a full spectrum of support to families to keep them together and connected—in short, a society where there is no need for a child welfare system.

To that end, we must reorient our understanding of "risk" away from a focus on the "risk" of child maltreatment by caregivers to instead focus on the "risks" to children and families caused by structural racism and economic hardship (Feely and Bosk 2021). This structural framework of maltreatment risk would entail conceptualizing social structures as potentially dangerous and harmful, especially for marginalized families, youth, and children. Understanding maltreatment in terms of structural risk, Megan Feely and Emily Adlin Bosk (2021) have argued, would shift the child welfare system's focus from individual parenting behaviors and choices to how those behaviors and choices unfold, not in a social vacuum but in a socioeconomic context of intersecting racism, capitalist economic exploitation, and patriarchy that shape social conditions of child maltreatment. This structural risk lens allows us to grasp how most system-involved children suffer abuse and neglect not as a result of living in families that seek to harm or deny them their needs but rather as a consequence of a society that stratifies access to resources and opportunities by race, class, gender, and other axes of inequality. Current risk assessments in the child welfare system misdiagnose "maltreatment" by focusing on individual-level evaluations and interventions, rather than the structural origins of neglect. Shifting the system's attention from one of individual- or family-level risk to structural risk is necessary to create a system that centers providing for families' needs as the solution to neglect rather than punishing those families for their poverty by pulling them apart.

Similar to assessing parental risk, efforts to reduce the biases of child welfare workers via diversity or anti-implicit-bias training frame racially disproportionate child welfare system involvement as the consequence of flawed individual decisions. Yet racial disproportionality in the family policing system is neither a product of individual parents' bad choices to harm or neglect their children nor the result solely of individual child welfare workers' racial biases.

Although race and class biases certainly play a role in decision-making points throughout the system, no implicit-bias training will fix the system's larger problem: child welfare workers often have only individualized and therapeutic interventions to offer families. Centering the elimination of implicit bias among social workers, however, absolves the child welfare system, other professionals and policy makers, and us all from dismantling systemic racism, colonialism, patriarchy, capitalist exploitation, and other oppressive social conditions that shape child "maltreatment"—which is more often the result of harmful and neglectful social conditions and policies than harmful or neglectful parents or families (see Dettlaff and Boyd 2020).

The structural risk perspective of child maltreatment points to feasible steps that can and should be taken immediately to promote child welfare, steps that we hope both abolitionists and critical reformists can support, even if these two groups do not agree on the end goal. Nearly every wealthy nation other than the United States provides families with children with some form of child allowance. The pandemic showed that doing so reduces child welfare system involvement. Building on this, we call for reestablishing the Child Tax Credit and guaranteeing basic income, housing, and health care for all families. Collectively, and with robust social service support in areas like child care, mental health care, and substance abuse treatment, these changes would eliminate poverty and much economic hardship. Investing in services in these areas—and decoupling such services from mandatory reporting and child welfare system involvement—are urgent. Programs that allow parents and children to stay together while seeking substance abuse and mental health treatment would strengthen families rather than force separation. Voluntary placement of children with family, friends, or social service agencies while parents seek help is another important option that should not be penalized by threat of or actual forced separation or termination of parental rights. We cannot know how much child welfare need would remain until we make significant progress in eliminating poverty and economic hardship and ensuring the availability and accessibility of a vast system of family supports. In the meantime, the US child welfare system fails families, and especially children, by embracing neoliberal policies and practices that fail to provide what families need to thrive, while furthering their hardships through policing and punitive measures.

ACKNOWLEDGMENTS

We wish to thank Daisy Rooks, Jennifer Sherman, and Jennifer Utrata for their feedback on the book proposal and introduction and the anonymous reviewers for their feedback on the manuscript. We also greatly appreciate the enthusiastic support and feedback from our editor, Ilene Kalish, and the NYU Press Critical Perspectives on Youth series editors, Amy Best, Lorena Garcia, and Jessica Taft.

Jennifer Randles: Thank you to all the parents I have had the privilege to meet and learn from through various research projects on the barriers and challenges, including child welfare system involvement, they encounter as they strive to raise and provide for their children.

To my coeditor, Kerry Woodward, thank you for inviting me to be part of this project and trusting me to help realize your vision for a much-needed volume on how the child welfare system policies families. I have enjoyed and learned so much from our collaboration.

To my colleagues, students, and friends at California State University, Fresno, thank you for providing the time and conversational space to contemplate why and how we can create a better system to support families. To Craig and Bridget, thank you for being my constant reminder for why everyone deserves to live in a safe, loving, and secure home. May we one day live in a world where everyone has what they need to do so.

Kerry Woodward: To all the mothers I have met who have feared, encountered, or had their children taken by the family policing system, thank you; I have learned so much from each of you, especially Danielle Rogers.

Thank you to my coeditor, Jennifer Randles, for her unwavering enthusiasm for this project and partnership through every stage of it. Working with you is always a pleasure!

I also want to thank the College of Liberal Arts, California State University, Long Beach for several Research, Scholarly and Creative Activity

Awards that have provided time to work on this book. I am grateful to Kris Zentgraf for her continuous support and the hours she spent listening to me talk about this project. I thank Andrea Ganz for providing the reproductive labor so that I could work long hours and for her patient mothering of our children. Thanks to my parents for their support and patience while I disappeared behind my computer for long stretches. And to my children, I thank you for all that you have taught me, and I wish for you a better, more just world.

RESOURCES

Alliance for Children's Rights, https://allianceforchildrensrights.org
American Bar Association Center on Children and the Law, Child Welfare
    and Immigration Project, www.americanbar.org
Center on Immigration and Child Welfare, www.cimmcw.org
Immigrant Legal Resource Center, www.ilrc.org
International Social Service, USA, www.iss-usa.org
Kids in Need of Defense Child Migrant Return and Reintegration Project,
    www.supportkind.org
Lakota People's Law Project, https://lakotalaw.org
Migration Policy Institute, www.migrationpolicy.org
National Alliance on Mental Health, www.nami.org
National Coalition for Child Protection Reform, https://nccpr.org/
National Indian Child Welfare Association, www.nicwa.org
Native American Rights Fund, www.narf.org
Substance Abuse and Mental Health Services Association, www.samhsa.gov
United States Department of Health and Human Services, Office on
    Trafficking in Persons—Victims Assistance, www.acf.hhs.gov/otip/
    victim-assistance
United States Immigration and Customs Enforcement, ICE Detained Parents
    Directive, www.ice.gov
upEND Movement (to abolish the family policing system), https://upend-
    movement.org
Young Center for Immigrant Children's Rights, www.theyoungcenter.org

REFERENCES

AAP (American Academy of Pediatrics). 2005. *Fostering Health: Health Care for Children and Adolescents in Foster Care*. 2nd ed. American Academy of Pediatrics, District II, New York State. www.aap.org.

Abdurahman, Khadijah. 2021. "Calculating the Souls of Black Folk: Predictive Analytics in New York City Administration for Children's Services." *Columbia Journal of Race and Law Forum* 11 (4): 75–109. https://doi.org/10.52214/cjrl.v11i4.8741.

Abramovitz, Mimi. 1996. *Regulating the Lives of Women: Social Welfare Policy from the Colonial Times to the Present*. Boston: South End.

ACF (Administration for Children and Families). 2019. "TANF and MOE Spending and Transfers by Activity, FY 2018." Office of Family Assistance, USDHHS, updated July 31, 2023. www.acf.hhs.gov.

———. 2020. "President Trump Signs Historic Child Welfare Executive Order." USDHHS, June 24, 2020. www.acf.hhs.gov.

———. 2023. "Separate Licensing or Approval Standards for Relative or Kinship Foster Family Homes." USDHHS. 45 CFR Part 1355, 1356. *Federal Register* 88 (187): 66700–66709. www.govinfo.gov.

Adams, David Wallace. 1995. *Education for Extinction: American Indians and the Boarding School Experience 1875–1928*. Lawrence: University Press of Kansas.

Ader, Sue. 2019. "Social Workers: First Responders to Wisconsin's Drug Epidemic." *Wisconsin Counties Magazine*, January 2019. www.wicounties.org.

Ahlstedt, Terry. 2016. "The General Allotment Act, 1887." In *50 Events That Shaped American Indian History: An Encyclopedia of the American Mosaic*, edited by Donna Martinez and Jennifer L. Williams Bordeaux, 335–50. Greenwood, CT: ABC-CLIO.

AIC (American Immigration Council). 2020. *Immigration Detention in the United States by Agency*. Washington, DC: AIC, January 2, 2020. http://americanimmigrationcouncil.org.

———. 2021. *U.S. Citizen Children Impacted by Immigration Enforcement*. Washington, DC: AIC, June 24, 2021. http://americanimmigrationcouncil.org.

Akee, Randall. 2018. "40 Years Ago We Stopped the Practice of Separating American Indian Families. Let's Not Reverse Course." Brookings, October 18, 2018. www.brookings.edu.

———. 2019. "How Does Measuring Poverty and Welfare Affect American Indian Children?" Brookings, March 12, 2019. www.brookings.edu.

Akin, Becci A. 2011. "Predictors of Foster Care Exits to Permanency: A Competing Risks Analysis of Reunification, Guardianship, and Adoption."

Children and Youth Services Review 33 (6): 999–1011. https://doi.org/10.1016/j.childyouth.2011.01.008.

Albert, Ashley, Tiheba Bain, Elizabeth Brico, Bishop Marcia Dinkins, Kelis Houston, Joyce McMillan, Vonya Quarles, Lisa Sangoi, Erin Miles Cloud, and Adina Marx-Arpadi. 2021. "Ending the Family Death Penalty and Building a World We Deserve." *Columbia Journal of Race and Law* 11 (3): 861–94. https://doi.org/10.52214/cjrl.v11i3.8753.

Alexander, Michelle. 2010. *The New Jim Crow: Mass Incarceration in the Age of Colorblindness*. New York: New Press.

Allen, Brian, Erica M. Cisneros, and Alexandra Tellez. 2015. "The Children Left Behind: The Impact of Parental Deportation on Mental Health." *Journal of Child and Family Studies* 24 (2): 386–92. https://doi.org/10.1007/s10826-013-9848-5.

Alphonso, Gwendoline M. 2021. "Political-Economic Roots of Coercion: Slavery, Neoliberalism, and the Racial Family Policy Logic of Child and Social Welfare." *Columbia Journal of Race and Law* 11 (3): 471–500. https://doi.org/10.52214/cjrl.v11i3.8742.

Anderson, Lydia, and Paul Hemez. 2022. "Over a Quarter of Children Lived with at Least One Foreign-Born Parent." US Census Bureau, February 3, 2022. www.census.gov.

Angwin, Julia, and Jeff Larson. 2016. "Bias in Criminal Risk Scores Is Mathematically Inevitable, Researchers Say." ProPublica, December 30, 2016. www.propublica.org.

Annie E. Casey Foundation. 2020. "Foster Care Race Statistics." Updated May 14, 2023. https://datacenter.kidscount.org.

———. 2021. "Who Are Children in Immigrant Families?" Updated August 28, 2023. www.aecf.org.

———. 2022. "Child Welfare and Foster Care Statistics." Updated April 7, 2024. www.aecf.org.

———. 2023a. "Children Who Are Confirmed by Child Protective Services as Victims of Maltreatment by Type of Maltreatment in the United States." Kids Count Data Center. Updated May 2023. https://datacenter.aecf.org.

———. 2023b. "Children Who Are Confirmed by Child Protective Services as Victims of Maltreatment in the United States." Kids Count Data Center. Updated May 2023. https://datacenter.aecf.org.

———. 2023c. "Children Who Are Subject to an Investigated Report in the United States." Kids Count Data Center. Updated May 2023. https://datacenter.aecf.org.

———. 2023d. "Child Welfare and Foster Care Statistics." www.aecf.org.

———. 2024. "Children in Extreme Poverty (50 Percent Poverty) by Race and Ethnicity." Kids Count Data Center. Updated January 2024. https://datacenter.aecf.org.

Aratani, Yumiko. 2009. *Homeless Children and Youth: Causes and Consequences*. New York: National Center for Children in Poverty, Columbia University, September 2009. www.nccp.org.

Arnold, Mildred. 1947. *Children's Services in the Public Welfare Agency*. Washington, DC: Federal Security Agency, Social Security Administration, Children's Bureau.

ASFA (Adoption and Safe Families Act of 1997). 1997. 42 U.S.C. § 629. www.govinfo.gov.

Asgarian, Roxanna. 2020. "The Forgotten Children of Texas." *The Imprint*, October 26, 2020. https://imprintnews.org.

Associated Press. 1989. "Firm Stole Indian Oil, Panel Told: $31 Million Owed, Investigators Tell Senate Committee." *Los Angeles Times*, May 9, 1989. www.latimes.com.

Austin, Lisette. 2009. "Serving Native American Children in Foster Care." *The Connection*, Winter 2009. http://nc.casaforchildren.org.

Ayón, Cecilia. 2009. "Shorter Time-Lines, Yet Higher Hurdles: Mexican Families' Access to Child Welfare Mandated Services." *Children and Youth Services Review* 31 (6): 609–16. https://doi.org/10.1016/j.childyouth.2008.11.004.

Ayón, Cecilia, Eugene Aisenberg, and Andrea Cimino. 2013. "Latino Families in the Nexus of Child Welfare Reform and Immigration Policies: Is Kinship a Lost Opportunity?" *Social Work* 58 (1): 91–94. https://doi.org/10.1093/sw/sws014.

Azevedo-McCaffrey, Diana. 2022. *States Should Use New Guidance to Stop Charging Parents for Foster Care, Prioritize Family Reunification.* Issue brief. Washington, DC: Center on Budget and Policy Priorities, October 13, 2022. www.cbpp.org.

Azevedo-McCaffrey, Diana, and Ali Safawi. 2022. *To Promote Equity, States Should Invest More TANF Dollars in Basic Assistance.* Washington, DC: Center on Budget and Policy Priorities, January 12, 2022. www.cbpp.org.

Azim, Katharina A., Laurie MacGillivray, and Donalyn Heise. 2019. "Mothering in the Margin." *Public Health Post*, Boston University School of Public Health, May 2, 2019. www.publichealthpost.org.

Bach, Wendy A. 2022. *Prosecuting Poverty, Criminalizing Care.* New York: Cambridge University Press.

Bai, Rong, Cyleste Collins, Robert Fischer, and David Crampton. 2019. "Pursuing Collaboration to Improve Services for Child Welfare-Involved Housing Unstable Families." *Children and Youth Services Review* 104:104405. https://doi.org/10.1016/j.childyouth.2019.104405.

Bai, Rong, Cyleste Collins, Robert Fischer, Victor Groza, and Liuhong Yang. 2020. "Exploring the Association between Housing Insecurity and Child Welfare Involvement: A Systematic Review." *Child and Adolescent Social Work Journal* 39 (2): 247–60. https://doi.org/10.1007/s10560-020-00722-z.

Baker, Regina S. 2022. "The Historical Racial Regime and Racial Inequality in Poverty in the American South." *American Journal of Sociology* 127 (6): 1721–81. https://doi.org/10.1086/719653.

Barker, Vanessa. 2009. *The Politics of Imprisonment: How the Democratic Process Shapes the Way America Punishes Offenders.* New York: Oxford University Press.

Barnard, Marina, and Neil McKeganey. 2004. "The Impact of Parental Problem Drug Use on Children: What Is the Problem and What Can Be Done to Help?" *Addiction* 99 (5): 552–59. https://doi.org/10.1111/j.1360-0443.2003.00664.x.

Barrow, Susan M., and Nicole D. Laborde. 2008. "Invisible Mothers: Parenting by Homeless Women Separated from Their Children." *Gender Issues* 25:157–72. https://doi.org/10.1007/s12147-008-9058-4.

Barth, Richard, Jill Duerr Berrick, Melissa Jonson-Reid, Brett Drake, Johanna Greeson, and Antonio Garcia. 2020. "The Research Doesn't Support Child Welfare Abolition." *The Imprint*, October 5, 2020. https://imprintnews.org.

Bartholet, Elizabeth. 2009. "The Racial Disproportionality Movement in Child Welfare: False Facts and Dangerous Directions." *Arizona Law Review* 51 (4): 871–932.

Bartholet, Elizabeth, Fred Wulczyn, Richard P. Barth, and Cindy Lederman. 2011. *Race and Child Welfare*. Issue brief. Chicago: Chapin Hall at the University of Chicago, June 2011. http://cap.law.harvard.edu.

BBC News. 2021. "Canada Mourns as Remains of 215 Children Found at Indigenous School." May 29, 2021. www.bbc.com.

Beall, Pat, Daphne Chen, and Josh Salman. 2020. "Florida Took Thousands of Kids from Families, Then Failed to Keep Them Safe." *USA Today*, October 15, 2020. www.usatoday.com.

Bear Runner, Julian. 2019. *Tribal Infrastructure: Roads, Bridges, and Buildings: Hearing Before the Subcommittee for Indigenous Peoples of the United States. House Natural Resources Committee*. Written testimony. 116th Cong. July 11, 2019. www.congress.gov.

Belanger, Kathleen, Becky Price-Mayo, and David Espinosa. 2008. "The Plight of Rural Child Welfare: Meeting Standards without Services." *Journal of Public Child Welfare* 1 (4): 1–19. https://doi.org/10.1080/15548730802118181.

Bell, Margaret. 2002. "Promoting Children's Rights through the Use of Relationship." *Child & Family Social Work* 7 (1): 1–11. https://doi.org/10.1046/j.1365-2206.2002.00225.x.

Bell, Monica C. 2017. "Police Reform and the Dismantling of Legal Estrangement." *Yale Law Journal* 126 (7): 2054–150.

Berger, Lawrence M., Maria Cancian, Laura Cuesta, and Jennifer L. Noyes. 2016. "Families at the Intersection of the Criminal Justice and Child Protective Services Systems." *Annals of the American Academy of Political and Social Science* 665 (1): 171–94. https://doi.org/10.1177/0002716216633058.

Berger, Lawrence M., Sarah A. Font, Kristen S. Slack, and Jane Waldfogel. 2017. "Income and Child Maltreatment in Unmarried Families: Evidence from the Earned Income Tax Credit." *Review of Economics of the Household* 15 (4): 1345–72. https://doi.org/10.1007%2Fs11150-016-9346-9.

Bernstein, Hamutal, Dulce Gonzalez, Michael Karpman, and Stephen Zuckerman. 2019. *One in Seven Adults in Immigrant Families Reported Avoiding Public Benefit Programs in 2018*. Washington, DC: Urban Institute, May 2019. www.urban.org.

Bernstein, Nina. 2002. *The Lost Children of Wilder: The Epic Struggle to Change Foster Care*. New York: Vintage.

Berrick, Jill. 2009. *Take Me Home: Protecting America's Vulnerable Children and Families*. New York: Oxford University Press.

Berry, William D., Evan J. Ringquist, Richard C. Fording, and Russell L. Hanson. 1998. "Measuring Citizen and Government Ideology in the American States, 1960–93." *American Journal of Political Science* 42 (1): 327–48. https://doi.org/10.2307/2991759.

Best, David, Melinda Beckwith, Catherine Haslam, S. Alexander Haslam, Jolanda Jetten, Emily Mawson, and Dan I. Lubman. 2016. "Overcoming Alcohol and Other Drug Addiction as a Process of Social Identity Transition: The Social Identity Model of Recovery (SIMOR)." *Addiction Research & Theory* 24 (2): 111–23. https://doi.org/10.3109/16066359.2015.1075980.

Billingsley, Andrew, and Jeanne M. Giovannoni. 1972. *Children of the Storm: Black Children and American Child Welfare.* New York: Harcourt, Brace, Jovanovich.

BJA (Bureau of Justice Assistance). 2023. "Substance Use and Pregnancy—Part 1: Current State Policies on Mandatory Reporting and Implementing Plans of Safe Care to Support Pregnant Persons with Substance Use Disorders." US Department of Justice, March 1, 2023. https://bja.ojp.gov.

Bjorum, Erika. 2014. "'Those Are Our People and That's Our Family': Wabanaki Perspectives on Child Welfare Practice in Their Communities." *Journal of Public Child Welfare* 8 (3): 279–303. https://doi.org/10.1080/15548732.2014.924893.

Black, Timothy, and Sky Keyes. 2021. *It's a Setup: Fathering from the Social and Economic Margins.* New York: Oxford University Press.

Blanco, Carlos, and Nora D. Volkow. 2019. "Management of Opioid Use Disorder in the USA: Present Status and Future Directions." *The Lancet* 393 (10182): 1760–72. https://doi.org/10.1016/S0140-6736(18)33078-2.

Bloemraad, Irene. 2006. "Becoming a Citizen in the United States and Canada: Structured Mobilization and Immigrant Political Incorporation." *Social Forces* 85 (2): 667–95. https://doi.org/10.1353/sof.2007.0002.

Boehm, Bernice. 1964. "The Community and the Social Agency Define Neglect." *Child Welfare* 43 (9): 453–64.

Bourdieu, Pierre. 1999. "The Abdication of the State." In *The Weight of the World: Social Suffering in Contemporary Society*, edited by Pierre Bourdieu et al., translated by Priscilla Parkhurst Ferguson, Susan Emanuel, Joe Johnson, and Shoggy T. Waryn, 181–88. Stanford, CA: Stanford University Press.

Brabeck, Kalina, and Qingwen Xu. 2010. "The Impact of Detention and Deportation on Latino Immigrant Children and Families: A Quantitative Exploration." *Hispanic Journal of Behavioral Sciences* 32 (3): 341–61. https://doi.org/10.1177/0739986310374053.

Brant, Kristina. 2022. "When Mamaw Becomes Mom: Social Capital and Kinship Family Formation amid the Rural Opioid Crisis." *RSF: The Russell Sage Foundation Journal of the Social Sciences* 8 (3): 78–98. https://doi.org/10.7758/RSF.2022.8.3.03.

Brayne, Sarah. 2014. "Surveillance and System Avoidance: Criminal Justice Contact and Institutional Attachment." *American Sociological Review* 79 (3): 367–91. https://doi.org/10.1177/0003122414530398.

Breitenbucher, Philip, Russ Bermejo, Colleen M. Killian, Nancy K. Young, Lisa Duong, and Ken DeCerchio. 2018. "Exploring Racial and Ethnic Disproportionalities and Disparities in Family Treatment Courts: Findings from the Regional Partnership Grant Program." *Journal for Advancing Justice* 1:35–62. https://advancejustice.org.

Brico, Elizabeth. 2019. "The Government Spends 10 Times More on Foster Care and Adoption than Reuniting Families." Talk Poverty, August 23, 2019. https://talkpoverty.org.

Bridges, Khiara M. 2017. *The Poverty of Privacy Rights*. Stanford, CA: Stanford University Press.

———. 2020. "Race, Pregnancy, and the Opioid Epidemic: White Privilege and the Criminalization of Opioid Use during Pregnancy." *Harvard Law Review* 133 (3): 770–851.

Briggs, Harold E., Kimberly Y. Huggins-Hoyt, Martell L. Teasley, and June Gary Hopps. 2022. "Poverty or Racism? Determinants of Disproportionality and Disparity for African American/Black Children in Child Welfare." *Research on Social Work Practice* 32 (5): 533–38.

Briggs, Laura. 2020. *Taking Children: A History of American Terror*. Oakland: University of California Press.

———. 2021. "Twentieth Century Black and Native Activism against the Child Taking System." *Columbia Journal of Race and Law* 11 (3): 611–38. https://doi.org/10.52214/cjrl.v11i3.8746.

Brown, Alleen, and Nick Estes. 2018. "An Untold Number of Indigenous Children Disappeared at U.S. Boarding Schools. Tribal Nations Are Raising the Stakes in Search of Answers." *The Intercept*, September 25, 2018. https://theintercept.com.

Brown, Caroline, and Lisa Rieger. 2001. "Culture and Compliance: Locating the Indian Child Welfare Act in Practice." *POLAR: Political and Legal Anthropology Review* 24 (2): 58–75.

Brown, Hana E. 2020. "Who Is an Indian Child? Institutional Context, Tribal Sovereignty, and Race-Making in Fragmented States." *American Sociological Review* 85 (5): 776–805. https://doi.org/10.1177/0003122420944165.

Buer, Lesly-Marie. 2020. *Rx Appalachia: Stories of Treatment and Survival in Rural Kentucky*. Chicago: Haymarket Books.

Bullinger, Lindsey Rose, and Angela Boy. 2023. "Association of Expanded Child Tax Credit Payments with Child Abuse and Neglect Emergency Department Visits." *JAMA Network Open* 6 (2): e2255639. https://doi.org/10.1001/jamanetworkopen.2022.55639.

Burns, Barbara J., Susan D. Phillips, H. Ryan Wagner, Richard P. Barth, David J. Kolko, Yvonne Campbell, and John Landsverk. 2004. "Mental Health Need and Access to Mental Health Services by Youths Involved with Child Welfare: A National Survey." *Journal of the American Academy of Child & Adolescent Psychiatry* 43 (8): 960–70. https://doi.org/10.1097/01.chi.0000127590.95585.65.

Burns, Stacy Lee, and Mark Peyrot. 2003. "Tough Love: Nurturing and Coercing Responsibility and Recovery in California Drug Courts." *Social Problems* 50 (3): 416–38. https://doi.org/10.1525/sp.2003.50.3.416.

Burrell, Michelle. 2019. "What Can the Child Welfare System Learn in the Wake of the Floyd Decision? A Comparison of Stop-and-Frisk Policing and Child Welfare Investigations." *City University of New York Law Review* 22 (1): 124–47.

Burrus, Scott W. M., Beth L. Green, Sonia Worcel, Michael Finigan, and Carrie Furrer. 2012. "Do Dads Matter? Child Welfare Outcomes for Father-Identified Families." *Journal of Child Custody* 9 (3): 201–16. https://doi.org/10.1080/15379418.2012.715550.

Byler, William. 1977. "The Destruction of American Indian Families." In *The Destruction of American Indian Families*, edited by Steven Unger, 1–11. New York: Association on American Indian Affairs.

Byrne, Thomas H., Benjamin F. Henwood, and Anthony W. Orlando. 2021. "A Rising Tide Drowns Unstable Boats: How Inequality Creates Homelessness." *Annals of the American Academy of Political and Social Science* 693 (1): 28–45. https://doi.org/10.1177/0002716220981864.

Bywaters, Paul, Lisa Bunting, Gavin Davidson, Jennifer Hanratty, Will Mason, Clair McCarta, and Nicole Steiles. 2016. *The Relationship between Poverty, Child Abuse and Neglect: An Evidence Review*. York, UK: Joseph Rowntree Foundation, March 3, 2016. www.jrf.org.uk.

Callahan, Jessica. 2020. *Mandated Reporters of Child Abuse and Neglect*. Hartford, CT: Office of Legislative Research, Connecticut General Assembly, November 25, 2020. https://cga.ct.gov.

Camp, Joy M., and Norma Finkelstein. 1997. "Parenting Training for Women in Residential Substance Abuse Treatment: Results of a Demonstration Project." *Journal of Substance Abuse Treatment* 14 (5): 411–22. https://doi.org/10.1016/S0740-5472(97)00004-4.

Campbell, Christina, A., Douglas Howard, Brett S. Rayford, and Derrick M. Gordon. 2015. "Fathers Matter: Involving and Engaging Fathers in the Child Welfare System Process." *Children and Youth Services Review* 53:84–91. https://doi.org/10.1016/j.childyouth.2015.03.020.

Cancian, Maria, Mi-Youn Yang, and Kristen Shook Slack. 2013. "The Effect of Additional Child Support Income on the Risk of Child Maltreatment." *Social Service Review* 87 (3): 417–37. https://doi.org/10.1086/671929.

Canfield, Martha, Polly Radcliffe, Sally Marlow, Marggie Boreham, and Gail Gilchrist. 2017. "Maternal Substance Use and Child Protection: A Rapid Evidence Assessment of Factors Associated with Loss of Child Care." *Child Abuse & Neglect* 70:11–27. https://doi.org/10.1016/j.chiabu.2017.05.005.

Capacity Building Center for States. 2023. *Promoting Safe and Stable Families Program*. Children's Bureau, Administration for Children and Families, US Department of Health and Human Services. https://capacity.childwelfare.gov.

CAPTA Reauthorization Act of 2010. 2010. 42 U.S.C. § 5101. www.govinfo.gov.

Carson, E. Ann. 2022. *Prisoners in 2021—Statistical Tables*. Bureau of Justice Statistics, Office of Justice Programs, US Department of Justice, December 2022. https://bjs.ojp.gov.

Carter, Lucy Salcido. 2010. *Doing the Work and Measuring the Progress: A Report on the December 2009 Experts Roundtable*. National Institute of Justice and the Family Violence Prevention Fund. www.ojp.gov.

Casey Family Programs. 2011. *The Promoting Safe and Stable Families Program: Background and Context*. Seattle: Casey Family Programs. www.casey.org.

———. 2019. *What Are Some Examples of Real-Time Information Sharing between Child Protection and Law Enforcement?* Seattle: Casey Family Programs. www.casey.org.

———. 2020. *Strong Families: How Can Child Protection Agencies Support Families and Children Who Lack Lawful Immigration Status?* Strategy brief. Seattle: Casey Family Programs. www.casey.org.

Casselman, Amy L. 2016. *Injustice in Indian Country: Jurisdiction, American Law, and Sexual Violence against Native Women*. New York: Peter Lang.

CDC (Centers for Disease Control and Prevention). 2023. *Fast Facts: Preventing Adverse Childhood Experiences*. Atlanta: National Center for Injury Prevention and Control, Division of Violence Prevention, June 29, 2023. www.cdc.gov.

Center for the Study of Social Policy. 2020. "What Does It Mean to Abolish the Child Welfare System as We Know It?" June 29, 2020. https://cssp.org.

Chaffin, Mark, David Bard, Debra Hecht, and Jane Silovsky. 2011. "Change Trajectories during Home-Based Services with Chronic Child Welfare Cases." *Child Maltreatment* 16 (2): 114–25. https://doi.org/10.1177/1077559511402048.

Chaiyachati, Barbara H., Joanne N. Wood, Nandita Mitra, and Krisda H. Chaiyachati. 2020. "All-Cause Mortality among Children in the US Foster Care System, 2003–2016." *JAMA Pediatrics* 174 (9): 896–98. https://doi.org/10.1001/jamapediatrics.2020.0715.

Chang, Andrea. 2023. "Low Wages, Short Hours Drive Many Fast-Food Workers into Homelessness." *Los Angeles Times*, May 2, 2023. www.latimes.com.

Chaudry, Ajay, and Karina Fortuny. 2010. *Children of Immigrants: Economic Well-Being*. Brief No. 4. Washington DC: Urban Institute, November 2010. www.urban.org.

Chen, Vivia. 2021. "Gibson Dunn Pro Bono Case Draws Ire of Some Native Americans." *Bloomberg Law*, November 23, 2021. https://news.bloomberglaw.com.

Child Support Enforcement Amendments of 1984. 1984. Public Law 98-378. www.govinfo.gov.

Cho, Minhae, Eric Harlin, Jungjoon Ihm, and Chi Hyun Lee. 2023. "Event History Analysis on Racial Disparities in the Path to Adoption for Black and White Children." *Child Abuse & Neglect* 141:106231. https://doi.org/10.1016/j.chiabu.2023.106231.

City Council of Philadelphia. 2022. *Special Committee on Child Separations in Philadelphia: Report and Recommendations*. Philadelphia: City Council of Philadelphia, April 2022. https://phila.legistar.com.

Clarren, Rebecca. 2017. "A Right-Wing Think Tank Is Trying to Bring Down the Indian Child Welfare Act. Why?" *The Nation*, April 6, 2017. www.thenation.com.

Clifford, Stephanie, and Jessica Silver-Greenberg. 2017. "Foster Care as Punishment: The New Reality of 'Jane Crow.'" *New York Times*, July 21, 2017. www.nytimes.com.

Coakley, Jennifer F., and Jill D. Berrick. 2008. "Research Review: In a Rush to Permanency: Preventing Adoption Disruption." *Child & Family Social Work* 13 (1): 101–12. https://doi.org/10.1111/j.1365-2206.2006.00468.x.

Coakley, Tanya M. 2013. "The Influence of Father Involvement on Child Welfare Permanency Outcomes: A Secondary Data Analysis." *Children and Youth Services Review* 35 (1): 174–82. https://doi.org/10.1016/j.childyouth.2012.09.023.

Cohen, Wilbur J., and Robert M. Ball. 1962. "Public Welfare Amendments of 1962 and Proposals for Health Insurance for the Aged." *Social Security Bulletin* 25 (10): 3–22.

Collins, Cyleste C., Rong Bai, David Crampton, and Robert L. Fischer. 2022. "Families with Black Caregivers Were More Likely to Reunify? Explaining Findings from a RCT for Families Who Are Housing-Unstable and Have Children in Foster Care." *Child Welfare* 100 (2): 27–49.

Collins, Cyleste C., Rong Bai, David Crampton, Robert Fischer, Rebecca D'Andrea, Kendra Dean, Nina Lalich, Tsui Chan, and Emily Cherney. 2019. "Implementing Housing First with Families and Young Adults: Challenges and Progress toward Self-Sufficiency." *Children and Youth Services Review* 96:34–46. https://doi.org/10.1016/j.childyouth.2018.11.025.

Collins, Cyleste C., Rebecca D'Andrea, Kendra Dean, and David Crampton. 2016. "Service Providers' Perspectives on Permanent Supportive Housing for Families." *Families in Society* 97 (3): 243–52. https://doi.org/10.1606/1044-3894.2016.97.27.

Collins, Patricia Hill. 2000. *Black Feminist Thought: Knowledge, Consciousness, and the Politics of Empowerment.* 2nd ed. New York: Routledge.

Collins, Patricia Hill, and Valerie Chepp. 2013. "Intersectionality." In *The Oxford Handbook of Gender and Politics*, edited by Georgina Waylen, Karen Celis, Johanna Kantola, and S. Laurel Weldon, 31–61. New York: Oxford University Press.

Congressional Budget Office. 2023. "The Federal Budget in Fiscal Year 2022: An Infographic." March 28, 2023. www.cbo.gov.

Congressional Research Service. 2023. "Child Welfare: Purposes, Federal Programs, and Funding." CRS Reports, updated January 5, 2023. https://sgp.fas.org.

Connecticut General Statutes § 17a-106a. 2018. www.cga.ct.gov.

Conrad-Hiebner, Aislinn, and Elizabeth Byram. 2020. "The Temporal Impact of Economic Insecurity on Child Maltreatment: A Systematic Review." *Trauma, Violence, and Abuse* 21 (1): 157–78. https://doi.org/10.1177/1524838018756122.

Corwin, Tyler W. 2012. *Strategies to Increase Birth Parent Engagement, Partnership, and Leadership in the Child Welfare System: A Review.* Seattle: Casey Family Program, July 2012. www.casey.org.

Corwin, Tyler W., Erin J. Maher, Monica Idzelis Rothe, Maggie Skrypek, Caren Kaplan, Dan Koziolek, and Brenda Mahoney. 2014. "Development and Evaluation of the Family Asset Builder: A New Child Protective Services Intervention to Address Chronic Neglect." *Journal of Family Strengths* 14 (1): 4. https://doi.org/10.58464/2168-670X.1244.

Cosgrove, Lisa, and Cheryl Flynn. 2005. "Marginalized Mothers: Parenting without a Home." *Analyses of Social Issues and Public Policy* 5 (1): 127–43. https://doi.org/10.1111/j.1530-2415.2005.00059.x.

Couch, Kenneth A., Robert W. Fairlie, and Huanan Xu. 2020. "Early Evidence of the Impacts of COVID-19 on Minority Unemployment." *Journal of Public Economics* 192:104287. https://doi.org/10.1016/j.jpubeco.2020.104287.

Courtney, Mark E., Amy Dworsky, Adam Brown, Colleen Cary, Kara Love, and Vanessa Vorhies. 2011. *Midwest Evaluation of the Adult Functioning of Former Foster Youth: Outcomes at Age 26*. Chicago: Chapin Hall at the University of Chicago. www.chapinhall.org.

Courtney, Mark E., Amy Dworsky, Joann S. Lee, and Melissa Raap. 2010. *Midwest Evaluation of the Adult Functioning of Former Foster Youth: Outcomes at Age 23 and 24*. Chicago: Chapin Hall at the University of Chicago. www.chapinhall.org.

Cox, Kris, Samantha Jacoby, and Chuck Marr. 2022. *Stimulus Payments, Child Tax Credit Expansion Were Critical Parts of Successful COVID-19 Policy Response*. Washington, DC: Center on Budget and Policy Priorities, June 22, 2022. www.cbpp.org.

Crampton, David, and Wendy Lewis Jackson. 2007. "Family Group Decision Making and Disproportionality in Foster Care: A Case Study." *Child Welfare* 86 (3): 51–69.

Crofoot, Thomas L., and Marian S. Harris. 2012. "An Indian Child Welfare Perspective on Disproportionality in Child Welfare." *Children and Youth Services Review* 34 (9): 1667–74. https://doi.org/10.1016/j.childyouth.2012.04.028.

Cross, Courtney. "Criminalizing Battered Mothers." 2018. *Utah Law Review* 2018 (2): 259–305.

Cross, Theodore P., David Finkelhor, and Richard Ormrod. 2005. "Police Involvement in Child Protective Services Investigations: Literature Review and Secondary Data Analysis." *Child Maltreatment* 10 (3): 224–44. https://doi.org/10.1177/1077559505274506.

Culhane, Jennifer F., David Webb, Susan Grim, Stephen Metraux, and Dennis Culhane. 2003. "Prevalence of Child Welfare Services Involvement among Homeless and Low-Income Mothers: A Five-Year Birth Cohort Study." *Journal of Sociology & Social Welfare* 30 (3): 79–95. https://doi.org/10.15453/0191-5096.2918.

Cunningham, Mary, Martha R. Burt, Molly Scott, Gretchen Locke, Larry Buron, Jacob Klerman, Nicole Fiore, and Lindsey Stillman. 2015. *Homelessness Prevention Study: Prevention Programs Funded by the Homelessness Prevention and Rapid Re-Housing Program*. Washington, DC: HUD, August 2015. www.huduser.gov.

CWIG (Child Welfare Information Gateway). 2018. *State vs. County Administration of Child Welfare Services*. USDHHS, Children's Bureau, March 2018. www.childwelfare.gov.

———. 2019a. *Penalties for Failure to Report and False Reporting of Child Abuse and Neglect*. USDHHS, ACF, Children's Bureau, February 2019. www.childwelfare.gov.

———. 2019b. "Plans of Safe Care for Infants with Prenatal Substance Exposure and Their Families—Kentucky." USDHHS, ACF, Children's Bureau, August 2019. www.childwelfare.gov.

———. 2020a. *Adoption Assistance for Children Adopted from Foster Care*. USDHHS, ACF, Children's Bureau, 2020. www.childwelfare.gov.

———. 2020b. *How the Child Welfare System Works*. USDHHS, ACF, Children's Bureau, October 2020. www.childwelfare.gov.

———. 2022a. *Definitions of Child Abuse and Neglect*. USDHHS, ACF, Children's Bureau, May 2022. www.childwelfare.gov.

———. 2022b. *Extension of Foster Care Beyond Age 18*. USDHHS, ACF, Children's Bureau. https://www.childwelfare.gov.

———. 2023. *Mandatory Reporting of Child Abuse and Neglect*. USDHHS, ACF, Children's Bureau, May 2023. www.childwelfare.gov.

CWLA (Child Welfare League of America). 1951. "Basic Principles Applicable to All Child Welfare Agencies." *Child Welfare* 30 (9): 9, 14–16.

———. 1958. *A Statement of Principles and Policies on Administration of Voluntary and Public Child Welfare Agencies*. New York: CWLA.

———. 1996. *Alcohol and Other Drugs: A Study of State Child Welfare Agencies' Policy and Programmatic Response*. Washington, DC: CWLA.

D'Andrade, Amy C., and Ruth M. Chambers. 2012. "Parental Problems, Case Plan Requirements, and Service Targeting in Child Welfare Reunification." *Children and Youth Services Review* 34 (10): 2131–38. https://doi.org/10.1016/j.childyouth.2012.07.008.

Daro, Deborah, and Kenneth A. Dodge. 2009. "Creating Community Responsibility for Child Protection: Possibilities and Challenges." *Future of Children* 19 (2): 67–93. https://doi.org/10.1353/foc.0.0030.

Davidson, Ryan D., Meredith W. Morrissey, and Connie J. Beck. 2019. "The Hispanic Experience of the Child Welfare System." *Family Court Review* 57 (2): 201–16. https://doi.org/10.1111/fcre.12404.

Day, Elizabeth, Brittany Mihalec-Adkins, Mary Beth Morrissey, Francesca Vescia, and Laura Tach. 2023. "I Was a Soccer Mom—High or Not: The Intersecting Roles of Parenting and Recovery." *Family Relations* 72 (4): 1827–44. https://doi.org/10.1111/fare.12780.

DePanfilis, Diane. 2006. *Child Neglect: A Guide for Prevention, Assessment, and Intervention*. Washington, DC: USDHHS, January 2006. www.govinfo.gov.

———. 2018. *Child Protective Services: A Guide for Caseworkers*. Capacity Building Center for States. Washington, DC: USDHHS, ACF, Children's Bureau. https://capacity.childwelfare.gov.

Desmond, Matthew. 2015. "Severe Deprivation in America: An Introduction." *RSF: The Russell Sage Foundation Journal of the Social Sciences* 1 (2): 1–11. https://doi.org/10.7758/RSF.2015.1.2.01.

Dettlaff, Alan J. 2012. "Immigrant Children and Families and the Public Child Welfare System: Considerations for Legal Systems." *Juvenile & Family Court Journal* 63 (1): 19–30. https://doi.org/10.1111/j.1755-6988.2011.01069.x.

———. 2023. *Confronting the Racist Legacy of the American Child Welfare System*. New York: Oxford University Press.

Dettlaff, Alan J., and Reiko Boyd. 2020. "Racial Disproportionality and Disparities in the Child Welfare System: Why Do They Exist, and What Can Be Done to Address

Them?" *Annals of the American Academy of Political and Social Science* 692 (1): 253–74. https://doi.org/10.1177/0002716220980329.

Dettlaff, Alan J., Reiko Boyd, Darcey Merritt, Jason Plummer, and James D. Simon. 2021. "Racial Bias, Poverty, and the Notion of Evidence." *Child Welfare* 99 (3): 61–90.

Dettlaff, Alan J., and Megan Finno-Velasquez. 2013. "Child Maltreatment and Immigration Enforcement: Considerations for Child Welfare and Legal Systems Working with Immigrant Families." *Children's Legal Rights Journal* 33 (1): 37–63.

Dettlaff, Alan J., and Rowena Fong. 2016. "Practice with Immigrant and Refugee Children and Families in the Child Welfare System." In *Immigrant and Refugee Children and Families: Culturally Responsive Practice*, edited by Alan J. Dettlaff and Rowena Fong, 285–317. New York: Columbia University Press.

Dettlaff, Alan J., Stephanie R. Rivaux, Donald J. Baumann, John D. Fluke, Joan R. Rycraft, and Joyce James. 2011. "Disentangling Substantiation: The Influence of Race, Income, and Risk on the Substantiation Decision in Child Welfare." *Children and Youth Services Review* 33 (9): 1630–37. https://doi.org/10.1016/j.childyouth.2011.04.005.

Dettlaff, Alan J., Kristen Weber, Maya Pendleton, Reiko Boyd, Bill Bettencourt, and Leonard Burton. 2020. "It Is Not a Broken System, It Is a System That Needs to Be Broken: The UpEND Movement to Abolish the Child Welfare System." *Journal of Public Child Welfare* 14 (5): 500–517. https://doi.org/10.1080/15548732.2020.1814542.

Dickerson, Caitlin. 2022. "The Secret History of the U.S. Government's Family-Separation Policy: 'We Need to Take Away Children.'" *The Atlantic*, August 7, 2022. www.theatlantic.com.

Dickerson, Kelli L., Jennifer Lavoie, and Jodi A. Quas. 2020. "Do Laypersons Conflate Poverty and Neglect?" *Law and Human Behavior* 44 (4): 311–26. https://doi.org/10.1037/lhb0000415.

Dolan, Melissa, Kieth Smith, Cecilia Casanueva, and Heather Ringeisen. 2011. *NSCAW II Baseline Report: Introduction to NSCAW II*. #2011-27a. Washington, DC: USD-HHS, ACF, Office of Planning, Research and Evaluation. www.acf.hhs.gov.

Doran, Morgan B. Ward, and Dorothy E. Roberts. 2002. "Welfare Reform and Families in the Child Welfare System." *Maryland Law Review* 61:386–435.

Dotson, Hilary M. 2011. "Homeless Women, Parents, and Children: A Triangulation Approach Analyzing Factors Influencing Homelessness and Child Separation." *Journal of Poverty* 15 (3): 241–58. https://doi.org/10.1080/10875549.2011.588489.

Doyle, Joseph J., Jr. 2007. "Child Protection and Child Outcomes: Measuring the Effects of Foster Care." *American Economic Review* 97 (5): 1583–1610. https://doi.org/10.1257/aer.97.5.1583.

———. 2008. "Child Protection and Adult Crime: Using Investigator Assignment to Estimate Causal Effects of Foster Care." *Journal of Political Economy* 116 (4): 746–70. https://doi.org/10.1086/590216.

Drake, Brett, Jennifer M. Jolley, Paul Lanier, John Fluke, Richard P. Barth, and Melissa Jonson-Reid. 2011. "Racial Bias in Child Protection? A Comparison of Competing

Explanations Using National Data." *Pediatrics* 127 (3): 471–78. https://doi.org/10.1542/peds.2010-1710.

Dreby, Joanna. 2012. "The Burden of Deportation on Children in Mexican Immigrant Families." *Journal of Marriage and Family* 74 (4): 829–45. https://doi.org/10.1111/j.1741-3737.2012.00989.x.

Duffy, Maureen 2010. "Writing about Clients: Developing Composite Case Material and Its Rationale." *Counseling and Values* 54 (2): 135–53. https://doi.org/10.1002/j.2161-007X.2010.tb00011.x.

Dunlap, Justine A. 2004. "Sometimes I Feel Like a Motherless Child: The Error of Pursuing Battered Mothers for Failure to Protect." *Loyola Law Review* 50:565–622.

Dworsky, Amy. 2014. "Families at the Nexus of Housing and Child Welfare." First Focus and the State Policy Advocacy Reform Center, November 2014. https://firstfocus.org.

———. 2015. "Child Welfare Services Involvement among the Children of Young Parents in Foster Care." *Child Abuse & Neglect* 45:68–79. https://doi.org/10.1016/j.chiabu.2015.04.005.

Eamon, Mary Keegan, and Sandra Kopels. 2004. "'For Reasons of Poverty': Court Challenges to Child Welfare Practices and Mandated Programs." *Children and Youth Services Review* 26 (9): 821–36. https://doi.org/10.1016/j.childyouth.2004.02.023.

Echo-Hawk, Walter R. 2010. *In the Courts of the Conqueror: The 10 Worst Indian Law Cases Ever Decided.* Golden, CO: Fulcrum.

Eck, Allison. 2018. "Psychological Damage Inflicted by Parent-Child Separation Is Deep, Long-Lasting." *NOVA*, June 20, 2018. www.pbs.org.

Economic Research Service. 2023. "Rural Poverty and Well-Being." November 15, 2023. US Department of Agriculture. www.ers.usda.gov.

Edwards, Frank. 2016. "Saving Children, Controlling Families: Punishment, Redistribution, and Child Protection." *American Sociological Review* 81 (3): 575–95. https://doi.org/10.1177/0003122416638652.

———. 2019. "Family Surveillance: Police and the Reporting of Child Abuse and Neglect." *RSF: The Russell Sage Foundation Journal of the Social Sciences* 5 (1): 50–70. https://doi.org/10.7758/RSF.2019.5.1.03.

Edwards, Frank, Theresa Rocha Beardall, and Hannah Curtis. 2023. "American Indian and Alaska Native Overexposure to Foster Care and Family Surveillance in the US: A Quantitative Overview of Contemporary System Contact." *Children and Youth Services Review* 149:106915. https://doi.org/10.1016/j.childyouth.2023.106915.

Edwards, Frank, Sara Wakefield, Kieran Hiely, and Christopher Wildeman. 2021. "Contact with Child Protective Services Is Pervasive but Unequally Distributed by Race and Ethnicity in Large U.S. Counties." *Proceedings of the National Academy of Sciences* 118 (30): e2106272118. https://doi.org/10.1073/pnas.2106272118.

Edwards, Mark Evan, Melissa Torgerson, and Jennifer Sattem. 2009. "Paradoxes of Providing Rural Social Services: The Case of Homeless Youth." *Rural Sociology* 74 (3): 330–55. https://doi.org/10.1526/003601109789037204.

E.E.G. 1962. "Action to Improve Our Welfare Programs." *Child Welfare* 41 (2): 50, 89.

Elgin, Dallas J., and David P. Carter 2020. "Higher Performance with Increased Risk of Undesirable Outcomes: The Dilemma of U.S. Child Welfare Services Privatization." *Public Management Review* 22 (11): 1603–23. https://doi.org/10.1080/14719037.2019.1 637013.

Eliot, Martha M. 1954. "Child Welfare Priorities in 1954." *Child Welfare* 33 (8): 3–7.

Erney, Rosalynd, and Kristen Weber. 2018. "Not All Children Are Straight and White: Strategies for Serving Youth of Color in Out-of-Home Care Who Identify as LG-BTQ." *Child Welfare* 96 (2): 151–77.

Esping-Andersen, Gøsta. 1990. *The Three Worlds of Welfare Capitalism*. Princeton, NJ: Princeton University Press.

Estes, Nick. 2016. "Native Liberation: The Way Forward." The Red Nation, August 17, 2016. http://therednation.org.

Evangelist, Michael, Margaret M. C. Thomas, and Jane Waldfogel. 2023. "Child Protective Services Contact and Youth Outcomes." *Child Abuse & Neglect* 136:105994. https://doi.org/10.1016/j.chiabu.2022.105994.

Ezell, Jerel M., Suzan Walters, Samuel R. Friedman, Rebecca Bolinski, Wiley D. Jenkins, John Schneider, Bruce Link, and Mai T. Pho. 2021. "Stigmatize the Use, Not the User? Attitudes on Opioid Use, Drug Injection, Treatment, and Overdose Prevention in Rural Communities." *Social Science & Medicine* 268:113470. https://doi.org/10.1016/j.socscimed.2020.113470.

Fagan, Jeffrey. 1996. *The Criminalization of Domestic Violence: Promises and Limits*. Washington, DC: US Department of Justice, January 1996. www.ojp.gov.

Fagan, Jeffrey, and Tom R. Tyler. 2005. "Legal Socialization of Children and Adolescents." *Social Justice Research* 18 (3): 217–41. https://doi.org/10.1007 /s11211-005-6823-3.

Family First Prevention Services Act. 2018. Public Law No. 115-123. www.acf.hhs.gov.

Farrell, Justin, Paul Berne Burow, Kathryn McConnell, Jude Bayham, Kyle Whyte, and Gal Koss. 2021. "Effects of Land Dispossession and Forced Migration on Indigenous Peoples in North America." *Science* 374 (6567): eabe4943. https://doi.org/10.1126/ science.abe4943.

Fauci, Jennifer E., and Lisa A. Goodman. 2020. "'You Don't Need Nobody Else Knocking You Down': Survivor-Mothers' Experiences of Surveillance in Domestic Violence Shelters." *Journal of Family Violence* 35 (3): 241–54. https://doi.org/10.1007 /s10896-019-00090-y.

Feely, Megan, and Emily Adlin Bosk. 2021. "That Which Is Essential Has Been Made Invisible: The Need to Bring a Structural Risk Perspective to Reduce Racial Disproportionality." *Race and Social Problems* 13 (1): 49–62. https://doi.org/10.1007 /s12552-021-09313-8.

Ferraro, A. C., Erin J. Maher, and Claudette Grinnell-Davis. 2022. "Family Ties: A Quasi-Experimental Approach to Estimate the Impact of Kinship Care on Child Well-Being." *Children and Youth Services Review* 137:106472. https://doi. org/10.1016/j.childyouth.2022.106472.

Finck, Kara, Marcia Hopkins, Courtney G. Joslin, Catherine Sakimura, L. Frunel, Sarah Lorr, and Sacha Coupet. 2021. "Looking through Client Lenses: Youth of Color, LGBT Parents and Youth, Disabled Parents." Presented at Strengthened Bonds: Abolishing the Child Welfare System and Re-Envisioning Child Well-Being, Columbia University, New York, June 16, 2001.

Finno-Velasquez, Megan, and Sophia Sepp. 2022. *The New Mexico Children, Youth, and Families Department Immigration Unit: A Model for Child Welfare and Juvenile Justice Systems Serving Immigrant Children and their Families.* Berkeley, CA: Center on Immigration and Child Welfare and New Mexico Children, Youth, and Families Department, November 2022. https://cimmcw.org.

Fischer, Robert L., and Francisca García-Cobián Richter. 2017. "SROI in the Pay for Success Context: Are They at Odds?" *Evaluation and Program Planning* 64:105–9. https://doi.org/10.1016/j.evalprogplan.2016.11.012.

Fish, Jessica N., Laura Baams, Armeda Stevenson Wojciak, and Stephen T. Russell. 2019. "Are Sexual Minority Youth Overrepresented in Foster Care, Child Welfare, and Out-of-Home Placement? Findings from Nationally Representative Data." *Child Abuse & Neglect* 89:203–11. https://doi.org/10.1016/j.chiabu.2019.01.005.

Fitzgerald, Michael. 2020. "Rising Voices for 'Family Power' Seek to Abolish the Child Welfare System." *The Imprint*, July 8, 2020. https://imprintnews.org.

Fix, Michael, ed. 2009. *Immigrants and Welfare: The Impact of Welfare Reform on America's Newcomers.* New York: Russell Sage Foundation.

Flasch, Paulina, Maria Haiyasoso, Kevin Fall, Kaylyn Evans, Colleen Dunlap, and Tal Nesichi. 2021. "State Standards for Batterer Intervention Programs: A Content Analysis." *Violence and Victims* 36 (6): 683–705. https://doi.org/10.1891/VV-D-20-00079.

Fong, Kelley. 2017. "Child Welfare Involvement and Contexts of Poverty: The Role of Parental Adversities, Social Networks, and Social Services." *Children and Youth Services Review* 72:5–13. https://doi.org/10.1016/j.childyouth.2016.10.011.

———. 2019a. "Concealment and Constraint: Child Protective Services Fears and Poor Mothers' Institutional Engagement." *Social Forces* 97 (4): 1785–810. https://doi.org/10.1093/sf/soy093.

———. 2019b. "Neighborhood Inequality in the Prevalence of Reported and Substantiated Child Maltreatment." *Child Abuse & Neglect* 90:13–21. https://doi.org/10.1016/j.chiabu.2019.01.014.

———. 2020. "Getting Eyes in the Home: Child Protective Services Investigations and State Surveillance of Family Life." *American Sociological Review* 85 (4): 610–38. https://doi.org/10.1177/0003122420938460.

———. 2023. *Investigating Families: Motherhood in the Shadow of Child Protective Services.* Princeton, NJ: Princeton University Press.

Font, Sarah A., Lawrence M. Berger, Maria Cancian, and Jennifer L. Noyles. 2018. "Permanency and the Educational and Economic Attainment of Former Foster Children in Early Adulthood." *American Sociological Review* 83 (4): 716–43. https://doi.org/10.1177/0003122418781791.

Font, Sarah A., Lawrence M. Berger, and Kristen S. Slack. 2012. "Examining Racial Disproportionality in Child Protective Services Case Decisions." *Children and Youth Services Review* 34 (11): 2188–200. https://doi.org/10.1016/j.childyouth.2012.07.012.

Font, Sarah A., Maria Cancian, Lawrence M. Berger, and Anna DiGiovanni. 2020. "Patterns of Intergenerational Child Protective Services Involvement." *Child Abuse & Neglect* 99:104247. https://doi.org/10.1016/j.chiabu.2019.104247.

Font, Sarah A., and Kathryn Maguire-Jack. 2020. "It's Not 'Just Poverty': Educational, Social, and Economic Functioning among Young Adults Exposed to Childhood Neglect, Abuse, and Poverty." *Child Abuse & Neglect* 101:104356. https://doi.org/10.1016/j.chiabu.2020.104356.

Foster, Carley Hayden. 2012. "Race and Child Welfare Policy: State-Level Variations in Disproportionality." *Race and Social Problems* 4 (2): 93–101. https://doi.org/10.1007/s12552-012-9071-9.

Foucault, Michel. 1982. "The Subject and Power." *Critical Inquiry* 8 (4): 777–95.

———. 2008. *The Birth of Biopolitics: Lectures at the Collège de France, 1978–1979.* Edited by Michel Senellart. Translated by Graham Burchell. New York: Picador.

Fowler, Patrick J. 2017. "U.S. Commentary: Implications from the Family Options Study for Homeless and Child Welfare Services." *Cityscape: A Journal of Policy Development and Research* 19 (3). www.huduser.gov.

Fowler, Patrick J., Derek S. Brown, Michael Schoeny, and Saras Chung. 2018. "Homelessness in the Child Welfare System: A Randomized Controlled Trial to Assess the Impact of Housing Subsidies on Foster Care Placements and Costs." *Child Abuse & Neglect* 83:52–61. https://doi.org/10.1016/j.chiabu.2018.07.014.

Fowler, Patrick J., and Anne F. Farrell. 2017. "Housing and Child Well Being: Implications for Research, Policy, and Practice." *American Journal of Community Psychology* 60 (1–2): 3–8. https://doi.org/10.1002%2Fajcp.12154.

Fowler, Patrick J., Anne F. Farrell, Katherine E. Marcal, Saras Chung, and Peter S. Hovmand. 2017. "Housing and Child Welfare: Emerging Evidence and Implications for Scaling Up Services." *American Journal of Community Psychology* 60 (1–2): 134–44. https://doi.org/10.1002/ajcp.12155.

Fowler, Patrick J., David B. Henry, Michael Schoeny, John Landsverk, Dina Chavira, and Jeremy J. Taylor. 2013. "Inadequate Housing among Families under Investigation for Child Abuse and Neglect: Prevalence from a National Probability Sample." *American Journal of Community Psychology* 52 (1–2): 106–14. https://doi.org/10.1007/s10464-013-9580-8.

Fowler, Patrick J., Katherine E. Marcal, Saras Chung, Derek S. Brown, Melissa Jonson-Reid, and Peter S. Hovmand. 2020. "Scaling Up Housing Services within the Child Welfare System: Policy Insights from Simulation Modeling." *Child Maltreatment* 25 (1): 51–60. https://doi.org/10.1177/1077559519846431.

Fowler, Patrick J., and Michael Schoeny. 2015. "The Family Unification Program: A Randomized-Controlled Trial of Housing Stability." *Child Welfare* 94 (1): 167–87.

———. 2017. "Permanent Housing for Child Welfare-Involved Families: Impact on Child Maltreatment Overview." *American Journal of Community Psychology* 60 (1–2): 91–102. https://doi.org/10.1002/ajcp.12146.

Fox, Cybelle. 2010. "Three Worlds of Relief: Race, Immigration, and Public and Private Social Welfare Spending in American Cities, 1929." *American Journal of Sociology* 116 (2): 453–502. https://doi.org/10.1086/653836.

Frame, Laura. 1999. "Suitable Homes Revisited: An Historical Look at Child Protection and Welfare Reform." *Children and Youth Services Review* 21 (9–10): 719–54. https://doi.org/10.1016/S0190-7409(99)00052-3.

Frederick, Angela. 2014. "Mothering While (Dis)Abled." *Contexts* 13 (4): 30–35. https://doi.org/10.1177/1536504214558214.

Freundlich, Madelyn, and Kathy Barbell. 2001. *Foster Care Today*. Washington, DC: Casey Family Programs.

Fuller, Tamara, and Martin Nieto. 2014. "Child Welfare Services and Risk of Child Maltreatment Rereports: Do Services Ameliorate Initial Risk?" *Children and Youth Services Review* 47 (pt. 1): 46–54. https://doi.org/10.1016/j.childyouth.2013.11.015.

Futures Without Violence. 2022. *Child Care as a Domestic Violence Issue*. Policy brief. San Francisco: Futures Without Violence, June 2022. www.futureswithoutviolence.org.

Ganasarajah, Shemini, Gene Siegel, and Melissa Sickmund. 2017. *Disproportionality Rates for Children in Foster Care: Fiscal Year 2015*. Reno, NV: National Council of Juvenile and Family Court Judges, September 2017. www.ncjfcj.org.

Garland, Patricia. 1966. "Illegitimacy—A Special Minority-Group Problem in Urban Areas: New Social Welfare Perspectives." *Child Welfare* 45 (2): 81–88, 100.

Garriott, William. 2013. "Methamphetamine in Rural America: Notes on Its Emergence." *Anthropology Now* 5 (1): 27–35. https://doi.org/10.5816/anthropologynow.5.1.0027.

Gaughan, Beatrice A. 1954. "Serving the Child through the Public Welfare Program." *Child Welfare* 33 (6): 10–15.

Gelles, Richard. 2003. Interview for "Failure to Protect." *Frontline*. Boston: WBGH, Public Broadcasting Service. www.pbs.org.

Gelman, Andrew, Jeffrey Fagan, and Alex Kiss. 2007. "An Analysis of the New York City Police Department's 'Stop and Frisk' Policy in the Context of Claims of Racial Bias." *Journal of the American Statistical Association* 102 (479): 813–23. https://doi.org/10.1198/016214506000001040.

Ghertner, Robin, Melinda Baldwin, Gilbert Crouse, Laura Radel, and Annette Waters. 2018. *The Relationship between Substance Use Indicators and Child Welfare Caseloads*. Washington, DC: USDHHS, revised March 9, 2018. https://aspe.hhs.gov.

Ghertner, Robin, Annette Waters, Laura Radel, and Gilbert Crouse. 2018. "The Role of Substance Use in Child Welfare Caseloads." *Children and Youth Services Review* 90:83–93. https://doi.org/10.1016/j.childyouth.2018.05.015.

Gil, David G. 1970. *Violence against Children: Physical Child Abuse in the United States*. Cambridge, MA: Harvard University Press.

———. 1971. "Violence against Children." *Journal of Marriage and Family* 33 (4): 637–48. https://doi.org/10.2307/349436.

Gilbert, Neil, Nigel Parton, and Marit Skivenes, eds. 2011. *Child Protection Systems: International Trends and Orientations.* New York: Oxford University Press.

Gilbert, Ruth, Cathy Spatz Widom, Kevin Browne, David Fergusson, Elspeth Webb, and Staffan Janson. 2009. "Burden and Consequences of Child Maltreatment in High-Income Countries." *The Lancet* 373 (9657): 68–81. https://doi.org/10.1016/S0140-6736(08)61706-7.

Gilmore, Ruth. 2007. *Golden Gulag: Prisons, Surplus, Crisis, and Opposition in Globalizing California.* Berkeley: University of California Press.

Ginther, Donna K., and Michelle Johnson-Motoyama. 2022. "Associations between State TANF Policies, Child Protective Services Involvement, and Foster Care Placement." *Health Affairs* 41 (12): 1744–53. https://doi.org/10.1377/hlthaff.2022.00743.

Goffman, Alice. 2014. *On the Run: Fugitive Life in an American City.* New York: Picador.

Goldstein, Joseph, Anna Freud, and Albert J. Solnit. 1973. *Beyond the Best Interests of the Child.* New York: Free Press.

———. 1979. *Before the Best Interests of the Child.* New York: Free Press.

Gomez, Laura E. 1997. *Misconceiving Mothers: Legislators, Prosecutors, and the Politics of Prenatal Drug Exposure.* Philadelphia: Temple University Press.

Goodmark, Leigh. 2011. *A Troubled Marriage: Domestic Violence and the Legal System.* New York: New York University Press.

———. 2018. *Decriminalizing Domestic Violence.* Berkley: University of California Press.

———. 2022. *Law Enforcement Experience Report: Domestic Violence Survivors' Survey Regarding Interaction with Law Enforcement.* Austin, TX: National Domestic Violence Hotline. www.thehotline.org.

Gordon, Derrick M., Arazais Oliveros, Samuel W. Hawes, Derek K. Iwamoto, and Brett S. Rayford. 2012. "Engaging Fathers in Child Protection Services: A Review of Factors and Strategies across Ecological Systems." *Child and Youth Service Review* 34 (8): 1399–417. https://doi.org/10.1016/j.childyouth.2012.03.021.

Gordon, Linda. 1988. *Heroes of Their Own Lives: The Politics and History of Family Violence, Boston, 1880–1960.* New York: Penguin Books.

———. 1994. *Pitied but Not Entitled: Single Mothers and the History of Welfare, 1890–1935.* Cambridge, MA: Harvard University Press.

———. 1999. *The Great Arizona Orphan Abduction.* Cambridge, MA: Harvard University Press.

Gottlieb, Chris. 2010. "Reflections on Judging Mothering." *University of Baltimore Law Review* 39 (3): 371–88.

Goudarzi, Sara. 2018. "Separating Families May Cause Lifelong Health Damage," *Scientific American,* June 20, 2018. www.scientificamerican.com.

Gowan, Teresa, and Sarah Whetstone. 2012. "Making the Criminal Addict: Subjectivity and Social Control in a Strong-Arm Rehab." *Punishment & Society* 14 (1): 69–93. https://doi.org/10.1177/1462474511424684.

Gowan, Teresa, Sarah Whetstone, and Tanja Andic. 2012. "Addiction, Agency, and the Politics of Self-Control: Doing Harm Reduction in a Heroin Users' Group." *Social Science & Medicine* 74 (8): 1251–60. https://doi.org/10.1016/j.socscimed .2011.11.045.

Graham, J. Christopher, Alan J. Dettlaff, Donald J. Baumann, and John D. Fluke. 2015. "The Decision Making Ecology of Placing a Child into Foster Care: A Structural Equation Model." *Child Abuse & Neglect* 49:12–23. https://doi.org/10.1016/j .chiabu.2015.02.020.

Greenberg, Mark, Randy Capps, Andrew Kalweit, Jennifer Grishkin, and Ann Flagg. 2019. *Immigrant Families and Child Welfare Systems: Emerging Needs and Promising Policies*. Washington, DC: Migration Policy Institute, May 2019. www.migrationpol-icy.org.

Greenberg, Max A. 2021. "Not Seeing Like a State: Mandated Reporting, State-Adjacent Actors and the Production of Illegible Subjects." *Social Problems* 68 (4): 870–85. https://doi.org/10.1093/socpro/spab003.

Greenfield, Lawrence, Kenneth Burgdorf, Xiaowu Chen, Allan Porowski, Tracy Roberts, and James Herrell. 2009. "Effectiveness of Long-Term Residential Substance Abuse Treatment for Women: Findings from Three National Studies." *American Journal of Drug and Alcohol Abuse* 30 (3): 537–50. https://doi.org/10.1081 /ADA-200032290.

Greeson, Johanna K. P., Antonio R. Garcia, Fei Tan, Alexi Chacon, and Andre J. Ortiz. 2020. "Interventions for Youth Aging Out of Foster Care: A State of the Science Review." *Children and Youth Services Review* 113:105005. https://doi.org/10.1016/j .childyouth.2020.105005.

Grella, Christine E., Barbara Needell, Yifei Shi, and Yih-Ing Hser. 2009. "Do Drug Treatment Services Predict Reunification Outcomes of Mothers and Their Children in Child Welfare?" *Journal of Substance Abuse Treatment* 36 (3): 278–93. https://doi. org/10.1016/j.jsat.2008.06.010.

Gubits, Daniel, Marybeth Shinn, Stephen Bell, Michelle Wood, Samuel Dastrup, Claudia Solari, Scott Brown, et al. 2015. *Family Options Study: Short-Term Impacts of Housing and Services Interventions for Homeless Families*. Washington, DC: HUD, July 2015. www.huduser.gov.

Gubits, Daniel, Marybeth Shinn, Michelle Wood, Stephen Bell, Samuel Dastrup, Clau-dia Solari, Scott Brown, Debi McInnis, Tom McCall, and Utsav Kattel. 2016. *Family Options Study: 3-Year Impacts of Housing and Services Interventions for Homeless Families*. Washington, DC: HUD, October 2016. www.huduser.gov.

Gubrium, Aline. 2008. "Writing against the Image of the Monstrous Crack Mother." *Journal of Contemporary Ethnography* 37:511–27. https://doi.org/10.1177/ 0891241607309891.

Guggenheim, Martin. 2021. "How Racial Politics Led Directly to the Enactment of the Adoption and Safe Families Act of 1997—The Worst Law Affecting Families Ever Enacted by Congress." *Columbia Journal of Race and Law* 11 (3): 711–32. https://doi. org/10.52214/cjrl.v11i3.8749.

Hagan, Jacqueline Maria, Nestor Rodriguez, and Brianna Castro. 2011. "Social Effects of Mass Deportations by the United States Government, 2000–10." *Ethnic & Racial Studies* 34 (8): 1374–91. https://doi.org/10.1080/01419870.2011.575233.

Hahn, Heather, Laudan Aron, Cary Lou, Eleanor Pratt, and Adaeze Okoli. 2017. *Why Does Cash Welfare Depend on Where You Live? How and Why State TANF Programs Vary*. Washington, DC: Urban Institute, June 5, 2017. www.urban.org.

Haider, Areeba, and Lorena Roque. 2021. New Poverty and Food Insecurity Data Illustrate Persistent Racial Inequities." Center for American Progress, September 29, 2021. www.americanprogress.org.

Haight, Wendy, Teresa Jacobsen, James Black, Linda Kingery, Kathryn Sheridan, and Cray Mulder. 2005. "'In These Bleak Days': Parent Methamphetamine Abuse and Child Welfare in the Rural Midwest." *Children and Youth Services Review* 27 (8): 949–71. https://doi.org/10.1016/j.childyouth.2004.12.025.

Haight, Wendy, Cary Waubanascum, David Glesener, and Scott Marsalis. 2018. "A Scoping Study of Indigenous Child Welfare: The Long Emergency and Preparations for the Next Seven Generations." *Children and Youth Services Review* 93:397–410. https://doi.org/10.1016/j.childyouth.2018.08.016.

Hall, Martin T., Jordan Wilfong, Ruth A. Huebner, Lynn Posze, and Tina Willauer. 2016. "Medication-Assisted Treatment Improves Child Permanency Outcomes for Opioid-Using Families in the Child Welfare System." *Journal of Substance Abuse Treatment* 71:63–67. https://doi.org/10.1016/j.jsat.2016.09.006.

Hamilton, Leah, Stephen Roll, Mathieu Despard, Elaine Maag, Yung Chun, Laura Brugger, and Michal Grinstein-Weis. 2022. *The Impacts of the 2021 Expanded Child Tax Credit on Family Employment, Nutrition, and Financial Well-Being*. Washington, DC: Brookings. www.brookings.edu.

Haney, Lynne. 2018. "Incarcerated Fatherhood: The Entanglements of Child Support Debt and Mass Imprisonment." *American Journal of Sociology* 124 (1): 1–48. https://doi.org/10.1086/697580.

———. 2022. *Prisons of Debt: The Afterlives of Incarcerated Fathers*. Oakland: University of California Press.

Hanks, Angela, Danyelle Solomon, and Christian E. Weller. 2018. *Systemic Inequality: How America's Structural Racism Helped Create the Black-White Wealth Gap*. Washington, DC: Center for American Progress, February 21, 2018. www.americanprogress.org.

Hanna, Michele D. 2021. "Child Welfare System Issues as Explanatory Factors for Racial Disproportionality and Disparities." In *Racial Disproportionality and Disparities in the Child Welfare System*, edited by Alan J. Dettlaff, 177–98. New York: Springer.

Hansen, Helena. 2017. "Assisted Technologies of Social Reproduction: Pharmaceutical Prosthesis for Gender, Race, and Class in the White Opioid 'Crisis.'" *Contemporary Drug Problems* 44 (4): 321–38. https://doi.org/10.1177/0091450917739391.

Harp, Kathi L. H., and Amanda M. Bunting. 2020. "The Racialized Nature of Child Welfare Policies and the Social Control of Black Bodies." *Social Politics:*

International Studies in Gender, State, & Society 27 (2): 258–81. https://doi.org/10.1093/sp/jxz039.

Harrington, Ben. 2020. *PRWORA's Restrictions on Noncitizen Eligibility for Federal Public Benefits: Legal Issues*. Washington, DC: Congressional Research Service, R46510, September 3, 2020. https://crsreports.congress.gov.

Harris, Alexes. 2016. *A Pound of Flesh: Monetary Sanctions as Punishment for the Poor*. New York: Russell Sage Foundation.

Harris, Alexes, Heather Evans, and Katherine Beckett. 2011. "Courtesy Stigma and Monetary Sanctions toward a Socio-cultural Theory of Punishment." *American Sociological Review* 76 (2): 234–64. https://doi.org/10.1177/0003122411400054.

Harris, Marian S. 2014. *Racial Disproportionality in Child Welfare*. New York: Columbia University Press.

Harris, Maxine, and Roger D. Fallot. 2001. "Envisioning a Trauma-Informed Service System: A Vital Paradigm Shift." *New Directions for Mental Health Services* 2001 (89): 3–22. https://doi.org/10.1002/yd.23320018903.

Hart, Carl L., Joanne Csete, and Don Habibi. 2014. *Methamphetamine: Fact vs. Fiction and Lessons from the Crack Hysteria*. New York: Open Society Foundations, February 2014. www.opensocietyfoundations.org.

Hartigan, John. 2005. *Odd Tribes: Toward a Cultural Analysis of White People*. Durham, NC: Duke University Press.

Harvey, Brianna, Josh Gupta-Kagan, and Christopher Church. 2021. "Reimagining Schools' Role outside the Family Regulation System." *Columbia Journal of Race and Law* 11 (3): 575–610. https://doi.org/10.52214/cjrl.v11i3.8745.

Hatcher, David L. 2016. *The Poverty Industry: The Exploitation of America's Most Vulnerable Citizens*. New York: New York University Press.

Havlicek, Judy, and Mark E. Courtney. 2016. "Maltreatment Histories of Aging Out Foster Youth: A Comparison of Official Investigated Reports and Self-Reports of Maltreatment prior to and during Out-of-Home Care." *Child Abuse & Neglect* 52:110–22. https://doi.org/10.1016/j.chiabu.2015.12.006.

Hawkins, Mildred. 1960. "Negro Adoptions—Challenge Accepted." *Child Welfare* 39 (10): 22–27.

Hays, Sharon, 1996. *The Cultural Contradictions of Motherhood*. New Haven, CT: Yale University Press.

Henry, Colleen. 2017. "Expanding the Legal Framework for Child Protection: Recognition of and Response to Child Exposure to Domestic Violence in California Law." *Social Service Review* 91 (2): 203–32. https://doi.org/10.1086/692399.

Henry, Colleen, Nicole Liner-Jigamian, Sarah Carnochan, Sarah Taylor, and Michael J. Austin. 2018. "Parental Substance Use: How Child Welfare Workers Make the Case for Court Intervention." *Children and Youth Services Review* 93:69–78. https://doi.org/10.1016/j.childyouth.2018.07.003.

Henry, Meghan, Tanya de Sousa, Caroline Roddey, Swati Gayen, Thomas Joe Bednar. 2021. *The 2020 Annual Homeless Assessment Repot (AHAR) to Congress*. Washington, DC: HUD, January 2021. www.huduser.gov.

Henry, Meghan, Tanya de Sousa, Colette Tano, Nathaniel Dick, Rhaia Hull, Meghan Shea, Tori Morris, Sean Morris. 2022. *The 2021 Annual Homeless Assessment Report (AHAR) to Congress*. Washington, DC: HUD, February 2022. www.huduser.gov.

Herbert, James Leslie, and Leah Bromfield. 2019. "Better Together? A Review of Evidence for Multi-disciplinary Teams Responding to Physical and Sexual Child Abuse." *Trauma, Violence, & Abuse* 20 (2): 214–28. https://doi.org/10.1177/1524838017697268.

Hill, Robert B. 2004. "Institutional Racism in Child Welfare." *Race and Society* 7 (1): 17–33. https://doi.org/10.1016/j.racsoc.2004.11.004.

Hilleary, Cecily. 2021. "Indian Boarding Schools 'Outings': Apprenticeships or Indentured Servitude?" *Voice of America News*, updated November 14, 2021. www.voanews.com.

Hinton, Elizabeth. 2016. *From the War on Poverty to the War on Crime: The Making of Mass Incarceration in America*. Cambridge, MA: Harvard University Press.

Hinton, Elizabeth, and DeAnza Cook. 2021. "The Mass Criminalization of Black Americans: A Historical Review." *Annual Review of Criminology* 4:261–86. https://doi.org/10.1146/annurev-criminol-060520-033306.

Hixenbaugh, Mike, Suzy Khimm, and Agnel Philip. 2022. "Mandatory Reporting Was Supposed to Stop Severe Child Abuse. It Punishes Poor Families Instead." ProPublica, October 22, 2022. www.propublica.org.

Hoffman, Jan. 2019. "Who Can Adopt a Native American Child? A Texas Couple v. 573 Tribes." *New York Times*, June 5, 2019. www.nytimes.com.

Hollander, Sidney. 1960. "Aid to Dependent Children: Introduction." *Child Welfare* 39 (5): 26–27.

Holt, Stephanie, Helen Buckley, and Sadhbh Whelan. 2008. "The Impact of Exposure to Domestic Violence on Children and Young People: A Review of the Literature." *Child Abuse & Neglect* 32 (8): 797–810. https://doi.org/10.1016/j.chiabu.2008.02.004.

Hope, Elan C., Lori S. Hoggard, and Alvin Thomas. 2015. "Emerging into Adulthood in the Face of Racial Discrimination: Physiological, Psychological, and Sociopolitical Consequences for African American Youth." *Translational Issues in Psychological Science* 1 (4): 342–51. https://doi.org/10.1037/tps0000041.

Hopkins, Ruth. 2018. "How Foster Care Has Stripped Native American Children of Their Own Cultures." *Teen Vogue*, May 22, 2018. www.teenvogue.com.

Howell, Kathryn H., Sarah E. Barnes, Laura E. Miller, and Sandra A. Graham-Bermann. 2016. "Developmental Variations in the Impact of Intimate Partner Violence Exposure during Childhood." *Journal of Injury and Violence* 8 (1): 43–57. https://doi.org/10.5249%2Fjivr.v8i1.663.

Hudson, Pete, and Karen Levasseur. 2002. "Supporting Foster Parents: Caring Voices." *Child Welfare* 81 (6): 853–77.

Huggins-Hoyt, Kimberly Y., Orion Mowbray, Harold E. Briggs, and Junior Lloyd Allen. 2019. "Private vs. Public Child Welfare Systems: A Comparative Analysis of

National Safety Outcome Performance." *Child Abuse & Neglect* 94:104024. https://doi.org/10.1016/j.chiabu.2019.104024.

Hughes, Sean, and Naomi Schaefer Riley. 2023. "Five Years On, the Family First Act Has Failed in Its Aims." *The Hill*, April 18, 2023. https://thehill.com.

Human Rights Watch. 2022. *"If I Wasn't Poor, I Wouldn't Be Unfit": The Family Separation Crisis in the US Child Welfare System.* New York: Human Rights Watch and ACLU, November 2022. www.hrw.org.

Humphreys, Cathy, Kristin Diemer, Anna Bornemisza, Anneliese Spiteri-Staines, Rae Kaspiew, and Briony Horsfall. 2018. "More Present than Absent: Men Who Use Domestic Violence and Their Fathering." *Child and Family Social Work* 24 (2): 321–29. https://doi.org/10.1111/cfs.12617.

Hunter, David R. 1962. "Slums and Social Work." *Child Welfare* 41 (9): 387–93, 410.

Hupe, Tess M., and Margaret C. Stevenson. 2019. "Teachers' Intentions to Report Suspected Child Abuse: The Influence of Compassion Fatigue." *Journal of Child Custody* 16 (4): 364–86. https://doi.org/10.1080/15379418.2019.1663334.

Hutchinson, Janet R. 2002. *Failed Child Welfare Policy: Family Preservation and the Orphaning of Child Welfare.* Lanham, MD: University Press of America.

Hyde, Justeen, and Nina Kammerer. 2009. "Adolescents' Perspectives on Placement Moves and Congregate Settings: Complex and Cumulative Instabilities in Out-of-Home Care." *Children and Youth Services Review* 31 (2): 265–73. https://doi.org/10.1016/j.childyouth.2008.07.019.

Immigrant Legal Resource Center. 2022. *The ICE Parental Interests Directive: How Child Welfare Agencies Can Advocate with ICE to Ensure Fair Treatment of Detained or Deported Parents.* San Francisco: Immigrant Legal Resource Center, August 2022. www.ilrc.org.

Indian Child Welfare Act of 1978. 1978. 25 U.S.C. §§ 1901–63.

Ismail, Tarek Z. 2023. "Family Policing and the Fourth Amendment." *California Law Review* 111:1485–550. https://doi.org/10.15779/Z38DV1CP78.

Jacobs, David, and Daniel Tope. 2007. "The Politics of Resentment in the Post–Civil Rights Era: Minority Threat, Homicide, and Ideological Voting in Congress." *American Journal of Sociology* 112 (5): 1458–94. https://doi.org/10.1086/511804.

Jacobs, Margaret D. 2009. *White Mother to a Dark Race: Settler Colonialism, Maternalism, and the Removal of Indigenous Children in the American West and Australia, 1880–1940.* Lincoln: University of Nebraska Press.

———. 2014. *A Generation Removed: The Fostering and Adoption of Indigenous Children in the Postwar World.* Lincoln: University of Nebraska Press.

Jaros, David Michael. 2010. "Unfettered Discretion: Criminal Orders of Protection and Their Impact on Parent Defendants." *Indiana Law Journal* 85 (4): 1445–76.

Jeter, Helen Rankin. 1960. *Children Who Receive Services from Public Child Welfare Agencies.* Washington, DC: US Department of Health, Education, and Welfare.

———. 1962. *Services in Public and Voluntary Child Welfare Programs.* Washington, DC: US Department of Health, Education, and Welfare.

———. 1963. *Children, Problems, and Services in Child Welfare Programs*. Washington, DC: US Department of Health, Education, and Welfare.

Johansen, Bruce E. 1998. "Reprise/Forced Sterilizations: Native Americans and the 'Last Gasp of Eugenics.'" *Native Americas* 15 (4): 44.

Johnson, Carrie. 2022. "Flaws Plague a Tool Meant to Help Low-Risk Federal Prisoners with Early Release." *Morning Edition*, National Public Radio, January 6, 2022. www.npr.org.

Johnson, Elizabeth I., and Beth Easterling. 2012. "Understanding Unique Effects of Parental Incarceration on Children: Challenges, Progress, and Recommendations." *Journal of Marriage and Family* 74 (2): 342–56. https://doi.org/10.1111/j.1741-3737.2012.00957.x.

Johnson-Motoyama, Michelle, Donna K. Ginther, Patricia Oslund, Lindsay Jorgenson, Yoonzie Chung, Rebecca Phillips, Oliver W. J. Beer, Starr Davis, and Patricia L. Sattler. 2022. "Association between State Supplemental Nutrition Assistance Program Policies, Child Protective Services Involvement, and Foster Care in the US, 2004–2016." *JAMA Network Open* 5 (7): e2221509. https://doi.org/10.1001/jamanetworkopen.2022.21509.

Jones, Jo, and William D. Mosher. 2013. *Fathers' Involvement with Their Children: United States, 2006–2010*. National Health Statistics Reports No. 71. Hyattsville, MD: National Center for Health Statistics. www.cdc.gov.

Jonson-Reid, Melissa, Brett Drake, Sulki Chung, and Ineke Way. 2003. "Cross-Type Recidivism among Child Maltreatment Victims and Perpetrators." *Child Abuse & Neglect* 27 (8): 899–917. https://doi.org/10.1016/S0145-2134(03)00138-8.

Jonson-Reid, Melissa, Clifton R. Emery, Brett Drake, and Mary Jo Stahlschmidt. 2010. "Understanding Chronically Reported Families." *Child Maltreatment* 15 (4): 271–81. https://doi.org/10.1177/1077559510380738.

Jordan, Elizabeth, and Dana Dean Connelly. 2016. *An Introduction to Child Welfare Funding, and How States Use It*. Research brief #2016-01. Rockville, MD: Child Trends, January 2016. https://cms.childtrends.org.

Joslin, Courtney G., and Catherine Sakimura. 2022. "Fractured Families: LGBTQ People and the Family Regulation System." *California Law Review* 13:78–107.

Kaba, Mariame. 2020. "Yes, We Mean Literally Abolish the Police: Because Reform Won't Happen." *New York Times*, June 12, 2020. www.nytimes.com.

———. 2021. *We Do This 'Til We Free Us: Abolitionist Organizing and Transforming Justice*. Chicago: Haymarket Books.

Kaiser, Jeanne M., and Caroline M. Foley. 2021. "The Revictimization of Survivors of Domestic Violence and Their Children: The Heartbreaking Unintended Consequence of Separating Children from Their Abused Parent." *Western New England Law Review* 43 (1): 167–87.

Kandel, William A. 2021. *Unaccompanied Alien Children: An Overview*. Congressional Research Service Report. R43599. Washington, DC: Congressional Research Service. https://crsreports.congress.gov.

Kang, Ji Young, Jennifer Romich, Jennifer L. Hook, JoAnn Lee, and Maureen Marcenko. 2019. "Family Earnings and Transfer Income among Families Involved with Child Welfare." *Child Welfare* 97 (1): 61–84.

Kang-Brown, Jacob, Chase Montagnet, and Jasmine Heiss. 2021. *People in Jail and Prison in Spring 2021.* New York: Vera Institute of Justice, June 2021. https://vera.org.

Kanstroom, Daniel. 2010. *Deportation Nation: Outsiders in American History.* Cambridge, MA: Harvard University Press.

Kaplan, Caren, Patricia Schene, Diane DePanfilis, and Debra Gilmore. 2009. "Introduction: Shining Light on Chronic Neglect." *Protecting Children: A Professional Publication of American Humane* 24 (1): 2–9.

Kappelman, Murray M., Eugene Kaplan, Milton Markowitz, and Janice D. Richmond. 1970. "Public Welfare in a Health Setting for Children." *Child Welfare* 49 (2): 89–93.

Katz, Colleen C., Mark E. Courtney, and Elizabeth Novotny. 2017. "Pre-Foster Care Maltreatment Class as a Predictor of Maltreatment in Foster Care." *Child and Adolescent Social Work Journal* 34:35–49. https://doi.org/10.1007/s10560-016-0476-y.

Katz, Michael B. 1996. *In the Shadow of the Poorhouse: A Social History of Welfare in America.* 2nd ed. New York: Basic Books.

———. 2013. *The Undeserving Poor: America's Enduring Confrontation with Poverty.* Oxford: Oxford University Press.

Kavaler, Florence, and Margaret R. Swire. 1972. "Health Services for Foster Children: An Approach to Evaluation." *Child Welfare* 51 (9): 574–84.

Kelly, Peggy. 2020. "Risk and Protective Factors Contributing to Homelessness among Foster Care Youth: An Analysis of the National Youth in Transition Database." *Children and Youth Services Review* 108:104589. https://doi.org/10.1016/j.childyouth.2019.104589.

Kempe, C. Henry, Frederic N. Silverman, Brandt F. Steele, William Droegemueller, and Henry K. Silver. 1962. "The Battered-Child Syndrome." *JAMA* 181 (1): 17–24. https://doi.org/10.1001/jama.1962.03050270019004.

Kenny, Kathleen S., and Clare Barrington. 2018. "'People Just Don't Look at You the Same Way': Public Stigma, Private Suffering and Unmet Social Support Needs among Mothers Who Use Drugs in the Aftermath of Child Removal." *Children and Youth Services Review* 86:209–16. https://doi.org/10.1016/j.childyouth.2018.01.030.

Kentucky Youth Advocates. 2018. *2018 Kids Count County Data Book.* Jeffersontown, KY: Kentucky Youth Advocates. https://kyyouth.org.

Kesner, John E., and Margaret Robinson. 2002. "Teachers as Mandated Reporters of Child Maltreatment: Comparison with Legal, Medical, and Social Services Reporters." *Children & Schools* 24 (4): 222–31. https://doi.org/10.1093/cs/24.4.222.

KFF. 2023. "Key Facts on Health Coverage of Immigrants." September 17, 2023. www.kff.org.

Kim, Hyunil, and Brett Drake. 2018. "Child Maltreatment Risk as a Function of Poverty and Race/Ethnicity in the USA." *International Journal of Epidemiology* 47 (3): 780–87. https://doi.org/10.1093/ije/dyx280.

Kim, Hyunil, Christopher Wildeman, Melissa Jonson-Reid, and Brett Drake. 2017. "Lifetime Prevalence of Investigating Child Maltreatment among US Children." *American Journal of Public Health* 107 (2): 274–80. https://doi.org/10.2105/AJPH.2016.303545.

King, Barbara. 1966. "Activity Group Therapy of Deprived Children in a Family Service Agency." *Child Welfare* 45 (9): 525–32.

Kingfisher, Catherine Pélissier. 2012. *Women in the American Welfare Trap.* Philadelphia: University of Pennsylvania Press.

Klevens, Joanne, Feijun Luo, Likang Xu, Cora Peterson, and Natasha Latzman. 2016. "Paid Family Leave's Effect on Hospital Admissions for Pediatric Abusive Head Trauma." *Injury Prevention* 22 (6): 442–45. https://doi.org/10.1136/injuryprev-2015-041702.

Koenen, Karestan C., Terrie E. Moffitt, Avshalom Caspi, Alan Taylor, and Shaun Purcell. 2003. "Domestic Violence Is Associated with Environmental Suppression of IQ in Young Children." *Development and Psychopathology* 15 (2): 297–311. https://doi.org/10.1017/S0954579403000166.

Kolivoski, Karen M., Jeffrey J. Shook, Heath C. Johnson, Sara Goodkind, Rachel Fusco, Matt DeLisi, and Michael G. Vaughn. 2016. "Applying Legal Socialization to the Child Welfare System: Do Youths' Perceptions of Caseworkers Matter?" *Child & Youth Care Forum* 45:65–83. https://doi.org/10.1007/s10566-015-9317-y.

Kolodny, Andrew, David T. Courtwright, Catherine S. Hwang, Peter Kreiner, John L. Fadie, Thomas W. Clark, and G. Caleb Alexander. 2015. "The Prescription Opioid and Heroin Crisis: A Public Health Approach to an Epidemic of Addiction." *Annual Review of Public Health* 36:559–74. https://doi.org/10.1146/annurev-publhealth-031914-122957.

Kovski, Nicole L., Heather D. Hill, Stephen J. Mooney, Frederick P. Rivara, and Ali Rowhani-Rahbar. 2022. "Short-Term Effects of Tax Credits on Rates of Child Maltreatment Reports in the United States." *Pediatrics* 150 (1): e2021054939. https://doi.org/10.1542/peds.2021-054939.

Kraft, Colleen. 2018. "AAP Statement Opposing Separation of Children and Parents at the Border." American Academy of Pediatrics, May 8, 2018. www.aap.org.

Krane, Julia, and Linda Davies. 2000. "Mothering and Child Protective Practice: Rethinking Risk Assessment." *Child and Family Social Work* 5 (1): 35–45. https://doi.org/10.1046/j.1365-2206.2000.00142.x.

Lakota People's Law Project. 2013. *Reviewing the Facts: An Assessment of the Accuracy of NPR's "Native Foster Care: Lost Children, Shattered Families."* A Report to US Congress from the Coalition of Sioux Tribes for Children and Families, January 22, 2013. http://lakotalaw.org.

Landsman, Miriam J. 2002. "Rural Child Welfare Practice from an Organization-in-Environment Perspective." *Child Welfare* 81 (5): 791–819.

Lara-Millán, Armando. 2017. "States as a Series of People Exchanges." In *The Many Hands of the State: Theorizing Political Authority and Social Control*, edited by Kimberly J. Morgan and Ann Shola Orloff, 81–102. Cambridge: Cambridge University Press.

Lareau, Annette. 2011. *Unequal Childhoods: Class, Race, and Family Life.* 2nd ed. Berkeley: University of California Press.

Larson, Neota. 1950. "Midcentury Planning for Children: A Look Back and a Look Ahead." *Child Welfare* 29 (9): 3–7.

Lash, Don. 2017. *When the Welfare People Come: Race and Class in the US Child Protection System.* Chicago: Haymarket Books.

Lawrence, Catherine K., Wendy Zeitlin, Sreyashi Chakravarty, Angela DeCristofano, and Salvador Armendariz. 2020. "Racial Diversity and Inclusive Representation in Urban Public Child Welfare." *Journal of Public Child Welfare* 14 (1): 38–59. https://doi.org/10.1080/15548732.2019.1674232.

Lee, Hedwig, Tyler McCormick, Margaret T. Hicken, and Christopher Wildeman. 2015. "Racial Inequalities in Connectedness to Imprisoned Individuals in the United States." *Du Bois Review* 12 (2): 269–82. https://doi.org/10.1017/S1742058X15000065.

Lee, Tina. 2016. *Catching a Case: Inequality and Fear in New York City's Child Welfare System.* New Brunswick, NJ: Rutgers University Press.

———. 2022. "Foreword: Response to the Symposium." *Columbia Journal of Race and Law* 12 (1). https://doi.org/10.52214/cjrl.v12i1.9932.

Legewie, Joscha, and Jeffrey Fagan. 2019. "Aggressive Policing and the Educational Performance of Minority Youth." *American Sociological Review* 84 (2): 220–47. https://doi.org/10.1177/0003122419826020.

Lewis, Oscar. 1968. "Culture of Poverty." In *On Understanding Poverty: Perspectives from the Social Sciences,* edited by Daniel P. Moynihan, 187–220. New York: Basic Books.

Lichtenstein, Matty, and Zawadi Rucks-Ahidiana. 2020. "Contextual Text Coding: A Mixed Methods Approach for Large-Scale Textual Data." *Sociological Methods & Research* 52 (2): 605–41. https://doi.org/10.1177/0049124120986191.

Lightfoot, Elizabeth. 2014. "Children and Youth with Disabilities in the Child Welfare System: An Overview." *Child Welfare* 93 (2): 23–46.

Lilley, David R., Kristen DeVall, and Kasey Tucker-Gail. 2019. "Drug Courts and Arrest for Substance Possession: Was the African American Community Differentially Impacted?" *Crime & Delinquency* 65 (3): 352–74. https://doi.org/10.1177/0011128718789856.

Linjean, Meschelle, and Hilary N. Weaver. 2022. "The Indian Child Welfare Act (ICWA): Where We've Been, Where We're Headed, and Where We Need to Go." *Journal of Public Child Welfare* 17 (5): 1034–57. https://doi.org/10.1080/15548732.2022.2131696.

Linnemann, Travis. 2013. "Governing through Meth: Local Politics, Drug Control and the Drift toward Securitization." *Crime, Media, Culture: An International Journal* 9 (1): 39–61. https://doi.org/10.1177/1741659012454125.

Linnemann, Travis, and Tyler Wall. 2013. "'This Is Your Face on Meth': The Punitive Spectacle of 'White Trash' in the Rural War on Drugs." *Theoretical Criminology* 17 (3): 315–34. https://doi.org/10.1177/1362480612468934.

Littner, Ner. 1972. "Violence as a Symptom of Childhood Emotional Illness." *Child Welfare* 51 (4): 208–19.

Lloyd, Margaret H. 2018. "Poverty and Family Reunification for Mothers with Substance Use Disorders in Child Welfare." *Child Abuse Review* 27 (4): 301–16. https://doi.org/10.1002/car.2519.

Lockwood, Kelly. 2018. "Disrupted Mothering: Narratives of Mothers in Prison." In *Marginalized Mothers, Mothering from the Margins*, edited by Tiffany Taylor and Katrina Bloch, 157–73. Bingley, UK: Emerald.

Loman, Anthony. 2006. *Families Frequently Encountered by Child Protection Services: A Report on Chronic Child Abuse and Neglect*. St. Louis: Institute of Applied Research, February 2006. www.iarstl.org.

Lorr, Sarah H., and L. Frunel. 2022. "Lived Experience and Disability Justice in the Family Regulation System." *Columbia Journal of Race and Law* 12 (1): 477–95. https://doi.org/10.52214/cjrl.v12i1.9924.

Loudenback, Jeremy. 2021. "Color-Blind Ambition." *The Imprint*, April 1, 2021. https://imprintnews.org.

———. 2022. "Nebraska Governor Signs Law to End Private Foster Care." *The Imprint*, April 26, 2002. https://imprintnews.org.

Lovato, Kristina. 2019. "Forced Separations: A Qualitative Examination of How Latino/a Adolescents Cope with Parental Deportation." *Children and Youth Services Review* 98:42–50. https://doi.org/10.1016/j.childyouth.2018.12.012.

Lovato, Kristina, and Laura S. Abrams. 2021. "Enforced Separations: A Qualitative Examination of How Latinx Families Cope with Family Disruption Following the Deportation of a Parent." *Families in Society* 102 (1): 33–49. https://doi.org/10.1177/1044389420923470.

Lovato, Kristina, Megan Finno-Velasquez, Sophia Sepp, Effie Clayton and Kelechi Chinyere Wright. 2024. "An Examination of Child Welfare Agency Models That Serve Immigrant Children and Families." *Journal of Public Child Welfare*. March, 1–24. https://doi.org/10.1080/15548732.2024.2320278.

Lovato, Kristina, and Jesse Jeffrey Ramirez. 2022. "Addressing the Social Service Needs of Latinx Families Impacted by COVID-19 and Immigration Related Stressors." *Journal of Social Service Research* 48 (5): 617–32. https://doi.org/10.1080/01488376.2022.2097359.

Lowenstein, Kate. 2018. *Shutting Down the Trauma to Prison Pipeline: Early, Appropriate Care for Child-Welfare Involved Youth*. Boston: Citizens for Juvenile Justice. www.cfjj.org.

Lundy, Marta, and Susan F. Grossman. 2005. "The Mental Health and Service Needs of Young Children Exposed to Domestic Violence: Supportive Data." *Families in Society* 86 (1): 17–29. https://doi.org/10.1606/1044-3894.1873.

Luu, Betty, Susan Collings, and Amy Conley Wright. 2022. "A Systematic Review of Common Elements of Practice that Support Reunification." *Children and Youth Services Review* 133:106342. https://doi.org/10.1016/j.childyouth.2021.106342.

Lyon, David, ed. 2002. *Surveillance as Social Sorting: Privacy, Risk and Automated Discrimination*. London: Routledge.

Lyon, Eleanor, Shannon Lane, and Anne Menard. 2008. *Meeting Survivors' Needs: A Multi-state Study of Domestic Violence Shelter Experiences, Final Report*. Harrisburg, PA: National Resource Center on Domestic Violence, February 2008. www.ojp.gov.

Lyon-Callo, Vincent. 2004. *Inequality, Poverty, and Neoliberal Governance: Activist Ethnography in the Homeless Sheltering Industry*. Peterborough, ON: Broadview.

Magura, Stephen. 1979. "Trend Analysis in Foster Care." *Social Work Research & Abstracts* 15 (4): 29–36. https://doi.org/10.1093/swra/15.4.29.

Maclean, Miriam, Scott Sims, Melissa O'Donnell, and Ruth Gilbert. 2016. "Out-of-Home Care versus In-Home Care for Children Who Have Been Maltreated: A Systematic Review of Health and Wellbeing Outcomes." *Child Abuse Review* 25 (4): 251–72. https://doi.org/10.1002/car.2437.

Maddali, Anita Ortiz. 2014. "The Immigrant 'Other': Racialized Identity and the Devaluation of Immigrant Family Relations." *Indiana Law Journal* 89:643–702. https://doi.org/10.2139/ssrn.2390223.

Maguire-Jack, Kathryn, Brooke Jespersen, Jill E. Korbin, and James C. Spilsbury. 2020. "Rural Child Maltreatment: A Scoping Literature Review." *Trauma, Violence, & Abuse* 22 (5): 1316–25. https://doi.org/10.1177/1524838020915592.

Maguire-Jack, Kathryn, and Hyunil Kim. 2021. "Rural Differences in Child Maltreatment Reports, Reporters, and Service Responses." *Children and Youth Services Review* 120:105792. https://doi.org/10.1016/j.childyouth.2020.105792.

Malm, Karin E. 2003. "Getting Noncustodial Dads Involved in the Lives of Foster Children." *Caring for Children: Facts and Perspectives*, Brief No. 3. Washington, DC: Urban Institute, November 1, 2003. www.urban.org.

Malm, Karin E., Erica Zielewski, and Henry Chen. 2008. *More about the Dads: Exploring Associations between Nonresident Father Involvement and Child Welfare Case Outcomes*. Washington, DC: USDHHS, ACF. https://aspe.hhs.gov.

Marcenko, Maureen O., Sandra J. Lyons, and Mark Courtney. 2011. "Mothers' Experiences, Resources and Needs: The Context for Reunification." *Children and Youth Services Review* 33 (3): 431–38. https://doi.org/10.1016/j.childyouth.2010.06.020.

Mateos, Ainoa, Eduard Vaquero, M. Angels Balsells, and Carmen Ponce. 2017. "'They Didn't Tell Me Anything; They Just Sent Me Home': Children's Participation in the Return Home." *Child & Family Social Work* 22 (2): 871–80. https://doi.org/10.1111/cfs.12307.

Mauer, Marc, Cathy Potler, and Richard Wolf. 1999. *Gender and Justice: Women, Drugs, and Sentencing Policy*. NCJ Number 182148. www.ojp.gov.

Maxwell, Nina, Jonathan Scourfield, Brid Featherstone, Sally Holland, and Richard Tolman. 2012. "Engaging Fathers in Child Welfare Services: A Narrative Review of Recent Research Evidence." *Child & Family Social Work* 17 (2): 160–69. https://doi.org/10.1111/j.1365-2206.2012.00827.x.

May, Peter J., and Ashley E. Jochim. 2013. "Policy Regime Perspectives: Policies, Politics, and Governing." *Policy Studies Journal* 41 (3): 426–52. https://doi.org/10.1111/psj.12024.

Mayo, Leonard W., Lawrence E. Higgins, Christine F. Adams, William I. Lacy, Callman Rawley, Ralph S. Barrow, Lawrence C. Cole, et al. 1950. "Editorial Comments: A Statement of Principles and Policies on Public Child Welfare." *Child Welfare* 29 (5): 10–16.

Mays, Jenni. 2021. "Reframing a New Politics of Distributive Justice and Housing Equity in Australia: How Lessons from Postwar and Neoliberal Eras Provide Opportunities for a Reinvigorated Political Commitment to Universal, Socially Just Alternatives." *Social Alternatives* 40 (4): 40–47. https://doi.org/10.3316/informit.324319830156547.

McCabe, Katharine. 2022. "Criminalization of Care: Drug Testing Pregnant Patients." *Journal of Health and Social Behavior* 63 (2): 162–76. https://doi.org/10.1177/00221465211058152.

Meinhofer, Angélica, and Yohanis Angleró-Díaz. 2019. "Trends in Foster Care Entry among Children Removed from Their Homes Because of Parental Drug Use, 2000 to 2017." *JAMA Pediatrics* 173 (9): 881–83. https://doi.org/10.1001/jamapediatrics.2019.1738.

Melo, Sara, Joana Guedes, and Sandra Mendes. 2019. "Theory of Cumulative Disadvantage/Advantage." In *Encyclopedia of Gerontology and Population Aging*, edited by Danan Gu and Matthew E. Dupre, 1–8. Cham, Switzerland: Springer. https://doi.org/10.1007/978-3-319-69892-2_751-1.

Menifield, Charles E., Geiguen Shin, and Logan Strother. 2019. "Do White Law Enforcement Officers Target Minority Suspects?" *Public Administration Review* 79 (1): 56–68. https://doi.org/10.1111/puar.12956.

Merritt, Darcey H. 2021. "Lived Experiences of Racism among Child Welfare-Involved Parents." *Race and Social Problems* 13 (1): 63–72. https://doi.org/10.1007/s12552-021-09316-5.

Mink, Gwendolyn. 1990. "The Lady and the Tramp: Gender, Race, and the Origins of the American Welfare State." In *Women, the State, and Welfare*, edited by Linda Gordon, 92–122. Madison: University of Wisconsin Press.

Minoff, Elisa. 2018. *Entangled Roots: The Role of Race in Policies That Separate Families.* Washington, DC: Center for the Study of Social Policy, October 2018. https://cssp.org.

Minoff, Elisa, and Alexandra Citrin. 2022. *Systemically Neglected: How Racism Structures Public Systems to Produce Child Neglect.* Washington, DC: Center for the Study of Social Policy, March 2022. https://cssp.org.

Mitchell, Monique B., and Leon Kuczynski. 2010. "Does Anyone Know What Is Going On? Examining Children's Lived Experience of the Transition into Foster Care." *Children and Youth Services Review* 32 (3): 437–44. https://doi.org/10.1016/j.childyouth.2009.10.023.

Mittelstadt, Jennifer. 2005. *From Welfare to Workfare: The Unintended Consequences of Liberal Reform, 1945–1965.* Chapel Hill: University of North Carolina Press.

Moore, Dawn. 2011. "The Benevolent Watch: Therapeutic Surveillance in Drug Treatment Court." *Theoretical Criminology* 15 (3): 255–68. https://doi.org/10.1177/1362480610396649.

Moreno, Christopher M., and Giorgio H. Curti. 2012. "Recovery Spaces and Therapeutic Jurisprudence: A Case Study of the Family Treatment Drug Courts." *Social & Cultural Geography* 13 (2): 161–83. https://doi.org/10.1080/14649365.2012.655768.

Morgan, Danielle Fuentes. 2018. "Visible Black Motherhood Is a Revolution." *Biography* 41 (4): 856–75. https://doi.org/10.1353/bio.2018.0082.

Moylan, Carrie A., Todd Herrenkohl, Cindy Sousa, Emiko A. Tajima, Roy C. Herrenkohl, and M. Jean Russo. 2010. "The Effects of Child Abuse and Exposure to Domestic Violence on Adolescent Internalizing and Externalizing Behavior Problems." *Journal of Family Violence* 25 (1): 53–63. https://doi.org/10.1007%2Fs10896-009-9269-9.

Muhammad, Khalil Gibran. 2011. *The Condemnation of Blackness: Race, Crime, and the Making of Modern Urban America*. Cambridge, MA: Harvard University Press.

Mullings, Leith. 2003. "Losing Ground: Harlem, the War on Drugs, and the Prison Industrial Complex." *Souls* 5 (2): 1–21. https://doi.org/10.1080/714044626.

Munro, Eileen. 2019. "Decision-Making under Uncertainty in Child Protection: Creating a Just and Learning Culture." *Child & Family Social Work* 24 (1): 123–30. https://doi.org/10.1111/cfs.12589.

Murakawa, Naomi. 2011. "Toothless: The Methamphetamine 'Epidemic,' 'Meth Mouth,' and the Racial Construction of Drug Scares." *Du Bois Review: Social Science Research on Race* 8 (1): 219–28. https://doi.org/10.1017/S1742058X11000208.

———. 2014. *The First Civil Right: How Liberals Built Prison America*. New York: Oxford University Press.

Murakawa, Naomi, and Katherine Beckett. 2010. "The Penology of Racial Innocence: The Erasure of Racism in the Study and Practice of Punishment." *Law & Society Review* 44 (3–4): 695–730. https://doi.org/10.1111/j.1540-5893.2010.00420.x.

Murphey, David, and P. May Cooper. 2015. *Parents Behind Bars: What Happens to Their Children?* Rockville, MD: Child Trends, October 2015. www.childtrends.org.

Myers, John E. B. 2006. *Child Protection in America: Past, Present, and Future*. New York: Oxford University Press.

Myers, Carly, Alexis Robles-Fradet, Abigail Coursolle, and T. Nancy Lam. 2023. *Foster Youth Access to Medi-Cal Specialty Mental Health Services in the California Counties with the Largest Foster Care Populations*. Los Angeles: National Health Law Program. https://healthlaw.org.

NABSW (National Association of Black Social Workers). 1972. *Position Statement on Trans-racial Adoptions*. New York: National Association of Black Social Workers. www.nabsw.org.

Nagle, Rebecca, host. 2021. *This Land*. Season 2. Crooked Media. https://crooked.com.

National Children's Alliance. n.d. "How the CAC Model Works." Accessed June 21, 2024. www.nationalchildrensalliance.org.

National Immigrant Justice Center. 2023. *ICE's Family Expedited Removal Management (FERM) Program Puts Families at Risk*. Chicago: National Immigrant Justice Center, August 2023. https://immigrantjustice.org.

National Immigration Law Center. 2022. *The 2022 Public Charge Regulations.* Los Angeles: National Immigration Law Center. www.nilc.org.

National Native American Boarding School Healing Coalition. n.d. "US Indian Boarding School History." Accessed December 23, 2023. https://boardingschoolhealing.org.

National Scientific Council on the Developing Child. 2012. "The Science of Neglect: The Persistent Absence of Responsive Care Disrupts the Developing Brain." Working Paper 12. Center on the Developing Child, Harvard University, Cambridge, MA. www.developingchild.harvard.edu.

Neal, Odeana R. 1995. "Myths and Moms: Images of Women and Termination of Parental Rights." *Kansas Journal of Law & Public Policy* 5:61–76.

Nelson, Barbara J. 1984. *Making an Issue of Child Abuse.* Chicago: University of Chicago Press.

Netherland, Julie, and Helena Hansen. 2017. "White Opioids: Pharmaceutical Race and the War on Drugs That Wasn't." *BioSocieties* 12:217–38. https://doi.org/10.1057/biosoc.2015.46.

Neubeck, Kenneth J., and Noel A. Cazenave. 2001. *Welfare Racism: Playing the Race Card Against America's Poor.* New York: Routledge.

Newland, Bryan. 2022. *Federal Indian Boarding School Initiative Investigative Report.* Washington, DC: US Department of the Interior, Bureau of Indian Affairs, May 2022. www.bia.gov.

Newman, Bernie Sue, and Paul L. Dannenfelser. 2005. "Children's Protective Services and Law Enforcement: Fostering Partnerships in Investigations of Child Abuse." *Journal of Child Sexual Abuse* 14 (2): 97–111. https://doi.org/10.1300/J070v14n02_06.

New York City Administration for Children's Services. n.d. "ACS—Data & Analysis." Accessed August 27, 2023. www.nyc.gov.

NICWA (National Indian Child Welfare Association). 2021. *Disproportionality in Child Welfare Fact Sheet.* Portland, OR: National Indian Child Welfare Association, October 2021. www.nicwa.org.

Nieweglowski, Katherine, Patrick W. Corrigan, Tri Tyas, Anastasia Tooley, Rachel Dubke, Juana Lara, Lorenzo Washington, Janis Sayer, and Lindsay Sheehan. 2018. "Exploring the Public Stigma of Substance Use Disorder through Community-Based Participatory Research." *Addiction Research & Theory* 26 (4): 323–29. https://doi.org/10.1080/16066359.2017.1409890.

Nourie, Amy E. 2022. "Child Welfare Abolition: Critical Theories, Human Rights, and Heteronormativity." *Journal of Human Rights and Social Work* 7:3–12. https://doi.org/10.1007/s41134-021-00168-y.

NRCPD (National Research Center for Parents with Disabilities). 2022. "Map of State Termination of Parental Rights Laws that Include Parental Disability." Heller School for Social Policy and Management, Brandeis University. https://heller.brandeis.edu.

ODI (Overseas Development Institute) and UNICEF (United Nations Children's Fund). 2020. *Universal Child Benefits: Policy Issues and Options.* London: ODI; and New York: UNICEF, June 2020. www.unicef.org.

O'Donnell, John M., Waldo E. Johnson, Lisa Easley D'Aunno, Helen L. Thornton. 2005. "Fathers in Child Welfare: Caseworkers' Perspectives." *Child Welfare* 84 (3): 387–414.

Office of Public Affairs, US Department of Justice (USDOJ). 2022. "Domestic and Sexual Violence on the 28th Anniversary of the Violence Against Women Act." Press release, September 13, 2022. https://www.justice.gov.

Ogbonnaya, Ijeoma Nwabuzor, and Annie J. Keeney. 2018. "A Systematic Review of the Effectiveness of Interagency and Cross-System Collaborations in the United States to Improve Child Welfare Outcomes." *Children and Youth Services Review* 94:225–45. https://doi.org/10.1016/j.childyouth.2018.10.008.

O'Hare, William. 2001. *The Child Population: First Data from the 2000 Census.* Baltimore: Annie E. Casey Foundation and the Population Reference Bureau, June 2001. www.aecf.org.

O'Hear, Michael M. 2009. "Rethinking Drug Courts: Restorative Justice as a Response to Racial Injustice." *Stanford Law & Policy Review* 20 (2): 463–500.

Ohio Domestic Violence Network. 2022. *Seeking Safety, Equity, and Justice: 2021 Ohio Statewide Survey Results: Domestic Violence Survivors' Experiences with Law Enforcement, Courts, Child Welfare and Social Services Systems.* Columbus: Ohio Domestic Violence Network, Ohio State Bar Foundation, and Office of Criminal Justice Services, February 2022. www.odvn.org.

OJJDP (Office of Juvenile Justice and Delinquency Prevention). 2021. "Family Drug Court Program." US Department of Justice, May 25, 2021. https://ojjdp.ojp.gov.

Olivet, Jeffrey, Catriona Wilkey, Molly Richard, Marc Dones, Julia Tripp, Maya Beit-Arie, Svetlana Yampolskaya, and Regina Cannon. 2021. "Racial Inequity and Homelessness: Findings from the SPARC Study." *Annals of the American Academy of Political and Social Science* 693 (1): 82–100. https://doi.org/10.1177 /0002716221991040.

Omi, Michael, and Howard Winant. 1994. *Racial Formation in the United States: From the 1960s to the 1990s.* 2nd ed. New York: Routledge.

Onarheim, Kristine Husøy, Andrea Melberg, Benjamin Mason Meier, and Ingrid Miljeteig. 2018. "Towards Universal Health Coverage: Including Undocumented Migrants." *BMJ Global Health* 3:e001031. https://doi.org/10.1136/bmjgh-2018 -001031.

Ono, Azusa. 2016a. "Child Welfare in Urban American Indian Communities." In *Urban American Indians: Reclaiming Native Space*, edited by Donna Martinez, Grace Sage, and Azusa Ono, 107–28. New York: Bloomsbury.

———. 2016b. "Indian Child Welfare Act of 1978." In *50 Events That Shaped American Indian History: An Encyclopedia of the American Mosaic*, edited by Donna Martinez and Jennifer L. Williams Bordeaux, 596–612. Greenwood, CT: ABC-CLIO.

O'Reilly, Rebecca, Lesley Wilkes, Lauretta Luck, and Debra Jackson. 2010. "The Efficacy of Family Support and Family Preservation Services on Reducing Child Abuse and Neglect: What the Literature Reveals." *Journal of Child Health Care* 14 (1): 82–94. https://doi.org/10.1177/1367493509347114.

Orloff, Ann Shola. 1993. "Gender and the Social Rights of Citizenship: The Comparative Analysis of Gender Relations and Welfare States." *American Sociological Review* 58 (3): 303–28. https://doi.org/10.2307/2095903.

Orsi, Rebecca, Lauren Boissy, Paula Yuma, Fred Palmer, and Stephanie Torres-Molinar. 2021. "Child Welfare in Non-metro and Rural Communities: Experiences of Child-Serving Professionals Addressing Substance Use." *Child & Family Social Work* 26 (4): 696–707. https://doi.org/10.1111/cfs.12850.

Osofsky, Joy D. 1999. "The Impact of Violence on Children." *Future of Children* 9 (3): 33–49. https://doi.org/10.2307/1602780.

Oudshoorn, Abe, Tracy Smith-Carrier, Jodi Hall, Cheryl Forchuk, Deanna Befus, Susana Caxaj, Jean Pierre Ndayisenga, and Colleen Parsons. 2023. "Understanding the Principle of Consumer Choice in Delivering Housing First." *Housing Studies* 38 (5): 841–59. https://doi.org/10.1080/02673037.2021.1912713.

Pac, Jessica, Sophie Collyer, Lawrence Berger, Kirk O'Brien, Elizabeth Parker, Peter Pecora, Whitney Rostad, Jane Waldfogel, and Christopher Wimer. 2023. "The Effects of Child Poverty Reductions on Child Protective Services Involvement." *Social Service Review* 97 (1): 43–91. https://doi.org/10.1086/723219.

Pac, Jessica, Irwin Garfinkel, Neeraj Kaushal, Jaehyun Nam, Laura Nolan, Jane Waldfogel, and Christopher Wimer. 2020. "Reducing Poverty among Children: Evidence from State Policy Simulations." *Children and Youth Services Review* 115:105030. https://doi.org/10.1016/j.childyouth.2020.105030.

Padgett, Deborah K., Benjamin F. Henwood, and Sam J. Tsemberis. 2016. *Housing First: Ending Homelessness, Transforming Systems, and Changing Lives*. New York: Oxford University Press.

Paik, Leslie. 2021. *Trapped in a Maze: How Social Control Institutions Drive Family Poverty and Inequality*. Oakland: University of California Press.

Park, Jung Min, Stephen Metraux, Gabriel Brodbar, and Dennis P. Culhane. 2004. "Child Welfare Involvement among Children in Homeless Families." *Child Welfare* 83 (5): 423–36.

Park, Kathy. 2015. "Why Structure Decisions in Child Welfare?" *The Imprint*, August 12, 2015. https://imprintnews.org.

Parolin, Zachary, Megan Curran, and Christopher Wimer. 2020. "The CARES Act and Poverty in the COVID-19 Crisis: Promises and Pitfalls of the Recovery Rebates and Expanded Unemployment Benefits." Poverty and Social Policy Brief 2048. Center on Poverty and Social Policy, Columbia University, New York. www.povertycenter.columbia.edu.

Paxson, Christina, and Jane Waldfogel. 2002. "Welfare Reforms, Family Resources, and Child Maltreatment." *Journal of Policy Analysis and Management* 22 (1): 85–113. https://doi.org/10.1002/pam.10097.

Pecora, Peter J., Ronald C. Kessler, Jason Williams, Kirk O'Brien, Chris Downs, Diana J. English, James White, et al. 2005. *Improving Family Foster Care: Findings from the Northwest Foster Care Alumni Study*. Seattle: Casey Family Programs, April 5, 2005. www.casey.org.

Pelton, Leroy H. 1978. "Child Abuse and Neglect: The Myth of Classlessness." *American Journal of Orthopsychiatry* 48 (4): 608–17. https://doi.org/10.1111/j.1939-0025.1978.tb02565.x.

———. 2015. "The Continuing Role of Material Factors in Child Maltreatment and Placement." *Child Abuse & Neglect* 41:30–39. https://doi.org/10.1016/j.chiabu.2014.08.001.

Pember, Mary Annette. 2019. "The New War on the Indian Child Welfare Act." Political Research Associates, November 11, 2019. https://politicalresearch.org.

Pergamit, Michael, Mary Cunningham, and Devlin Hanson. 2017. "The Impact of Family Unification Housing Vouchers on Child Welfare Outcomes." *American Journal of Community Psychology* 60 (1–2): 103–13. https://doi.org/10.1002/ajcp.12136.

Perrone, Jaime. 2012. "Failing to Realize Nicholson's Vision: How New York's Child Welfare System Continues to Punish Battered Mothers." *Journal of Law and Policy* 20 (2): 641–75.

Peterson, Ruth D., and Lauren J. Krivo. 2010. *Divergent Social Worlds: Neighborhood Crime and the Racial-Spatial Divide*. New York: Russell Sage Foundation.

Pettit, Becky. 2012. *Invisible Men: Mass Incarceration and the Myth of Black Progress*. New York: Russell Sage Foundation.

Pevar, Stephen. 2012. *The Rights of Indians and Tribes*. 4th ed. Oxford: Oxford University Press.

———. 2017. "In South Dakota, Officials Defied a Federal Judge and Took Indian Kids Away from Their Parents in Rigged Proceedings." American Civil Liberties Union, February 22, 2017. www.aclu.org.

Pharris, Angela B., Ricky T. Munoz, and Chan M. Hellman. 2022. "Hope and Resilience as Protective Factors Linked to Lower Burnout among Child Welfare Workers." *Children and Youth Services Review* 136:106424. https://doi.org/10.1016/j.childyouth.2022.106424.

Phillips, Susan D., and Alan J. Dettlaff. 2009. "More than Parents in Prison: The Broader Overlap between the Criminal Justice and Child Welfare Systems." *Journal of Public Child Welfare* 3 (1): 3–22. https://doi.org/10.1080/15548730802690718.

Phillips, Susan D., Alan J. Dettlaff, and Melinda J. Baldwin. 2010. "An Exploratory Study of the Range of Implications of Families' Criminal Justice System Involvement in Child Welfare Cases." *Children and Youth Services Review* 32 (4): 544–50. https://doi.org/10.1016/j.childyouth.2009.11.008.

Pierce, Sarah, and Jessica Bolter. 2020. *Dismantling and Reconstructing the U.S. Immigration System: A Catalog of Changes under the Trump Presidency*. Washington, DC: Migration Policy Institute, July 2020. www.migrationpolicy.org.

Pimentel, David. 2019. "Punishing Families for Being Poor: How Child Protection Interventions Threaten the Right to Parent While Impoverished." *Oklahoma Law Review* 71 (3): 885–922.

Piven, Frances Fox, and Richard A. Cloward. 1971. *Regulating the Poor: The Functions of Public Welfare*. New York: Pantheon Books.

Poehlmann, Julie. 2005. "Representations of Attachment Relationships in Children of Incarcerated Mothers." *Child Development* 76 (3): 679–96. https://doi.org/10.1111/j.1467-8624.2005.00871.x.

Polikoff, Nancy D. 2018. "Neglected Lesbian Mothers." *Family Law Quarterly* 52 (1): 87–122.

Polikoff, Nancy D., and Jane Spinak. 2021. "Foreword." *Columbia Journal of Race and Law* 11 (3): 533–74. https://doi.org/10.52214/cjrl.v11i3.8737.

Polsky, Andrew J. 1991. *The Rise of the Therapeutic State.* Princeton, NJ: Princeton University Press.

Popple, Philip R. 2018. *Social Work Practice and Social Welfare Policy in the United States: A History.* New York: Oxford University Press.

Prasad, Mona, and Megan Jones. 2019. "Medical Complications of Opioid Use Disorder in Pregnancy." *Seminars in Perinatology* 43:162–67. https://doi.org/10.1053/j.semperi.2019.01.005.

Pryce, Jessica. 2018. "To Transform Child Welfare, Take Race Out of the Equation." TED Conference video, May 2018, 7:32. www.ted.com.

Putnam-Hornstein, Emily, Eunhye Ahn, John Prindle, Joseph Magruder, Daniel Webster, and Christopher Wildeman. 2021. "Cumulative Rates of Child Protection Involvement and Terminations of Parental Rights in a California Birth Cohort, 1999–2017." *American Journal of Public Health* 111 (6): 1157–63. https://doi.org/10.2105/AJPH.2021.306214.

Putnam-Hornstein, Emily, James David Simon, Andrea Lane Eastman, and Joseph Magruder. 2015. "Risk of Re-reporting among Infants Who Remain at Home Following Alleged Maltreatment." *Child Maltreatment* 20 (2): 92–103. https://doi.org/10.1177/1077559514558586.

Puzzanchera, Charles, Marly Zeigler, Moriah Taylor, Wei Kang, and Jason Smith. 2023. *Disproportionality Rates for Children of Color in Foster Care Dashboard.* Reno, NV: National Council of Juvenile and Family Court Judges. https://ncjj.org.

Quadagno, Jill. 1994. *The Color of Welfare: How Racism Undermined the War on Poverty.* New York: Oxford University Press.

Rabuy, Bernadette, and Daniel Kopf. 2015. *Prisons of Poverty: Uncovering the Pre-Incarceration Incomes of the Imprisoned.* Northampton, MA: Prison Policy Institute, July 9, 2015. www.prisonpolicy.org.

Radel, Laura, Melinda Baldwin, Gilbert Crouse, Robin Ghertner, and Annette Waters. 2018. *Substance Use, the Opioid Epidemic, and the Child Welfare System: Key Findings from a Mixed Methods Study.* Washington, DC: USDHHS, March 7, 2018. https://aspe.hhs.gov.

Raissian, Kerri M., and Lindsey Rose Bullinger. 2017. "Money Matters: Does the Minimum Wage Affect Child Maltreatment Rates?" *Children and Youth Services Review* 72:60–70. https://doi.org/10.1016/j.childyouth.2016.09.033.

Randles, Jennifer M. 2020. *Essential Dads: The Inequalities and Politics of Fatherhood.* Oakland: University of California Press.

Randles, Jennifer M., and Kerry Woodward. 2018. "Learning to Labor, Love, and Live: Shaping the Good Neoliberal Citizen in State Work and Marriage Programs." *Sociological Perspectives* 61 (1): 39–56. https://doi.org/10.1177/0731121417707753.

Rascoe, Ayesha. 2022. "Incarcerated People Pay about 5 Dollars for a 30-Minute Phone Call. A New Bill Wants to Change That." *Weekend Edition Sunday*, National Public Radio, October 23, 2022. www.npr.org.

Rauktis, Mary E., Rachael A. Fusco, Helen Cahalane, Ivory Kierston Bennett, and Shauna M. Reinhart. 2011. "'Try to Make It Seem like We're Regular Kids': Youth Perceptions of Restrictiveness in Out-of-Home Care." *Children and Youth Services Review* 33 (7): 1224–33. https://doi.org/10.1016/j.childyouth.2011.02.012.

Raz, Mical. 2020. *Abusive Policies: How the American Child Welfare System Lost Its Way*. Chapel Hill: University of North Carolina Press.

———. 2022. "Our Adoption Policies Have Harmed Families and Children." *Washington Post*, November 18, 2022. www.washingtonpost.com.

Rebbe, Rebecca. 2018. "What Is Neglect? State Legal Definitions in the United States." *Child Maltreatment* 23 (3): 303–15. https://doi.org/10.1177/1077559518767337.

Reich, Jennifer A. 2005. *Fixing Families: Parents, Power, and the Child Welfare System*. New York: Routledge.

Reid, Joseph H. 1956a. "Editorial Comment." *Child Welfare* 35 (1): 16–17.

———. 1956b. "Ensuring Adoption for Hard-to-Place Children." *Child Welfare* 35 (3): 4–8.

———. 1962. "The Emotion and Logic of Structure." *Child Welfare* 41 (10): 477–83.

Richter, Kimber Paschall, and Gabriele Bammer. 2000. "A Hierarchy of Strategies Heroin-Using Mothers Employ to Reduce Harm to Their Children." *Journal of Substance Abuse Treatment* 19 (4): 403–13. https://doi.org/10.1016/S0740-5472(00)00137-9.

Rigg, Khary K., Shannon M. Monnat, and Melody N. Chavez. 2018. "Opioid-Related Mortality in Rural America: Geographic Heterogeneity and Intervention Strategies." *International Journal of Drug Policy* 57:119–29. https://doi.org/10.1016/j.drugpo.2018.04.011.

Rios, Victor M. 2011. *Punished: Policing the Lives of Black and Latino Boys*. New York: New York University Press.

Rise. 2021. "Why We're Using the Term 'Family Policing System.'" *Rise Magazine*, May 7, 2021. www.risemagazine.org.

Rivaux, Stephanie L., Joyce James, Kim Wittenstrom, Donald J. Baumann, Janess Sheets, Judith Henry, and Victoria Jeffries. 2008. "The Intersection of Race, Poverty, and Risk: Understanding the Decision to Provide Services to Clients and to Remove Children." *Child Welfare* 87 (2): 151–68.

Rivera, Marny, and Rita Sullivan. 2015. "Rethinking Child Welfare to Keep Families Safe and Together: Effective Housing-Based Supports to Reduce Child Trauma, Maltreatment Recidivism, and Re-entry to Foster Care." *Child Welfare* 24 (4): 185–204.

Roberts, Dorothy E. 1997. *Killing the Black Body: Race, Reproduction, and the Meaning of Liberty*. New York: Pantheon Books.

———. 2001. "Kinship Care and the Price of State Support." *Chicago-Kent Law Review* 76:1619–42.

———. 2002. *Shattered Bonds: The Color of Child Welfare*. New York: Basic Civitas Books.

———. 2007. "Child Welfare's Paradox." *William & Mary Law Review* 49 (3): 881–901.

———. 2012. "Prison, Foster Care, and the Systemic Punishment of Black Mothers." *UCLA Law Review* 59 (6): 1474–500.

———. 2014. "Complicating the Triangle of Race, Class and State: The Insights of Black Feminists." *Ethnic and Racial Studies* 37 (10): 1776–82. https://doi.org/10.1080/01419 870.2014.931988.

———. 2019. "Digitizing the Carceral State." Review of *Automating Inequality: How High-Tech Tools Profile, Police, and Punish the Poor*, by Virginia Eubanks. *Harvard Law Review* 132 (6): 1695–729.

———. 2020. "Abolishing Policing Also Means Abolishing Family Regulation." *The Imprint*, June 16, 2020. https://imprintnews.org.

———. 2021. "Keynote: How I Became a Family Policing Abolitionist." *Columbia Journal of Race and Law* 11 (3): 455–70. https://doi.org/10.52214/cjrl.v11i3.8738.

———. 2022. *Torn Apart: How the Child Welfare System Destroys Black Families—And How Abolition Can Build a Better World*. New York: Basic Books.

Robinson, Brandon Andrew. 2018. "Child Welfare Systems and LGBTQ Youth Homelessness: Gender Segregation, Instability, and Intersectionality." *Child Welfare* 96 (2): 29–46.

Rocha Beardall, Theresa, and Frank Edwards. 2021. "Abolition, Settler Colonialism, and the Persistent Threat of Indian Child Welfare." *Columbia Journal of Race and Law* 11 (3): 533–74. https://doi.org/10.52214/cjrl.v11i3.8744.

Rolnick, Addie C. 2016. "Locked Up: Fear, Racism, Prison Economics, and the Incarceration of Native Youth." *American Indian Culture and Research Journal* 40 (1): 55–92. https://doi.org/10.17953/aicrj.40.1.rolnick.

Rolock, Nancy, and Mark Testa. 2005. "Indicated Child Abuse and Neglect Reports: Is the Investigation Process Racially Biased?" In *Race Matters in Child Welfare: The Overrepresentation of African American Children in the System*, edited by Dennette Derezotes, John Poertner, and Mark Testa, 119–30. Washington, DC: CWLA Press.

Rome, Sunny Harris, and Miriam Raskin. 2019. "Transitioning Out of Foster Care: The First 12 Months." *Youth & Society* 51 (4): 529–47. https://doi.org/10.1177 /0044118X17694968.

Rose, Nikolas. 2000. "Government and Control." *British Journal of Criminology* 40 (2): 321–39. https://doi.org/10.1093/bjc/40.2.321.

Rose, Susan J., and William Meezan. 1993. "Defining Child Neglect: Evolution, Influences, and Issues." *Social Service Review* 67 (2): 279–93. https://doi.org/10.1086 /603982.

Rosinsky, Kristina, Megan Fischer, and Maggie Haas. 2023. *Child Welfare Financing SFY 2020: A Survey of Federal, State, and Local Expenditures.* Rockville, MD: Child Trends, May 2020. www.childtrends.org.

Ross, Luana. 1998. *Inventing the Savage: The Social Construction of Native American Criminality.* Austin: University of Texas Press.

Rouse, Heather L., Tera R. Hurt, Janet N. Melby, Maya Bartel, Bethany McCurdy, Emily McKnight, Feng Zhao, Carol Behrer, and Carl F. Weems. 2021. "Pregnancy and Parenting among Youth Transitioning from Foster Care: A Mixed Methods Study." *Child & Youth Care Forum* 50:167–97. https://doi.org/10.1007/s10566-020-09567-0.

Rymph, Catherine E. 2012. "From 'Economic Want' to 'Family Pathology': Foster Family Care, the New Deal, and the Emergence of a Public Child Welfare System." *Journal of Policy History* 24 (1): 7–25. https://doi.org/10.1017/S0898030611000352.

———. 2017. *Raising Government Children: A History of Foster Care and the American Welfare State.* Chapel Hill: University of North Carolina Press.

Ryo, Emily, and Ian Peacock. 2018. "A National Study of Immigration Detention in the United States." *Southern California Law Review* 92 (1): 1–68.

Sampson, Jerome N. 1962. "Is Child Welfare a Specialty?" *Child Welfare* 41 (9): 394–97.

Sampson, Robert J. 2012. *Great American City: Chicago and the Enduring Neighborhood Effect.* Chicago: University of Chicago Press.

Sanchirico, Andrew, and Kary Jablonka. 2000. "Keeping Foster Children Connected to Their Biological Parents: The Impact of Foster Parent Training and Support." *Child and Adolescent Social Work Journal* 17 (3): 185–203. https://doi.org/10.1023/A:1007583813448.

Sankaran, Vivek, Christopher Church, and Monique Mitchell. 2019. "A Cure Worse than the Disease? The Impact of Removal on Children and Their Families." *Marquette Law Review* 102 (4): 1161–94.

Scales, T. Laine, and H. Stephen Cooper. 1999. "Family Violence in Rural Areas: Law Enforcement and Social Workers Working Together for Change." In *Preserving and Strengthening Small Towns and Rural Communities*, edited by Iris Carlton-LaNey, Richard L. Edwards, and P. Nelson Reid, 104–16. Washington DC: National Association of Social Workers.

Scannapieco, Maria, Kirstin R. Painter, and Gary Blau. 2018. "A Comparison of LGBTQ Youth and Heterosexual Youth in the Child Welfare System." *Children and Services Review* 91:39–46. https://doi.org/10.1016/j.childyouth.2018.05.016.

Schneiderman, Janet U., John Prindle, and Emily Putnam-Hornstein. 2021. "Infant Deaths from Medical Causes after a Maltreatment Report." *Pediatrics* 148 (3): e2020048389. https://doi.org/10.1542/peds.2020-048389.

Schomburg, Aysha E. 2021a. "Equity Is a Right." *Children's Bureau Express* 22 (8). https://cbexpress.acf.hhs.gov.

———. 2021b. "Letter from Aysha E. Schomburg on Equity in Child Welfare." Official memorandum. USDHHS, ACF. www.acf.hhs.gov.

Schottland, Charles I. 1955. "Trends Affecting Public and Voluntary Welfare Planning." *Social Security Bulletin* 18 (2): 3–6.

Schram, Sanford F. 2018. "Neoliberalizing the Welfare State: Marketizing Social Policy/ Disciplining Clients." In *The SAGE Handbook of Neoliberalism*, edited by Damien Cahill, Melinda Cooper, Martijn Konings, and David Primrose, 308–22. Los Angeles: Sage. https://doi.org/10.4135/9781526416001.n25.

Schuck, Amie M., and Cathy Spatz Widom. 2021. "The Roles of Housing, Financial, and Food Insecurities in Understanding the Relationship between Childhood Neglect and Violence in Adulthood." *PLoS One* 16 (3): e0246682. https://doi.org/10.1371/journal.pone.0246682.

Schuerman, John R., Tina L. Rzepnicki, and Julia H. Littell. 1994. *Putting Families First: An Experiment in Family Preservation*. New York: Aldine de Gruyter.

Schwartz, Ira M., Peter York, Eva Nowakowski-Sims, and Ana Ramos-Hernandez. 2017. "Predictive and Prescriptive Analytics, Machine Learning and Child Welfare Risk Assessment: The Broward County Experience." *Children and Youth Services Review* 81:309–20. https://doi.org/10.1016/j.childyouth.2017.08.020.

Sedlak, Andrea, Jane Mettenburg, Monica Basena, Ian Petta, Karla McPherson, Angela Greene, and Spencer Li. 2010. *Fourth National Incidence Study of Child Abuse and Neglect (NIS-4): Report to Congress*. Washington, DC: USDHHS, ACF. www.acf.hhs.gov.

Segal, Leonie, Jason M. Armfield, Emmanuel S. Gnanamanickam, David B. Preen, Derek S. Brown, James Doidge, and Ha Nguyen. 2021. "Child Maltreatment and Mortality in Young Adults." *Pediatrics* 147 (1): e2020023416. https://doi.org/10.1542/peds.2020-023416.

Sege, Robert, and Allison Stephens. 2022. "Child Physical Abuse Did Not Increase during the Pandemic." *JAMA Pediatrics* 176 (4): 338–40. https://doi.org/10.1001/jamapediatrics.2021.5476.

Seim, Josh. 2020. *Bandage, Sort, and Hustle: Ambulance Crews on the Front Lines of Urban Suffering*. Oakland: University of California Press.

Selleck, Kristen, Jeannie Newman, and Debra Gilmore. 2018. *Child Protection in Families Experiencing Domestic Violence*. 2nd ed. Capacity Building Center for States. Washington, DC: USDHHS, ACF, Administration on Children, Youth and Families, Children's Bureau. https://cwlibrary.childwelfare.gov.

Sepulveda, Kristin, and Sarah Catherine Williams. 2019. "One in Three Children Entered Foster Care in 2017 Because of Parental Drug Abuse." Child Trends, February 25, 2019. www.childtrends.org.

Shachar, Carmel, Tess Wise, Gali Katznelson, and Andrea Louise Campbell. 2020. "Criminal Justice or Public Health: A Comparison of the Representation of the Crack Cocaine and Opioid Epidemics in the Media." *Journal of Health Politics, Policy, and Law* 45 (2): 211–39. https://doi.org/10.1215/03616878-8004862.

Shah, Purvi. 2017. *Seeding Generations: Fostering Innovations in Accountability with Healing*. Booklet 2 of 3. New York: Coalition on Working with Abusive Partners, October 2017. www.innovatingjustice.org.

Sharff, Jagna W. 1998. *King Kong on 4th Street: Families and the Violence of Poverty on the Lower East Side*. Boulder, CO: Westview.

Shedd, Carla. 2015. *Unequal City: Race, Schools, and Perceptions of Injustice.* New York: Russell Sage Foundation.

Sheeran, Alyssa M., and Amanda J. Heideman. 2021. "The Effects of Race and Ethnicity on Admission, Graduation, and Recidivism in the Milwaukee County Adult Drug Treatment Court." *Social Sciences* 10 (7): 261. https://doi.org/10.3390/socsci10070261.

Shelton, Katherine H., Pamela J. Taylor, Adrian Bonner, and Marianne van den Bree. 2009. "Risk Factors for Homelessness: Evidence from a Population-Based Study." *Psychiatric Services* 60 (4): 465–72. https://doi.org/10.1176/ps.2009.60.4.465.

Sheridan, Kathryn. 2014. "A Systematic Review of the Literature Regarding Family Context and Mental Health of Children from Rural Methamphetamine-Involved Families: Implications for Rural Child Welfare Practice." *Journal of Public Child Welfare* 8 (5): 514–38. https://doi.org/10.1080/15548732.2014.948584.

Shinn, Marybeth, Scott R. Brown, and Daniel Gubits. 2017. "Can Housing and Service Interventions Reduce Family Separations for Families Who Experience Homelessness?" *American Journal of Community Psychology* 60 (1–2): 79–90. https://doi.org/10.1002/ajcp.12111.

Shrider, Emily A., and John Creamer. 2023. *Poverty in the United States: 2022.* Current Population Reports, P60-280. Washington, DC: US Census Bureau, September 12, 2023. www.census.gov.

Shyne, Ann W. 1951. *Analysis of Family Service Agency Operation; Casework Statistics: 1951. Data from 60 Private Member Agencies of the Family Service Association of America.* New York: Family Service Association of America.

———. 1953. *Statistics of Family Casework: 1952. Data from 60 Private Agencies of the Family Service Association of America.* New York: Family Service Association of America.

Shyne, Ann W., and Anita G. Schroeder. 1978. *National Study of Social Services to Children and Their Families: Overview.* Washington, DC: Prepared for National Center for Child Advocacy, Children's Bureau; US Department of Health, Education, and Welfare, July 1978.

Simmons, Michaela Christy. 2020. "Becoming Wards of the State: Race, Crime, and Childhood in the Struggle for Foster Care Integration, 1920s to 1960s." *American Sociological Review* 85 (2): 199–222. https://doi.org/10.1177/0003122420911062.

Skolnick, Arlene. 1975. "The Limits of Childhood: Conceptions of Child Development and Social Context." *Law and Contemporary Problems* 39 (3): 38–77. https://doi.org/10.2307/1191268.

Slayter, Elspeth. 2016. "Youth with Disabilities in the United States Child Welfare System." *Children and Youth Services Review* 64:155–65. https://doi.org/10.1016/j.childyouth.2016.03.012.

Smith, Andrea. 2005. *Conquest: Sexual Violence and American Genocide.* Durham, NC: Duke University Press.

Smith, Brenda D., Qingyi Li, Kun Wang, and Angela M. Smith. 2021. "A National Study of Child Maltreatment Reporting at the County Level: Interactions among Race/

Ethnicity, Rurality and Poverty." *Children and Youth Services Review* 122:105925. https://doi.org/10.1016/j.childyouth.2021.105925.

Smith, Dorothy E. 1993. "The Standard North American Family: SNAF as an Ideological Code." *Journal of Family Issues* 14 (1): 50–65. https://doi.org/10.1177/01925 13X93014001005.

Smith, Lynne M., and Lucinda S. Santos. 2016. "Prenatal Exposure: The Effects of Prenatal Cocaine and Methamphetamine Exposure on the Developing Child." *Birth Defects Research Part C: Embryo Today: Reviews* 108 (2): 142–46. https://doi.org/10.1002/bdrc.21131.

Smith, Rebecca. 1968. "'For Every Child': A Commentary on Developments in Child Welfare 1962–1967." *Child Welfare* 47 (3): 125–32, 149.

Song, Sarah, and Irene Bloemraad. 2022. "Immigrant Legalization: A Dilemma between Justice and the Rule of Law." *Migration Studies* 10 (3): 484–509. https://doi.org/10.1093/migration/mnac014.

Sonik, Rajan Anthony, Susan L. Parish, Monika Mitra, and Joanne Nicholson. 2018. "Parents with and without Disabilities: Demographics, Material Hardship, and Program Participation." *Review of Disability Studies: An International Journal* 14 (4): 1–20.

Soss, Joe, Richard C. Fording, and Sanford F. Schram. 2011. *Disciplining the Poor: Neoliberal Paternalism and the Persistent Power of Race*. Chicago: University of Chicago Press.

Spade, Dean. 2020. *Mutual Aid: Building Solidarity During This Crisis (and the Next)*. London: Verso.

Spar, Karen. 2004. *Child Welfare: Implementation of the Adoption and Safe Families Act (P.L. 105-89)*. Washington, DC: Congressional Research Service.

Stark, Evan. 2005. "*Nicholson v. Williams* Revisited: When Good People Do Bad Things." *Denver Law Review* 82 (4): 691–721.

———. 2008. *CPS: Reforming Child Protective Services through Advocacy for Battered Women*. Seattle: Washington State Coalition Against Domestic Violence, July 2008. https://wscadv.org.

Stein, Theodore J. 2003. "The Adoption and Safe Families Act: How Congress Overlooks Available Data and Ignores Systemic Obstacles in Its Pursuit of Political Goals." *Children and Youth Services Review* 25 (9): 669–82. https://doi.org/10.1016/S0190-7409(03)00066-5.

Stoltzfus, Emilie. 2013. *Child Welfare: Structure and Funding of the Adoption Incentives Program along with Reauthorization Issues*. Washington, DC: Congressional Research Service, April 18, 2013.

Sullivan, Andrew Alfred. 2022. "What Does It Mean to Be Homeless? How Definitions Affect Homelessness Policy." *Urban Affairs Review* 59 (3): 728–58. https://doi.org/10.1177/10780874221095185.

Sullivan, Laura, and Amy Walters. 2011. "Native Foster Care: Lost Children, Shattered Families." *All Things Considered*, National Public Radio, October 25, 2011. www.npr.org.

Sutton, John R. 2013. "The Transformation of Prison Regimes in Late Capitalist Societies." *American Journal of Sociology* 119 (3): 715–46. https://doi.org/10.1086/675300.

Swann, Christopher, and Michelle Sheran Sylvester. 2006. "The Foster Care Crisis: What Caused Caseloads to Grow?" *Demography* 43 (2): 309–35. https://doi.org/10.1353/dem.2006.0019.

Swift, Karen J. 1995. *Manufacturing "Bad Mothers": A Critical Perspective on Child Neglect.* Toronto: University of Toronto Press.

Sykes, Jennifer. 2011. "Negotiating Stigma: Understanding Mothers' Responses to Accusations of Child Neglect." *Children and Youth Services Review* 33 (3): 448–56. https://doi.org/10.1016/j.childyouth.2010.06.015.

Tach, Laura, Mary Beth Morrissey, Elizabeth Day, Francesca Vescia, and Brittany Mihalec-Adkins. 2022. "Experiences of Trauma-Informed Care in a Family Drug Treatment Court." *Social Service Review* 96 (3): 465–506. https://doi.org/10.1086/721234.

Therolf, Garrett. 2013. "Special Report: Private Foster Care System, Intended to Save Children, Endangers Some." *Los Angeles Times*, December 18, 2013. www.latimes.com.

Thomas, Margaret M. C., and Jane Waldfogel. 2022. "What Kind of 'Poverty' Predicts CPS Contact: Income, Material Hardship, and Differences among Racialized Groups." *Children and Youth Services Review* 136:106400. https://doi.org/10.1016/j.childyouth.2022.106400.

Tidwell, Amelia. 2023. "The Heart of the Matter: ICWA and the Future of Native American Child Welfare." *Journal of the National Association of Administrative Law Judiciary* 43 (2): 126–89.

Tiger, Rebecca. 2011. "Drug Courts and the Logic of Coerced Treatment." *Sociological Forum* 26 (1): 169–82. https://doi.org/10.1111/j.1573-7861.2010.01229.x.

Tobis, David. 1989. "The New York City Foster Care System, 1979–1986: The Rise and Fall of Reform." PhD diss., Yale University. ProQuest.

Toensing, Gale Courey. 2018. "Indian-Killer Andrew Jackson Deserves Top Spot on List of Worst US Presidents." *Indian Country Today*, updated September 13, 2018. https://indiancountrytoday.com.

Trans Legislation Tracker. n.d. "Tracking the Rise of Anti-Trans Bills in the U.S." Accessed June 15, 2024. https://translegislation.com.

Trattner, Walter I. 1999. *From Poor Law to Welfare State: A History of Social Welfare in America.* New York: Free Press.

Trisi, Danilo, and Matt Saenz. 2020. "Deep Poverty among Children Rose in TANF's First Decade, Then Fell as Other Programs Strengthened." Center on Budget and Policy Priorities, February 27, 2020. www.cbpp.org.

Trivedi, Shanta. 2019. "The Harm of Child Removal." *New York University Review of Law & Social Change* 43:523–80. https://doi.org/10.2139/ssrn.3341033.

———. 2023. "The Adoption and Safe Families Act Is Not Worth Saving: The Case for Repeal." *Family Court Review* 61 (2): 315–40. https://doi.org/10.1111/fcre.12711.

Turitz, Zitha R. 1962. "Discussion." *Child Welfare* 41 (9): 397–99.

United Nations. 1989. *Convention on the Rights of the Child*. United Nations, Treaty Series 1577. November 20, 1989. www.refworld.org.

———. 1990. *International Convention on the Protection of the Rights of All Migrant Workers and Members of Their Families*. UN Human Rights Office of the High Commissioner, United Nations, December 18, 1990. www.ohchr.org.

UN OHCHR (United Nations Office of the High Commissioner for Human Rights). 2018. "UN Experts to US: 'Release Migrant Children from Detention and Stop Using Them to Deter Irregular Migration.'" Press release. June 22, 2018. www.ohchr.org.

upEND. 2022. *Help Is NOT on the Way: How Family Policing Perpetuates State Directed Terror*. Houston: upEND. https://upendmovement.org.

———. n.d. "Family Policing Definition." Accessed December 28, 2021. https://upend-movement.org.

US Census Bureau. 1968. "The Extent of Poverty in the United States: 1959–1968." Current Population Reports. Series P-60, no. 54. May 31, 1968. www2.census.gov.

———. 2020. "Poverty Thresholds for 2019 by Size of Family and Number of Related Children Under 18 Years." Poverty Thresholds. www.census.gov.

———. 2021. "National Population Estimates by Age, Sex, and Race: 1900–1979." National Intercensal Tables: 1900–1990. Updated October 8, 2021. www.census.gov.

———. 2022a. "The Current Population Survey Historical Poverty Tables." Historical Poverty Tables: People and Families, 1959 to 2021. Table 3: "Poverty Status of People by Age, Race, and Hispanic Origin: 1959 to 2021." www.census.gov.

———. 2022b. "SAIPE State and County Estimates for 2021." Small Area Income and Poverty Estimates. www.census.gov.

———. 2022c. "U.S. Census Bureau QuickFacts: Dunn County, Wisconsin." www.census.gov.

US Children's Bureau. 1949. *Trends and Developments in Public Child Welfare Services*. Washington, DC: Federal Security Agency, Social Security Administration, Children's Bureau.

———. 1949–69. *Children's Bureau Statistical Series*. Washington, DC: US Children's Bureau, 1949–69.

———. 1957. *Educational Leave in Public Child Welfare Programs: A Way to Better Services for Children*. Washington, DC: US Department of Health, Education, and Welfare, Social Security Administration, Children's Bureau.

———. 2022. "8.4C Title IV-E, General Title IV-E Requirements, Child Support." Question 5 in *Child Welfare Policy Manual*. Washington, DC: Office of the Administration for Children and Families, US Department of Health and Human Services. www.acf.hhs.gov.

USCIS (US Citizenship and Immigration Services). 2019. "Inadmissibility on Public Charge Grounds." Final Rule by the US Department of Homeland Security. 84 FR 4192. CIS No. 2637-19, August 14, 2019. www.federalregister.gov.

US Department of the Interior, Bureau of Indian Affairs. n.d. "Frequently Asked Questions." Accessed June 15, 2024. www.bia.gov.

USDHHS (US Department of Health and Human Services). 1988. *Study of National Incidence and Prevalence of Child Abuse and Neglect 1988*. Washington, DC: USDHHS. www.ojp.gov.

———. 1999. *Blending Perspectives and Building Common Ground: A Report to Congress on Substance Abuse and Child Protection*. Washington, DC: USDHHS, Substance Abuse and Mental Health Services Administration, March 31, 1999. https://aspe.hhs.gov.

———. 2006. *The AFCARS Report #12*. Final estimates for FY 1998 through FY 2002. Washington, DC: USDHHS, Children's Bureau, October 2006. www.acf.hhs.gov.

———. 2021. *Child Maltreatment 2019*. Washington, DC: USDHHS, Children's Bureau. www.acf.hhs.gov.

———. 2022a. *The AFCARS Report #29*. Preliminary estimates for FY 2021. Washington, DC: USDHHS, Children's Bureau, June 28, 2022. www.acf.hhs.gov.

———. 2022b. *Child Maltreatment 2020*. Washington, DC: USDHHS, Children's Bureau. www.acf.hhs.gov.

———. 2023. *Child Maltreatment 2021*. Washington, DC: USDHHS, Children's Bureau. www.acf.hhs.gov.

USDHS (US Department of Homeland Security). 2022. "DHS Publishes Fair and Humane Public Charge Rule." Press release. September 8, 2022. www.dhs.gov.

———. 2023a. *Family Unit Actions Report: October 1, 2021–September 30, 2022*. Fiscal year 2022 report to Congress. Washington, DC: US Department of Homeland Security, April 4, 2023. www.dhs.gov.

———. 2023b. *Interagency Task Force on the Reunification of Families: Interim Progress Report*. Washington, DC: Interagency Task Force on the Reunification of Families, Department of Homeland Security, September 20, 2023. www.dhs.gov.

USDOJ (US Department of Justice). 2016. *Review of the Federal Bureau of Prisons' Monitoring of Contract Prisons*. Washington, DC: US Department of Justice, Office of the Inspector General, Evaluations and Inspections Division 16-06, August 2016. https://oig.justice.gov.

USGAO (US Government Accountability Office). 2021. *Pandemic Posed Challenges, but Also Created Opportunities for Agencies to Enhance Future Operations*. GAO Report 2021-483.Washington, DC: USGAO. www.gao.gov.

US House of Representatives. 1998. *Regarding the Importance of Fathers in the Raising and Development of Their Children*. H.R. Res. 417. 105th Congress. www.govinfo.gov.

US House of Representatives, Committee on Ways and Means. 2012. *Green Book*.

———. 2018. "Figure 11.3: Trends in Foster Care Use, FY 1982-FY2016." *Green Book*.

USHUD (US Department of Housing and Urban Development). 2022. "FUP Awards All Years." Spreadsheet available at "Family Unification Program (FUP)." September 2022. www.hud.gov.

US Immigration and Customs Enforcement. 2021. *U.S. Immigration and Customs Enforcement Fiscal Year 2020 Enforcement and Removal Operations Report*. Washington, DC: US Immigration and Customs Enforcement. www.ice.gov.

US Senate, Committee on Finance. 2017. *An Examination of Foster Care in the United States and the Use of Privatization*. 115th Congress, 1st sess. (October 2017). Committee print. S. Prt. 115-18. www.finance.senate.gov.

Vandivere, Sharon, Karin Malm, and Laura Radel. 2009. *Adoption USA. A Chartbook Based on the 2007 National Survey of Adoptive Parents*. Washington, DC: USDHHS. https://aspe.hhs.gov.

Vasquez-Tokos, Jessica, and Priscilla Yamin. 2021. "The Racialization of Privacy: Racial Formation as a Family Affair." *Theory and Society*. 50: 717–40. doi.org/10.1007/s11186-020-09427-9.

Victor, Bryan G., Ashley N. Rousson, Colleen Henry, Haresh B. Dalvi, and E. Susana Mariscal. 2021. "Child Protective Services Guidelines for Substantiating Exposure to Domestic Violence as Maltreatment and Assigning Caregiver Responsibilities: Policy Analysis and Recommendations." *Child Maltreatment* 24 (4): 452–63. https://doi.org/10.1177/10775595211002639.

Vivrette, Rebecca, Amy McKlindon, Elizabeth Jordan, Maggie Haas, Ja'Chelle Ball, Gina Mueterthies, Jaclyn Szrom, and Torey Silloway. 2023. *Using the Family First Act to Grow and Nurture Support Systems for Families of Young Children: A Look at Promotion, Prevention, and Family First Act Implementation in Six States*. Rockville, MD: Child Trends, October 2023. https://doi.org/10.56417/1882r3831m.

Wacquant, Loïc. 2009. *Punishing the Poor: The Neoliberal Government of Social Insecurity*. Durham, NC: Duke University Press.

———. 2010. *Urban Outcasts: A Comparative Sociology of Advanced Marginality*. Cambridge, UK: Polity.

———. 2012. "Three Steps to a Historical Anthropology of Actually Existing Neoliberalism." *Social Anthropology* 20 (1): 66–79. https://doi.org/10.1111/j.1469-8676.2011.00189.x.

Wan, William. 2018. "What Separation from Parents Does to Children: 'The Effect Is Catastrophic.'" *Washington Post*, June 18, 2018. www.washingtonpost.com.

Washington, S. Lisa. 2022. "Survived and Coerced: Epistemic Injustice in the Family Regulation System." *Columbia Law Review* 122 (4): 1097–163.

Weithorn, Lois A. 2001 "Protecting Children from Exposure to Domestic Violence: The Use and Abuse of Child Maltreatment." *Hastings Law Journal* 53 (1): 1–156.

Wessler, Seth F. 2011. *Shattered Families: The Perilous Intersection of Immigration Enforcement and the Child Welfare System*." Washington, DC: Applied Research Center (now Race Forward), November 2011. www.raceforward.org.

Whitehead, Sam. 2022. "'Desperate Situation': States Are Housing High-Needs Foster Kids in Offices and Hotels." *KFF Health News*, June 1, 2022. https://kffhealthnews.org.

Wildeman, Christopher, Frank R. Edwards, and Sara Wakefield. 2020. "The Cumulative Prevalence of Termination of Parental Rights for U.S. Children, 2000–2016." *Child Maltreatment* 25 (1): 32–42. https://doi.org/10.1177/1077559519848499.

Wildeman, Christopher, and Natalia Emanuel. 2014. "Cumulative Risks of Foster Care Placement by Age 18 for U.S. Children, 2000–2011." *PLoS ONE* 9 (3): e92785. https://doi.org/10.1371/journal.pone.0092785.

Williams, Sarah Catherine, Reva Dalela, and Sharon Vandivere. 2022. "In Defining Maltreatment, Nearly Half of States Do Not Specifically Exempt Families' Financial Inability to Provide." Child Trends, February 23, 2022. www.childtrends.org.

Williams, Sarah Catherine, Rachel Rosenberg, and Valerie Martinez. 2023. "State-Level Data for Understanding Child Welfare in the United States." Child Trends, April 27, 2023. www.childtrends.org.

Williams, Sarah Catherine, and Kristin Sepulveda. 2019. "Infants and Toddlers Are More Likely than Older Children to Enter Foster Care Because of Neglect and Parental Drug Abuse." Child Trends, March 11, 2019. www.childtrends.org.

Wilson, Bianca D. M., and Angeliki A. Kastanis. 2015. "Sexual and Gender Minority Disproportionality and Disparities in Child Welfare: A Population-Based Study." *Children and Youth Services Review* 58:11–17. https://doi.org/10.1016/j.childyouth.2015.08.016.

Wilson, Dee, and William Horner. 2005. "Chronic Child Neglect: Needed Developments in Theory and Practice." *Families in Society* 86 (4): 471–81. https://doi.org/10.1606/1044-3894.3452.

Wilson, Samita, Sarah Hean, Tatek Abebe, and Vanessa Heaslip. 2020. "Children's Experiences with Child Protection Services: A Synthesis of Qualitative Evidence." *Children and Youth Services Review* 113:104974. https://doi.org/10.1016/j.childyouth.2020.104974.

Wilson, Starsky. 2021. "Letter to Dr. Naomi Goldstein Re: Title IV-E Prevention Services Clearinghouse Handbook of Standards and Procedures (86 FR 37332)." Children's Defense Fund, August 15, 2021. https://cdfohio.org.

Winston, Ellen. 1960. "What Lies Ahead in Public Services for Children." *Child Welfare* 39 (7): 1–5.

———. 1966. "The Shape of Things to Come in Child Welfare: The Broad Outline." *Child Welfare* 45 (1): 5–11.

Wisconsin Department of Children and Families. 2024. "Child Protective Services (CPS) Reports Dashboard." Last updated January 10, 2024. https://dcf.wisconsin.gov.

Wisconsin Statewide Intelligence Center, Southeast Wisconsin Threat Analysis Center, Federal Bureau of Investigation—Milwaukee Field Division. 2016. *Wisconsin Methamphetamine Study*. Milwaukee: FBI Milwaukee, November 21, 2016. www.doj.state.wi.us.

Wise, Paul II., and Lisa J. Chamberlain. 2022. "Adversity and Opportunity—The Pandemic's Paradoxical Effect on Child Health and Well-Being." *JAMA Pediatrics* 176 (7): e220063. https://doi.org/10.1001/jamapediatrics.2022.0063.

Witt, Jason. 2019. "Counties Take Action to Save a System in Crisis." *Wisconsin Counties Magazine*, January 2019. www.wicounties.org.

Wobie, Kathleen, Fonda Davis Eyler, Michael Conlon, Leslie Clarke, and Marylou Behnke. 1997. "Women and Children in Residential Treatment: Outcomes for Mothers and Their Infants." *Journal of Drug Issues* 27 (3): 585–606. https://doi.org/10.1177/002204269702700309.

Wolfe, Patrick. 2006. "Settler Colonialism and the Elimination of the Native." *Journal of Genocide Research* 8 (4): 387–409. https://doi.org/10.1080/14623520601056240.

Wong, Julia Carrie. 2021. "The Fight to Whitewash US History: 'A Drop of Poison Is All You Need.'" *The Guardian*, May 25, 2021. www.theguardian.com.

Woodward, Kerry. 2016. "Marketing Black Babies versus Recruiting Black Families: The Racialized Strategies Private Adoption Agencies Use to Find Homes for Black Babies." *Sociology of Race and Ethnicity* 2 (4): 482–97. https://doi.org/10.1177/2332649215627820.

———. 2021. "Race, Gender, and Poverty Governance: The Case of the U.S. Child Welfare System." *Social Politics: International Studies in Gender, State & Society* 28 (2): 428–50. https://doi.org/10.1093/sp/jxz036.

Wray, Matt. 2006. *Not Quite White: White Trash and the Boundaries of Whiteness.* Durham, NC: Duke University Press.

Wray, Matt, and Annalee Newitz, eds. 1997. *White Trash: Race and Class in America.* New York: Routledge.

Wrieden, Jane E. 1960. "Illegitimacy and ADC." *Child Welfare* 39 (6): 27–30.

WSDCYF (Washington State Department of Children, Youth, and Families). 2021. *2022 Annual Progress and Services Report (APSR).* Olympia: WSDCYF. www.dcyf.wa.gov.

Wulczyn, Fred, Lijun Chen, and Mark Courtney. 2011. "Family Reunification in a Social Structural Context." *Children and Youth Services Review* 33 (3): 424–30. https://doi.org/10.1016/j.childyouth.2010.06.021.

Wulczyn, Fred, Arno Parolini, Florie Schmits, Joseph Magruder, and Daniel Webster. 2020. "Returning to Foster Care: Age and Other Risk Factors." *Children and Youth Services Review* 116:105166. https://doi.org/10.1016/j.childyouth.2020.105166.

Wulczyn, Fred, Xiaomeng Zhou, Jamie McClanahan, Scott Huhr, Kristen Hislop, Forrest Moore, and Emily Rhodes. 2023. "Race, Poverty, and Foster Care Placement in the United States: Longitudinal and Cross-Sectional Perspectives." *International Journal of Environmental Research and Public Health* 20 (16): 6572. https://doi.org/10.3390/ijerph20166572.

Yale Child Study Center. n.d. "The Child Development–Community Policing Program." Child Study Center, Yale School of Medicine. Accessed February 15, 2022. https://medicine.yale.edu.

Yang, Mi-Youn, Kathryn Maguire-Jack, Kathryn Showalter, Youn Kyoung Kim, and Kristen Shook Slack. 2019. "Child Care Subsidy and Child Maltreatment." *Child & Family Social Work* 24 (4): 547–54. https://doi.org/10.1111/cfs.12635.

Yi, Youngmin, Frank R. Edwards, and Christopher Wildeman. 2020. "Cumulative Prevalence of Confirmed Maltreatment and Foster Care Placement for US Children by Race/Ethnicity, 2011–2016." *American Journal of Public Health* 110 (5): 704–9. https://doi.org/10.2105/AJPH.2019.305554.

Zayas, Luis H., Sergio Aguilar-Gaxiola, Hyunwoo Yoon, and Guillermina Natera Rey. 2015. "The Distress of Citizen-Children with Detained and Deported Parents." *Journal of Child and Family Studies* 24 (11): 3213–23. https://doi.org/10.1007/s10826-015-0124-8.

Zaza, Stephanie, Laura Kann, and Lisa C. Barrios. 2016. "Lesbian, Gay, and Bisexual Adolescents: Population Estimate and Prevalence of Health Behaviors." *Journal of American Medical Association* 316 (22): 2355–56. https://doi.org/10.1001/jama.2016.11683.

Zerai, Assata, and Rae Banks. 2002. *Dehumanizing Discourse, Anti-Drug Law, and Policy in America: A "Crack Mother's" Nightmare*. Aldershot, UK: Ashgate.

Zulliger, Katharina, Erin Maher, Mary Myslewicz, Tyler Corwin, Dee Wilson, Stephanie Jones-Peguero, Jason Williams, and Lyscha Marcynyszyn. 2015. *Prioritizing Early Childhood to Safely Reduce the Need for Foster Care: A National Scan of Interventions*. Seattle: Casey Family Programs, March 2015. www.casey.org.

ABOUT THE CONTRIBUTORS

RONG BAI is Assistant Professor of Social Work at East Carolina University. Her research and publications focus on the intersections of housing instability and child welfare and their effects on families.

KRISTINA P. BRANT is Assistant Professor of Rural Sociology and a Co-Funded Faculty Member in the Consortium of Substance Use and Addiction at Pennsylvania State University. Her research concerns how rural families experience substance use and how the rural risk environment shapes vulnerabilities to substance-use-related harms.

STEPHANIE A. BRYSON is Professor and Associate Dean of Academic Affairs in the School of Social Work at Portland State University. Her research aims to reduce coercive, stigmatizing, and carceral practices within public systems.

AMY CASSELMAN-HONTALAS is a PhD candidate in sociology at Stanford University and a lecturer in American Indian history and federal Indian policy at San Francisco State University. Prior to her career in academia, she was a caseworker for the Washoe Tribe of Nevada and California, where she provided support services for Native children and families.

CYLESTE C. COLLINS is Associate Professor of Social Work at Cleveland State University. Her research examines health disparities, the social determinants of health, and the effectiveness of community-based interventions in affecting health disparities.

ELIZABETH DAY is Research Assistant Professor with the HEDCO Institute for Evidence-Based Educational Practice at the University of Oregon. Her research focuses on understanding best practices for connecting research, practice, and policy with a focus on social policy and educational practice.

ALAN J. DETTLAFF is Professor at the University of Houston Graduate College of Social Work, where he also served as Dean from 2015 to 2022. In 2020, he helped to create and launch the upEND movement, a collaborative effort dedicated to abolishing the family policing system and building alternatives that focus on healing and liberation. He is the author of *Confronting the Racist Legacy of the American Child Welfare System: The Case for Abolition.*

FRANK EDWARDS is a sociologist broadly interested in social control, the welfare state, racism, and applied statistics. His research explores the causes and consequences of the social distribution of state violence. He is Assistant Professor of Criminal Justice at Rutgers University–Newark.

KELLEY FONG is Assistant Professor of Sociology at the University of California, Irvine. She is the author of *Investigating Families: Motherhood in the Shadow of Child Protective Services.*

TINA LEE is Professor of Anthropology at the University of Wisconsin–Stout and an applied anthropologist whose research focuses on how state bureaucracies, policies, and practices contribute to the construction and reinforcement of race, class, and gender inequalities in the United States. She is the author of *Catching a Case: Inequality and Fear in New York City's Child Welfare System.* In addition to her work on child welfare, she has conducted research about environmental policy and practice in rural Wisconsin and how projects conducted through Engineers Without Borders shape the professional identities and ethics of engineering students. She is currently working on an ethnography of child welfare in western Wisconsin.

MATTY LICHTENSTEIN is Assistant Professor at Florida Atlantic University, where her research focuses on maternal health disparities, gendered regulation of families, and social policy development. She completed a postdoctoral research fellowship at Brown University in

2023. Her recent publications have appeared in the *American Journal of Sociology, Sociological Methods and Research*, and *Health Equity*.

KRISTINA K. LOVATO is Assistant Professor of Social Welfare at the University of California–Berkeley and the Director of the Center on Immigration and Child Welfare. Her scholarly work focuses on enhancing the well-being of Latine and immigrant families at risk of immigration enforcement and/or public child welfare involvement. Her research aims to better understand the lived experiences of immigrant communities to develop policies, systems, and services that are culturally responsive and equity-based regardless of legal status.

ERIN J. MAHER is Associate Professor of Sociology and Associate Director of the Data Institute for Societal Challenges at the University of Oklahoma. Her research focuses on the intersection of poverty and child maltreatment, child well-being, and family functioning. She works with state agencies to evaluate social programs in these areas. She brings an applied focus to her scholarship and an emphasis on using and communicating research results in policy and practice. She has also served as Director of Research for a national foundation conducting large-scale program evaluations in child welfare organizations.

BRITTANY MIHALEC-ADKINS is a research scientist at Child Trends. She is a family scientist focused on experiences and well-being among children and caregivers impacted by state-mandated interventions in the child welfare and carceral systems. She holds a PhD in human development and family studies from Purdue University.

MAYA PENDLETON is a cofounding member of the upEND movement, contributing to upEND as a researcher and writer focused on dismantling the family policing system. She brings her expertise to Alan J. Dettlaff's book *Confronting the Racist Legacy of the American Child Welfare System: The Case for Abolition*. Additionally, Pendleton serves as Adjunct Professor at American University, guiding students in transformative justice and abolition studies.

ASHLEE SMITH is Associate Researcher at Abt Associates, working on projects related to economic mobility, criminal justice, child welfare, and housing. She holds a PhD in public policy.

ERIN CARRINGTON SMITH has a JD from the University of Baltimore School of Law. She has worked extensively with Shanta Trivedi on issues related to the family policing system and the harm of child removal, including their recent piece in the *Family Justice Journal*, "'How Will I Get Back?': The Enduring Pain of Family Separation."

LAURA TACH is Professor of Public Policy and Sociology at Cornell University. Her research examines poverty and social policy, using quantitative and qualitative methods to study how social policies can alleviate poverty among disadvantaged families and communities.

SHANTA TRIVEDI is Assistant Professor of Law and Faculty Director of the Sayra and Neil Meyerhoff Center for Families, Children and the Courts at the University of Baltimore School of Law. She teaches family law, children's and parents' rights, and child welfare law. She is a widely published legal scholar and policy advocate in popular media, focusing on promoting policies to reduce family separation by the family policing system.

DEE WILSON worked as a child welfare CPS caseworker supervisor, area manager, regional administrator, and training director in Washington State's child welfare system for twenty-six years. He has been writing and training on child welfare policy and practice issues for more than three decades. Wilson has disseminated monthly *Sounding Board* commentaries on a wide range of child welfare subjects since 2010. He has also directed a child welfare training and research institute, taught classes in the MSW program at the University of Washington School of Social Work, and worked for several years in Casey Family Programs' Knowledge Management unit.

JENNIFER RANDLES is Interim Associate Dean of the College of Social Sciences and Professor of Sociology at California State University, Fresno. Her research focuses on how policies and community-based organizations support poor and low-income families and how intersecting inequalities of class, race, and gender shape parenting experiences. She is the author of *Proposing Prosperity: Marriage Education Policy and Inequality in America* and *Essential Dads: The Inequalities and Politics of Fathering*.

KERRY WOODWARD is Professor of Sociology at California State University, Long Beach. Her research focuses on the child welfare system; poverty and public policy; and race, class, and gender inequities. She is the author of *Pimping the Welfare System: Empowering Participants with Economic, Social, and Cultural Capital*.

INDEX

Page numbers in *italics* indicate Figures.